INSTRUCTIONAL STRATEGIES
for
BRAILLE LITERACY

DIANE P. WORMSLEY & FRANCES MARY D'ANDREA
Editors

AFB PRESS
American Foundation for the Blind

Printed in the United States of America
2010 reprint

Library of Congress Cataloging-in-Publication Data

Wormsley, Diane P., 1946—
    Instructional strategies for braille literacy / Diane P. Wormsley and Frances Mary D'Andrea.
        p.   cm.
    Includes bibliographical references and index.
    ISBN 978-0-89128-936-4
    1. Braille—Study and teaching—United States. 2. Children, Blind—Education—United States. 3. Visually handicapped children—Education—United States. 4. Teachers of the blind—Training of—United States. 5. Teaching—United States—Aids and devices—Evaluation. I. D'Andrea, Frances Mary, 1960-. II. American Foundation for the Blind. III. Title.
HV1672.D35   1997
411—DC21

                                    97-22030
                                          CIP

Photo Credits
American Foundation for the Blind, 113; American Printing House for the Blind, 96; Blazie Engineering, 272; Janet Charles, 173; Bradford Herzog, 181, 283; Nolan Hulsey, Kentucky School for the Blind, 64, 90, 91, 147; Jewish Guild for the Blind, 35, 62; Neldine Nichols, Wisconsin Department of Public Instruction, 135; Pinellas Center for the Visually Impaired, 66, 137.

The mission of the American Foundation for the Blind (AFB) is to enable persons who are blind or visually impaired to achieve equality of access and opportunity that will ensure freedom of choice in their lives.

CONTENTS

FOREWORD

The history of the teaching of braille reading and writing is essentially an oral tradition that began when braille became the literacy medium for children and adults who are blind or visually impaired. Teachers of children in residential schools and, later, itinerant teachers and resource room teachers developed a variety of successful instructional strategies for teaching braille literacy. They shared their successes with few individuals, for there were few with which to share them. Many of these "front line" braille literacy instructors, teachers with years of experience relating to braille literacy, are now retired or are retiring from the field, taking with them much that they have learned about instructing students in the reading and writing of braille. This volume, *Instructional Strategies for Braille Literacy,* is an attempt to capture this oral tradition before it dies out and to pass critical knowledge and skills on to present and future teachers.

A companion volume, *Foundations of Braille Literacy,* was published by the American Foundation for the Blind (AFB) in 1994. That text delves into the theoretical background for braille literacy instruction and includes present-day approaches to teaching print reading and writing to sighted children, at the same time pointing out the challenges these various approaches present for the teacher of a child who reads braille. Taken together, these two books represent both a foundation and a summary of what is currently known about teaching braille literacy from theoretical and practical perspectives. Through these books and the creation of bridges and networks among experienced braille teachers and other braille users, AFB hopes to ensure that future generations of teachers will be able to share in the successes of the past and educate the children of the future to be literate adults.

Carl R. Augusto
President
American Foundation for the Blind

Susan Jay Spungin, Ed.D.
Vice President, National Programs and Initiatives
American Foundation for the Blind

EDITORS' PREFACE

In past years, an emphasis by the blindness field on the use and training of residual vision, combined with the capability of technology for enlarging print, established a general preference for print over braille. Although technological advances created options for literacy that had not been previously possible for children and adults who were blind or visually impaired, these same advances also led many people to dismiss braille as an option for children who were capable of reading print. The existence of other literacy channels such as tape recorded materials, speech synthesis programs used in combination with computer screen readers, and scanners made it appear to some observers that braille was becoming outmoded.

In the late 1980s a reemphasis on braille emerged among various organizations that were strongly concerned about providing blind and visually impaired individuals with as wide a variety of options for literacy as possible. The Braille Revival League was formed as a subgroup of the American Council of the Blind. They and the National Federation of the Blind began promoting legislation to encourage the use of braille in the education of all legally blind students. In many states around the country, blind people let it be known that braille was an important literacy medium for them.

This renewed interest in braille fueled the establishment in 1989 of the National Braille Literacy Mentor Project, which was part of the American Foundation for the Blind (AFB)'s National Initiative on Literacy. Out of this project came *Understanding Braille Literacy,* a videotape produced in 1993, and *Foundations of Braille Literacy,* published in 1994. This volume, *Instructional Strategies for Braille Literacy,* is the third major component of this project. It represents the compilation of successful instructional strategies for teaching braille to blind and visually impaired students that will allow them to achieve braille literacy to the best of their abilities.

The editors are aware that the strategies provided in this volume are not an exhaustive list. However, the national dissemination of strategies for effective teaching was a primary concern. Other publications refer to games and activities and guidelines for teaching braille reading and to additional important information relating to braille. For this reason, a number of valuable materials are reprinted later in this volume. As teachers and other readers of this book develop effective instructional strategies, the editors hope that they will contact the AFB National Braille Literacy Mentor Project. These vital educational resources may then be recorded and passed on, perhaps in future editions of this book, or in other ways, such as in the *DOTS* newsletter published by AFB. In this way, teachers, children, parents, and others working with students may benefit from a rich and growing body of knowledge.

ACKNOWLEDGMENTS

Some of the following individuals contributed strategies, suggestions, and ideas, while others served as sounding boards or provided critiques of the material in this text. This book is a product of all of them, and we cannot thank them enough: Patty Arnold, Joan Bliss, Joyce Burnett, Beth Caruso, Laraine Caton, Brian Charlson, Mary J. Clark, Kathy Coffey, Alison Colbs, Judy Colbs, Chrissy Cowan, Joanne Davidoff, Kristine Davis, Kay Dennis, Liz DePiero, Cheri DeWaard, Frances Dibble, Beth Ann DiFabio, Judy Dixon, Debbie Doe, Winifred Downing, Suzanne Dudley, Carolyn Dullard, Joy Effron, E. L. Eveland, June Feigenblatt, Betsy Feinberg, Olivia Ferrante, Kathie Frankel-Mislinski, Sharon Fridley, Kathleen Geiger, Jay Gense, Nancy Godfrey, Holly Guinan, Debbie Harlin, Kathryn Heller, John Hernandez, Cay Holbrook, Penny Hoover, Kathleen M. Huebner, Nada Hyman, Janet Jasko, Tammy Johnson, Lynda Jones, Janet Kieck, Marie Knowlton, Alan Koenig, Lynne Laird, Emily Leyenberger, Sally Mangold, Scott Marshall, Barbara Mattson, Michelle McCallion, Doug McJannet, Kathy McKinsey, Donna McNear, Jeanne Meyer, Diane Mitchell, Susan Anne Mooney, Judy Van Naerssen, Grace D. Napier, Sandra Nevins, Martha Pamperin, Barbara Paton, Beth Paul, Sue Ponchillia, William R. Powell, Betsey Presley, Ike Presley, Therese Rafalowski-Welch, Linda Ray, Evelyn Rex, Mary Rich, LaRhea Sanford, Paul Schroeder, Christine M. Schumacher, Liz Seger, Bonnie Simons, Patricia Bussen Smith, Michelle Smithdas, Lisa-Anne Soucey, Claudell Stocker, Janice Strassman, Rose-Marie Swallow, Anna Swenson, Cath Tendler, Dawn Turco, Lois Wencil, Joan Whartnaby, Sue White, Miriam Whitman, Mary Wilmeth, Carla Wirzburger, Ellyn York-Ross, and Penny Zibula.

In addition, we would like to thank all the authors and publishers of the material in the Reprints section for generously sharing their resources with the readers of this book. The Jewish Guild for the Blind and the Kentucky School for the Blind also deserve special recognition for their cooperation and graciousness in helping to provide some of the photographs appearing in these pages.

The editors would also like to thank family and friends for patiently waiting while we were unavailable because we were "working on the book." We would like to thank Bill Wormsley and Pat Wormsley for their support and willingness to have just one more "nuked" dinner. We also want to thank Stephen D'Andrea for his graphic design assistance and his unfailing sense of humor and Margaret D'Andrea for her loving support. Our editors, Natalie Hilzen and Ellen Bilofsky of AFB Press, deserve thanks for their tireless efforts and many hours of work to get this book finished. Thanks again to all.

ABOUT THE CONTRIBUTORS

Diane P. Wormsley, Ph.D., is Coordinator of the Education of Children and Youth with Visual and Multiple Impairments Program at the Pennsylvania College of Optometry. At the time of writing, she was Education Manager at Overbrook School for the Blind in Philadelphia, Pennsylvania, and, previously, Director of the American Foundation for the Blind's National Initiative on Literacy. Dr. Wormsley was co-author of *Foundations of Braille Literacy* and the *Understanding Braille Literacy* video.

Frances Mary D'Andrea, M.Ed., is Director of the Southeast office and the National Literacy Program for the American Foundation for the Blind in Atlanta, Georgia. She is editor of *DOTS for Braille Literacy* and was previously a teacher of visually impaired students and has worked in residential, itinerant, and other settings.

Kitch Barnicle, M. S., is Senior Project Engineer at the American Foundation for the Blind in New York City and Research Associate, Center for Opportunities and Outcomes for People with Disabilities, Teachers College, at Columbia University in New York City. She is the author of several consumer guides on evaluating and selecting assistive technology.

Carol Ann Layton, Ph.D., is Assistant Professor in Special Education, College of Education, at Texas Tech University in Lubbock, Texas. She also works as a private consultant assessing students who are visually impaired and has conducted numerous workshops on the assessment of students with visual impairments. Dr. Layton is the author of articles on analysis of reading skills and low vision.

Madeline Milian, Ed.D., is Assistant Professor, Division of Special Education, at the University of Northern Colorado in Greeley, and has authored articles on the education of young students with visual impairments who speak English as a second language.

CHAPTER 1

BRAILLE AS THE PRIMARY LITERACY MEDIUM: GENERAL GUIDELINES AND STRATEGIES

DIANE P. WORMSLEY

Cassandra, a student with low vision, is in the 6th grade. She uses braille to read the written information on graphs in her mathematics homework but often uses a felt-tipped pen to fill in the worksheets that her teacher makes to accompany the graphs. She thus uses print and braille in the same assignment.

At a recent annual meeting of a national organization, one of the keynote speakers began his address by reading from his brailled notes. When he introduced some statistics during the presentation, he picked up the print copy of a chart, held it close to his face, and read it aloud. That concluded, he went back to his braille notes and continued. His use of braille during his presentation was particularly effective because it allowed him to maintain eye contact with the audience—something he could not do while he was reading from the print copy of the chart.

Like everyone else, people who are blind or visually impaired need to be able to obtain information in an effective and timely way, exchange information with others accurately and to a desired end, and, in general, read and write with fluency. But when someone cannot use print with ease to perform these activities, alternatives need to be found. Braille, along with other options such as tapes, personal readers, and computers equipped with adaptive equipment, presents an effective alternative, and its use can enable the individual who is blind or visually impaired to be a fully literate participant in today's information-driven society. For people who are blind or visually impaired, braille serves essentially the same function today that it has since raised-type alphabets and codes were invented in the mid-1800s. It provides a means of *independent* literacy—that is, it permits them to read and write without being dependent on anyone else to do it for them.

A number of developments over recent years have made braille literacy perhaps more important today than it has ever been. First, the significance of being literate is greater than ever in today's world, in which the quantity of information available to those who are print and computer literate continues to grow exponentially—while the availability of work *not* requiring literacy continues to diminish almost as rapidly. Second, legislation has been passed in many states that guarantees access to assessment and educational services for students who would benefit from learning to read and write in braille. Finally, the availability of computer and telecommunications technology that allows braille users access to more information makes braille literacy an increasingly powerful tool.

The ability of literacy and specifically braille literacy to increase one's potential for independence through employment, creativity, and other forms of success has never been greater. The availability of braille as a tool for literacy allows a choice for adults and children who are blind or visually impaired. Each individual has unique needs that may be met with various combinations of the available options, and braille can often be the most suitable and effective channel for written information for a child.

Thinking of braille as a literacy tool has an additional implication: teachers of braille need to be teachers of reading and writing as well as of the braille code. The companion volume to this handbook, *The Foundations of Braille Literacy* (Rex, Koenig, Wormsley & Baker, 1994), discussed the main theoretical approaches to teaching reading and writing and the implications of each for teaching reading and writing in braille. It will be helpful for readers of this book to have this theoretical perspective, although it is not necessary in order for this book to be useful.

The information and strategies in this book apply to the teaching of reading and writing to the child who will be using braille. The remainder of this book assumes that the decision has already been made to use braille as the child's primary tool for literacy. It is important to make the decision regarding braille as a primary literacy and learning medium for a child who is visually impaired as early as possible, but what exactly is meant by the term "primary literacy medium"?

PRIMARY LITERACY MEDIUM

When a child who is visually impaired is capable of reading and writing in both braille and print, a decision needs to be made about which medium is the most appropriate in which to conduct the bulk of the child's instruction. Mangold and Mangold (1989) differentiate between a primary and secondary learning medium. In their words, the primary learning medium is that which

1. is most frequently used during classroom instruction,
2. allows access to the greatest variety of educational materials,

3. is utilized in a wide variety of settings inside and outside the classroom, and

4. permits both reading and writing.

It must accommodate academic, nonacademic, and vocational needs.

A secondary learning medium may also be learned and used to complement the primary medium when

1. It allows a student to perform specific tasks not easily performed in the primary learning medium.

2. It alleviates fatigue (Mangold and Mangold, 1989).

Thus, deciding to make braille the primary learning and literacy medium does not rule out the teaching of print reading and writing; nor does deciding to make print the primary literacy medium rule out instruction in braille as a secondary medium. Many children who attended residential schools in the mid-1960s and the 1970s learned both print and braille. Like the speaker at the annual meeting in the first vignette, those children can now choose in which medium to read, depending on the situation and the need at hand. As their needs—and, perhaps, their vision—changes, these individuals have the power to maintain their own literacy. Therefore, the goal to strive for in regard to an individual is to have as many options as possible available for literacy.

Determining the primary medium for reading and writing may be the most important decision a teacher will make with respect to a particular child, and the decision needs to be made as early as possible if the medium is to be braille so that the child will have the benefit of early instruction in the tactile skills he or she will need. Although people can and do learn braille at any age, there is no question that the younger an individual is when learning braille, the easier it is for him or her to attain reasonably fast reading speeds.

Every student is unique and brings his or her own individual strengths and needs to the learning task, but there are some questions that the teacher of every visually impaired child will need to ask before beginning to teach:

• Should I teach this child braille or some other medium?

• How do I determine which medium this child will read?

• What characteristics of this student will be important in making this decision?

Although this book is not intended to be used as a "cookbook" for every child, there are some general guidelines that the teacher can use as a starting point to answer these questions. Determining the primary literacy medium for a child who is totally blind is usually easy. For a child who has some vision, the task can become more complicated. It is important to stress to all concerned that the decision needs to be based upon what will ultimately be in the best interest of the child, not the parents, the teacher, the school district, or any other individuals or organizations who might have a vested interest in the decision.

The choice of a primary literacy medium is a far-reaching decision and must take into consideration the future as well as current needs of the child. The student may do well in first grade with short reading assignments and the relatively large print size of most texts. By the time the student is confronted with the smaller print size and increased demands for reading and writing that are typical of the third grade, however, he or she may find it increasingly difficult to keep up with academic requirements. Teachers should remember that students and their needs change over time, and the more skills they learn, the more prepared they will be for independence and adulthood. Some adults who have been visually impaired all their lives were able to read some print when they were young, but lost more vision as they aged and now rely solely on braille.

Until recently, there were few published guidelines for teachers to use in supporting and documenting their decision to use a particular learning medium with a student. However, a number of articles and manuals have now provided assessments or guidelines for making the determination for print or braille or both, filling the previous gap in this area (Caton, 1991, 1994; Koenig & Holbrook, 1989, 1991, 1995; Sanford and Burnett, 1996). The manual *Learning Media Assessment of Students with Visual Impairments* (Koenig & Holbrook, 1995) suggests an initial in-depth learning media assessment, with continuous subsequent assessment to determine whether a change in primary learning media would be beneficial (see Chapter 4). (*Learning Media Assessment* also contains easy-to-use forms that can become part of a student's ongoing record to document the decision.) The initial media assessment is a joint effort of the child's educational team to determine whether the child is collecting information in a primarily visual, tactile, or auditory manner. The box on page 5 summarizes the characteristics of students who may be candidates for either print reading or braille reading programs. This information is combined with what is known about the etiology and stability of the child's eye condition to determine whether the primary literacy medium will be print or braille and whether to teach a secondary medium as well.

VARIABLES IN TEACHING BRAILLE

If it has been established that a child's primary literacy medium is braille, the teacher is then confronted with the question that sums up the essence of this book: "How do I teach reading and writing using braille?" But the answer to this question is filled with variables. How the teacher teaches depends on many factors, including:

- the age of the child at the onset of the visual impairment
- the level of the student's literacy at the onset of the visual impairment
- the student's functional vision and options for other literacy media
- the motivation of the student and his or her parents for learning braille

CHARACTERISTICS OF STUDENTS WHO MAY BE CANDIDATES FOR PRINT READING AND BRAILLE READING PROGRAMS

CHARACTERISTICS OF A LIKELY PRINT READER

- Uses vision efficiently to complete tasks at near distances.

- Shows interest in pictures and demonstrates the ability to identify pictures or elements within pictures.

- Identifies his or her name in print and/or understands that print has meaning.

- Uses print to perform other prerequisite reading skills.

- Has a stable eye condition.

- Has an intact central visual field.

- Shows steady progress in learning to use his or her vision as necessary to ensure efficient print reading.

- Is free of additional disabilities that would interfere with progress in a developmental reading program in print.

CHARACTERISTICS OF A LIKELY BRAILLE READER

- Shows a preference for exploring the environment tactilely.

- Uses the tactile sense efficiently to identify small objects.

- Identifies his or her name in braille and/or understands that braille has meaning.

- Uses braille to acquire other prerequisite reading skills.

- Has an unstable eye condition or a poor prognosis for retaining his or her current level of vision in the near future.

- Has a reduced or nonfunctional central field to the extent that print reading is expected to be inefficient.

- Shows steady progress in developing tactile skills that are necessary for efficient braille reading.

- Is free of additional disabilities that would interfere with progress in a developmental reading program in braille.

Source: Adapted from A. J. Koenig and M. C. Holbrook, *Learning Media Assessment of Students with Visual Impairments: A Resource Guide for Teachers* (2nd ed.) (Austin: Texas School for the Blind and Visually Impaired, 1995), p. 43.

- the student's tactile and perceptual abilities
- the student's primary language
- the student's intellectual capabilities
- any additional disabilities that the student has
- the setting in which the literacy instruction is to take place

There are also a host of other variables related to how the student learns. The nearly infinite combinations of these factors are what make the teaching of braille reading and writing both so demanding and so rewarding, and they will be discussed in detail throughout this book.

Despite the great variation in the needs that students bring to learning braille—and therefore in the strategies that are required to teach it—there are certain items that all teachers of braille must know, and there are certain basic guidelines and strategies that will apply to any student. In addition to variables related to the students, the skills and experience of the teacher also affect the way that braille is taught. Teachers of braille reading and writing must of necessity know all the symbols and rules of the braille code. (A list of braille refresher courses is included in the Resources section of this book for teachers who may need to brush up on their skills.) They also need to have some knowledge of how reading and writing are taught to sighted students. This is discussed in more detail in Chapter 3.

In addition, it is important for the teacher of braille reading and writing to understand some basic differences between braille and print that determine the skills braille readers and writers need to learn. This knowledge will also suggest some general guidelines and strategies for teachers to follow in providing instruction in braille reading and writing.

GENERAL GUIDELINES: DIFFERENCES BETWEEN BRAILLE AND PRINT READING

Tactile versus Visual Reading

The most basic and obvious way in which reading braille differs from reading print is in the sensory modality used. Braille readers read tactilely, and print readers read visually. Kusajima (1974) conducted a comprehensive investigation of both tactile and visual reading. His findings are still valid, and they are important for teachers of reading to consider in understanding the two processes. Kusajima summarized the different characteristics of efficient visual and tactile reading as follows:

> Good visual reading is characterized by a small number of short, regular pauses, no regressive movements, and well-adjusted return sweeps—combined with a deep and accurate understanding of the meaning of a text. Good braille reading is characterized by few zig-zag, up-and-down, or fluttering movements, uniform pressure of the finger on the page, no regressive movements, and well-adjusted movements between lines with the help of both hands—combined with a deep and accurate understanding of the meaning of the text. (p. 57)

A summary of Kusajima's conclusions is presented in Table 1-1.

Kusajima's findings demonstrated that perception is tied to movement in braille reading; in fact, without movement, perception cannot occur. Subsequent research also demonstrated the key importance of an individual reader's tactile perceptual abilities in developing good braille reading skills, such as how the reader moves his or her hands (Mangold 1976; Wormsley, 1979). This difference in perception from print reading has significant implications for the skills braille readers need to learn, and teachers must make sure that their instructional strate-

Table 1-1. Differences Between Visual and Tactile Reading in Regard to Selected Variables

Variable	Visual Reading	Tactile Reading
Pauses	The eye does not move smoothly.	Pauses are rare; fingers read through movement.
Movement	No perception of words and letters occurs during movement because movement is too rapid.	Perception occurs *only* through movement.
Pause time	92–98% of reading time is spent in pauses.	Pause time is minimal.
Number of pauses	As reading skill improves, the number of pauses declines.	Better readers have smooth movements.
Span[a]	Covered three to five words (with Japanese subjects).	Not relevant.
Locations of pauses	Pauses occur irrespective of meaning, grammar or rhetoric, or length of a sentence in lines.	Pauses occur rarely; they are found near word intervals or at beginnings of words.
Functions of pauses	Readers perceive during pauses.	Pauses are halting points, "rallying points for understanding."
Functions of "flying" movements—movements from one fixation point to another	Links between pauses.	Of paramount significance—perception occurs through movement.
Methods of perception	Several letters or words are perceived all at once in pauses.	Letters are perceived successively through the movement of the fingers and become grouped in perception.
Word cues	The average reader reads sentences with the help of small cues, such as the size and shape of letters and words.	The average reader uses the first and second and sometimes the third braille character in words as cues to predict or anticipate the remainder of the word.
Dominant and subordinate letters	Word recognition depends on context and letter shapes.	The first three characters or letters are dominant, along with some characters that are also tactilely characteristic or peculiar.
Sensory channel	Both eyes work together involuntarily, without conscious knowledge of the activity.	Both hands are entirely under voluntary control, especially in the early stages of learning braille.[b]

Source: Diane P. Wormsley, *The Effects of a Hand Movement Training Program on the Hand Movements and Reading Rates of Young Braille Readers* (Ann Arbor, MI: University Microfilms International, 1979); adapted from T. Kusajima, *Visual Reading and Braille Reading: An Experimental Investigation of the Physiology and Psychology of Visual and Tactual Reading* (New York: American Foundation for the Blind, 1974).
[a]Span refers to the amount of information that can be perceived at one time. Braille readers perceive one character at a time and "chunk" what they read into meaningful units.
[b]Many experienced braille readers disagree with Kusajima on this point. They feel as if their hands are not under their voluntary control while reading.

gies are consistent with the way braille readers process information. In print reading, the teacher pays little attention to the mechanics of reading—that is, the movements of the eyes—but the braille teacher must help students develop good hand movements if they are to become efficient readers. Teachers must also be able to recognize inefficient hand movements and learn how to eliminate them and replace them with efficient ones.

Many teachers think that they can teach tracking, or the ability to follow a line of braille across the page and down to the next line, by itself. When the task goes from tracking a line of dots to actual reading, however, tracking cannot be separated from the perception of the braille characters. Therefore, no matter how much "tracking practice" the child has been given, if it does not incorporate recognition of braille characters, the child's tracking skills will not usually improve (Wormsley, 1979). As a general rule, therefore, teachers should pay close attention at the beginning of braille reading instruction to teaching the child how to move his or her hands on the braille materials and to constructing materials that allow for movement across lines and characters in the manner of the most efficient readers. More specific strategies for teaching efficient hand movements are discussed in Chapter 3.

Complexity of the Code

Another difference between learning to read and write in braille and in print that affects the development of instructional programs is the fact that braille readers have more symbols to learn than do print readers, and they do not learn all the elements of the code until long after print readers have learned theirs. Generally, all of the print symbols, with the exception of certain standardized marks such as the ampersand (&) and certain punctuation signs such as the semicolon, are introduced by the end of first grade. However, the vocabulary in children's reading materials will not contain all of the braille contractions until they have reached a third-grade reading level. Conversely, providing material at a first-, second-, or third-grade reading level may not ensure that the child will be able to recognize or interpret the braille symbols that do appear. And, in addition to the symbols themselves, braille readers must learn rules of usage of the braille symbols that print readers do not have to contend with. This means that braille readers have an extended period of time during which they are still learning their literacy medium, while their sighted classmates have moved on beyond learning their code.

As a result of this difference, teachers need to be aware of the actual symbol knowledge of their students and to examine all materials for unfamiliar contractions or symbols before the student reads them. When a student does encounter an unfamiliar contraction or use of a braille symbol, someone familiar with braille needs to be close by to help the student interpret the symbol, just as a teacher familiar with print needs to help a beginning print reader interpret symbols when he or she needs help. More specific strategies for dealing with this difference are presented in Chapter 3.

Availability of Materials

Another important guideline for teachers relates to differences in the availability of braille and print materials. Because there is less material available for braille readers than for print readers, many braille students may come to school less well prepared in their experiences with the written medium than print readers. Print readers may also have the opportunity to practice reading on a wider variety of materials. Since the amount of independent silent reading children do both in school and out of school is related to gains in reading achievement (Anderson, Hiebert, Scott & Wilkinson, 1985), the lack of reading material for braille readers can significantly affect their progress in achievement when compared with print readers. It is important, therefore, to immerse the child in braille material that is written at the child's level of understanding. Regardless of the type of reading materials used in the regular classroom, the visually impaired child must have all books and other reading matter materials in braille, in order to learn to read. This includes texts for health, social studies, math, and any other content area (as well as the basal readers, literature anthologies, or novels). It is not acceptable for sighted children to be reading from print books, while the blind child is "listening." Following are some suggestions for ensuring that students have all their materials in braille.

STRATEGIES

OBTAINING MATERIALS IN BRAILLE

✛ Utilize the state network of instructional materials centers for obtaining braille books and materials (see the *AFB Directory of Services,* 1997, for the nearest center). See "Sources of Braille Books for Children" in this chapter for additional resources.

✛ Find out if the reading series or books that are being used are already in braille. The American Printing House for the Blind (APH; see the Resources section at the end of this book) maintains a central catalog of braille books with 128,000 listings from over 200 volunteer and commercial agencies in North America, as well as an on-line search service known as CARL ET AL (http//www.aph.org). Be sure to order in plenty of time to receive the books prior to the beginning of the school year.

✛ Become familiar with the local transcriber groups in your area. In addition to those listed in the Resources section of this book and the *AFB Directory of Services,* (1997), the National Braille Association or the Library of Congress National Library Service for the Blind and Physically Handicapped (NLS) will provide a listing of local transcriber groups. NLS has compiled a free directory, *Volunteers Who Produce*

SOURCES OF BRAILLE BOOKS FOR CHILDREN

The place to start searching for braille children's books is the Library of Congress National Library Service for the Blind and Physically Handicapped (NLS). (See the Resources section for all contact information.) NLS offers braille books on loan, and its directory, *Library Resources for the Blind and Physically Handicapped,* provides a listing of all the regional Libraries for the Blind and Physically Handicapped as well as several additional libraries of braille books.

Another source for children who may wish to borrow books is the American Action Fund for Blind Children and Adults (formerly the American Brotherhood for the Blind), which has a lending library of TWIN-VISION books (books in both print and braille) as well as books all the way up to 12th-grade reading and interest levels. Books are mailed to the child's home.

For children who wish to have their books "for keeps," the National Braille Press sells books and also offers a Children's Braille Book Club aimed especially at preschool and primary grade children. These are popular picture books with clear plastic sheets inserted that contain the braille translation. There is no fee to join the club, and you can buy as few or as many books as you wish.

Seedlings Braille Books for Children also carries beginner books that include braille and print text together. In addition, they sell books through the sixth-grade reading level on many different topics, with more than 160 titles available.

Expectations, published in braille by the Braille Institute of America, is a free volume that contains about 12 stories for elementary school-age children, plus some scratch-and-sniff pages. The book is sent out once a year around Christmastime, to anyone who contacts them.

Braille International's William T. Thomas Bookstore carries books for both children and adults. They offer the children's State Books Series, with information about the geography, history, economy, and culture of each state, Washington, DC, and Puerto Rico, and the One to Grow On! series of children's print-braille books with read-along cassettes.

Frances Mary D'Andrea

Books, available in large print and braille, of volunteer groups and individuals that transcribe and record books.

✢ Ask the National Braille Association for help in starting a transcription group if there is none close by. Until the local group is up and running, consider working with a more distant group through fax or express delivery services as a short-term alternative. The Resources section has sources for people who wish to teach themselves braille for purposes of transcription, if you do not have the time to teach them yourself.

✢ Materials can sometimes be transcribed using braille software translation packages (see Chapter 8). The print is entered either by scanning or by typing it into a computer equipped with the software. A braille printer is required for this as well as the computer and the braille translation software. The translation is best done by someone who has a knowledge of braille as well as how the particular software package translates the print into braille to avoid presenting poorly produced braille to the beginning reader.

✛ Take a trip with the student to the nearest Library for the Blind and Physically Handicapped (see Resources) to discuss its services and the availability of different types of braille material.

✛ Inform parents about sources for obtaining braille books (see "Sources of Braille Books for Children").

✛ Meet with the classroom teacher regularly to find out far in advance the materials that will need to be translated into braille, including the teacher's own handouts and any outside reading that will be assigned.

Opportunities for Sharing

A child who is visually impaired today most often learns to read and write braille in a setting where he or she is the only child receiving instruction in his or her primary reading medium. This means that the child will have limited ability to read what others in the class have written or to share his or her writings with classmates. The classroom teacher will most likely not be able to read the child's braille writing or to interpret what the child is reading in order to give assistance. The teacher of a child who is learning to read braille in such a setting, therefore, needs to provide the student with exposure to other children who read and write braille in as many ways as possible. Older children, for example, can locate "pen" pals with whom to correspond through organizations such as the American Council for the Blind, National Federation of the Blind, or the National Association for Parents of the Visually Impaired (see Resources), or make friends at a summer camp for children who are blind or visually impaired.

A related guideline is to promote braille to the child's sighted peers and the classroom teacher and to encourage everyone involved with the child to learn braille. Kindergarten or first grade is a good time to introduce the teacher and classmates to Grade 1 braille and to have a Perkins brailler and slates and styli available for the students to practice on. As contractions are introduced in the reading materials, the teacher of visually impaired students can plan ahead and teach all the students what is coming up. Even if the sighted students and teachers learn only grade 1 braille, they will be able to communicate with the visually impaired child in writing. And as they see their classmate learning more and more contractions, they will have increased respect for his or her learning task.

STRATEGIES

TEACHING EVERYONE BRAILLE

✛ Have teaching assistants learn braille to help the blind child in the classroom, while you monitor for correctness.

✛ Set up a bulletin board with the letters of the alphabet and numbers in braille and print. You can use cotton balls or halves of styrofoam balls to form the braille dots.

✛ Braille students' names to have on their desks.

✛ Give the classroom teacher and students braille alphabet cards from the nearest local agency for the blind.

✛ Purchase a braille labeler for the classroom and teach the teacher and students how to use it to mark things.

✛ Braille things that are used on a daily basis (months and days on the calendar, numbers, bathroom passes, children's job charts, and so forth).

✛ Have a desk set aside for students to use to braille notes to each other. Have several types of slates and styli available as well as a Perkins brailler. Above the wall behind the desk have poster-size cues about how to use them; and have a swing cell handy for students to practice with, as well as the peg slate from American Printing House for the Blind. Another useful tool to have available would be the Swail Dot Inverter for making raised lines without either a braillewriter or slate and stylus.

✛ Let the students take turns trying to read braille characters tactilely to help them understand the difference between reading braille tactilely and visually. This should help them grasp that they are more efficient at recognizing the characters visually, just as their blind friend is more efficient tactilely.

✛ Start a braille club for students. An example of one teacher who did that successfully is presented in "How to Make a Braille Wave," by Bonnie Simons, which is reprinted at the end of this volume.

Not all regular classroom teachers may want to learn braille, but those who can be encouraged to do so and whose classes take part will have a unique skill. A selling point for the regular classroom teacher is the wonderful enthusiasm and excitement that it generates among the students in the class.

Even if the sighted students are not learning braille, a mini-lesson about the intricacies of the code and the various contractions and rules would help provide them with an idea of what the task of learning to read is like for their classmate. If the visually handicapped student or an older blind child can provide this information, the result may be increased respect for the student rather than the perception that he or she is "slow" and always needs extra help. Teachers and students need to recognize that it "takes time to be blind."

PARENTS AS PARTNERS

Unlike sighted children, whose parents will most likely be able to read print, children learning braille will not be able to share their reading and writing experiences with their parents unless the parents make a special effort to learn braille. Teachers must make an ongoing effort to lend parents support for learning braille. Parents may think learning braille is difficult, may have little time to devote to the effort, or may simply feel resistant to the idea for their own personal reasons. The teacher can explain the significance it would have for the child if the parents were able to communicate with him or her in braille. There are a variety of strategies teachers can use to get parents more involved with their children's reading and writing experiences.

STRATEGIES

ENLISTING THE HELP OF PARENTS

✦ Get to know the parents. Until you know the kinds of constraints under which the parents are operating, you will not know how much or how little you can ask of them. Asking a family to learn braille when they are having difficulty paying the bills or providing child care for their children will only alienate them from the teacher and will not help the teacher to help their child. The family needs to develop trust in the teacher, to know that the teacher cares about them and their child and that any suggestions he or she makes will be reasonable for them.

✦ Establish a parents' support group. Parents of children who are visually impaired find ongoing support groups helpful for any number of reasons. Initially, such groups may be just for meeting other parents who have children who are blind or visually impaired so they can exchange experiences and provide mutual support. Sometimes it takes a teacher or other facilitator to provide the impetus for the parents to get together. As such groups evolve, they often seek out information about braille and its uses. At this point, bringing in a speaker to talk about learning braille may be just what some parents are looking for. For example, the teacher can invite one or more braille users to talk to parents about what braille means to them or show one of several videotapes that show the expanded options that braille offers (see "Resources for Parents" in this chapter) and follow up with a discussion.

✦ Ask parents who resist allowing their child to learn braille to let you start teaching the child and to see how the child reacts. Ask them to withhold judgment and

---

MATERIALS

RESOURCES FOR PARENTS

The following resources are helpful to show parents or parents' groups how people who are blind or visually impaired use braille or both print and braille:

✦ *Personal Touch: Braille for Lifelong Enrichment* (Mangold & Pesavento, 1994) is an informative and upbeat videotape showing how braille is used throughout the lifespan.

✦ *Understanding Braille Literacy* (1993) is a motivational video featuring students demonstrating how braille is learned and teachers, parents, and school administrators talking about how braille skills contribute to literacy, independence, and educational success.

✦ *Braille: The Key to Literacy and Independence* (Braille Revival League of California, 1991), a 19-page booklet, provides a brief description of braille, its importance as a literacy medium, and the variety of ways braille is used in everday activities.

The following materials are useful for parents who are learning braille:

Beginners

✦ *Just Enough to Know Better* (Curran, 1988), was designed to help the parents of blind children to acquire a general understanding of the braille code. It presents opportunities to read and learn braille through a series of stories, with the print text on the back of each braille page for checking purposes.

Advanced Users

✦ Braille Reading for Family Members is a correspondence course in Grade 2 braille offered by the Hadley School for the Blind specifically for family members of students who are learning braille (see Resources).

✦ *New Programmed Instruction in Braille* (Ashcroft, Henderson, Sanford, & Koenig, 1991) is a programmed instruction course designed to teach the braille code in 10 chapters. It incorporates all the changes in the code through 1991.

---

keep any negative feelings about braille to themselves during a long enough period for the child to learn some basic braille—perhaps a third to a half of the school year. Make plans to review the decision with them after this time. Make sure they know that teaching braille does not mean that you will stop any teaching of print.

✦ Teach parents the basics of grade 1 braille using *Just Enough to Know Better* (Curran, 1988; see "Resources for Parents") as a starting point. Suggest that they purchase a slate and stylus to use to write to their child. This will give them enough to communicate with their child in braille, and supports the child's learning of braille. Even if they learn nothing more, they will always be able to leave their child a note or write a letter. Some parents may wish to sign up with the Hadley School for the Blind to learn braille and may wish to take other parenting courses they offer (see Resources).

✛ Take parents who are willing into advanced courses. Teach them how to use the Perkins brailler with the correct fingering, so that they can monitor their child's ability to write, just as a sighted parent monitors how a child holds a pencil. Teach them more contractions. Break the code into sections and teach a little bit at a time. Knowing just the alphabet word contractions will allow them to write fewer characters.

✛ Encourage children to teach their parents.

NEXT STEPS IN TEACHING BRAILLE

Understanding the differences between primary and secondary learning media and between reading in print and in braille is the first step in mastering the teaching of braille reading and writing. The next step is to understand how to deal with the differences in the learners themselves, which were referred to earlier in this chapter. To address these variables, the succeeding chapters of this book deal with different types of learners. Thus, Chapter 2 discusses the emergent literacy needs of young children, usually those with congenital vision loss, who are not yet ready to learn to read and write but whose primary learning medium will be braille. Chapter 3 addresses the core strategies of teaching reading and writing in braille, primarily for students who have never learned any other literacy medium. Strategies to address the needs of students who learned to read and write in print but need to make the transition to braille are presented in Chapter 4. Students with special needs and other disabilities in addition to vision loss are discussed in Chapter 5, and students who are learning English as a second language are covered in Chapter 6.

Two additional areas related to the teaching of braille are covered in the final chapters of this book. All students need to be assessed both initially and on an ongoing basis to make sure that instruction is addressing their needs. Assessment strategies are discussed in Chapter 7. Finally, as noted at the beginning of this chapter, the rapid growth of computer technology is opening up new possibilities for people who use braille for reading and writing. An overview of this technology, as well as strategies for teaching its use to visually impaired students, is presented in Chapter 8. Sources for obtaining more information and materials mentioned in all of the chapters are found in the Resources section at the end of the book.

Enabling students who are blind or visually impaired to attain the highest possible degree of literacy is a large part of enabling them to be fully independent individuals. In the constellation of alternatives for literacy, braille can assume a commanding position for a child. Effective ways of fostering a knowledge of braille and instructing students in its use are explored in the chapters that follow.

REFERENCES

AFB directory of services for blind and visually impaired persons in the United States and Canada (25th ed.). (1997). New York: AFB Press.

Anderson, R. D., Hiebert, E. H., Scott, J. A., & Wilkinson, I. A. G. (1985). *Becoming a nation of readers. The report of the commission on reading.* Washington, DC: National Academy of Education, National Institute of Education.

Ashcroft, S.C., Henderson, F. M., Sanford, L. R., & Koenig, A. J. (1991). *New programmed instruction in braille.* Nashville, TN: SCALARS.

Braille Revival League of California. (1991). *Braille: The key to literacy and independence.* Danville, CA: Braille Publishers. (Available from the American Council for the Blind.)

Caton, H. D. (Ed.). (1991). *Print and braille literacy: Selecting appropriate learning media.* Louisville, KY: American Printing House for the Blind.

Caton, H. D. (Ed.). (1994). *TOOLS for selecting appropriate learning media.* Louisville, KY: American Printing House for the Blind.

Curran, E. P. (1988). *Just enough to know better.* Boston: National Braille Press.

Koenig, A. J., & Holbrook, M. C. (1989). Determining the reading medium for students with visual impairments: A diagnostic teaching approach. *Journal of Visual Impairment & Blindness, 83,* 296–302. (Reprinted in this volume).

Koenig, A. J., & Holbrook, M. C. (1991). Determining the reading medium for visually impaired students via diagnostic testing. *Journal of Visual Impairment & Blindness, 85*(2), 61–68.

Koenig, A. J., & Holbrook, M. C. (1995). *Learning media assessment of students with visual impairments: A resource guide for teachers* (2nd ed.). Austin: Texas School for the Blind and Visually Impaired.

Kusajima, T. (1974). *Visual reading and braille reading: An experimental investigation of the physiology and psychology of visual and tactual reading.* New York: American Foundation for the Blind.

Mangold, S. S. (1976). *The effects of a developmental teaching approach of tactile perception and braille letter recognition based on a model of precision teaching.* Unpublished doctoral dissertation, California State University, San Francisco.

Mangold, S. S. (Ed.). (1982). *A teacher's guide to the special educational needs of blind and visually handicapped children.* New York: American Foundation for the Blind.

Mangold, S. S. (1989). *The Mangold developmental program of tactile perception and braille letter recognition.* Castro Valley, CA: Exceptional Teaching Aids.

Mangold, S. S., & Mangold, P. (1989). Selecting the most appropriate learning medium for students with functional vision. *Journal of Visual Impairment & Blindness, 83*(6), 294–296.

Mangold, S. S., & Pesavento, M. E. (1994). *Personal touch: Braille for lifelong enrichment* [videotape]. Winnetka, IL: Hadley School for the Blind.

Rex, E. J., Koenig, A. J., Wormsley, D. P., & Baker, R. L. (1994). *Foundations of braille literacy.* New York: AFB Press.

Sanford, L., & Burnett, R. (1996). *Functional vision and media assessment* [checklist]. Hermitage, TN: Consultants for the Visually Impaired.

Understanding braille literacy [videotape]. (1993). New York: AFB Press.

Wormsley, D. P. (1979). *The effects of a hand movement training program on the hand movements and reading rates of young braille readers.* Ann Arbor, MI: University Microfilms International.

CHAPTER 2
FOSTERING EMERGENT LITERACY

DIANE P. WORMSLEY

Vanessa is almost 2 and is legally blind as a result of retinopathy of prematurity. An early childhood caseworker for visually impaired youngsters comes to her home on a weekly basis to help her family and provide information. This week, Vanessa's mother wants to know what she can do to begin getting Vanessa ready to learn to read. Her sister's child, who is 3, is in a regular preschool and is already learning to recognize her alphabet.

Jeremy is 4½, legally blind from glaucoma, and in a regular preschool setting with support from an itinerant teacher of visually impaired students. The regular preschool teacher is concerned because he doesn't seem to interact with his toys and peers as she feels he should.

Children know about reading and writing long before they actually learn to read. The process of becoming familiar with written language is generally known as *emergent literacy*—the term refers to the time during which literacy is "emerging" in the child. Generally, emergent literacy is the stage in which infants and toddlers begin to develop concepts related to reading and writing and participate in activities or have experiences that can lead to the later development of literacy. Among other experiences, it includes "early interactions with written language—for example, scribbling, telling stories from pictures, and recognizing logos of favorite restaurants" (Rex, Koenig, Wormsley, & Baker, 1994, p. 9). Anderson, Hiebert, Scott, and Wilkinson (1985, p. 21) have commented, "Early development of the knowledge required for reading comes from experience talking and learning about the world and talking and learning about written language."

Although this stage is generally thought of as beginning with the preschool years, it actually starts in infancy. All parents contribute to the early growth of literacy by talking to and reading to their infants and teaching them about themselves and their ever-expanding world (their bodies, rooms, families, neighborhoods, and communities). Parents and caregivers also shape their children's cognitive and sensorimotor development. All this is part of an essential developmental process. Learning about the world, formulating concepts about how it works, and developing the ability to interact with the people and objects in the environment are prerequisites to developing spoken language and, eventually, written language.

However, because children who are blind or visually impaired lack sight, they may miss out on certain experiences and opportunities for learning that other children have available more or less incidentally as part of their everyday lives—unless a deliberate attempt is made to provide those experiences. Moreover, because people who are visually impaired need to make greater use of their senses other than vision to learn about the world around them, they need experiences that focus on developing those senses. This chapter presents strategies for making sure that visually impaired children undergo the experiences they need to develop the prerequisites for later literacy.

EARLY DEVELOPMENT AND LANGUAGE

Some parents of infants who are blind may lack confidence in their parenting abilities. Because many visually impaired babies tend not to establish eye contact, it is often more difficult to engage them in communication. Their parents may need help to understand that they should talk to blind infants just as to sighted babies. It is through hearing, feeling, smelling, and tasting, and through talking about what they hear, feel, smell, and taste, that blind children learn concepts—that is, the organization of information into generalizations about the world. They may learn, for example, that furry creatures are *animals*, and animals with four legs and a tail that bark are *dogs*. When talking is paired with what children are feeling, smelling, touching, and hearing, children can begin to develop language concepts that are based upon their reality. Early intervention specialists trained to work with visually impaired children and their families can help parents to cope with their fears and learn strategies to assist their children in preparing to acquire literacy.

In this regard, it is important for parents and teachers to train themselves to "get inside the children's heads," imagine what the children are experiencing, and try to think as they do by watching how the children react to things around them and by imagining the environment from their viewpoint. In short, it is necessary to turn off awareness of visual stimuli, tune in to what the children may be sensing, and then judge their reactions on the basis of this new understanding of what they are perceiving.

Parents and caretakers can be taught strategies to develop the precursors of language and concepts necessary for braille reading and writing. Providing experiences with a variety of stimuli fosters infants' cognitive, auditory, and sensorimotor development so that they progress through the developmental stages from passive recipients of stimuli to active explorers and interpreters. (For detailed discussions of early development in infants who are blind and visually impaired, see

Ferrell, 1985; Pogrund, Fazzi, & Lampert, 1992.) As infants mature, they will start to develop concepts and the ability to reason abstractly, and to classify objects and living things into categories.

All infants and young children learn and develop through interaction with their parents and others and their environment, but because visual information is not available to young children who are blind, they are likely to need more active instruction in these areas. This instruction does not have to be presented in formal teaching sessions, however, since young children learn mainly through taking part in everyday activities, such as getting dressed, having their diapers changed, eating, playing, and going to the store. The important difference for children who are blind is that because they cannot learn visually from the environment, their parents or caregivers must offer a good deal of information by commenting verbally on the environment and events taking place, by providing extra physical contact, and by deliberately introducing objects and experiences that children with vision can discover by themselves.

Specific strategies are presented here for fostering early development and the acquisition of language and concepts. In addition, "Providing Guidance about Early Development for Parents, Caretakers, and Teachers" notes some resources that will be useful to both parents and teachers. While these strategies emphasize the senses other than vision, it is also important to provide visually stimulating objects for children who have some vision or who are suspected to have vision.

STRATEGIES

PROMOTING EARLY LEARNING EXPERIENCES

Cognitive Development

Specific strategies can help infants to develop movement and tactile function—grasping, reaching, releasing, and wrist rotation; to develop concepts of objects, actions, three-dimensional space, and cause-and-effect relationships; and to move from experience of the self to experience of the outside world.

Sources: Adapted from Karen M. Finello, Nancy Hedlund Hanson, and Linda S. Kekelis, "Cognitive Focus: Developing Cognition, Concepts, and Language in Young Blind and Visually Impaired Children," in Rona L. Pogrund, Diane L. Fazzi, and Jessica S. Lampert, eds., *Early Focus: Working with Young Blind and Visually Impaired Children and Their Families* (New York: American Foundation for the Blind, 1992), pp. 34–49; Kay Alicyn Ferrell, *Reach Out and Teach: Meeting the Training Needs of Parents of Visually and Multiply Handicapped Young Children, Parent Handbook* (New York: American Foundation for the Blind, 1985); and Myrna R. Olson, *Guidelines and Games for Teaching Efficient Braille Reading* (New York: American Foundation for the Blind, 1981).

Grasping

✛ Encourage awareness of the hands and arms by stretching and massaging them using different textures—a washcloth; a blanket; a piece of corduroy, velvet, or nylon; socks; and brushes.

✛ Encourage opening of the palms and weight bearing and give feedback about the use of the hands and arms by placing the baby on his or her stomach and pushing his or her palms against the floor.

✛ Hang stimulating objects securely in the crib or hang a "baby gym" of objects over the infant when he or she is lying on the floor or in an infant seat so the infant will make contact accidentally; this will foster the expectation of encountering objects in the environment and help the baby get the idea of locating objects. Objects that respond when touched, such as a mobile that makes musical sounds when pulled or batted, are particularly useful.

✛ Place a variety of objects in the infant's hands that are of different shapes, weights, and textures, but that are about the size of the baby's hands—small enough to grasp but not to swallow. Some examples are a small wooden block, hard plastic rattle, chewy teething ring, or fuzzy stuffed animal.

✛ Tie toys to the infant's chair with a short string; gradually lengthen the string to encourage the infant to search for the object.

✛ As the baby develops the use of the thumb, gradually provide objects that are smaller and thinner, such as teething rings or plastic keys.

✛ As the infant develops a pincer grasp, allow the infant to feed himself or herself small pieces of food like crackers, banana, cheese, and dry cereal Os.

✛ Give the baby toys that can be filled and dumped, such as a box of blocks or clothespins and a plastic milk bottle.

✛ Provide toys with crevices, recessed parts, or moving parts, such as a telephone dial, peg board, or a "busy box" or pop-up toy with a number of activities, that encourage exploration with the index finger and separation of the index finger from the rest of the hand.

Reaching

✛ Encourage the infant to reach and investigate nearby objects and people by moving his or her hand to the object and showing the infant how to pick it up (working from behind). Gradually reduce the amount of guidance by shifting your grasp first to the baby's wrist and then to the elbow and finally lightly touching the upper arm as a reminder to move.

✛ Gradually increase the distance of the objects, stretching the infant's arm or bending him or her forward, if necessary, to give encouragement.

✛ Take advantage of everyday opportunities to have the infant reach for food, diapers, a sock on a foot, or soap in the bathtub.

✛ Choose toys that make a variety of interesting sounds—squeaks, rattles, bells—that will not frighten or overload the infant with stimuli.

Releasing

✛ To encourage the baby to release objects, use hand-over-hand modeling for demonstration, working from behind, to stack blocks; fill containers with sand, cookies, or beads; or share food and toys with others.

✛ Offer the infant sticky food, such as honey or peanut butter, that exaggerates the motion and sensation of release.

Developing concepts of object permanence and constancy

✛ Continue to talk to the baby when you approach and leave, so you do not suddenly appear and disappear.

✛ Encourage the baby to search for dropped objects, using the strategies for searching and reaching, such as tying toys to strings.

✛ Help the baby to feel that he or she has control over objects disappearing and reappearing by including activities that involve filling and dumping from containers.

✛ Roll a ball with a continuous beeping tone back and forth to provide auditory feedback that the ball still exists when it is out of the baby's grasp and tactile feedback that it has returned.

✛ Let the child know that an object remains the same even when certain characteristics have changed. For example, a potato is still a potato, whether it is hard when raw or soft, warm, and fragrant after cooking; the hall clock is the same whether it chimes loudly when you are right next to it or softly when you are in another room.

Teaching cause and effect

✛ Many of the activities just described will encourage an understanding of the notion of cause and effect: hitting crib toys; shaking rattles that produce sound; and playing with busy boxes, sorting toys, or any other toys that respond to the baby's actions.

✛ Encourage the baby to use words or gestures to produce an effect, such as pointing to a cookie jar or saying "cookie" to get one. Avoid anticipating the baby's needs, desires, likes, and dislikes to encourage the baby to take action to get what he or she wants.

✛ Build towers of blocks, bowls, or cookies that the baby can knock over.

✛ Make sure to explain what is happening in the environment, so the baby knows where things come from—for example, that Sister picked up the toy he dropped or that Daddy brought her bottle—and that things do not seem to appear and disappear as if by magic.

Sensory Development

The activities used to encourage cognitive development in infants will implicitly stimulate sensory development. There are specific strategies for helping parents develop their infants' auditory and tactile skills that are crucial for learning.

Auditory development

Infants who are blind need to learn that sound signifies an object with specific properties and to use sound cues to locate and track objects.

✤ Limit the distraction from sounds of stimuli not actually present in the environment, such as sounds from a television or radio.

✤ Speak to the baby whenever you enter the room.

✤ Introduce a variety of sound-producing toys and objects. Pay attention to the infant's preferences.

✤ To encourage an infant to turn toward a sound, start by making the sound at ear level on the side. If the infant does not turn his or her head, gently turn his or her head toward the sound, then touch the object to the infant's hand and repeat the sound. When the infant turns his or her head to sounds made at the side, move the sound below ear level till he or she turns toward it and down; then follow with sounds above ear level and in front of the infant.

✤ Identify sounds that occur in everyday activities, explaining both what they are and what is producing them. For example, "Yes, that's the sound of the toilet flushing. Jenny just flushed the toilet." Other sounds include water running in a sink, drawers closing, paper crinkling, a vacuum cleaner running, a refrigerator humming, a clock ticking or chiming, a furnace humming, cars honking, dogs barking, and wind rustling the leaves of a tree.

✤ Play sound-identification games to help the infant learn to distinguish sounds in the environment and pick out the important ones.

Tactile development

✤ Use a firm, not "tickly" touch.

✤ Present a variety of textures in clothes, toys, and food and identify them, paying attention to the infant's preferences.

✤ Allow the infant to be touched and caressed by different people.

✤ Provide objects and toys that require finer motor manipulations—pots and lids, large nuts and bolts, keys and locks, fasteners and hooks, beads for stringing, and blocks for building.

✤ Glue materials with different textures to a deck of playing cards for sorting activities.

✤ Provide a model for the child of systematic scanning and searching of objects such as from top to bottom and left to right or in widening concentric circles.

✛ Teach concepts and parts of large objects using real objects, when possible.

Language Development

Early language development involves stimulating the infant's *receptive* language (understanding) by constant exposure to language and nonverbal (physical) communication and the infant's *expressive* language by responding to his or her nonverbal communications: crying, gurgling, laughing, babbling, and the like.

✛ From the baby's earliest moments, talk to him or her. Describe and explain what is happening and what the infant is experiencing: "You're drinking your milk. It's warm and sweet. Mommy's holding you. You feel safe and warm."

✛ Since the baby cannot see you smiling back at him or her, reinforce communication with extra physical contact.

✛ Listen to and watch the infant: Give the infant a chance to talk to *you*, and take time to find out what he or she is trying to communicate. Then give feedback by expressing his or her communications in words.

✛ Express your feelings in words and put the baby's feelings into words.

✛ Both name and describe the infant's toys. For instance, say "Here is your teddy bear. It's furry and squishy. Listen! It makes a jingly sound when you shake it. That's because it has a bell inside."

✛ Encourage the infant to communicate his or her needs, likes, and dislikes; do not anticipate them. Give the infant a chance to say "ba-ba" instead of placing the bottle in his or her hands as soon as it is ready.

EXPERIENCING THE WORLD

Expanding Early Learning Experiences

Even past the stage of infancy, congenital blindness or severely reduced vision can have a tremendous impact on a child's early learning experiences, which, in turn, may lead to difficulty in learning to read and write. Lowenfeld (1973) categorized these impediments as limitations in

- the range and variety of experiences,
- the ability to get about, and
- interaction with the environment.

He urged those who work with young blind and visually impaired children to address these limitations by providing concrete and unifying experiences and opportunities for learning by doing. (Although activities to implement these strategies are discussed separately, there is considerable overlap among them.) These strategies can be applied to helping all children learn, but they are critical for children who were born blind. Vision is the sense through which children learn most easily and vicariously. The other senses give information, but not to the degree that the sense of vision does.

For example, sighted children can watch a nature program about lions in Africa on television and immediately form a concept of the environment in which lions live, what lions look like, how lion cubs play, and so forth. Children who are blind who are exposed to the same nature program will come away with much less information, received mainly from the narrator's voice and the sounds they heard. Thus, blind children need to have the environment explained to them in terms that they already understand. For example, to understand what a lion looks like, children need to have the visual information translated into meaningful tactile information. A cat can be used as a living model of a small lion without a mane, a stuffed model of a real lion can give them a better idea of a lion's size, and experience with a variety of house cats will help generalize the concept. For congenitally blind children, limitations in the range and variety of experiences, in the ability to get about, and in interactions with the environment can severely restrict the development of concepts and language.

It requires considerable thought and planning to provide a child who is blind or visually impaired with the same range and variety of experiences that a sighted child can have vicariously. Devising ways to give a congenitally blind child the same amount of information and experiences is perhaps the biggest challenge for parents and teachers not only in the preschool years but throughout the school years. The following strategies will help parents and other caregivers provide children with a rich variety of experiences, for the most part in the course of their daily activities.

STRATEGIES

EXPANDING THE RANGE AND VARIETY OF EXPERIENCES

✛ Take the child on errands in the community and talk about the places you are going. Use words to describe what you feel, hear, smell, and taste (when appropriate). Among the places you would go with children are
- stores (pharmacy, grocery store, mall, pet store, clothing store, bakery, flower shop, gift shop)
- the post office
- doctors' or dentists' offices
- a gas station
- a dry cleaner's, laundromat
- the library.

✛ Make outings a part of weekly family activities, for example to
- a zoo, especially a petting zoo
- a park (feed the ducks)
- a train, bus, trolley, or wagon ride
- a swimming pool
- a lake, river, the ocean
- a farm
- a factory (for example, a candy or toy factory)
- a picnic
- a restaurant
- relatives' or friends' homes
- museums, especially those geared to children (such as the Please Touch Museum in Philadelphia) that allow them to touch the exhibits.

✛ Use the home and neighborhood to expand the child's environment.

✛ Help the child develop concepts about his or her room—its furniture, door, closet, and windows, and position in the house or apartment (upstairs, downstairs, down the hall).
- Expand the explorations to the rest of the rooms and their contents.
- Take the child outside and explore the perimeter of the house, including steps or stoop, the entranceway, and the adjacent sidewalks, and relate it to the rooms inside.
- If the family has a yard, use it to talk about bushes, flowers, trees, grass, sidewalks, stoops, birds, and insects.
- Take walks with the child from the house or apartment to visit neighbors and then expand outward. All the while, help the child develop the vocabulary to describe his or her world and let the child experience as much as possible through touching, hearing, smelling, and tasting.

A child who is blind or visually impaired needs to be allowed the experience of exploring his or her world independently. A child's opportunities to experience his or her environment will be greatly expanded by helping him or her to develop independent mobility skills.

S T R A T E G I E S

EXPANDING THE ABILITY TO GET ABOUT

✛ Some children enjoy using a rolling walker that they can sit in when they are first learning to walk. Although children in walkers must be carefully supervised, walkers provide some children with a sense of security because the padded bumpers absorb any bumps, so the children can scoot around a room with ease and without fear of falling or banging into things themselves.

✛ Once the child learns to walk, have a mobility specialist provide an appropriate precane device to allow the child to further expand and refine his or her skills in exploring the environment.

✛ Help the child to become as independent as possible in negotiating the environment by always keeping furniture in the same place.

Lowenfeld (1973) pointed out that people who cannot see what is going on around them may tend to feel a sense of detachment from their environment. But people cannot interact with something that they are not aware of. Part of the limitation in interaction with the environment comes simply from not being able to see what is there. Providing a broad range and variety of experiences will help children know what to expect and what is expected of them. But parents also need to teach and encourage appropriate interactions with environment.

STRATEGIES

INCREASING INTERACTION WITH THE ENVIRONMENT

✛ Point out what is in the child's surroundings. For example, at a playground, show the child where all the play equipment is—climbing bars, slides, and sandboxes as well as the swings—and help him or her gradually learn how to use each piece of equipment.

✛ Help the child anticipate what to expect in various environments. For example, in the grocery store, explain how food is located on the shelves and let the child explore the shelves nearby. Ask the child to go ahead to find a display that sticks out in the aisle. Explain the coldness of the frozen foods aisle and the smells of the fish and meat counters. Have the child help push the cart, help put food in the cart, take food out and put it on the conveyor belt, talk to the checkout person, and so forth.

Lowenfeld (1973) suggested that children who are blind need a variety of direct, concrete experiences with objects and situations in their immediate environment. Special attention is required to make sure that they are familiar with ideas and concepts that sighted children usually absorb without special effort either through observation of real life or from picture books, television, or movies.

Then, when blind children begin to encounter such concepts in their reading materials, they have a realistic frame of reference based on genuine experiences.

Koenig and Farrenkopf (1997) examined 254 stories from three basal reading series to identify the types of meaningful experiences that would help a reader understand the stories. Their list of global experiences, from the most to the least frequently mentioned, was as follows:

Exploring nature/plants/insects
Experiences with living creatures
Experiencing emotions/sense of well being
Experiences with family/family traditions
Experiences in the community
Experiences at home
Experiences with friends/pretending
Experiences with eating
School experiences
Experiences with books
Experiences with weather
Using different forms of transportation
Enjoying the arts
Going to a farm
Working together/sharing/helping
Doing/making things
Learning about people who are different
Getting into trouble
Looking for/finding something
Traveling/visiting others

This list could serve as a beginning outline of experiences that would help visually impaired children to develop concepts needed to comprehend the books and stories they are likely to encounter at the beginning level.

Whenever possible, the real object should be used when teaching concepts to blind children. But when this is not possible because real objects are too hot or otherwise dangerous, too small, or large, or far away, it is necessary to use models. Children need to learn what models are before teachers or parents can use them meaningfully. Teaching the concept of models needs to take place gradually over time during the child's preschool years. The best way to teach the notion of a model is to use a concept that the child has already developed from experiencing the real thing. This can take a bit of creativity on the part of parents or teachers, as in the following example:

Ronny loved his wagon and loved to have his sister pull him around in it. He had explored the wagon from front to back, knew about the wheels and the handle, and had a firm concept of "wagon." His parents gave him a miniature toy wagon for Christmas, helped him compare the parts with those on his real wagon, and talked to him about how much the toy wagon looked like his real one. Then they put a stylized toy person in the wagon to represent Ronny, explaining that though the toy did not look much like Ronny, he had to imagine that it was because it was the right size for the miniwagon, just as Ronny was the right size for the real wagon. Next, they tried to put his sister's Barbie doll in the mini-wagon, but it was too big for the wagon, just as Ronnie's mother was too big for the real wagon. But, they explained, even though the Barbie was too big for the miniwagon, it was a better model than the first toy person, and they asked Ronny why. He said, "Because it has arms and legs like real people."

This type of activity has to be repeated again and again using other objects to establish a firm concept of a model. Children need to be able to experience models that are both larger and smaller than the real objects so they can recognize that the concept operates in both directions.

STRATEGIES

PROVIDING CONCRETE EXPERIENCES

✛ Bring the experience physically close to the child so he or she can smell, touch, feel, hear, and see as much as his or her vision permits. For example, make sure to take the child to the petting zoo, where he or she can touch, smell, and interact with the animals, rather than just listening to them from a distance. Continually broaden the range and variety of common experiences. Emphasize the quality and depth of the experiences, rather than simply highlighting many superficial experiences.

✛ Refer to Koenig and Farrenkopf's (1997) list of experiences commonly discussed in children's reading materials and use it as a guide when planning trips or other experiences to ensure that when the child reads the stories he or she will be bringing the appropriate mind-set to them.

✛ Teach the child the necessary vocabulary to describe what he or she is experiencing through the senses. Create a list of concepts for the experience and teach the concepts to the child, relating each to what he or she has already learned and experienced (see "Activities for Developing Concepts" and "Record Keeping" in this chapter).

✛ Provide the child with real objects or things whenever possible. A *real* caterpillar feels very different from a foot-long stuffed toy caterpillar wearing sneakers!

✛ Be creative in using models when real objects are not feasible—for example, the cat as a model of a lion, fuzzy pipe cleaners to represent a caterpillar, large doilies cut to resemble snowflake, a bonsai plant to represent a tree, or a dollhouse to give the idea of an entire house.

✛ Expand on concepts already learned to include a wider range of experiences or activities. For example, once the child has learned the concept of "boat," it can be expanded to include other vehicles that float, such as canoes, kayaks, tugboats, ocean-going vessels, etc. Models that are proportionate in size to the real objects can be used once the child has had the initial experience.

It is easy for children who are visually impaired to miss part of an experience because they are focusing on only part of what is happening. Remember the story of the blind men and the elephant? Each touched only one part of the animal, and each had a severely limited and completely different impression of the beast. It is important for parents and teachers to find ways to present situations in their entirety—what Lowenfeld (1973) termed a unifying experience.

STRATEGIES

PROVIDING UNIFYING EXPERIENCES

✛ Try to create the whole experience for the child. For example, a child who sits in one place in a rowboat is gaining a limited experience of a boat ride. To make the experience more meaningful, he or she needs to reach into the water from the boat, hear the waves, trail (on dry land or near the shore) the perimeter and interior of the boat, feel how far down the boat sits in the water, and so forth.

✛ Teach the child how to explore objects (large and small) with his or her hands so none of the parts of the objects are missed. If children are hesitant to explore objects in their environment, teach them how to curl their fingers under and use the backs of their fingers initially to explore something in the same way they are taught to trail walls in mobility lessons. They can use this technique to explore as much of objects as possible; then, once they have an idea of the size and shape of the objects, they can go back and use their fingertips to explore the objects more thoroughly.

✛ Whenever a child has one experience, think of ways to relate that experience or link it to other things he or she is interested in. For instance, when planting a small tree, show the child the root ball, the branches, the leaves, and the trunk and compare this tree and its parts to those of a full-grown tree. Cooking offers many opportunities to show how objects may change form—for example, make the connection between the hard potato dug up from the dirt on a farm visit to warm, fluffy mashed potatoes or between a hard, cold egg from the refrigerator and scrambled eggs on a plate.

✛ Make certain a child is not missing things around him or her that one may take for granted that the child knows. For example, to show where and how high the ceiling is, lift the child up to explore and walk on the ceiling with his or her hands or feet. To show what the windows open out to, open a window on the ground floor and help the child climb outside, if possible, so he or she can understand where the one side of the window leads to. Shout to the child from an upstairs window to let the child hear how high up your voice is.

There is no doubt that learning by doing provides a more engaging and memorable experience and is a better teaching tool than merely hearing or reading about something. For blind children it is even more important, since the "doing" of an activity allows them to develop an understanding of the activity based upon kinesthetic and other sensory experiences related to the performance of the activity. A good example of this is taking care of plants. A child who plants the seeds, waters, and cares for her own tomato plant and then later eats the tomatoes feels engaged with the activity. She knows the pungent smell of its leaves and has seen how it grows from a tiny seed to a large plant. By taking care of the plant, she learns about responsibility, about the needs of organisms, and about how to water a plant, and she feels good about her ability. She learns that she is able to do things. Parents, caregivers, and teachers can provide children who are congenitally blind with opportunities to engage in functional experiences. The list that follows provides a sample of experiences around the home in which children can become involved.

STRATEGIES

PROVIDING OPPORTUNITIES TO LEARN BY DOING

Beginning Household Tasks

✛ sweeping the sidewalk

✛ washing yard furniture

✛ emptying wastebaskets

✛ folding towels

✛ setting the table

Source: Adapted from Sally S. Mangold, "Nurturing High Self-Esteem in Visually Handicapped Children," in Mangold (Ed.), *A Teachers' Guide to the Special Educational Needs of Blind and Visually Handicapped Children* (New York: American Foundation for the Blind, 1982), p. 99.

- ✛ bringing in the mail every day
- ✛ making the bed
- ✛ taking the silverware from the dishwasher and putting it away
- ✛ washing the dishes
- ✛ cleaning the sink and bathtub
- ✛ changing light bulbs
- ✛ collecting dirty towels from the bathroom
- ✛ opening and closing windows
- ✛ unlocking and locking the door with a key
- ✛ straightening magazines in a pile or in a rack
- ✛ changing the toilet paper

Beginning Cooking Skills

- ✛ washing little tomatoes and taking off the stems
- ✛ making frozen lemonade or juice
- ✛ opening potato chips and filling a bowl
- ✛ making toast
- ✛ buttering toast
- ✛ arranging pre-sliced cheese on a plate
- ✛ pouring breakfast cereal into a bowl
- ✛ taking ice cubes out of the tray and refilling the tray
- ✛ making instant pudding
- ✛ baking cookies:
    - ▪ frozen prepared cookies—just bake
    - ▪ prepared cookie dough in the refrigerator of the store—cut and bake

Fostering Essential Concepts

Many of the skills that are part of any good preschool curriculum are especially crucial to help children who are congenitally blind develop so they will have the foundation to comprehend what they will read later. For example, special attention needs to be given to developing concepts, abstractions, classifications, and problem-solving skills. Some concepts that a child must learn, such as up, down, right, left, top, bottom, page, line, beginning, and end, relate directly to the reading process itself. Other concepts relate to descriptions of what is found in the environment. Mangold (1982) suggested compiling lists of adjectives found in beginning readers and using them to reinforce meanings. She gave the following examples:

The way things feel: rough, smooth, hard, soft, bumpy, spongy.

The size of things: small, little, tiny, big, fat, huge, gigantic, long, narrow, thick, thin, fat, wide.

The way things smell: sweet, sour, good, icky, awful, wonderful, terrible, delightful. (p. 2)

Hall (1982) presented an extensive list of crucial concepts that children must understand to be able to participate fully in daily life. Children also need these concepts to be able to comprehend both reading instruction and what they read. Hall believed these concepts need to be taught in a systematic way to visually impaired children. (Hall's entire article, including a complete listing of her crucial concepts, is reprinted at the back of this volume.) She organized them into the following categories:

1. Body awareness (concepts pertaining to the body)
   a. kinesthetic awareness
   b. proprioceptive awareness
   c. sensations
   d. facial expressions
   e. gestures
2. Environmental awareness (crucial objects in the environment and specific relationships among elements in the environment)
3. Awareness of object characteristics (general properties of objects)
   a. size
   b. shape
   c. sound
   d. color
   e. texture
   f. comparative characteristics
4. Time awareness (concepts pertaining to time)
5. Spatial awareness (concepts related to position in space)
6. Actions (concepts pertaining to movement)
7. Quantity (concepts associated with numbers and number combinations)
8. Symbol awareness (crucial symbolic concepts)
9. Emotional and social awareness (concepts associated with psychosocial adjustment)
10. Reasoning (thought processes in which concepts are used)

Children's understanding progresses from the concrete object ("my play table in the kitchen") to its function (a place to put things) to an abstraction (objects with flat tops and four legs that are used as a place to put things)—at which point the object has evolved into a concept (Lydon & McGraw, 1973). Hall (1982) stressed that to teach a concept, it is first necessary to assess a child's current understanding of it. The concept must be defined precisely in order to teach it, because concepts are often used in different ways (the *front* of one's body versus the *front* of a line or the *front* of a book, for example). Then it must be analyzed into any component concepts that must be taught first.

In addition to the general strategies for teaching early concepts, Lydon and McGraw (1973) presented many activities for teaching a variety of specific concepts. The following strategies usually work well with children ages 3 to 6. However, all children develop at different rates, and some blind children may not be developmentally ready or able to perform all of the activities until they are older.

STRATEGIES

ACTIVITIES FOR DEVELOPING CONCEPTS

Body Image

Body parts

Teaching concepts related to body parts generally also entails introducing such notions as open-closed, apart-together, forward-backward, raise, lower, bend, alike-different, circle, and straight. It will also develop *kinesthetic perception,* or knowing where one's body and its parts are in relation to space.

✛ Explore with the child the range of motion of each body part, including the hand and fingers, wrist, forearm, elbow joint, shoulder joint, shoulders, head and neck, lower back and waist, hip joint, knee joint, ankle joint, and foot and toes.

✛ Compare and contrast different body parts. For example, how many parts can be bent? How many can be bent in more than one direction?

✛ Explore the function of each body part.

✛ Play games like Simon Says and Here We Go Loopedy Loo.

Directionality

In the course of the following activities, teach the child how what is on his or her left and right will change as the child's position changes.

✛ Identify either the left or right side by a distinguishing mark, such as a ribbon tied around the hand on that side.

✛ Play games involving left and right, such as "Pick up the book with your left hand," in addition to Simon Says and Loopedy Loo.

Source: Adapted from William T. Lydon and M. Loretta McGraw, *Concept Development for Visually Handicapped Children: A Resource Guide for Teachers and Other Professionals Working in Educational Settings* (New York: American Foundation for the Blind, 1973).

✛ Arrange objects in different ways and have the child identify which is on the left and the right. Start with objects of the same size and shape, progress to different sizes, different sizes and shapes, textured objects, and combinations of all these variations.

✛ Have the child move toward his or her left and right and respond to directions, such as "Go left to the window" and "Pick up the book on your right."

✛ Stand in front of the child and hold out your left hand. Show the child that to touch it, the child extends his or her right hand. Repeat with the other side.

✛ Discuss the child's idea of up and down.

✛ Introduce the idea of top and bottom in relation to body parts: Where is the top of the body? the bottom? Which parts are above the waist and which are below?

✛ Discuss daily activities that involve up and down, such as getting up in the morning, going up and down stairs, standing up, sitting down, and reaching up or down.

✛ Discuss the child's idea of front and back.

✛ Identify body parts that are in front of the body and in back.

✛ Talk about who sits in front and in back of the child, who is in front or in back of the child on line, the front and back of the classroom, the front and back of books, and items that are in front or in back of the child.

Gross motor movement

The following activities develop balance, coordination, flexibility, and strength; contribute to the child's spatial awareness; reinforce concepts of body image; develop kinesthetic perception; and allow for free expression and exploration of the body's capabilities.

✛ Practice basic locomotor patterns, including walking, running, hopping, jumping, leaping, galloping, skipping, and sliding.

✛ Practice a variety of movements, starting with easy ones and progressing to more difficult ones, such as log rolls, crab walk, bear walk, duck walk, crane hop, elevator (deep knee bends), seesaw (alternating deep knee bends while holding hands with a partner), frog hop, and modified and regular push-ups.

✛ Additional gross motor activities include jumping jacks, toe touches, roller skating, climbing, balance-beam exercises, sit-ups, forward and back rolls, arm wrestling, and throwing and catching balls.

Tactile discrimination

Tactile discrimination includes becoming familiar with different textures and surfaces, weights, sizes, shapes, temperatures and other atmospheric conditions and being able to identify objects by touch.

✛ To refine muscle movements, have the child practice such activities as manipulating fasteners (buttons, zippers, and snaps), stringing beads of various sizes and

Exploring objects of different shapes and textures helps develop tactile discrimination.

shapes, manipulating locks and cabinet fixtures, dressing and undressing, using eating utensils, washing hands and face, finger painting, stretching a rubber band, using Scotch tape, using scissors, and folding paper in half by placing the corners together.

✢ Allow the child to play with various surfaces like dirt, grass, and mud.

✢ Play games involving the identification of objects through tactile exploration.

✢ Practice identifying objects in a smaller play version, such as recognizing doll house furniture and appliances, before locating the real thing.

Sound discrimination

Sound discrimination involves being aware of, identifying, localizing, and discriminating among sounds.

✛ Have the child listen to sounds coming from inside and outside and describe them. Then have the child move toward the sounds.

✛ Move about the room making natural sounds and have the child point to where you are and identify them.

✛ Bounce a ball and have the child count the bounces.

✛ Touch one child and have him or her say a word; have the other children identify him or her by voice.

✛ Fill several glasses with various depths of water and have the child note the change in sound.

✛ Play recordings of sounds the child would not normally hear, such as crickets chirping (for city dwellers) and rush hour traffic (for country dwellers).

✛ Record a segment of a class and play it back to allow the children to hear all the sounds they make.

✛ Have the child explore a building and several rooms, noting the changes in resonance in rooms of different sizes and the different types of sounds in different rooms.

✛ Have the child pay attention to the different sounds on days with different types of weather.

✛ Ask the child to distinguish different types of vehicles by the sound.

✛ Have the child provide sound effects for a story.

✛ Play recordings of various sounds and have the child identify them.

✛ Have the child attempt to identify a dropped object, such as a book or a pencil, by the sound it makes when dropped.

Olfactory discrimination

Olfactory discrimination involves being aware of, discriminating, and localizing odors.

✛ Have the child become aware of different odors in the environment, identify them, and go to the sources.

✛ Provide a number of containers with different odors and set up a contest between two teams to identify the most odors. Use cotton balls soaked with various scents in baby food jars, or put different spices in the jars.

✛ Have the child note odors in different rooms at home and when riding in a car or train or taking a walk and suggest adjectives to describe the odors.

✛ Take the child on trips to a bakery, butcher shop, pizza parlor, hair salon, hospital, and florist. Go to a place with no special odor, such as the canned goods section of a supermarket, and ask the child why there are no odors.

Time and Distance

✛ Discuss the time it takes to perform everyday activities like dressing or eating. Have the child estimate the time and then time him or her to see the difference. While this activity will be difficult for preschoolers, it starts them thinking about time.

Keeping Track of Experiential Learning

As children get older, it becomes difficult for their parents and teachers to remember what experiences they have had. In assuming that children have had a real, concrete experience with something just because they seem to use the words correctly in talking about it, parents or teachers may be reinforcing what is referred to as "verbalism" (Cutsforth, 1972)—using words without a real understanding of what they mean. In the preschool years it is essential for teachers to communicate frequently with parents so they can refer to experiences that the child may have had while at home or on summer vacation. Record keeping becomes even more valuable as children get older and change teachers. Keeping file folders of the language and concept experiences that children have had can help teachers determine whether the children will be able to understand a particular reading passage. As the children progress through the preschool years, this record of experiences can be expanded and used as a guide to influence the activities in which they participate and to which teachers direct their attention.

STRATEGIES

RECORD KEEPING

✛ Maintain a language and concept development folder or an experiences journal for each child. The folder would contain short descriptions of experiences the child has had that can be referred to and built on when the child is learning new language concepts. The journal could contain a set of stories written in braille and print for someone to read to the child and for the child eventually to read independently. Miller (1985) suggests having the child keep an experiences journal. The child can even use a tape recorder to record sounds he or she likes (such as birds calling to each other or the monkeys chattering at a zoo). After listening to the tapes of the sounds, the teacher and the child could construct a story about visiting the place where the sounds were taped that could be used to help the child remember the outing. Having children tape-record their recounting of an experience is a fun way to remember what happened, and children are delighted to hear what they sounded like when they were younger. This is like creating an auditory scrapbook.

CONCEPT CHECKLIST

Student _____ Date _____

Environmental Awareness

Concepts	Date Achieved	Comments on the Experience

Body Awareness

top _____

bottom _____

middle _____

back _____

front _____

left-right _____

names of body parts _____

Environmental Awareness

yard _____

backyard _____

stairs _____

doorbell _____

house _____

porch _____

tree _____

Figure 2-1. Sample Concept Checklist

Source: Adapted from Amanda Hall, "Teaching Specific Concepts to Visually Handicapped Students," in Sally S. Mangold, Ed., *A Teacher's Guide to the Special Educational Needs of Blind and Visually Handicapped Children* (New York: American Foundation for the Blind, 1982), pp. 10–19.

If you are reading a story and the word *wet* is in it, you could remind children of how they felt when they fell into a puddle: *That* is wet. At the same time, you can provide additional experience with the word *wet* by taking a bath, wetting a cloth, or taking the children out in the rain.

✦ Keep records of concept development by adapting lists of concepts that congenitally blind children need to learn and placing them in the child's folder on language and concept development. The sample form in Figure 2-1, which is adapted from Hall (1982), is an example of such a checklist. Depending on how many teachers work with a child, there may need to be a column for the teachers' names or initials.

DEVELOPING AWARENESS OF READING AND WRITING

Developing a Concept of Written Language

An important part of developing language and concepts is to understand what written language is. This concept can be partly taught by reading aloud to a child, but the child must also encounter the writing where it would normally be placed: in books, on cereal boxes, on posters, on automatic teller machines, in elevators, and so on. When the child cannot see the writing because it is print, parents or teachers may want to alert the child that they are reading from signs that have print on them. These signs could be anything from labels on packages to street signs to road maps to the sign for a McDonald's restaurant.

There is no hard and fast rule about when to begin exposing a child to reading and writing, but in general all the strategies should be implemented as early as possible and the child's attention gradually focused on them.

STRATEGIES

EXPOSING A CHILD TO WRITTEN LANGUAGE (BRAILLE AND PRINT)

✦ Let children know where print writing appears in the environment. Children need to know where sighted people get their information, so they can grasp how print is used to communicate. Young sighted children may learn to recognize letters from signs, such as for K-Mart. Young blind children do not have any idea how sighted people know one store from another, so they have to be told. When you are walking in the neighborhood, for example, say, "I know we are on Juniper Street because we just passed the street sign," and show where the street signs are placed.

✤ Provide a child with lots of braille. Many teachers recommend labeling everything in a child's environment in braille. They use vinyl labeling tape with an adhesive backing, and braille labelers (similar to those used to create print labels with vinyl tape). These products are available from various consumer product catalogs (see the Resources section). Some teachers use premade labels from the American Printing House for the Blind (APH) to label sofas, chairs, tables, and other objects. The labels expose the children to braille and to the words that represent the objects as they encounter them. Using this technique can also provide the child with a reason to explore an object carefully to find the braille on it. One drawback to this approach is that it creates an impression that a child would normally find braille labels in these places and perhaps that print labels may also appear where there is braille. Labeling the objects in a child's environment is not harmful, but the following approach may be more functional.

✤ Provide braille in places where there may normally be print. You might label such objects such as:

- the on and off positions on a light switch
- the words on refrigerator magnets
- a child's name on his or her door, toy box, wagon, audiotapes, and books
- titles on the covers of books
- the backs of cereal boxes, recipe cards, and grocery lists, using plastic overlay sheets of braille
- playing cards for games (bought or made)

✤ Incorporate the use of signs in braille and large print, as well as simulated reading and writing activities, in preschool classrooms (see "Incorporating Environmental Literacy in Preschool Play Centers" in this chapter).

✤ Provide books in braille or print-braille. Print-braille books are written in both print and braille, with the braille either directly on the print page or on a clear plastic overlay so that the print and picture can be seen as the braille is read. Sighted children love to "read" books to their dolls, pets, and stuffed animals. Give visually impaired children the same opportunity to read braille books to theirs. The Resources section at the end of this book lists sources for finding books in braille and print-braille, so that young children who are blind can be exposed to braille stories just as their sighted peers are exposed to print stories.

There are two additional reasons for the strong emphasis on exposing blind children to print and where it is found in their environment. First, blind children who are aware of how sighted people gain information can more readily participate in conversations with their sighted friends. Second, they have more control over their environment when they know how it is structured.

Reading Aloud

"The single most important activity for building the knowledge required for eventual success in reading is reading aloud to children." (Anderson, Heibert, Scott, & Wilkinson, 1985, p. 23)

As important as reading aloud is to all children from the earliest possible age to establish the foundation for later learning, it is even more crucial for children who are blind or visually impaired, who will not see others reading unless their

---

INCORPORATING ENVIRONMENTAL LITERACY IN PRESCHOOL PLAY CENTERS

Incorporating braille, large print, and everyday uses of reading and writing into play centers—such as the housekeeping area that is a standard feature of most preschools—provides a way to expose children who are blind or visually impaired to written language in a meaningful way. Not only do these centers increase literacy behaviors such as scribbling, but they are also fun for children and stimulate their creative play.

These play centers can be set up using simple materials such as blocks for their construction, with brailled and/or large print signs and other materials that are used for reading and writing in real life. Teachers model literacy activities such as "reading" a menu and "writing" orders on a pad in a restaurant play center. Pairing the construction of a play center with a field trip to the real-life location makes it more exciting and meaningful for the children and allows the teacher to point out the use of environmental print.

For example, one preschool class discussed making a fire station play center. First they took a field trip to a real fire station. Then they constructed their play center out of blocks, based on what they had seen. They included a print and braille sign for the fire station; a toy telephone, paper and pencil, and slate and stylus for taking 911 calls; a print and tactile map for locating fires; a living area with books, magazines, and a cookbook; a fire hat with a print and braille label on it; toy fire trucks to "ride" to the fire; and street signs made from blocks with print and braille taped to them. The teacher modeled taking the emergency call, writing the address, and checking the map.

Examples of play centers in which literacy could be effectively and meaningfully integrated include:

- airport
- art gallery
- beauty shop
- doctor's office
- post office
- restaurant
- train station
- fire station
- bakery
- bank
- fix-it shop
- flower shop
- grocery
- ice cream parlor
- library
- travel agency
- veterinarian's office

Source: Joyce Burnett, "Play Centers for Preschool Visually Impaired Children," unpublished manuscript, May 1995.

attention is called to it. Reading aloud should be a pleasurable part of the daily routine.

The videotape *Discovering the Magic of Reading: Elizabeth's Story* (1995), available from APH, provides some simple guidelines for reading aloud to children who are blind or visually impaired from infancy through the preschool years (see "Guidelines for Reading Aloud"). It stresses that reading to children who are blind or visually impaired is even more important than reading to sighted children, since books provide another way for blind and visually impaired children to interact with their world.

Miller (1985) also suggests ideas and activities for helping to promote language and concept growth, especially through the use of storybooks. In working with her preschool-age daughter, who was born blind, Miller found that the most effective reading-readiness tool was an actual braille book, because "the motivation is intrinsic in the words that tell a story" (p. 3). (The article is reprinted in full in this book because, in addition to providing a wealth of activities, it captures the experiences that parents have in trying to locate and adapt appropriate stories for their blind children.)

STRATEGIES

READING ALOUD

✢ When reading books in braille or print-braille format, move your hands across the braille as you read and have the child place his or her hands on yours so the child can get an idea of how people read braille. Or, you can place the child's fingers on the braille and move them as you read the print. (You may need to get a copy of the print if the braille covers it.)

✢ Make use of anticipation and redundancy in language when reading aloud to children. Let children complete sentences, especially with stories in which the endings repeat or rhyme. Once they are familiar with a story, substitute words that do not make sense. For example, in the nursery rhyme "Humpty Dumpty," you might say, "and Humpty Dumpty had a great autumn. Oops, wrong kind of 'fall'!" Or "Humpty Dumpty had a great banana." Children delight in being giving words that do not make sense. They think this kind of game is hilarious, and while you are providing the fun, you are teaching them that they understand what words make sense and what words do not.

✢ Relate what you are reading to children's previous experiences. Children often do not relate their own knowledge to what they are reading (Anderson, Hiebert, Scott and Wilkinson, 1985). When reading aloud to children or when discussing what has been read, teachers and parents should ask questions that help children recognize the relationship between what they are reading and what they already know. This practice is particularly important with congenitally blind children who may have limitations in their experiences to begin with. They should be reminded of how things felt, smelled, or tasted instead of what things looked like. They need to believe that knowledge gained through these other senses is important knowledge that they can rely on.

For example, when reading aloud the story "Rumplestiltskin," you might ask the child if he or she remembers what straw and gold feel like and what a spinning wheel is. (As discussed earlier in this chapter, you would have exposed the children to such objects or concepts before reading the book.) You can then ask the child how easy he or she thinks it would be to take straw and spin it into gold.

If you are reading aloud a story that has a description of a barn and hayloft, ask the child to tell you whether he or she has had any experience with barns and haylofts. This is where knowledge of a child's experiences becomes important. You may need to remind the child that on a visit to relatives who live on a farm, he or she climbed a ladder into the hayloft that had wooden planks on it. Have the child relate his or her experiences with haylofts and barns to the barn and loft in the story you are reading. Are the experiences similar? If not, then the child is learning about another kind of loft or barn, but such concrete experiences are the building blocks for developing a broader meaningful concept.

USING TOOLS FOR WRITING AND DRAWING

In addition to developing a concept of written language, in the emergent literacy stage children need to develop a concept of the act of writing. Why do people write? What do they write with? What is drawing, and how is it different from writing? Parents can help children develop these concepts as early as possible by letting the children in on what they are doing. ("I'm writing a letter to Grandma." "I'm making a grocery list. I use my pencil and make marks on the paper to help me remember what I need to buy.")

Congenitally blind children cannot "visualize" things the way adventitiously blinded children or adults may be able to do. The notion of "writing" has meaning to sighted children who see it demonstrated, but congenitally blind children do not necessarily know what writing is unless someone models it for them. Thus, just as it is important for them to know that their parent is writing a grocery list using a pen or pencil, they also need to know that grocery lists, letters, telephone numbers, and messages can be produced in braille. Parents and teachers need to provide a lot of modeling for young blind children using the various tools for writing braille to get across the idea of how writing is accomplished, as well as the purposes of writing.

GUIDELINES FOR READING ALOUD

INFANCY

- Read to a child in a cozy place.

- Read and sing rhymes to help soothe a child.

- Use your voice in a dramatic way to make the words of the story exciting.

- Read anything, as long as you enjoy it.

- Choose books with simple, bright illustrations in case the child has some vision; outline the illustrations with a dark felt-tip pen to provide contrast, if necessary.

TODDLER YEARS

- Give the child objects to feel in place of the pictures that may be in the books.

- Collect objects in a story box to accompany stories; explore the objects before reading a story

- Make your own books with objects for each page, using sturdy cardboard for the pages.

- Give the child plenty of opportunities to handle books.

- Look for and use commercial books that have things for touching and looking.

- Keep books in a location where the child can have access to them.

- Involve the child in the story; encourage him or her to repeat words or rhymes and ask the child simple questions.

ALMOST PRESCHOOL

- Read stories that are predictable.

- Use tactile symbols for the covers of books.

- Use books with tactile illustrations that are in print and braille.

- Let the child's interest in braille develop naturally.

- Let the child know what you use print for.

PRESCHOOL

- Enroll the child in a preschool story-hour program at a local library.

- Review books to see if they depend on pictures before reading them to the child.

- Consider if the concepts presented in the books are familiar to the child; if not, help the child learn the concepts by relating them to things the child knows. Books then begin to broaden the child's learning.

- Use tactile-visual storybooks or books with raised-line drawings, such as those published by APH.

- Use print-braille books.

Source: Adapted from *Discovering the Magic of Reading: Elizabeth's Story* (videotape) (Louisville, KY: American Printing House for the Blind, 1995).

Scribbling is also a natural part of any child's evolution into a writer. Sighted children use pencils or crayons to imitate their parents' writing or to draw pictures. Children who are blind need to be encouraged to scribble by using tools that produce braille, which they themselves will later read.

These activities can occur at the same time teachers are using some of the strategies for providing experiences and learning about print. Some of the same activities that let children know where print exists in the environment will give them an idea of what writing is all about. The difference is that in the first instance, children are being introduced to writing that was "put there" by someone unknown (Where did the print on the cereal box come from?), whereas in the second, they are learning how adults in their environment use writing to communicate with others and with themselves.

STRATEGIES

FOSTERING THE CONCEPTS OF WRITING AND DRAWING

Model the activity of writing using a variety of tools, including the tools children will use to produce braille and tools that sighted people use to produce print. Use a variety of methods such as the following to demonstrate what writing is:

✛ Use a screen board, paper, and crayon (see "How to Make a Screen Board" in this chapter). Put a piece of paper on top of the screen and secure it in place with rubber bands or tape. Have the child draw a line across the paper with a crayon and then feel that line with his or her fingers. Let the child know that just as he or she can feel the line, sighted people can see the line. Lines like that are called print lines. Many of these lines exist on paper, but cannot be felt. If you use scented crayons, you can create a multisensory experience for the child.

✛ Make a line of braille characters. Explain that this is a line of braille that can be felt. Print readers read lines of print characters that are formed on the paper using ink that cannot be felt but can be seen. (Remind the child of the crayon line that was drawn and could be felt and seen.)

✛ Various substances that form lines can be glued down on paper, including lines of colored glue (let the glue dry before touching the lines), puff paint, or yarn, or use Wikki Stix (available from Exceptional Teaching Aids; see Resources). (Wikki Stix are like sticky pipe cleaners of all colors; they are flexible, can be bent into any shape, will stick to paper until pulled off, and can be cut into smaller lengths.) Plastic alphabet letters can be glued onto paper or magnetic alphabet letters can be arranged in a line on a magnetic tray, thus forming a line of print letters. These letters can be likened to letters made by using a pen on paper and related to the line of print found in a book.

✛ Give children writing tools and allow them to scribble. Children who are blind or visually impaired need to have hands-on access to their unique writing implements.

✛ Use a brailler. In general, the best tool to start with is the Perkins brailler, because it gives a child immediate access to what he or she has written without having to remove the paper or turn it over as one does when writing with the slate and stylus. Using the Perkins brailler to scribble also teaches children the amount of strength they will need to write braille on it. Children can be taught to make tactile designs using the brailler, such as the "braille wave" (Simons, 1994), which is made by brailling dots 3, 2, 1, 4, 5, and 6 over and over across the page to create a curving tactile line. Help them learn to put the paper in the braillewriter and in the slate and stylus as early as possible. Also encourage them to use the correct fingers on the braillewriter as early as possible, so they can achieve accuracy once they are actually writing braille.

✛ Use a Peg Slate. The Peg Slate, available from APH, consists of 10 cells, each of which has six pegs that can be pushed down with the finger from one side of the slate to the other. On the Peg Slate, braille characters are created by pushing selected pegs down with the index finger from one side, and then turning the Peg Slate over to feel what characters have been made. The connection between making and reading braille characters on a braille slate can be made easily.

✛ Use the Swail Dot Inverter. In conjunction with the Peg Slate, the teacher may want to teach children to use a Swail Dot Inverter (also available from APH) for scribbling and to eventually teach the proper way to hold the stylus. The Swail Dot Inverter is shaped like a stylus, except that instead of a point at the base, it has a small cylinder with a sharp point inside. Pushing down on the stylus and pulling it up creates a single raised dot that can be felt without turning the paper over. This is a good drawing and scribbling tool for young blind children. Using it helps them develop a good hold on the stylus and allows them to practice making dots and writing braille. They can make lines of pictures, dots, circles, and other shapes with this tool and feel everything they have made.

✛ Use a slate and stylus. These tools are often referred to as the blind person's pencil. A slate is made of metal or plastic hinged on the left side and opening on the right. The top of the slate has rectangular holes that match indentations for the six dots of the braille cell on the bottom of the slate. Paper is inserted between the two parts of the slate. The stylus consists of a handle from which an elongated metal point sticks out. The writer uses the metal point to punch holes in the paper in the recesses in each hole corresponding to the six dots of the braille cell. The writer moves from right to left on the slate, and the dots are felt by taking the paper out of the slate and turning it over. For young children's scribbling practice, you should provide as many types of slates and styli as you can purchase (see Chapter 3).

✛ Use pencils and crayons. Blind children should also scribble using tools that sighted children use. Although they will eventually need to learn to hold them properly so they can be taught signature writing, at this stage they do not have to know the proper way of holding pencils and crayons (just as sighted children do not).

✛ Use kits with raised-line drawing boards, which generally have a clipboard with a rubbery surface on which a sheet of plastic is placed. Using a pen or the pointed stylus that comes with these kits (which are available from some specialty catalogs; see Resources), children can write or draw on the plastic; the stylus creates a raised line that can be felt. Have children make lines using the pen or stylus and then feel the line. Use a ballpoint pen on regular paper and tell them that, although they cannot feel the line, the line can be seen because there is ink in the pen. Children can also use a screen board to make drawings with crayons they can feel.

✛ Use raised-line coloring books are similar to regular coloring books, except that the outlines of the pictures are raised. Although they are not as meaningful for visually impaired children as they are for sighted children, visually impaired children like to be able to color when their siblings and friends do. Also, the raised lines give them some ideas of what pictures are. You can create coloring books using lines of glue over the main lines of a picture or purchase a raised-line coloring book from Exceptional Teaching Aids (see Resources).

✛ Try other devices. A more expensive way to make raised-line pictures to color is by using a Tactile Image Enhancer (manufactured by Repro-Tronics; see the Resources section). This machine makes raised-line drawings that correspond to the lines in a drawing or picture. A page from a coloring book can be photocopied onto the special paper purchased from the company. When this special paper is then fed into the Tactile Image Enhancer, a raised-line image of the page is created. The raised lines can be felt, but the images are not always easy to discriminate tactilely. The paper has a waxy or rubbery feel and requires simple line drawings in order to be discriminated easily.

PROMOTING TACTILE DEVELOPMENT

Developing Strength and Dexterity in Hands and Fingers
Children who are blind need to develop enough strength and dexterity in their hands and fingers to use the slate and stylus and the Perkins brailler. The types of scribbling activities just mentioned can also foster strength and dexterity. In addi-

HOW TO MAKE A SCREEN BOARD

A screen board that allows a child to feel what he or she has written can easily be assembled using readily available materials. Place a section of window screening, which is available from a hardware store, over a piece of cardboard backing, and tape the two together using heavy electrical or duct tape. The screen board should be 8½ x 11 inches or larger. Make the card-board slightly larger than the screen so the screen's prickly edges don't poke through the tape. Then take a sheet of regular paper and place it over the screen, using rubber bands on the top and bottom to hold the paper in place. When a child uses a crayon on the paper, the lines are raised because of the texture of the screen underneath.

tion to encouraging children to scribble, however, teachers need to help children develop the proper hold on the stylus, the proper placement of their hands on the slate, and the proper finger position on the Perkins brailler. Giving children activities that develop strength in their hands and fingers while teaching them the proper placement of fingers and hands will prevent them from establishing bad habits simply because their fingers and hands are not strong enough to write correctly.

No matter how teachers help children build strength in their hands and fingers, tying the activity to something practical and meaningful is a challenge. One creative preschool teacher used eggs produced by the chicken who had visited her class. The class hard boiled the eggs, peeled them, and then crushed the shells between their fingertips to create smaller and smaller pieces. The children then made a tactile pattern out of the crushed shells, as a mosaic art project, using egg whites from uncooked eggs as glue. In addition, they got to eat the hard-boiled eggs while listening to the story of Humpty Dumpty. This teacher had incorporated language and concept development, development of finger and hand dexterity, a tactile art project, and reading aloud to children into one set of activities.

STRATEGIES

DEVELOPING STRENGTH AND DEXTERITY IN HANDS AND FINGERS
✛ Have the child squeeze modeling clay with his or her hands and fingers, roll it into balls, and pinch off bits of clay to make smaller and smaller balls or snakes.

ACTIVITIES FOR DEVELOPING DEXTERITY

- simple finger plays, such as "Where Is Thumbkin?"
- using finger puppets on several fingers
- twisting small knobs on the radio, TV, or a toy
- dialing a toy telephone
- "plunking" the keys of a toy piano or a real piano
- spinning the wheels of a toy car with a finger
- using a flour sifter
- pulling up a zipper after it is started
- putting small toys into a small hole in a container
- pushing a large button through a buttonhole
- clipping spring clothespins on the edge of a box
- putting pegs or peg "toys" into their holes
- winding up a toy or a music box

Source: Reprinted with permission from J. M. Stratton and S. Wright, *On the Way to Literacy* (Louisville, KY: American Printing House for the Blind, 1991), p. 49.

✛ Have the child play a variety of games that involve pinching the end of a clothes-pin and putting it on a clothesline (real or pretend).

✛ Have the child prepare a variety of foods.

- *Bread.* Have the child help knead the dough.
- *Cookies.* Have the child use a cookie cutter to cut out the shapes of cookies and use a pincer grasp to grip and press small candies into the dough.
- *Marshmallow taffy.* Have the child squeeze a large marshmallow between the thumbs and index fingers of both hands, pull it apart, and then stick it back together a number of times until the texture of the marshmallow becomes like that of taffy. This can be difficult for preschoolers unless they can rotate their fingers and thumbs, but they usually obtain the desired results with some help (or they can eat the marshmallow and start again).
- *Potato chip crust.* Have the child crush potato chips with both hands into a bowl to be used as a topping for a casserole.

✛ Many daily living skills promote finger dexterity and the use of both hands together:

- lacing shoes
- tying knots
- buttoning
- zipping
- snapping

ACTIVITIES FOR BUILDING FINGER AND HAND STRENGTH

Provide materials and opportunities for the child to

- pull apart and push together locking blocks, Tinkertoys, and pop-beads
- wind up a music box or a Jack-in-the-box
- open jars with screw-on lids or pop-up plastic lids
- push a lever, as on a gumball machine
- pull a string to activate a "talking" toy
- climb up play equipment, such as a ladder to a slide

- carry a pail full of blocks
- lift a heavy toy box lid
- open a sticky cabinet door
- pull open dresser drawers
- grip tightly while riding a rocking horse or "Big Wheel"
- shovel sand and lift pails filled with sand
- hammer on a toy workbench
- squeeze and mold clay or dough

Source: Reprinted with permission from J. M. Stratton and S. Wright, *On the Way to Literacy* (Louisville, KY: American Printing House for the Blind, 1991), p. 51.

Some additional activities for developing dexterity and strength in the hands and fingers are listed in the accompanying sidebars. For children who seem to need an unusual amount of help, occupational therapists can provide activities to promote strong hands and fingers (see "The Occupational Therapist's Role in Promoting Strength and Dexterity in Hands and Fingers" in this chapter).

Developing Tactile Sensitivity and Perception

Blind children need to learn how to use their hands to manipulate and explore objects and the environment, as well as to develop flexibility and strength in their hands and fingers. Blind children are not born knowing how to use their hands to discriminate among objects; they need to be taught. Children often touch only part of an object unless they are encouraged to move their hands all over and around it. Furthermore, because young children are frequently forbidden to touch objects, parents or teachers will have to overcome this taboo in order to help blind children develop their sense of touch. They also have to be taught how to scan an object with their hands and fingertips to learn as much as possible about it. For example, in exploring a wagon, a child needs to be shown how to

THE OCCUPATIONAL THERAPIST'S ROLE IN PROMOTING STRENGTH AND DEXTERITY IN HANDS AND FINGERS

For a child who needs extra, individual attention and activities to be prepared for learning to read and write braille, a teacher can consult an occupational therapist. The occupational therapist will help the instructor evaluate the child's overall readiness for the process, as well as positional requirements, strength, dexterity, and fine motor skills.

Readiness varies from child to child, fluctuates throughout the day, and is dependent on internal factors, such as the arousal level of the central nervous system and emotional stress, and environmental factors, such as temperature and noise. A blind child may have difficulty interpreting sensory information because of his or her inability to filter out nonrelevant sensory information. As a result, the child may appear distractible or easily excited. The occupational therapist will use inhibitory or stimulating techniques to promote an alert, calm, focused state of being.

Muscle tone refers to a muscle's ability to resist a counterforce without changing length. A normally toned muscle is slightly contracted and requires only slight additional effort to cause movement on preset stable joints. Various factors affect muscle tone and can positively or negatively influence the motor performance of a child who is learning to braille.

Brailling requires normal postural tone, and the child's muscles should be "preset" for function. The high-toned child may benefit from activities that promote relaxation, and the low-toned child may benefit from activities that promote muscle tone. An occupational therapist will individualize a child's program and ensure that certain activities are not contraindicated.

Kinesthetic awareness refers to the unconscious awareness of where body parts are in space and the motions involved in follow the handle down to the seat of the wagon and to feel around the outside of the wagon to see how big it is. He or she should be shown how to explore the way the wheels are attached and how they move. This type of exploration will give the child a picture of the entire wagon. Riding in it or pulling someone else in it will give him or her the idea of its utility.

Children who are blind also need to be taught how to explore small objects. The adjectives they learn for what objects feel like (their shapes, sizes, textures, and temperatures) are part of the concepts that are necessary for language development. As a child moves his or her hands around and over an object, the teacher can point out the features and discuss what they feel like and that they make the object different from other objects. For example, in comparing an apple and an orange, the child can differentiate their smells, shapes (the orange is rounder than the apple, but the apple has an indentation at the stem and perhaps at the bottom), and textures (the skin of the apple is smoother than the skin of the orange). In addition, the teacher can point out that the skin of an orange can be peeled with the fingers (another activity for building dexterity and strength in fingers),

THE OCCUPATIONAL THERAPIST'S ROLE (continued)

such positioning. Understanding one's position in space develops gradually over time and relies less and less on visual and auditory input. Acute kinesthetic awareness is essential for blind children to participate in all aspects of daily living, movement, and communication, including brailling. As children internalize kinesthetic awareness, their motoric speed improves, key pressure is more accurately adjusted, and brailling becomes more automatic and efficient. An occupational therapist can introduce supplemental sensory input through activities to enhance kinesthetic awareness.

Arm strength develops gradually from birth. Through play and exploration, children learn to use their arms for body support, protection, and movement. As coordination improves with age, so does strength and stability at the shoulder, elbow, and wrist. Often children who are congenitally blind have weak large and small upper-body muscles. As a result, their balance and

bilateral integration may be compromised. The occupational therapist can suggest many activities to strengthen a child's arms.

The *fine finger functioning* that a child needs to operate a brailler and to read braille is dependent on intact sensory and motor controls in the trunk, shoulders, elbows, and wrists. Weakness in the fingers may not be the sole reason why a child has difficulty operating a brailler. The lack of shoulder, elbow, and wrist stability; limited forearm movement; and poor finger isolation may be contributing factors, along with depressed kinesthetic awareness and generalized muscle weakness. An occupational therapist individualizes remedial activities to improve a child's upper-body, arm, and hand skills for brailling, including weight-bearing activities, pressing and squeezing activities, and sensory stimulation activities.

—*Judy Van Naerssen*
Overbrook School for the Blind

but the skin of an apple has to be peeled with a peeler or knife. Thus, exploring two types of fruit can give a blind child a great deal of information and an opportunity to use his or her senses to gain the information.

Tactile sensitivity is developed through many of the same techniques that are used in developing finger and hand dexterity. However, the purpose of tactile-sensitivity activities is to refine the sense of touch to allow children to discriminate among or perceive smaller and smaller stimuli and eventually to discriminate among the characters of the braille code. Tactile discrimination activities that help children differentiate among textures, sizes, shapes, and temperatures, such as those suggested earlier in this chapter, will help them in learning the adjectives that describe these features. (These activities will help to develop concepts as well as tactile skills.) Such activities fit readily into everyday activities such as getting dressed or bathing and lend themselves easily to games. Following are some additional activities that promote the development of the sense of touch in young children.

STRATEGIES

DEVELOPING TACTILE SENSITIVITY

✛ Give the child opportunities to play with a variety of toys that are tactilely interesting—stuffed toys with all kinds of textures, textured blocks, balls with different textures.

✛ Have the child use, touch, and talk about the feel of a hairbrush, toothbrush, wet and dry bath items (towels, soap, sponges), the lather of shampoo.

✛ Let the child eat with his or her fingers—pieces of cracker, ice cream cone, spaghetti.

✛ Give the child a chance to try finger painting with shaving cream or pudding.

✛ Let the child crawl around or play on carpets and floors, tile, wet and dry grass, mud, sand, pavement.

✛ Have the child find his or her own clothing by touch—T-shirts, sweatshirts, sweaters, jeans.

✛ Give the child opportunities to feel temperatures—warm and cold water on his or her hands, ice cubes, hot sun.

Source: Adapted with permission from J. M. Stratton and S. Wright, *On the Way to Literacy* (Louisville, KY: American Printing House for the Blind, 1991), p. 50.

The accompanying box suggests sources of commercially available materials and games to teach tactile discrimination, as well as ideas for many activities that teachers can create themselves.

M A T E R I A L S

DEVELOPING TACTILE SENSITIVITY AND PERCEPTION

✛ The back pages of the APH catalog (see Resources) include a chart of the various tactile discrimination tasks and recommendations of various products in the catalog that may be used to teach specific tasks at specific ages, including a sensory stimulation kit.

✛ The Exceptional Teaching Aids catalog has a variety of kits of materials for teaching tactile discrimination, including Jumbo Tactile Mat Pattern Blocks, Touch Game, What Is What, and Shape Stacker.

✛ Several commercial programs are available to teach the skills leading to recognition of braille characters. The *Mangold Developmental Program of Tactile Perception and Braille Letter Recognition* (Mangold, 1977) builds on tactile discrimination skills and introduces proper hand positions and rapid tracking techniques for recognizing braille. (This program is discussed in more detail in Chapter 3.)

✛ APH offers the *Preparatory Reading Program for Visually Handicapped Children* and the *Patterns Prebraille Program* series that can be used along with its *Touch and Tell* books.

✛ Barraga, Dorwood, and Ford's (1973) *Aids for Teaching Basic Concepts of Sensory Development* presents many activities for tactile discrimination and suggests materials that teachers and parents can create from easily available objects.

✛ Some materials that teachers have used and objects they have made to teach tactile discrimination or sensitivity skills include the following:

  • textures glued to both ends of popsicle sticks or tongue depressors for playing a form of dominoes
  • sand paper (fine to rough), silk, flannel, burlap, corduroy, glue, glue with sand, aluminum foil, screening, toothpicks, straws, buttons, bingo chips, coins, string, cotton, and yarn for a variety of activities

✛ Teachers have incorporated these materials into a variety of games and activities, such as the following:

  • a bingo game in which children have to match textures on a board to win
  • a spinner game in which children twirl a spinner to locate the textures on the spinner board, and match them to texture squares they were dealt or move pieces on a board to get to the texture at which the arrow is pointing
  • an Old Maid card game whose cards have different textures glued to them

---

MATERIALS

PROVIDING GUIDANCE ABOUT EARLY DEVELOPMENT FOR PARENTS, CAREGIVERS, AND TEACHERS

✤ The pamphlet *Touch the Baby: Blind and Visually Impaired Children as Patients: Helping Them Respond to Care* (Harrell, 1984), although directed specifically at medical professionals, gives a good, brief overview of how to establish and maintain contact with children at different developmental stages through the appropriate use of extra physical contact and speech.

✤ *On the Way to Literacy* (Stratton and Wright, 1991) is an easy-to-follow guide for parents and teachers of children who are congenitally blind. It contains many illustrations and examples of how to provide the stimulation blind children need throughout their early years.

✤ The Hadley School for the Blind has a number of correspondence courses in Parent/Family Education for parents of children who are blind or visually impaired (see the Resources section for contact information).

A discussion of tactile sensitivity and perception cannot be separated from a consideration of the ways children use their hands to explore objects and ultimately to read braille. Perception of braille is tied to movement; it occurs only when the fingers are moving over the braille characters. Once a finger comes to rest on a character, no perception occurs. Strategies for developing perception of braille characters while encouraging proper hand movements or mechanics in reading braille are presented in Chapter 3, which looks at the formal teaching of reading and writing to congenitally blind children.

REFERENCES

Anderson, R. D., Hiebert, E. H., Scott, J. A., & Wilkinson, I. A. G. (1985). *Becoming a nation of readers. The report of the commission on reading.* Washington, DC: National Academy of Education, National Institute of Education.

Barraga, N., Dorwood, B., & Ford P. (1973). *Aids for teaching basic concepts of sensory development.* Louisville, KY: American Printing House for the Blind.

Cutsforth, T. D. (1972). *The blind in school and society.* New York: American Foundation for the Blind.

Discovering the magic of reading: Elizabeth's story [videotape]. (1995). Louisville, KY: American Printing House for the Blind.

Ferrell, K. A. (1985). *Reach out and teach: Meeting the training needs of parents of visually and multiply handicapped young children. Parent handbook.* New York: American Foundation for the Blind.

Hall, A. (1982). In S. Mangold (Ed.), *A teacher's guide to the special educational needs of blind and visually handicapped children.* (pp. 10–19). (Reprinted in this volume.) New York: American Foundation for the Blind.

Harrell, L. (1984). *Touch the baby–Blind and visually impaired children as patients: Helping them respond to care.* New York: American Foundation for the Blind.

Koenig, A. J., and Farrenkopf, C. (1997). Essential experiences to undergird the early development of literacy. *Journal of Visual Impairment & Blindness, 91*(1), pp. 14–24.

Lowenfeld, B. (1973). Psychological considerations. In B. Lowenfeld (Ed.), *The visually handicapped child in school* (pp. 27–60). New York: John Day.

Lydon, W. T., & McGraw, M. L. (1973). *Concept development for visually handicapped children: A resource guide for teachers and other professionals working in educational settings.* New York: American Foundation for the Blind.

Mangold, S. (1977). *The Mangold developmental program of tactile perception and braille letter recognition.* Castro Valley, CA: Exceptional Teaching Aids.

Mangold, S. S. (1982). Teaching reading via braille. In S. S. Mangold (Ed.), *A teacher's guide to the special educational needs of blind and visually handicapped children.* (pp. 1–6). New York: American Foundation for the Blind.

Miller, D. D. (1985). Reading comes naturally: A mother and her blind child's experiences. *Journal of Visual Impairment & Blindness, 79*, pp. 1–4. (Reprinted in this volume.)

Pogrund, R. L., Fazzi, D. L., & Lampert, J. S. (Eds.). (1992). *Early focus: Working with young blind and visually impaired children and their families.* New York: American Foundation for the Blind.

Rex, E. J., Koenig, A. J., Wormsley, D. P., & Baker, R. L. (1994). *Foundations of braille literacy.* New York: AFB Press.

Simons, B. (1994, July). *How to make a braille wave.* Paper presented at the meeting of the Association for Education and Rehabilitation of the Blind and Visually Impaired, Dallas, Texas. (Reprinted in this volume.)

Stratton, J. M., & Wright, S. (1991). *On the way to literacy.* Louisville, KY: American Printing House for the Blind.

CHAPTER 3

LEARNING TO READ, READING TO LEARN: TEACHING BRAILLE READING AND WRITING

Diane P. Wormsley

Brittany is 9 years old and in a regular third-grade class. She reads braille at about 45 words per minute. Her classroom teacher thinks this is too slow and wonders if she should give Brittany more material on tape, rather than in braille.

Rasheem, age 7, has learned how to read and write his braille alphabet and loves to make up stories using his own spelling of the words. One of his stories was in the class newsletter that was sent home to the parents. He was thrilled, because the teacher created a braille version of the newsletter, and he read it to his family.

In the emergent literacy stage discussed in the preceding chapter, literacy development is informal, growing out of a child's experiences and expanding knowledge. When children reach elementary school, they are faced with a more formal approach to reading and writing, which may begin in kindergarten, but certainly has begun by the time a child enters first grade (Anderson, Hiebert, Scott, & Wilkinson, 1985). Learning to read and write in this more formal setting sometimes poses different challenges for students who are learning braille than it does for those who are learning print. This chapter examines the processes of learning to read and write, considers the particular needs of children who are learning braille, and provides strategies for the teacher of visually impaired students.

Reading theorists refer to this stage of formal learning as "learning to read." This is followed by a stage termed "reading to learn," when the student has become a fluent reader and uses reading to acquire new knowledge (Chall, 1983; Samuels, Schermer, & Reinking, 1992). In fact, Chall (1983) posited five stages of reading development (see Table 3-1). The age groups that Chall specified are useful only as guidelines; the important information for teachers of children who are braille readers is what each stage entails, how the stages relate to one another, and

Table 3-1. Chall's Stages of Reading Development

Stage	Grade Range (Age)	Major Qualitative Characteristics and Masteries by End of Stage
1. Initial reading and decoding	Grade 1 and beginning grade 2 (ages 6–7)	Child learns relationship between letters and sounds and between printed and spoken words; child is able to read simple text containing high-frequency words and phonically regular words; uses skill and insight to "sound out" new one-syllable words.
2. Confirmation and fluency	Grades 2 and 3 (ages 7–8)	Child reads simple, familiar stories and selections with increasing fluency. This is done by consolidating the basic decoding elements, sight vocabulary, and meaning context in the reading of familiar stories and selections.
3. Reading for learning the new	Grades 4–8 (ages 9–14)	Reading is used to learn new ideas, to gain new knowledge, to experience new feelings, to learn new attitudes; generally from one viewpoint.
4. Multiple viewpoints	High school, grades 10–12 (ages 15–17)	Reading widely from a broad range of complex materials, both expository and narrative, with a variety of viewpoints.
5. Construction and reconstruction	College and beyond (age 18+)	Reading is used for one's own needs and purposes (professional and personal); reading serves to integrate one's knowledge with that of others, to synthesize it, and to create new knowledge. It is rapid and efficient.

Source: Adapted with permission from Jean Chall, *Stages of Reading Development* (New York, McGraw-Hill, 1983).

how this information can be put to practical use by a teacher of the visually impaired. This chapter focuses on the learning-to-read and reading-to-learn stages, and the strategies that need to be in place to allow braille readers to attain these stages. In the classroom, however, many types of learning go on at the same time; children are simultaneously learning to write, and that process is discussed in this chapter as well.

Some of the general strategies suggested in Chapter 2 are also relevant for the school setting and formal instruction in reading and writing. Two basic strategies in particular will be important throughout all the school years:

- Be sure that the student has a wealth of braille materials available to read both at home and in school. Bulletin boards, notices, students' names on desks, classroom signs, rules, posters, calendars, and so forth should be brailled for the student to read.
- Be alert to concepts that the student has formed and continue to provide concrete and unifying experiences and opportunities for learning by doing.

These strategies, like the others suggested in this chapter, are useful for all children who are blind or visually impaired. Corn and Koenig (1996) and Holbrook and Koenig (1992; reprinted in this volume) discuss considerations and strategies that are specific to teaching braille to children who have low vision.

LEARNING TO READ

The stage of learning to read, or beginning reading, is characterized by learning to decode, that is, learning sound-symbol relationships, how to blend sounds to form words, and the use of context (and, for children who have vision, pictures) to assist in recognizing words. This decoding process may be taught using any of a number of approaches to initial reading instruction, or a combination of methods, which will be presented in this chapter. Part of this process for braille readers is to develop the most efficient use of their hands in reading (often called reading mechanics). This is also discussed later in this chapter.

In addition, before students begin to learn, it is important to make sure that they have the most comfortable place possible for reading and writing. This as-

---

ENSURING THE PROPER FIT FOR FURNITURE

Students need to be able to have their hands at approximately waist or elbow height when brailling or reading braille so they do not have to lift their hands at the same time that they are trying to read. Thus, the desks at which they sit should be lower than the desks of students who are reading print. Since it may be difficult for a student to fit his or her knees under a desk of the correct height that contains a center drawer for books and papers, it may be necessary to place a small table of the proper height to the right or left of the desk to create an L-shaped area and to put a small bookshelf under the desk to accommodate the bulky braille books.

When a student is learning to read braille, the teacher may provide individual worksheets for him or her to read. As the student moves his or her hands across the pages, the pages may slip. A sheet of Dycem, a material that grips all surfaces and to which braille paper will adhere but can be easily removed (available from some specialty catalogs; see Resources; see also Chapter 5 for more details on nonslip materials), placed under a braille page, will keep the paper from slipping when the student moves his or her hands. A thick rubber mat (such as those available in hardware stores and from specialty catalogs) under a brailler will keep the brailler in place and muffle some of the noise it creates.

Teachers can help students recognize what feels comfortable for them when they are using their hands to read. Sighted students automatically raise themselves up in their seats when reading if their chairs and tables do not fit them properly so they can see the print better. However, blind students may adjust by raising their hands to reach the braille, which tires them sooner so they may not want to read for a long time. If they are shown how much easier it is to read when the braille is at the correct height for them, they will learn to ask for or make the adjustments themselves.

pect of reading instruction is particularly significant for students who are learning braille because the mechanics they use for reading are different from that of visual readers (see "Ensuring the Proper Fit for Furniture" in this chapter).

Learning the Code: Sound-Symbol Relationships

No matter what approach is used to teach reading in the classroom, all students need to learn the symbols used in reading and writing and the sounds that the symbols represent, generally referred to as phonics. Instruction in phonics can be *implicit* or *explicit* (Beck & Juel, 1992). In an implicit approach, it is assumed that students will generalize from the whole to the part, in other words, that they will learn that the letter *c* is pronounced /k/ in many words beginning with c after they have learned to read such words as *cat, car,* and *cap.* In the explicit phonics instruction, no such assumption is made; instead, students are explicitly taught the relationships between letters and sounds.

Since reading programs vary in how well they provide for phonics instruction, Beck and Juel (1992, pp. 112–119) suggest ways of adapting these approaches if teachers find them too restrictive. With implicit approaches, they suggest finding or developing materials that show the relationship of letter to sounds more closely:

- Create little books that incorporate sound-spelling patterns and revise some of the stories previously read.
- Use published children's stories, such as Dr. Seuss books, that incorporate rhyme and spelling patterns.
- Use nursery rhymes and tongue twisters to emphasize phonics.

With explicit approaches that concentrate on phonics:

- Incorporate high-frequency words that have lots of use for future reading but that may not fit the typical patterns.
- Include words of interest to the students, such as words that have appeared in their own writings.

In addition to instruction in phonics, blind children need to be taught how to blend the sounds of the letters. Beck and Juel's (1992) suggestions for teaching blending can be adapted easily for use with braille-reading students. These authors suggest the use of "successive blending." Rather than pronouncing *buh-eh-duh* to sound out the word *bed,* for example, students would think to themselves, /b/, /beh/, /bed/ in succession. This avoids the *uh* sound that children usually add to the pronunciation of each consonant when pronouncing them individually. The strategies for teaching the braille code and the relationships between the alphabet sounds and the symbols are probably as varied as the teachers themselves. The following are some tried-and-true suggestions.

STRATEGIES

TEACHING SYMBOL RECOGNITION AND SOUND-SYMBOL RELATIONSHIPS

✛ Teach the student the configuration of a letter by discussing where the dots are located in the braille cell. Help the student talk about the cell in terms of the top, bottom, and middle dots and the "first" and "second" (or "last") columns. These terms transfer well to the task of learning to write, whether with the Perkins brailler or with a slate and stylus. When you use terms such as these, you do not need to worry that using the slate will cause the student to reverse letters. Problems with reversals of letters in reading and writing may still occur, but they will not be related to a student trying to turn a braille character around in his or her head to write it using the slate and stylus.

✛ Show the student where the dots are located for the letter you are teaching by enlarging the braille cell. You can use the old stand-by of a six-cup muffin tin with tennis balls, TACK-TILES (distributed by Los Olvidados; see Resources), the Peg Slate, or the Swing Cell (discussed later under "Learning to Write") in a closed position, or create your own ways of representing braille. Other materials that can be used to represent braille for beginning readers are glue dots (made from dabs of glue that are allowed to dry), raised markers (from Exceptional Teaching Aids), small felt pads, buttons sewn onto a page, and small raised foam pads (HighDots, also available from Exceptional Teaching Aids). One caution when using any material that does not give consistent spacing is to attempt to keep the between-cell and within-cell spacing as closely proportional to the real braille as possible. Some teachers whose spatial perception is not perfect have used a slate to draw the dots with a pencil and then put glue over the pencil dots.

✛ Help the student create a book for each letter of the alphabet that has one braille letter to be learned on each page and objects that begins with the initial sound of the letter. For example, for the letter *s* a page may contain a small bar of soap, a rubber snake, a piece of sandpaper, a sock, or the number 6 in raised print and braille. Notice that all the objects are in a blind child's environment. Rather than search books that are used with sighted students for ideas of words beginning with *s*, it is preferable to think of words that are meaningful to the blind student. Instead of representing the sun by a raised-line drawing of the sun in this initial stage of learning to read, it is much more meaningful to have real objects that a child is familiar with.

It may seem that it is more difficult to apply an explicit phonics approach to braille, with its more than 180 contractions and short-form words, but braille ac-

There are many ways to create an enlarged braille cell.

tually lends itself well to this approach. Many of the contractions are related to the sounds of language (*sh, ch, th, wh, ou, ow, er, ar, ea, dis, in,* and *en,* for example). Words that are the most difficult contain contractions that disrupt their pronunciation. These alphabet signs, such as the letter words (*c* for can, *d* for do, and *p* for people), simply have to be memorized, although teachers can emphasize the beginning letter sounds of the words. Words in which the contraction does not make its usual sound (like *the* in *lathe, of* in *soft,* and *ar* in *rear* or *bear*), also present problems. Teachers need to be sure to provide additional practice with such words that are not easy to relate to phonics instruction.

Thus, as teachers read ahead to identify unfamiliar contractions, they also have to identify familiar contractions that, by virtue of being used in a nonphonetic way, may make the word more difficult to recognize. Providing practice with these words before students read them in a passage will help. One reason for starting with grade 2 braille is to ensure that students become familiar with the unphonetic aspects of the braille code as early as possible so they overlearn the frequently used words that contain contractions used in a nonphonetic way.

Although teachers can teach some sound-symbol relationships to braille readers at the preschool level, the use of additional braille contractions other than the letters of the alphabet requires teachers to continue building sound-symbol relationships well beyond first grade. While sighted students are learning that the letters *c* and *h* combined make the sound *ch*, braille-reading students are learning to identify an entirely new symbol *and* learn its sound. In some cases, the symbol may use an alphabet letter but bear no relationship to the initial sound of the letter (for example, dots 4-6 n = sion).

Developing Proper Reading Mechanics

Teaching letter or symbol identification in braille reading cannot be separated from teaching correct finger and hand use. At the same time the child is learning the sounds and names of the letters, contractions, and short-form words, it is important to incorporate a program to develop tactile perception (see Chapter 2) in addition to proper reading mechanics.

Although many of the activities that are used with sighted children can be easily adapted to blind children, a major difference between teaching sighted and blind students is that sighted students can learn to identify their symbols at a distance in a group, whereas blind students must have direct tactile contact with the symbols. Moreover, since braille cannot be perceived without movement of the fingers over the braille symbols, teaching braille readers the correct way to move their hands in order to locate and identify the symbols is a critical element of teaching beginning braille reading.

Blind people use different types of hand movement patterns in reading braille. In general, the most efficient pattern is moving the two hands like scissors—the left hand reads to the middle of the line, then the right hand takes over and reads to the end of the line while the left hand returns to the next line and begins to read independently of the right. The hands meet in the middle of the line of braille and then separate. Students gradually learn to use their hands independently. Initially, they may locate the beginning of the line with the left hand and read with both hands until they approach the end of the line, when they have the

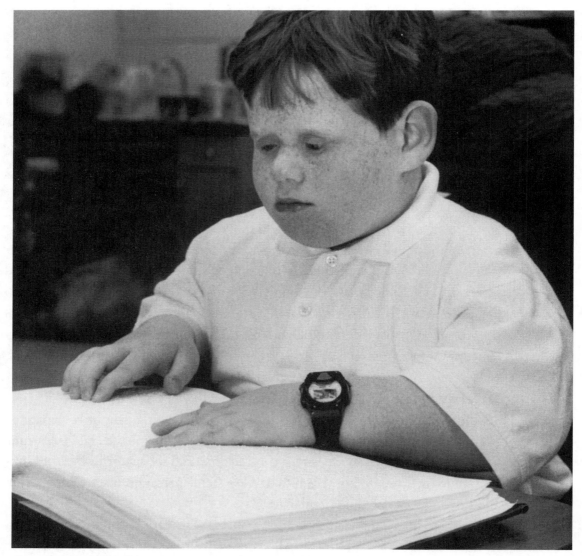

The most efficient pattern of hand movements for reading braille is to read with both hands independently and maintain contact with all four fingers of both hands.

left hand find the next line. This technique requires both hands to have fairly equal perceptual ability.

In addition to using their hands independently, the fastest braille readers maintain contact with the braille with all four fingers of both hands. The index or middle fingers may be key in the accurate recognition of characters, but the other fingers orient readers to such features as the end of the line, punctuation, and spatial orientation to the braille characters (whether the characters include dots in the upper or lower part of the cell or both).

In the development of hand-movement patterns in reading, the perception of braille characters is the most important ingredient (Wormsley, 1979). Therefore, a program such as the *Mangold Developmental Program of Tactile Perception and*

THE MANGOLD DEVELOPMENTAL PROGRAM OF TACTILE PERCEPTION AND BRAILLE LETTER RECOGNITION

The *Mangold Developmental Program of Tactile Perception and Braille Letter Recognition* (S. Mangold, 1977) is a complete curriculum that focuses specifically on the mechanical aspects of reading braille, including tracking, skimming, light finger touch, and left-to-right movement of the hands. The program's lessons include a sequence of criteria tests and worksheets that promote mastery of such skills as tracking from left to right across like and unlike symbols, tracking from top to bottom over like and unlike symbols, identifying whether two geometric shapes are the same or different, and identifying whether braille symbols are the same or different. The remaining lessons introduce the letters of the alphabet. Learning of the skills is motivated and reinforced through games scattered throughout the lessons and through charting of the student's achievement.

Braille Letter Recognition (S. Mangold, 1977; see sidebar) is needed to incorporate proper hand movements and a light finger touch with improving the ability to recognize and discriminate among braille characters with both hands. Applying this approach at the beginning will encourage students to adopt the most efficient hand-movement pattern: the use of both hands independently in reading. Teachers should encourage and model the independent use of the hands, as well as a light finger touch.

Beginning students initially tend to stop and move their fingers up and down on a character in an attempt to identify it. This practice, known as *scrubbing*, is a deterrent to smooth, efficient braille reading. Students need to learn to identify characters by moving their fingers across them from left to right without stopping. Therefore, teachers need to be sure that the materials they create allow students to keep their fingers moving from left to right over the braille characters. (Techniques for working with students who are already reading and continue to exhibit scrubbing are discussed later in the chapter.)

STRATEGIES

DEVELOPING GOOD READING MECHANICS

✛ Model the hand movements used by good braille readers. Young children can sit on your lap and place their hands on yours while you read from a braille book.

✛ Lay a pen or pencil horizontally across a sheet of paper. Have the child place his or her fingers on the paper, curving them until they are all lined up against the pen

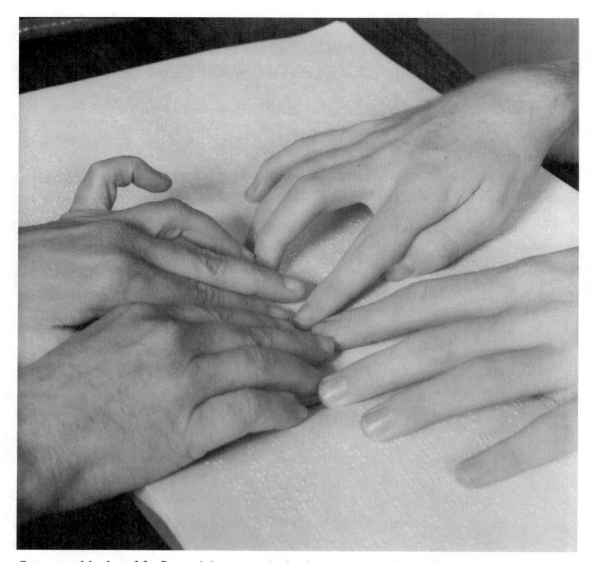

Correct positioning of the fingers is important in developing good braille reading mechanics.

and the pads of all the fingers are touching the paper. This technique requires a little practice, but you can start every lesson by lining up the fingers and do "finger checks" part way through the lesson. Have students practice this technique using the Mangold materials or other tracking and perception-building activities.

✛ When working with students on initial character recognition skills, provide them with lines of braille characters, rather than with the characters in isolation. This encourages students to keep their fingers moving from left to right and is a deterrent to scrubbing.

✛ Create exercises that encourage students to keep their fingers moving over the rows of words and letters to pick out one that is different, a particular letter, or one word from a group of words. This exercise encourages movement and helps students realize that they can indeed recognize the characters.

✛ When students begin to learn to read braille, watch for a sudden decrease in tactile sensitivity part way through the lessons. Students may make mistakes on characters that they previously identified correctly, and their fingers may become "numb" after a certain amount of stimulation (which may differ from child to child). Students should be helped to recognize when this is happening. After a break, the sensitivity should have returned to normal. You can keep track of how long students can read before beginning to make errors. Through practice, students will build up the ability to read for longer and longer periods of time without their fingers losing sensitivity.

Although the Mangold program is exceptionally good for the initial development of proper reading mechanics and braille perceptual abilities, some students may need more practice than those materials provide. When students are not perceiving the characters accurately, teachers can provide additional practice materials for those characters that students have difficulty recognizing. The materials can be modeled after the exercises in the Mangold materials.

Flash cards are one type of material that can be used to help students learn to recognize characters accurately, to discourage scrubbing, and to encourage proper reading mechanics. Teachers use flash cards to teach a number of important skills, including remembering number facts, recognizing letters and their sounds, and identifying words. Flash cards in print need to be big, bold, and recognizable from whatever distance the teacher intends to use them. Flash cards in braille are generally used for practicing either single symbols or words and require more thought because of the medium. The following are suggested guidelines to ensure the best use of flash cards.

STRATEGIES

CREATING AND USING FLASH CARDS

✛ Cutting off a corner of the flash cards helps students know how to position a card in space so the braille is not upside down (see Figure 3-1). It does not matter whether you cut off the top right corner or the left, as long as you are consistent.

✛ Use a lead-in line on a flash card, so that when the fingertips reach the symbol to be identified, they move in the correct direction (from left to right) over the braille symbol or symbols; then add a line following the symbols (see Figure 3-1). The lines are there to guide the fingers and to give a sense of the character's position. The lead-in and follow-out lines can be lines of full cells, a line of *c*'s, a line of middle *c*'s, or a line of dots 3-6. Using the full cell has the advantage of giving the student a ref-

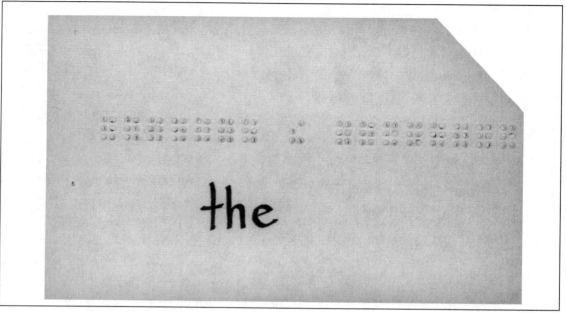

Figure 3-1. Sample Braille Flash Card
A regular 3" x 5" index card makes a fine braille flash card. Cutting off the same corner on each card allows the student to orient the card. Use a line of full cells to lead in to and away from the character, word, or contraction to be identified.

erence point for position in the cell, but as long as you use the same symbol consistently for the lead-in lines and the student knows what the symbol is, he or she can judge the position of the character. Be sure to leave some spaces before presenting the symbol or word for which the flash card is designed.

✛ Direct the student to keep his or her fingers moving across the flash card by starting the lead-in line on the far left and moving lightly across toward the symbol or symbols. Use Dycem or another nonslip material to keep the card from slipping. When the student reaches the space before the symbol, he or she should keep the fingers moving across the character to be recognized and continue to the follow-out line. If the student does not recognize the character on the first try, he or she should start again at the far left. Encouraging students to keep their fingers moving in this way prevents them from scrubbing.

✛ If a student does not recognize the character on the first or second try, ask the student where he or she feels the dots in the characters. Discuss the position of the dots in relation to the cell: top, bottom, middle, first column, second column, and so forth. Ask the student to run his or her fingers lightly from left to right following the lead-in and follow-out lines again to try to ascertain where the dots are. Verify whether the student is correct. Have the student go over the card several times until he or she has found where the dots are. If the student cannot identify the character after several tries, tell him or her what it is and show an enlarged version. You may want to give the student a page with lines of the character with spaces between them and have the student track the lines several times, keeping in mind what the character is. Then return to using the flash card in the same manner as before until the student recognizes the character.

If students continue to have difficulty recognizing certain characters, you may need to develop additional materials that present these characters as different from others in order for the student to begin to recognize the differences and distinguish among them.

STRATEGIES

TEACHING ACCURATE RECOGNITION OF CHARACTERS

✛ First be sure the student understands the configuration of the dots within the cell. Check his or her knowledge by using an enlarged model of a cell.

✛ Have the student use all six reading fingers on a page with lines (double spaced) of the character with a space in between each character. Ask the student to tell you what parts of the character he or she feels and what parts he or she does not and what the student feels as he or she moves his or her fingers across the characters one by one. Also ask the student to tell you where he or she feels the dots (first column, second column, top, middle, or left).

✛ If the student confuses the character with another braille symbol, repeat these steps with the other symbol. Then try interspersing the two symbols to help the student distinguish between them. Start with every other symbol being different, and then begin to intersperse the symbols more randomly, until you are certain that the student is identifying each of the symbols with 80 to 100 percent accuracy.

✛ Use the character in words in which it commonly appears. Take each word and repeat it as many times on a line as the line will allow and then repeat it over and over. Start with two-letter words, then proceed to three-letter words, and so on. Start with the character as the first letter in the words, and then include it at the end. Finally, intersperse the words on a line, two at a time and then three at a time, until you are sure that the student is not having difficulty recognizing the words and letters.

✛ Continue with this type of activity until the student has overlearned the letters or characters he or she had difficulty with.

✛ Flash cards can also be used with the Voxcom to enable students to check themselves (see "Using the Voxcom" in this chapter).

Teachers must carefully monitor the hand movements of their students for what they indicate about the students' perception and recognition of braille. To achieve the fastest reading speed possible, students must accurately recognize braille characters, so teachers should not worry that they are providing too much practice of this type.

Some students prefer to use the index fingers together, pointing toward each other. Nevertheless, teachers should still have students practice initial tracking and letter-recognition exercises using all four fingers of each hand with the index fingers side by side, to encourage the development of sensitivity with this orientation of the fingers to the characters. Teachers should keep track of the students'

MATERIALS

USING THE VOXCOM

The Voxcom (also known as the Language Master and available from specialty catalogs; see Resources) can be used for a variety of purposes and at a variety of levels. The Voxcom is a small recorder that is used with long cards, about 2½ inches by 6 inches, that have a strip of magnetic tape on the bottom, to record and play back short messages. The cards, which can be erased and reused, allow students to check themselves and study independently.

Teachers can create flash cards by brailling words or letters either on the Voxcom cards or on strips of labeling tape that can be attached to the cards. Students read the braille first and then run the card through the Voxcom to check if they have read it correctly. The following are just a few ways that students can use the Voxcom:

1. recognizing the names of classmates
2. recognizing familiar words that are part of the spoken vocabulary
3. drilling on words or letters that cause special difficulty
4. reading simple sentences
5. reading cards that make up a grocery list to the class
6. labeling CDs or audiotapes
7. labeling cereal packages
8. remembering math facts or symbols of the Nemeth code
9. practicing braille independently
10. learning which contractions are included in a word

accuracy with both techniques. If students persist in using their preferred technique and are more accurate with it than with the other technique past the stage of word recognition, then they will probably not change to the other technique, which is not necessarily a better system for them.

Some students are better at reading with one hand than with the other. A student who reads with the left hand should practice reading with the right hand to increase its sensitivity. Since braille is read from left to right, a student is at a disadvantage when he or she reads only with the left hand. Most braille readers can use the left hand as a marker at the beginning of the line, while reading across the page with the right; but if the left hand is the reading hand, there is no way to keep track of the lines that have been read, and it is easy to lose one's place. However, a teacher also has to be alert to a student who simply cannot read with the right hand and know when to stop attempting the impossible. (Photographs of Helen Keller show her to be a left-handed reader; she certainly seemed to do quite well with this one-handed system.)

Developing Skills of Anticipation and Prediction

In teaching reading, teachers generally urge students to recognize the meaning of unfamiliar words through the use of context (or, for early readers, pictures). For braille readers, anticipating or predicting what a word may be from its context, coupled with identification of the first two or three letters of a word, is also important.

The ability to anticipate a word from the first few characters is a trait commonly noted in good braille readers (Kusajima, 1974). Accuracy in predicting what will be coming next is a way to increase speed and efficiency in braille reading, which otherwise would consist of character-by-character reading. Teachers and parents can help braille-reading children develop skills of anticipation in a number of ways.

STRATEGIES

ENCOURAGING ANTICIPATION AND PREDICTION

✛ As described in Chapter 2, when reading to young children, pause to allow them to finish a sentence or fill in a rhyming word. Children enjoy doing this, and it helps them develop the ability to anticipate what is coming in a story.

✛ For older children who are reading by themselves, use of procedures such as the cloze procedure can achieve the same effect. The cloze procedure requires the reader to fill gaps that are introduced into a reading passage. The reader has to predict or anticipate what the word must be. The cloze procedure can be used to de-termine whether a particular passage is at a student's independent, instructional, or frustration reading level. It is discussed in more detail in Chapter 7 on assessment. There are many variations of the cloze procedure, but most delete every fifth word from a passage (leaving the first and last sentences intact). Some delete entire words, while others retain the first letter or letters of the word. Some delete partic-ular parts of speech (nouns, verbs, pronouns, adjectives) rather than every fifth word. (See Miller, 1993, and Koenig & Holbrook, 1995, for ways to use and score the cloze procedure and for ways to use it with children who are visually impaired.) If the cloze procedure were used with the beginning of this paragraph, it would look like this:

> The cloze procedure requires _____ reader to fill _____ that are introduced into a _____ passage. The reader has to _____ or anticipate what the _____ must be. It is generally used to _____ whether a particular passage _____ at a student's independent, _____ , or frustration reading level.

✛ Games such as Mad Libs and Rutabaga develop similar skills and are fun for chil-dren to play. Mad Libs is a party game that can be purchased in novelty stores in the form of a pad of stories. Words are deleted, and children must supply a word of the type requested (for example, a noun, adjective, or verb). When all the blanks are filled, the story is read aloud, with hilarious results. To adapt this game for braille readers, teachers have to transcribe the stories into braille. The blanks could be numbered in braille, and the words suggested for each blank could be numbered and written in braille on a separate sheet for when the stories are read back aloud. Two students could then read a story together, with one reading the story and the other supplying the words, one at a time, to fill in the blanks.

✛ The Rutabaga game is similar. In one version, every fifth word of a story is deleted. When the teacher or a student reads the story aloud and pauses at the blanks, the rest of the class shouts out "rutabaga." The cumulative effect is quite amusing. In another version, nouns or verbs are deleted from a story. The deleted words are then brailled on notecards. As a student reads the story aloud, he or she pauses at the blanks. The other students take turns drawing the cards with the deleted words and read the words they have picked. Although the words that are drawn sometimes make sense, usually they do not. The random drawing results in some ridiculous and humorous sentences. As the story progresses, the children find it more and more amusing. What they are learning, without anyone having to ex-press it for them, is that they can anticipate what should come next and that certain words not only do *not* make sense in certain places, but are ridiculous.

Evaluating Approaches to Teaching Reading

Every student who learns to read must learn the skills of decoding, and students who learn braille must also master the mechanics of reading. However, these basics may be presented within a variety of instructional approaches that are used to teach beginning reading in general, and blind children specifically. These include the basal reader approach, language experience approach, literature-based approach, and whole language approach. Because the basic approach to teaching reading and writing used in the classroom may be determined by the school authorities or by the classroom teacher, the teacher of visually impaired students needs to be aware of how all of these approaches may affect their learning.

Each of these approaches will be discussed in turn, along with its limitations or special considerations that need to be addressed and strategies for using that approach with braille-reading students. Holbrook and Koenig (1992; reprinted at the back of this volume) discuss the specific advantages and disadvantages of each approach for students with low vision who are learning braille.

Basal Reader Approach

A basal reader program consists of a comprehensive series of reading textbooks, workbooks, and teacher's guides, all arranged sequentially. The teacher's guide provides information on how to present each lesson, including specific skills to be taught and suggested activities. Instruction tends to be teacher directed, and the focus tends to be on reading skills, such as word recognition, vocabulary, and comprehension.

When standard basal reader series are transliterated into braille versions, they tend to have certain limitations, particularly when used in an inclusive setting:

- The stories at the early levels frequently convey meaning through pictures, which are not available to children who are blind.
- The vocabulary, which is selected for the print characteristics of words, may introduce difficult braille contractions early on, and there is no control for when specific contractions are introduced.
- The content of the material may not be congruent with the experiences of students who are blind or visually impaired.
- Not all series are available in braille. Even when a series is available, the braille edition may not match the current print edition.

The following strategies will help the teacher counteract each of the limitations of using transliterated-basal readers with children who are blind or visually impaired.

WORKING WITH A BASAL READER APPROACH

Pictures

✛ Evaluate how the braille version handles the pictures. Is there a transcriber's note? Have raised-line drawings been substituted? You may have to help a student ignore certain aspects of the braille version such as italics or other formatting symbols until he or she has learned to recognize them and their meaning. Or you can use them as "teachable moments" to explain these new symbols and formats. Teachers who can direct how books are transcribed should control when to introduce formatting in the materials they are using.

✛ When possible, substitute real objects for the pictures in the stories.

✛ Either describe the picture for the braille-reading student before he or she reads the story with the reading group or ask another student in the group to describe what is in the picture as part of reading the story. In any case, try to include the braille-reading student by describing the picture, since it will help set the scene for the story.

✛ Discuss the experience depicted in the pictures with the blind student and relate it to experiences the student has had. If the experience is not within the student's realm of experiences, provide something for him or her to replicate the experience (see "Expanding Early Learning Experiences" in Chapter 2).

Vocabulary

✛ Teachers should read each story ahead of time to determine the contractions that are introduced and teach the student any contractions he or she does not already know. Whereas basal reading series assume that print readers have been taught all the print symbols or provide guidelines for teaching new symbols that are introduced, no guidelines are presented for teaching new braille contractions. For example, the contraction *ed* may occur in the name Ted. The child needs to know the dot configuration and the letters for which the contraction stands. Referring to the contraction as the *e-d* sign will help the student remember the letters and spell the word.

✛ Provide additional practice with reading words with new contractions in them. With the *ed* sign, have the student help you think of words that have the *ed* sound at the end and write them out for the student to read. The student will not have had as much exposure to this contraction as to the letters of the alphabet, so he or she needs to see words in which this contraction will be used. When the contraction helps blend the sounds of the word, show the student the sound-symbol relationship; also help the student when the contraction does not fit this relationship (for example, the *ed* sign in *bleed*).

✛ Keep records of which contractions a student has learned (see "Keeping Track of Students' Learning" later in this chapter). Share them with the regular classroom teacher and the parents to show the progress the child is making toward the goal of fluent braille reading. Keeping them informed will help them support the student's progress.

Content

✛ If the parents or teacher have kept an experience log (see Chapter 2) for the student, it will be of great help in determining whether the story will be meaningful to him or her. The log is even more valuable if the student moves from one district to another or from one teacher to another. However, there are some experiences that blind children simply will not have been able to participate in, such as those which involve using sight to recognize objects or people. Thus, teachers need to be sensitive to the fact that students may be finding out for the first time that there are things their sighted classmates can do that they cannot or must do differently.

✛ Read ahead in the basal reader to determine the types of experiences included in the stories the child will be reading and provide these experiences before the blind student reads the story. For example, if a story involves a visit to a farm, suggest to the parents that they might take the child to visit a farm, or take the entire class on a field trip to a farm. The sighted children will also benefit from such a visit. Even though they can experience a farm vicariously by looking at pictures, nothing can replace the real experience of visiting an actual farm. If you know which basal reader will be used the next year, read the stories before school lets out so you can suggest activities and trips for the blind child to participate in during the summer.

Availability

✛ If the series is not available in braille, it will be necessary to get it transcribed. There is no alternative but to provide the braille copy. (See Chapter 1 for information on obtaining braille transcription.) Teachers need to know well in advance which materials will be used so the braille reader will be able to participate in reading.

✛ If braille and print books are different editions, the teacher must compare them to find the differences. If the differences are extensive (sometimes entire stories are removed from one edition and new ones inserted), the teacher will have to create either the print version for the print-reading students or the braille version for the braille-reading students.

✛ Check with the state's instructional materials centers or on-line catalogs to determine if there is another braille version that matches the print edition, before you spend time brailling the book.

Patterns: The Primary Braille Reading Program (Caton, Pester, & Bradley, 1980) is a basal reading series in braille that was developed by American Printing House for the Blind (APH) to address concerns about teaching blind and visually impaired students to read using braille. It provides for controlled introduction to the braille contractions and contains stories that are particularly meaningful to blind students and are not dependent on pictures. Teachers may still need to examine the stories in the series to determine if their students have had experiences that will allow them to understand the text.

Patterns is often the choice of teachers in residential and day programs for students who are blind or visually impaired. The approach is skills centered—that is, it concentrates on the component skills required to decode symbols into words. It includes supplementary reading materials—*The Patterns Library Series* and *Patterns: The Primary Braille Spelling and English Program*—that provide an integrated approach to language instruction. Teachers in residential and day programs can easily incorporate the language experience approach, described in the next section, with *Patterns*.

It is difficult to incorporate *Patterns* within a regular classroom, no matter what approach the classroom teacher is using. Using *Patterns* may necessitate pulling blind students out of the regular classroom or working with them in the classroom as a separate reading group. *Patterns* may also be used as a method of after-school tutoring in reading to ensure that students receive a consistent introduction to contractions, but the tutor must be familiar with both reading braille and with the braille code.

Language Experience Approach
In the language experience approach, the student dictates a text based on his or her own experiences. The teacher transcribes the student's story and helps the student to read it over a period of time. This approach guarantees that the text is meaningful to the student, that the vocabulary and complexity of the text are at the student's level, and that the student has the background to understand it. Because the approach is unstructured, it is up to the teacher to make sure that all reading skills are presented.

Although the language experience approach shows students how meaningful reading and writing can be, it does not expose them to any language other than what they have already acquired. Thus, if it is used in a classroom, it is generally used in addition to another approach to teaching reading. It should be noted, however, that this approach provides some students with the motivation to make the effort to become readers and writers.

One stipulation for using the language experience approach with blind children is that the stories must be brailled. Since the language is student generated, the vocabulary is not controlled, and braille-reading students do not get a consistent introduction to braille contractions (they may choose words with contractions they have not yet learned, a problem similar to the one that blind students have with basal reading series designed for print readers). As with the basal reader approach, record keeping is critical to determine which contractions and how much grade 2 braille students know.

Morris (1976) used experience stories for reading readiness, as an introduction to reading, and as a supplement to a basal reader. She modified the traditional language experience approach by suggesting topics or asking questions, so the words the students would use in writing the stories would be theirs, but they would also be words that would be included in the basal reader or vocabulary that the students needed to know. Morris stated that although this may have been a more controlled approach than strict adherence to the technique the language experience approach calls for, she did not find students less motivated to read.

Literature-Based Approach

The literature-based approach teaches reading using interesting children's literature. It focuses on meaning, interpretation, and enjoyment. Students may read books that they select themselves or choose from books selected around a theme. The teacher can generate a wide variety of activities in response to the readings. Skills are generally taught within the context of the literature. This approach is highly motivational but requires a good deal of individual attention.

Like the other approaches, the literature-based approach has certain requisites for braille readers:

- Since the approach is individualized, a teacher who knows and is able to teach braille reading and writing must be available to work with the student on a daily basis.
- The approach is based on having a large supply of books in the classroom, which would of necessity need to be in braille for the child who is a braille reader.
- Controlling for the introduction of contractions is as difficult to handle as it is with the basal reading approach and the language experience approach,

since the books that students choose to read may be at a variety of levels. Students need to be taught how to recognize contractions and their sound-symbol relationship just as with any other initial reading approach.

Following are some suggested strategies that address each of these limitations.

STRATEGIES

WORKING WITH A LITERATURE-BASED APPROACH

Individualized Approach

✤ If the blind student is in a regular classroom, it would be beneficial to help the regular classroom teacher—and even the sighted students in the classroom—to learn braille (see Chapter 1 for suggestions on how to teach everyone braille).

Supply of Books

✤ Obtain as many books in braille as are available. Print-braille books are especially important, so braille and print readers can share reading (see Resources section for sources of braille and print-braille books).

✤ Obtain braille copies of the print titles that are available for sighted students (see Chapter 1 for strategies for getting print materials transcribed into braille). Some teachers may use a literature-based textbook that is already available in braille.

✤ Teachers may have to exert more control over which books a student reads so that they can prepare the student for unfamiliar contractions. Reading the stories ahead of time allows the teacher to teach contractions or new usage rules before the student encounters them. If there are too many new symbols in a book, the student may become frustrated and develop a negative attitude toward reading. Reading materials that contain many unfamiliar contractions may also cause the student to scrub the letters in an attempt to recognize unfamiliar characters.

Whole Language Approach

Whole language is a philosophy of learning in which learning derives from the meaning, rather than from an assembly of individual parts, such as letters or words; and reading and writing are integrated into every aspect of the curriculum. Students learn through daily reading and writing activities, such as choral reading, journal writing, and language experience activities; and invented spellings or reading miscues are seen not as errors but as part of a developmental process. Skills are generally taught in the context of other literacy activities. It is a highly motivational and individualized approach and requires the teacher to produce a great deal of material.

Whole language is a "dynamic, evolving grassroots movement" (Goodman, 1992, p. 48), rather than just an approach to teaching reading. It is based on the philosophy that reading, writing, listening, speaking, and thinking cannot be separated and proposes a way of teaching that is based on integrating all aspects of learning through language while students learn language (Goodman, 1992).

A widely used book that exemplifies how the whole language approach works in a classroom is Routman's (1994) *Invitations: Changing as Teachers and Learners K–12*. This book contains over 250 pages of resources for teachers in addition to 500 pages of advice on how to apply the approach. Although reading and writing are not separated in practice in a whole language reading or writing program, this discussion focuses on the reading aspects. According to Routman, the components of a balanced reading program include reading aloud, shared reading, guided reading, independent reading, and language opportunities to respond critically and thoughtfully.

Koenig and Farrenkopf's (1994) *Providing Quality Instruction in Braille Literacy Skills: A Companion Guide to "Invitations: Changing as Teachers and Learners K–12"* suggests strategies that itinerant or consultant teachers of visually impaired students can use when working in collaboration with regular classroom teachers. Teachers must first read *Invitations* to learn the general guidelines and strategies of a whole language approach and then use the companion guide, which follows the same outline, to find suggested modifications for braille-reading students. Two overall strategies that can be derived from the companion guide are these:

- Braille-reading students must be given comparable experiences to those of their sighted peers: braille versions of books and stories, hand-over-hand modeling of reading, and adequate tactile representations or descriptions of pictures.
- Teachers of visually impaired children must be available to blind students and their regular classroom teachers on an as-needed basis.

Although many of the strategies suggested for overcoming the limitations of the other approaches can be used with this approach, the whole language approach requires teachers of the visually impaired to be much more readily available than do the other approaches, since reading instruction takes place literally throughout the school day and the approach is an integral part of the entire curriculum.

Whereas Koenig and Farrenkopf (1994) discuss strategies for implementing a whole language approach in a regular classroom, Swenson (1988), whose article "Using an Integrated Literacy Curriculum with Beginning Braille Readers" is reprinted in full in this volume, gives examples of how to use this approach to teach reading and writing braille in a resource room. Her suggestions can also be adapted for use in a residential or day program.

Developing Fluency and Automaticity

Chall's (1983) second stage of reading development is a "practice" stage to bridge the gap between the decoding stage and the subsequent stage, reading to learn. This stage is not for gaining new information, but for confirming what the reader already knows. In the practice stage, the reader reads materials that are familiar, which allows him or her to concentrate on the words and meaning and to become "fluent" in reading. The teacher's role during this stage is to provide reading materials and opportunities to read.

This stage is often referred to as attaining "automaticity" in decoding—that is, making the decoding of words automatic. For readers to be able to focus their energies on comprehending the meaning of what they are reading, decoding has to become automatic. "Automaticity is based on the principle that tasks become easier, requiring less attention through practice" (Samuels et al., 1992, p. 133).

Three indicators of automaticity are these:

1. Students can read passages out loud with expression.

2. Students can tell you about what they have read.

3. Students' listening comprehension and oral reading comprehension of similar passages demonstrate equal recall.

Given that the decoding stage ends earlier for print readers than for braille readers, it is especially important for the teachers of the visually impaired child to make sure that a braille-reading child has enough material to read during this practice stage. It is just at this stage, however, that it becomes more and more difficult to provide materials to read in braille, and some teachers may begin to compensate by emphasizing listening over reading. Thus, strategies for promoting fluency and helping students achieve automaticity usually involve providing sufficient time and materials for reading practice.

S T R A T E G I E S

DEVELOPING READING FLUENCY

✛ Encourage independent reading. Many elementary school classrooms now have what is referred to as sustained silent reading, a time when the students read silently to themselves from materials of their choice that they can read independently.

✛ Consult school librarians or reading teachers about books that students at different grade levels enjoy reading, so that you can supply students with the same books

their sighted peers are reading. To make sure materials are at a student's independent reading level (see Chapter 7), use the cloze procedure.

✛ Include braille-reading students in various local or statewide programs to promote reading, as well as school book weeks and book fairs.

✛ Have students practice a story to read to younger students.

✛ Have students read and reread simple, familiar nursery rhymes and fables.

✛ Interest students in summer braille reading programs sponsored by such groups
as the Braille Revival League, a subsidiary of the American Council of the Blind, and
the National Federation of the Blind.

✛ Review the strategies for obtaining materials in braille in Chapter 1, such as
searching out sources of braille books, transcription services, libraries for the blind,
and the National Library Service for the Blind and Physically Handicapped, and using technology to produce braille reading materials.

✛ Enroll children in a braille book club.

Braille readers' hand movements tell much about their abilities to recognize
and decode braille characters. Indeed, the smooth sweeps of fluent braille readers
are a visible demonstration of fluency in motion.

Because braille readers have more symbols to learn, it makes sense that they
will need extra practice in decoding and that it will take them longer than print
readers to develop fluency. Two characteristics of inefficient braille readers, scrubbing and backtracking, can alert teachers to the need for additional attention to
the decoding task.

Teachers very often complain about a student's scrubbing, but scrubbing is a
way of saying, "I can't recognize what this character is." It is a signal to the teacher
that he or she needs to offer more practice in recognizing whatever character or
characters the student is having difficulty with, using the methods discussed earlier in this chapter.

Backtracking is when the reader goes back in the text to search for characters or
words encountered earlier in a line or in previous lines. Backtracking is less of a
concern than scrubbing, but teachers need to understand what backtracking tells
them about a student's reading of particular material. Backtracking usually occurs
when a student recognizes that something he or she is reading did not make sense
and goes back to the point where the problem seems to lie. Although it detracts
from efficiency in reading, it is really no different from what many print readers
do when they suddenly lose the sense of a passage because the word they expected
to read was not the word they actually read or because the material contains new
ideas or unexpected thoughts. When a student backtracks a lot a teacher may need

METHODS OF BUILDING READING FLUENCY

REPEATED READINGS

Repeated readings is an effective way of enabling readers to gain fluency that can be used in many settings with students of diverse levels of ability. With this method, the student is provided with many opportunities to read a familiar passage, until reading sounds like oral language (Aulls, 1982) and he or she becomes an "expert" on that passage.

The method requires the teacher to prepare several short passages of approximately the same grade level. These passages should be of high interest and at an easy reading level for the student. The technique of repeated readings can be an empowering strategy, allowing the student to direct his or her own reading, and reading interesting materials will enhance the experience.

A convenient source of materials is the series *Dolch Classic Books* (Dolch & Dolch, 1961). Each book in the series consists of 15 to 17 short stories that are easily adapted to small passages of approximately the same number of words and the same difficulty; that is, the reading level of the stories does not increase throughout the book as it would in a basal reader. Paragraphs can also be chosen from an interesting children's book; the level of difficulty should remain relatively stable throughout the book.

The steps for implementing repeated readings are as follows:

1. Determine the student's average reading rate over a two- or three-day period.

2. Choose as a goal a modest reading rate that will be easily obtained after three or four readings, based on knowledge of the student and the data collected. It is crucial that the criterion not overwhelm the student. Explain the procedure to the student and discuss the selected criterion.

3. Present the passage to the student and allow him or her to read it and reread it aloud until the criterion rate is met. (The reading rate is calculated after each reading.) It is also helpful to tell the student that he or she may ask for help with a word between readings. Instead of correcting each mistake, allow the student to direct your help. Tell the student his or her rate after each rereading. Rereading stops when the criterion is achieved or the student becomes frustrated. If the student becomes frustrated, the student and teacher need to reevaluate and select a more modest criterion. If the student must read a passage more than five or six times, the teacher should reevaluate the criterion. Provide positive reinforcement when the criterion rate is achieved. Graphing the student's progress can also provide the student with reinforcement.

4. At the beginning of each session, present the student with a new reading selection and review the criterion rate for the session.

to determine whether the content of the reading material is too difficult for the student. Is the student recognizing the characters but not making sense of the material, or is there some concept or word that he or she does not understand?

Two additional techniques that can be used to help students become more fluent and increase their reading speed are repeated readings and Reading Recovery (see "Methods of Building Reading Fluency" in this chapter). Both methods have been highly successful with print readers and are easily adapted for braille. Both entail rereading the same material until the student masters it, and both require considerable individual attention.

METHODS OF BUILDING READING FLUENCY *(continued)*

5. After the student has met the criterion rate for several days (preferably five days), increase the criterion to another achievable goal. Be sure that the student has been able to feel successful at one criterion rate before raising the rate. As the repeated readings of the same passages increase the student's reading fluency over a period of time, small increments in the criterion rate build on this success.

READING RECOVERY

Reading Recovery is a highly successful intervention program that links assessment and reading instruction. It is an excellent example of using ongoing assessment (see Chapter 7) to determine the next step in daily instructional goals. Reading Recovery was developed by Marie Clay as an early intervention program for students having difficulty with reading in the first grade (Tierney, Readence, & Dishner, 1995). It involves one-on-one instruction for about 30 minutes daily and requires that teachers undergo extensive training by specialists in the program. Although the program cannot be taught without this training, a number of the strategies used in Reading Recovery can be adapted for braille readers who are experiencing difficulty in reading fluency.

Strategies adapted from the Reading Recovery system have been effective in assessing reading problems of students who use print and helping them use self-correction techniques to improve their reading skills (Miller, 1993). Among the questions used for assessment are these (Tierney, Readence, & Dishner, 1995):

- Does the student recognize all the letters of the alphabet, capitalization, and punctuation signs?

- Does the student recognize commonly used words?

- Does the student have basic concepts about reading, such as the title and author of the book, the concept of a word, left-to-right progression in reading, and the purpose of punctuation marks?

These assessment questions can be adapted for students who read braille as follows:

- Does the student recognize all of the characters in grade 2 braille?

- Does the student recognize words from the Dolch list?

- Can the student locate the title of the book? Does the student understand the concept of a word in braille? Does the student know where on the page to begin reading? Does he or she understand left-to-right progression?

(continued on next page)

Keeping Track of Students' Learning

Record keeping is just as important when children are learning to read in braille as it is in the emergent literacy stage. These records help teachers remember what students have learned and provide an anecdotal account of students' progress. Extensive record keeping may sometimes seem to place the focus on learning the code rather than learning to read. However, it helps parents and regular teachers realize that (1) blind children have more code to learn than sighted children do, (2) they also have to learn various braille formatting techniques that do not stand out tactilely from the page in the same way that print

METHODS OF BUILDING READING FLUENCY *(continued)*

Predictable books are used as the basic reading material in the program because repetitive language enables the child to read at an easy pace. The teacher and child need to have books available that range from easy to more difficult, as well as a number of books at the same level of difficulty. Thus, using these types of strategies with braille readers entails producing a significant amount of braille material. Teachers need to remember as well that a book that is simple in print may include many contractions and abbreviations in braille, making it more difficult to read. A list of predictable books at an easy reading level are found in the *Complete Reading Disabilities Handbook* (Miller, 1993).

Other helpful strategies from this program might include some of the following procedures. Students read and reread each book aloud until they become fluent—reading smoothly and meaningfully. Students commonly begin each lesson by rereading a book that was completed in a prior lesson. As the student reads, the teacher keeps a running record of the student's reading. Running records are quick, daily assessments used by the teacher to provide immediate feedback to the student. This motivating practice ensures daily success.

The teacher observes a student's reading behaviors and acts on his or her diagnosis of the student's reading problems by cueing the student in useful strategies, using such questions and comments as: "Does this word fit in the sentence?" "Does it make sense here?" "You read that sentence again to discover the words you didn't know." "You really sound like the reading makes sense to you."

The components that could be adapted from one reading lesson in Reading Recovery might include the following (Tierney, Readence & Dishner, 1995):
1. rereading prior books
2. writing stories and rereading them
3. isolating sounds and blending them
4. cutting up stories written by the student and reassembling them
5. reading new books

Strategies developed from the Reading Recovery program require both teacher and student to be cognitively involved in the reading process, assessing throughout reading instruction. The consistent tutoring sessions enable students to make remarkable progress. Adapting components from the program might prove beneficial for developing greater reading fluency for students who read braille.

—*Carol Ann Layton*

formats stand out visually, and (3) learning the braille code extends into the upper elementary grades, at a time when sighted students are no longer considered to be learning to read.

Each student's record should include the following types of information:
1. Concepts learned and experiences the student has had.
2. Tactile discrimination activities and the success the student has had with them.
3. Curriculum materials used and the student's success in using them.

4. The tracking and hand-movement patterns the student exhibits, any problems the student has had, and what has been done to remediate these problems with what success.

5. Words or letters that frequently cause problems in reading or writing, what remediation has been used, and with what success.

6. A record of the braille characters the student can read and write, including the meanings associated with those characters with which the student is familiar.

7. Any special adaptations that are necessary to help the student read and write braille.

8. Comprehension of reading material (see Figure 3-2 for an example of a checklist that can be used to track comprehension).

9. Reading rate. Establish the student's reading rate in number of words per minute by timing the student's reading. Take 2- to 5-minute samples, both silent and oral, and test for comprehension after reading. (See Chapter 7 for more details on establishing reading rates.) Having students record their rates on a chart helps them feel they are progressing.

10. Samples of the student's oral reading. Tape-record the student reading a passage he or she is familiar with at least three times a year. Keep the tapes on file for diagnosing problems and reporting progress to the student and his or her parents (see Anderson et al., 1985, p. 99).

The Comprehension Record Sheet (see Figure 3-2) can be used to keep track of the student's responses to comprehension questions asked orally by the teacher during the reading lesson. This form was originally designed to be used with the *Patterns* series. In the teacher's edition of the series, each story is accompanied by suggested comprehension questions and answers, and the skill assessed by each question is listed next to it—for example, use of context clues, sentence meaning, or forecasting. The categories for each column correspond to these skills. A simple key such as + for correct and – for incorrect can be used, or the teacher can devise other symbols that may be useful (such as © for self-corrected or *RO* for read over). The form also can be used with other questions devised by the teacher. For example, on the sample form shown in Figure 3-2, a column was added for "recall from previous day" for stories that are read over successive days. Before continuing to read on the second day, the teacher can ask the student to summarize the story so far or ask specific content questions about the action to this point. This form can also be used with other reading materials besides *Patterns,* and a teacher can adapt the columns to reflect the comprehension areas about which he or she is most concerned.

The teacher can use this form to obtain a daily percentage of correct responses. This can be useful to document changes that occur if, for example, the student is taking medication that affects memory or stamina and thus affects performance

COMPREHENSION RECORD SHEET

Student's name: Jason
Book: New Friends

Date	Story & page numbers	Characterization	Classification	Comparison	Conclusion	Context clues	Creative thinking	Detail	Emotional reaction	Empathy	Forecasting	Generalization	Inference	Literary point of view	Main idea	Paragraph meaning	Personal evaluation	Personal experience	Personal reaction	Pitch, stress, juncture	Previous knowledge	Recall	Relationship	Sentence meaning	Sequence	Summarizing	Word meaning	Recall from previous day	Total/%
4/1	Telling Time pp. 54–57 (1st ¶)				|			+			+				|						+		+	+ + + + +		| |			
4/2	Telling Time pp. 57–61				|				+	+			|		| | +	+	+		+		+		+	+ + + + + +	+	+		+ + +	
4/3	Sniff & Mr. Wells pp. 66–69			|	| |			+ + + | + +			+		| | + | |		|		|	+			+		+	+ + |	+			
4/4	Sniff & Mr. Wells pp. 70–74			+	+ | + | |			+ + + | + +					| | +	| +	+ +			+		+	+	+ + +	+ + + +	+		+	+ + | +
4/5	Poem p. 76				|		+						|		|						|			+				
	Total/%				2/10 20%			11/13 85%					2/10 20%											19/20 95%				

in class. The teacher can also look at the percentage of correct responses for each type of question over time to document the types of questions with which the student is having difficulty by tallying up the scores in each column. (This teacher only obtained totals for types of questions that had a sample of 10 or more responses.) This information can suggest activities that could help the student with specific comprehension problems. (A blank version of this form appears at the end of the Resources section.)

The example in Figure 3-2 shows how this form can be used over the course of a school week to keep data on a student's reading comprehension. Jason is reading in the first reader level of *Patterns*. He reads enthusiastically and enjoys talking about the stories he is reading. The teacher of visually impaired children, Ms. Marcus, had always felt that Jason was having no problem with comprehension because he could remember details so well about the stories he read. However, when she started keeping track of his responses, she realized that Jason was having difficulty putting the details together to reach conclusions and making inferences from the text. She was then able to devise some activities that focused on these skills to do in conjunction with Jason's other reading and writing lessons.

The Daily Record Sheet shown in Figure 3-3 incorporates several of the other points on the list of information that should be in students' records and can be used on an ongoing basis to keep a quick, daily record of a student's progress. It can be kept in a folder and used to record information as the student reads aloud. The teacher can keep track of the errors the student makes in reading to see if he or she consistently makes mistakes on the same word or words. The miscue column shows the student's misreading, and the next column shows the correct word. In the time column, the teacher can indicate the number of words per minute that the student reads on a particular page or pages that day. The comments column is useful for recording such information as reading behaviors, remarks the student makes about the story, or any other observations the teacher makes about the student's reading. The anecdotal information and other data on this form, such as troublesome vocabulary words, the student's reading rate, and the number of pages read, will be helpful in planning future lessons in reading. (A blank version of this form appears at the end of the Resources section.)

In the example in Figure 3-3, taken from a lesson using a story from the *Patterns* series, Ms. Marcus keeps track of the pages Jason is reading during this lesson. After he reads the page silently to himself and he and Ms. Marcus discuss the events in the story, Jason reads the page aloud. Ms. Marcus uses the © symbol to indicate when Jason corrects himself and the letters *ng* when he has no guess and she has to supply the word. If there is a page with no errors, she marks a dash as a placeholder. On the first day of this week, she noticed that some of the new words they went over at the beginning of the lesson are still somewhat trouble-

DAILY RECORD SHEET

Student's name: _Jason_ Book: _New Friends_

Date	Page #	Miscue	Actual Word	Time (wpm)	Comments
4/1	54	"Fras..."	Friend's		Thought title referred to learning to tell time, rather than show & tell.
		go	were		
		snails©	Snakes		
	55	hurt	harm		
		but©	be		
	56	(ng)	harmless	45 wpm	Needed some help on new vocabulary words. Seemed tired today.
		my©	may		
		(ng)	worms		
4/2	57	"Ned..."	Needlework	47 wpm	Good recall of new words, and of story events. Said he wanted to share his book with his class today!
	58	threed	thread		
		seeing	sewing		
	59	—	—		
	60	—	—		
	61	—	—		
	62	—	—		
4/3	66	some©	where	45 wpm	Says he doesn't know any one with a guide dog— see if R. can visit sometime. Jason was really
		keel...?	steel		
	67	kept	keeps		
4/4	68	on...	once		fascinated by this story.
		will guide	guides		
	69	careful	carefully		
	70	when	while	49 wpm	Said "Can't wait to finish story." Asked if Mr. Wells uses a computer, too! Now he wants a guide dog too.
		bes...©	beside		
	71	—	—		
	72	this©	through		
	73	home	house		
	74	—	—		
4/5	75	—	—		Talked about compound words. Made up more. Had some trouble with main idea of poem.
	76	—	—		

Figure 3-3. Sample Completed Daily Record Sheet

Source: Frances Mary D'Andrea, National Initiative on Literacy, American Foundation for the Blind, Atlanta, Georgia (n.d.).

some for Jason and that he had some difficulty with the apostrophe. Ms. Marcus decided to develop some games and activities that would reinforce the new vocabulary and punctuation marks. On another day, Jason showed great interest in the story about a dog guide, and Ms. Marcus wrote a few notes to herself as a reminder to plan other activities they could do based on this topic. (Chapter 7 provides information on other assessment tools for keeping track of students' progress in learning braille reading and writing.)

LEARNING TO WRITE

At the same time they are learning to read, students must also learn to write. Writing is both the mechanical production of the symbols of a language and a process by which meaning is conveyed to an audience of readers. This section first covers teaching the mechanics of writing braille using the Perkins brailler and the slate and stylus and then discusses teaching writing as an act of communication. (Writing using various technological devices, such as braille notetakers, computers, or printers, is discussed in Chapter 8.)

By the time a braille-reading child enters kindergarten or first grade, he or she should be familiar with the tools used for writing. The child will have had experience scribbling with the Perkins brailler and with a variety of different slates and styli. At this point, teachers need to help students learn the various parts of the braillewriter and how to insert paper, use the various keys, place fingers properly on the keys, and correctly form the letters and symbols they have learned. With the slate and stylus, teachers have to teach the students how to hold the stylus properly, how to use the desk slate, and how to correctly form the letters and symbols they have learned. Although students can learn both the Perkins brailler and the slate and stylus at the same time, many teachers prefer to begin the formal teaching of writing using the Perkins brailler because students can get immediate reinforcement of what they have written and it is easier to make corrections on it.

Using the Perkins Brailler

The Perkins brailler has six keys, each representing a single dot in the braille cell, and a space bar in the middle. In teaching students which key represents which part of the cell, teachers often use the Swing Cell, produced by APH. The Swing Cell is a device that represents a braille cell with six holes into which pegs can be placed to represent the braille dots. The cell consists of two vertical wooden bars, each with spaces for three pegs, representing the left and right columns of a braille cell. Each vertical bar is hinged so it can be swung open into a horizontal position. In the vertical or closed position, the pegs resemble the braille cell. In the horizontal or open position, the pegs resemble the six keys of the Perkins

The Swing Cell represents a braille cell when closed and the keys of a braillewriter when open, helping students to understand the relationship between the dots and the keys.

brailler. Thus, the Swing Cell facilitates understanding of the relationship between the dots in the braille character and the keys that create those dots when writing the character on the Perkins brailler.

Aside from knowing which keys represent which dots of the braille cell, students should also learn which fingers are used to press down each key. The index fingers of each hand are used for dots 1 and 4, respectively; the middle fingers, for dots 2 and 5; and the fourth fingers, for dots 3 and 6. Either thumb is used to press down the space bar. Fingers should be curved, as in typing or playing the piano, to allow eventually for more speed than when the fingers are extended and stiff. All fingers are to be on the keys at the same time and exert even pressure.

Proper finger placement is achieved more readily if students are strong enough to press the individual keys down with each finger separately and to press down different combinations of keys together at the same time, as will be required when they are actually writing braille. Until they achieve this strength they may develop their own "techniques" for getting all three keys on one side to press down, for example, or they may use their stronger fingers for more than the keys to which these fingers are appropriately assigned. The longer students are allowed to develop these bad habits, the more ingrained they will become, and they will lead to less accuracy in writing braille when the students develop some speed. Therefore, it is essential for teachers to monitor carefully students' finger placement on the Perkins brailler, and provide exercises for strengthening the fingers when students seem to be having difficulty pressing hard enough with one or more fingers. Preliminary exercises involve using fingers individually on the proper keys. If a student has an unusual amount of difficulty with finger strength or dexterity, consultation with an occupational therapist may be helpful, as described in Chapter 2.

The form shown in Figure 3-4, used for recording students' progress in learning to use a brailler, is a good way to keep track of the functions and parts of the

Using the correct fingers to press down different combinations of keys on the brailler may require the student to develop additional finger strength.

brailler that a student is familiar with or capable of using. The completed form can be kept in the student's folder as a permanent record of his or her abilities in using the brailler.

Students must also learn how to press down more than one key at once to form the various braille characters. Students need to practice pressing the keys down simultaneously without having one or two keys lag behind. Sometimes they will remember that they need an extra key after they have already pressed down the other keys and will try to add the key without releasing the others. This practice results in a distinct "scrunching" sound that lets both the teachers and students know that not all the keys have been pressed at the same time.

S T R A T E G I E S

PRACTICING ON THE PERKINS BRAILLER

✢ Create patterns like the "braille wave" mentioned in Chapter 2. Start with dots 3-2-1, then continue with dots 4-5-6-3-2-1, and keep repeating one dot at a time. In addition to being tactilely pleasing, the wave has students use all three fingers of each hand on the proper keys and lets them see if they have pressed hard enough for the keys to be felt.

✢ Isolate any fingers that students have difficulty using and have the students practice using only these fingers on the appropriate keys to create rows of dots for these keys. Be sure to have the students curve their fingers as if they were playing the piano while they are pressing down the keys.

✢ Add interest and motivation by using music, timing students to see if they can beat their own records, keeping the exercises brief and letting the students know that the exercises will be brief, and charting the students' progress.

✢ The Swing Cell can be used initially to help students know which keys to press down. Teachers should start with the Swing Cell in the closed position and have the students place the pegs to represent a braille character they want to write. The students can then swing the cell open to see which keys of the braillewriter they should press to create the character.

✢ To practice forming different characters, students can draw pictures using the brailler. They can use a character they are having difficulty with to create circles, Christmas trees, boxes, or random patterns on a page or use all the letters of the alphabet to create the patterns. Drawings like these also give students practice using all the parts of the Perkins brailler, such as the back space and line space and can be used to talk about the concepts of centering, margins, rows, and columns, among others.

MECHANICS OF USING A BRAILLEWRITER
Assessment and Sequence of Skills

Recording Procedures: I = Skill introduced
A = Skill achieved with assistance
M = Skill achieved with mastery

Skills	I	A	M
01. Identifies and uses the following parts of the brailer:			
embossing bar			
spacing keys			
backspacing key			
paper release levers			
paper feed knob			
embossing head lever			
line spacing key			
support bar			
feed roller			
left paper stop			
warning bell			
handle			
cover			
margin stop			
02. Operates braillewriter:			
Positions brailler correctly on work surface.			
Moves embossing head to correct positions.			
Rotates paper feed knob away from self.			
Pulls paper release levers all the way toward self.			
Holds paper against paper support with one hand and closes paper release with the other.			
Rolls paper into brailler until stopped by left paper stop.			
Depresses the line spacing key to lock paper position.			
Removes paper from the brailler.			
Leaves brailler in rest position when not in use (moves embossing head to the right as far as possible, leaves paper release lever open, and covers machine).			

Figure 3-4. Sample Form for Recording Students' Progress in Learning to Use a Brailler

Source: Reprinted from Rosemary Swallow, Sally S. Mangold, and Philip Mangold, Eds., *Informal Assessment of Developmental Skills for Visually Handicapped Students* (New York: American Foundation for the Blind, 1978). Copyright © 1978, American Foundation for the Blind.

Teaching the Slate and Stylus

The slate and stylus, often referred to as a braille writer's pencil, is probably the most inexpensive, portable writing tool for a blind person. It has been criticized for being difficult to learn and teach because it requires the writer to work from right to left, so the shapes of the braille characters are reversed when writing.

However, learning to use the slate and stylus is not difficult, and reversals can be handled by using the same terminology to describe a character whether one is writing from left to right or from right to left. For example, to describe the dots that make up the letter *r*, a teacher could say "first column, top, middle, bottom dots; second column, middle dot" or "first side, top, middle, bottom; and then second side, middle" (referring to what is felt first and second when reading braille in the normal way). One does not have to think of the shape of the character and reverse it to write it; instead, the configuration of the character dictates how to write it. Eliminating the idea that writing on the slate and stylus is a reversal of writing braille allows teachers to feel free to introduce the slate as early as possible and thus to give students the practice they need to become efficient.

P. Mangold's book, *Teaching the Braille Slate and Stylus* (1993), is a valuable resource for the bookshelf of every teacher of visually impaired students. It includes specific instructions for teaching the desk slate and the pocket slate and suggests ways to make the slate and stylus appealing to students. In it, Mangold (1993, p. 21) described the proper way to hold a stylus:

> The stylus is almost always held in the right hand and the way that it is held is extremely important. . . . The first, or index finger, of the right hand curls over the top of the handle so that the top of the stylus rests mainly between the second and third knuckles. If the stylus is positioned correctly, the index finger should be able to hold the stylus in the air without assistance from any of the other fingers. This test should be used frequently, at first, to insure the proper positioning of the first finger.

Some teachers prefer to use thermoform paper with a slate and stylus, since it makes dots that are more permanent and is very quiet. However, it takes slightly more effort to make the dots with thermoform paper than with lightweight paper. As students progress, let them experiment with various weights of paper so they can choose the types they prefer for different situations.

For students who are just in the scribbling stage, it is good to have a selection of as many kinds of slates as possible. Some different types of slates and their uses are described in Table 3-2. Slates are available from a variety of catalogs (see Resources). Teachers and students can discuss the differences among slates, including the types of materials, and students can explain which ones they like to use and why.

Table 3-2. Types of Slates and Their Uses

Types of Slates	*Uses and Features*
Single-line slate (25 cells)	Good for making labels with label tape.
Jumbo E-Z slate with stylus (18 cells, 4 lines)	Produces jumbo braille. Could be used in teaching the configuration of braille, but has not been shown to transfer to reading regular braille.
E-Z Read slates (come in various sizes with various numbers of lines and braille cells)	Special pins secure the paper, so the user can read braille by lifting the back away from the paper.
Pocket slates (multicell and line)	Good for taking notes.
Desk slate	The slate fits onto a board on which the paper is secured. The slate has pegs on the back of each side that fits into holes on the right and left sides of the board. As a writer finishes each set of four lines, he or she lifts the slate and moves it down into the next set of holes, thus positioning it farther down the paper. Good for beginning slate users.
Cassette slate	Used with labels that are specially designed for labeling cassette tapes in braille.
Playing-card slate	Used for embossing any standard size playing card.
Brown slate	Back can be opened, allowing braille to be read without removing the paper from the frame.
Interpoint slate	Can be used to produce interpoint braille (braille on both sides of a page).

For teaching beginning writing, the desk slate is probably the easiest to use. The paper stays in one place, so that students do not have to worry about paper falling out while they are still trying to master producing the dots using the stylus. But eventually they will want to learn to use one of the smaller, more lightweight slates, for its convenience. They will then have to learn to use the holes that the pins make in the paper to move the slate down on the paper.

Teaching Contractions

In addition to the mechanical act of creating braille dots, learning to write braille also involves a set of cognitive skills that are related to learning the rules of using the various braille contractions and that are not required of sighted print readers. Therefore, just as it takes blind students longer to learn to read braille symbols than sighted students to learn print symbols, it takes blind students longer to learn to write braille. Braille readers ultimately need to make decisions that print readers do not. For example, they need to decide whether to use the *ble* contraction in the word *bled* or to use the *in* sign by itself with a space on either side.

Students should learn to write the braille symbols as soon as possible after they have learned to read them. They may actually learn to read and write some contractions at the same time if they need the contractions to write their names or to write stories. However, it should be kept in mind that teaching students to write a

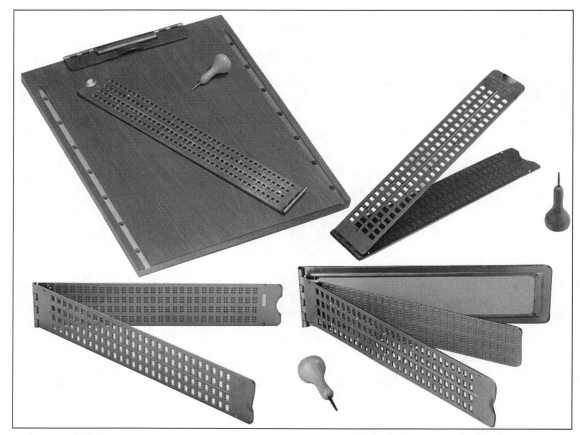

Different types of slates have a variety of uses. Clockwise from top left, 41-cell metal desk slate; metal pocket slate; Brown slate; interpoint pocket slate slotted for labeling tape.

braille contraction is not the same as teaching them to *read* it. Students may be able to write all the letters of the braille alphabet, but not be able to identify them tactilely unless they have been taught to do so.

S T R A T E G I E S

TEACHING STUDENTS TO WRITE BRAILLE CONTRACTIONS

The strategies provided here for teaching contractions can be implemental in addition to those used to provide information that students need to write stories. Rex et al. (1994, pp. 83–110) suggest ways to infuse this information as part of the meaning-centered approach to teaching writing.

✛ Use the Literary Braille Practice Sentences, sold by Exceptional Teaching Aids (see Resources), which are designed specifically for practice on particular types of words (short-form words, words preceded by dot 5, and so on) in the braille code. These sentences can be read aloud by a student or written by a student while listening to the recorded version. They can be used with a slate and stylus, Perkins brailler, or portable braille notetaker.

✢ Give dictation to students on a regular basis. The teacher and the students can correct their braille writing of the dictation, looking specifically for the errors they made.

✢ Use *Braille Writing Dot by Dot,* a program developed by APH, when working with older students.

✢ Use material that students have written to identify errors in writing braille that can be the basis of future lessons. The accurate use of grade 2 braille is essential when braille material is being back-translated into print for a sighted teacher. Although a sighted teacher may be able to recognize the invented spelling of a print writer, he or she will not know braille well enough to understand from the print version the student's errors in writing braille.

Evaluating Approaches to Teaching Writing

As with teaching reading, there are different approaches to teaching writing. The two basic approaches are the skills-centered approach and the meaning-centered approach (Rex et al., 1994). In the *skills-centered approach,* separate instruction and textbooks are generally provided for the three areas of writing: spelling, English (grammar, usage, and the like), and penmanship. The focus is the *product* of writing, with the teacher as audience, and the purpose of writing exercises is to teach specific skills. In the *meaning-centered approach,* writing is purposeful and functional. The audience is a real-world audience. The focus is on the *process* of writing, with the teacher as a supportive facilitator, and writing exercises are designed to be meaningful to students (Swenson, 1991). Consequently, the meaning-centered approach incorporates the writing process, which involves the following steps (Schroder & Lovett, 1993, p. 37):

- *Prewriting:* Brainstorming for ideas and refining writing topics and approaches, often by means of group discussion.
- *Drafting:* Preparing an initial written text.
- *Revising:* Working on aspects such as clarity and style through discussions with other students or the teacher.
- *Editing:* Checking the draft for spelling, punctuation, and grammatical errors.
- *Publishing:* Sharing the writing with the intended audience.

The whole language approach supports the meaning-centered approach, but differs from it in that in whole language there is no separation between reading and writing (Rex et al., 1994, p. 91; Routman, 1994, p. 31).

According to Routman (1994, pp. 51–69), a balanced writing program consists of the following components:

- *Writing aloud:* "The teacher writes in front of the students and also verbalizes what he is thinking and writing" (p. 51).
- *Shared writing:* The teacher and students compose together, making choices about words and other matters jointly, but the teacher is the actual writer.
- *Guided writing:* The teacher helps students to discover what they want to say and how to say it. The teacher is supportive; the student is the writer.
- *Independent writing:* The student writes without the teacher's intervention or evaluation. The purpose is to "build fluency and establish the writing habit" (p. 67).
- *Opportunities to respond critically and thoughtfully:* These opportunities for speaking, listening, sharing, and evaluating stem from integration of the whole language approach into the entire curriculum, and are provided by the teacher.

Teachers of braille-reading students in residential schools, day schools, or resource rooms will need strategies to implement their chosen approach with their students. As with the different approaches to reading, itinerant teachers will need to be familiar with a variety of teaching strategies so that they can adapt and implement the approach that is used by the regular classroom teacher for the braille-reading child. The strategies suggested here will be useful in any setting.

STRATEGIES

IMPLEMENTING THE SKILLS-CENTERED APPROACH

Because teachers who use the skills-centered approach frequently make use of a number of different workbooks, it is particularly important to keep in mind the basic strategy of providing all materials in braille.

Spelling

Because grade 2 braille contractions produce different spellings for some words, the focus on spelling in this approach requires some special strategies for braille-reading students.

✛ Look ahead in the spelling books for unfamiliar contractions so students can learn them before they encounter them in the spelling words.

✛ Keep abreast of the classroom teacher's plans for spelling lessons in order to provide the necessary materials in braille and prepare the student for new contractions.

Some regular classroom teachers do not work from spelling textbooks, but generate sets of spelling words for the students to study each week or every other week. Some have a set structure for the week, whereas others do not.

✛ Refer to contractions by their alphabet letters, whenever possible. For example, talk about the *f-o-r* sign, rather than the "full cell," and the *s-i-o-n* sign, rather than dots 4-6, *n*. With short-form words, refer to the *a-b* sign for *about,* or *a-c* for *according,* rather than spelling out the whole word.

✛ Give students extra help, if needed, in dealing with the braille formatting of spelling books, especially if there are many boxes or fill-in-the-blank exercises. Since braille-reading students cannot write in their spelling books as sighted students do, they may need help in organizing and keeping track of their papers and correcting their work (see strategies for "Submitting Written Work" in this chapter).

✛ Explain any special braille symbols that correspond to new print symbols that the regular classroom teacher has introduced (such as diacritical marks, slash marks around phonemes, and underlined words).

✛ Allow students some extra time when taking tests, since they generally have to spell the word using grade 2 braille contractions and then in full spelling (grade 1 braille).

English

✛ Use similar strategies regarding translation and formatting of materials and introducing new contractions with the English grammar books students are using.

Penmanship

The equivalent of penmanship for braille readers is the mechanics of braille writing, discussed earlier in this chapter. Although students who write in braille also need to learn signature writing, this is a separate skill for the specific purpose of being able to sign their name to produce a legal signature.

✛ Use the time when sighted students are practicing penmanship to work one-on-one with braille readers on writing skills, using either the slate and stylus or the Perkins brailler.

The meaning-centered approach is an excellent one to use with braille readers, since writing exercises are designed to relate to students' real-life experiences. Because the process approach to writing is such an integral part of the meaning-centered approach, the strategies for these approaches are presented together.

STRATEGIES

IMPLEMENTING THE WRITING PROCESS WITHIN A MEANING-CENTERED APPROACH

Prewriting

✛ If a list of possible topics for writing is written on a chalkboard for others to see, reproduce it in braille, preferably at the time it is developed.

✛ Since students who are blind or visually impaired may have had limited experiences, make sure that what the student chooses to write about is based on his or her experiences.

Drafting

✛ Model how to write a story, if necessary, as the student uses the braillewriter or slate and stylus to draft it. A braille reader must have tactile modeling, with his or her hands on the braillewriter to determine what the teacher is doing and to feel the braille.

Revising

✛ If the class is helping the teacher revise a story, give the blind student a braille copy to work from.

✛ Revising entails adding, deleting, and making changes to the text. There are several ways to accomplish this in braille.

- Have the student triple space all drafts, and add extra space between words, so the student can insert words and phrases between the lines of braille, and use HighDots or other tactile markers to signal an insertion. If a long paragraph is to be inserted, the student can identify it by a capital *A* and then braille the paragraph at the end of the draft, again identified by *A*.
- Have the student delete words or phrases by rubbing them out or brailling full cells over them. If the student wants to be able to review what he or she originally wrote, the student can place Wikki Stix just above or below the section of braille to be deleted.
- To change a word or phrase, have the student follow the strategies for deleting just mentioned and then braille the change above the deletion.
- Once the student has made changes on the draft, have the student rebraille the entire draft (still triple spacing it and leaving a lot of room between words) in preparation for editing.

Editing

✛ In addition to helping the student correct misspellings, incorrect punctuation or capitalization, and grammatical errors, check the student's use of contractions to ensure that they are correct and in the right places.

✛ Use tactile editing marks such as those suggested in Figure 3-5 for making corrections, or devise your own. These editing marks would generally be placed under or over the line of braille in a double- or triple-spaced draft. The key to using any form of editing marks is to use them consistently. Editing is usually done together with students, but the editing marks help them remember what they have to do.

Publishing

✛ Discuss with the student whether the writing should be reproduced in braille, print, large print, or a combination of media, depending on the audience.

✛ Write the print words over the braille (often called inkprinting or back-translating) for the student if no other means of producing a print-braille copy exists.

✛ If feasible, give the student a wider range of options for publishing the work by using a computer, braille-translation software, and a braille printer; an electronic device that produces print copies from a braillewriter; or other technology that can convert braille to print or print to braille (for descriptions, see Chapter 8).

Because in the whole language approach, reading and writing are integrated with other language activities throughout the day, many of the strategies that were discussed in relation to the whole language approach to reading will also apply to teaching writing. In addition, since the whole language approach supports the meaning-centered approach to teaching writing, many of the strategies offered for that approach will also be useful in a whole language classroom. (For information about using a whole language approach with braille readers, see Koenig and Farrenkopf, 1994; Rex et al., 1994, pp. 83–110; and Swenson, 1988.)

Submitting Written Work

Regardless of the approach used to teach writing, students will be taking tests and handing in homework to their teachers in braille. Tactical problems can arise when teachers have to correct work written in braille, and students may need special strategies to mark their answers on braille versions of multiple-choice or true-false questions. The following suggestions have worked well for some teachers.

S T R A T E G I E S

SUBMITTING WRITTEN WORK

Correcting Papers Written in Braille

✢ Use HighDots or dots made out of colored glue in front of answers that contain errors and need to be corrected.

✢ When teachers correct the papers of students who use print, they often create their own code for editing marks. Teachers who correct braille copies of work can use the tactile editing marks presented in Figure 3–5.

✢ Record students' grades in a consistent way. The number or percentage correct can be marked in the same place each time, such as the upper-right or left corner of the papers. Write the print numerals over the braille numbers so that parents can see the grade.

✢ Place a length of Wikki Stix or graphic arts tape under the section of the paper that needs to be corrected. Have the student correct that section on a new sheet of paper.

✢ Teach students to put a self-adhesive label over the error and braille over it.

Answering Multiple-Choice or True-False Questions

✢ Instruct students to rub out the letter for the correct choice with their finger or with a braille eraser.

✢ Teach students how to use a crayon (they can feel the wax), pencil, or bold or scented marker to circle the correct choices. Using a screen board (see Chapter 2) may make the wax from the crayon easier for young students to feel.

✢ Have students place the tip of one finger on the answers they choose and then trace around the fingertip with a pencil or crayon to create a curved line over the letter of their choice.

✢ When students are directed to underline words, they can use a pencil, crayon, marker, or even short, precut pieces of Wikki Stix, which can be reused.

It is important to stress that when students hand assignments in to their teachers in print, they should keep braille copies of everything for reference. When students turn in print copies of assignments to sighted teachers who then correct the print copies, the marks the teachers make need to be transferred to the students' braille copies, so they can make corrections, if required, or have tactile records of the errors they made for future reference.

TACTILE EDITING MARKS

Correction	Visual Symbols	Tactile Symbols	Comments
Capital letter	≡	■	Place a cutout square of graphic arts tape (available from art supply stores) or gummed paper; or braille a full cell or dot 6 either over or under the letter needing the capital.
Punctuation mark	. ? ! ,	●	Use circle stickers with the correct punctuation brailled next to or on the circle; or braille directly on the draft.
New paragraph	¶	★	Use a gummed star.
Correct spelling	⬭	▭ (file folder label)	Braille the correct spelling of the word on a file folder label and then affix it to the paper directly on top of the misspelled word or in the line above or under the word.
Space needed	|	| (graphic arts tape)	Use a narrow strip of graphic arts tape to indicate the need for a space.
Insert	∧	▮ (graphic arts tape)	Use graphic arts tape cut a bit wider to indicate where an insert should go; braille the material to be inserted in the space between the lines next to the strip of tape.
Cross out	—	▭ (piece of masking tape)	Place masking tape either directly over the words to be omitted or directly below or above the words (so that the student can see what he or she needs to omit).

Figure 3-5. Tactile Editing Marks

Source: Adapted with permission from Anna Swenson and Carol Norrish, "Braille Literacy: Teaching the Writing Process to Braille Readers at the Elementary Level," paper presented at an International Conference of the Association for Education and Rehabilitation of the Blind and Visually Impaired, July 9–13, 1994; and Swenson, "A Process Approach to Teaching Braille Writing at the Primary Level," *Journal of Visual Impairment & Blindness,* 85 (5) (May 1991), pp. 217–221. (Reprinted in this volume.)

READING TO LEARN

Once students in the primary grades have a strong basis in learning to read, they start to use their literacy skills to perform other academic tasks: they begin to read to learn. Each year, the amount of reading required of them grows. Increasingly, their assignments require students to read different types of materials and report back in a variety of ways, as in the following example:

Sylvia, a fifth grader, has just finished a research report in which she had to access 15 to 20 sources, take notes on the content, use the information she obtained from reading to decide on a science project, and create a report summarizing what she had learned. She has reached the point where she is reading to learn, rather than just learning to read. All students need to learn to use dictionaries, glossaries, encyclopedias, and on-line reference sources; to take notes; and to summarize and synthesize. The fact that Sylvia uses braille does not mean she is exempt from these activities.

By the time braille readers reach the fourth grade, it is imperative that they know all the grade 2 contractions and have become fluent in reading grade 2 braille. Although students may have been using some content books for science or social studies in the second or third grades, by fourth grade they usually will have content readers for every subject and possibly some workbooks, exercise books, or photocopied material to accompany the readers.

As students progress, the uses they make of literacy, both in and outside of school, become still more complex. And, as students begin reading more complex materials, they will encounter a variety of formats for braille that are designed to reflect what is in print documents, such as boxes, tables, flowcharts, pictures and captions, diagrams, and sidebars. Teachers of older students who read braille will continue to use some of the same strategies, but they will also need many new strategies to help students have access to the broadening variety of materials and experiences.

STRATEGIES

READING TO LEARN

General Guidelines

✛ In this stage, as previously, braille readers must have the same materials available to them in braille that their classmates have in print. Acquiring these books in braille is one of the more difficult tasks a teacher of students who are blind faces (see Chapter 1 for strategies for acquiring braille materials).

✛ If the classroom teacher is making the choice of which textbooks to use, the teacher of visually impaired students can sometimes work with him or her to suggest a particular content book that is already available in braille. The APH central catalog (see Resources) can identify what texts are available in braille in a particular subject area.

✛ Supplementary reading materials for students need to be obtained well in advance to have time to have braille copies transcribed. Developing good relationships with the classroom or subject teachers and stressing the importance of blind students' having materials in braille are essential in the quest to obtain these materials.

✛ A braille version of a previous edition of a print book is not as good as the edition the class is using. However, if a print copy of the previous edition is available to go along with it, teachers can note the differences and do additional brailling to "align" the copies. Changes from one edition to the next are not always extreme.

✛ Older braille readers still need help to relate vocabulary to real experiences and to improve their ability to learn through all their senses. Continue to provide concrete experiences whenever possible to illustrate the vocabulary that appears in the reading material. For example, when reading a story about painting a child's bedroom, the teacher took the entire class to a paint store, where they learned about mixing paint, smelled the odor of paint and turpentine, and felt brushes and rollers.

✛ Adapt the curricula used with sighted students for braille-reading students. For example, if the sighted students in a sixth-grade class are studying note-taking skills, modify the instruction so blind students can take notes in braille with a slate and stylus, Perkins brailler, or portable notetaker.

✛ Teach grade 3 braille, a form of braille used for notetaking that includes contractions and abbreviations—a shorthand version of braille. Grade 3 braille is especially useful for taking notes on a slate and stylus.

MATERIALS

MAKING TACTILE ADAPTATIONS

Sometimes the teacher has to be creative in adapting print materials that contain pictures, graphs, and other special-format items.

✛ The Tactile Image Enhancer (see Chapter 2) can be used to adapt workbook pages or mimeographed sheets. The Thermoform machine, produced and sold by American Thermoform Corporation (see Resources), uses a heating element to melt a sheet of plastic thermoform paper so that it takes the form of any shape that is placed under it during the heating process. The technique is useful for creating raised-line diagrams, graphs, maps, outline shapes, and even some three-dimensional shapes.

✛ The Tactile Graphics Kit (available from APH) contains tools and a guidebook to help the reader get started in adapting worksheets, as well as constructing maps, diagrams, charts, and the like.

✛ The book *Tactile Graphics* (Edman, 1992) includes over 500 pages of information on creating raised-line drawings and tactile graphics.

✛ Teachers may need to adapt certain graphic formats into tactile forms (see "Making Tactile Adaptations" in this chapter).

Magazines and Newspapers

✛ Information from or actual issues of many periodicals can be obtained on-line through the Internet and then transcribed into braille (see Chapter 8).

✛ Students can also subscribe to magazines in braille or borrow periodicals and books from state or regional Libraries for the Blind and Physically Handicapped (see Resources).

Encyclopedias

✛ Encyclopedias are expensive and difficult to obtain in braille. The braille encyclopedias that exist are not always current and are extremely bulky to store. Residential or day schools that teach academic subjects usually have the most current editions in their libraries. If the distance is not too great, teachers can arrange for a student to visit the reference collection at a residential or day school to give the student hands-on experience using the braille copies of these books.

✛ Seedlings, a publisher of braille books for children (see Resources section), has a service, known as the ROSE Project, that provides encyclopedia articles in braille for students' projects and reports.

✛ Another way to provide a student with information from encyclopedias is to use the CD-ROM version of an encyclopedia on a computer that is equipped with braille-translation software connected to a braille printer (see Chapter 8) and create the braille articles the student needs for an assignment. A student should learn how to gain access to information using speech or refreshable braille displays to select the articles and then braille hard copies of the articles.

Dictionaries

✛ Dictionaries are less bulky than encyclopedias in braille but still take up considerable space. One strategy for teaching dictionary skills is to show students how to use talking dictionaries, which are available from specialty catalogues.

✛ Students may be assigned to write their own dictionary entries, read from worksheets that have been brailled, or answer questions in which they must include the correct diacritical markings. To do so, they must be able to recognize and write the correct braille symbols. Therefore, regardless of the type of dictionary ordinarily used, teachers of students who are blind or visually impaired need to instruct the students in using the braille symbols for diacritical markings, guide words, and various parts of a dictionary entry.

✛ Dictionaries are also available on CD-ROM, so the teacher or the student can obtain hard copies of entries in the same way as for encyclopedia articles.

Other Reference Materials

✛ Many reference materials to which students are introduced are rarely available in braille because of the cost of production. These materials are often available in electronic format, however, which means that more information is available to students who are blind or visually impaired today than ever before. Teachers can check to see which CD-ROM versions of reference materials are available and purchase them for their students' use.

✛ On-line searching mechanisms allow users to access World Wide Web pages and many other new on-line sources of information (see Chapter 8).

✛ Works of classical literature can also be found on-line. Frequently, they can be downloaded and braille copies created in a much shorter time than it would take to locate books in a list of materials that have already been brailled.

Use of Libraries

✛ Although card catalogs are usually inaccessible for braille readers to use independently, students need to be taught how card catalogs are organized so they can use a reader to help them locate materials they may need for school or for leisure reading.

✛ Some local libraries have computerized their card catalogs, and it may be possible in the future for a braille reader to read the catalog entries and perform searches with a computer that has speech or refreshable braille access to the electronic database.

✛ Many libraries around the world have put their catalogs online so that they are accessible through the Internet. Students can use readers to read materials they have obtained from the library or scan them into a computer to be read with synthetic speech or refreshable braille (see Chapter 8).

Textbook Format Braille

✛ Help students become aware of the various formats used in print and how these formats are represented in braille, so that they can move easily, for example, from the main body of the text to a box and back to the text. The *Code of Braille Textbook Formats and Techniques* (1977) contains guidelines for transcribing textbooks. The more knowledge students have of print formats, including graphics and fonts, the easier it will be for them to recognize the special symbols of textbook formats. Students will also need to be familiar with print formats to use a scanner to transport a print document into a word-processing program for braille or speech output (see Chapter 8).

✛ Just as teachers need to read ahead in the braille books of beginning readers to determine what new contractions or symbols may be presented so they can prepare students for them, teachers need to examine the textbooks of older readers for new formatting techniques that students need to learn.

Although the task of teaching braille reading and writing can be challenging, there is nothing quite like the excitement of children at being able to read by themselves. The ability to read braille gives the person who is blind or visually impaired the ability to be literate, offers choices for a preferred and effective reading medium, and enables the person to be independent. One would no more exclude braille reading and writing from the curriculum for blind and visually impaired children than one could exclude teaching print reading and writing from the curriculum for sighted children.

Thus far, the discussion has focused on students who are learning to read and write for the first time when they learn braille. However, some children who lose their sight after they have already begun to read and write in print have to negotiate a transition as well as learn the fundamentals of braille. The special concerns that have to be considered for these students are discussed in Chapter 4.

REFERENCES

Anderson, R. D., Hiebert, E. H., Scott, J. A., & Wilkinson, I. A. G. (1985). *Becoming a nation of readers. The report of the commission on reading.* Washington, DC: National Academy of Education, National Institute of Education.

Aulls, M. W. (1982). *Developing readers in today's elementary school.* Boston: Allyn & Bacon.

Beck, I. L., & Juel, C. (1992). The role of decoding in learning to read. In Samuels, S. J., and Farstrup, A. E. (Eds.) *What research has to say about reading instruction* (pp. 101–123). Newark, DE: International Reading Association.

Caton, H. R., Pester, E., & Bradley, E. J. (1980). *Patterns: The primary braille reading program.* Louisville, KY: American Printing House for the Blind.

Chall, J. S. (1983). *Stages of reading development.* New York: McGraw-Hill.

Code of braille textbook formats and techniques. (1977). Louisville, KY: American Printing House for the Blind.

Corn, A., & Koenig, A. J. (1996). *Foundations of low vision.* New York: AFB Press.

Dolch, E. W., & Dolch, M. P. (1961). *Dolch classic books: A first reading book.* Allen, TX: DLM Teaching Resources.

Edman, P. K. (1992). *Tactile graphics.* New York: American Foundation for the Blind.

Goodman, K. S. (1992). Whole language research: Foundations and development. In Samuels, S. J., and Farstrup, A. E. (Eds.), *What research has to say about reading instruction* (pp. 46–69). Newark, DE: International Reading Association.

Holbrook, M. C., & Koenig, A. J. (1992). Teaching braille reading to students with low vision. *Journal of Visual Impairment & Blindness, 86,* pp. 44-48. (Reprinted in this volume.)

Koenig, A. J., & Farrenkopf, C. (1994). *Providing quality instruction in braille literacy skills: A companion guide to "Invitations: Changing as Teachers and Learners K–12."* Houston: Region IV Education Service Center.

Koenig, A. J., & Holbrook, M. C. (1995). *Learning media assessment of students with visual impairments: A resource guide for teachers* (2nd ed.). Austin: Texas School for the Blind and Visually Impaired.

Kusajima, T. (1974). *Visual reading and braille reading: An experimental investigation of the physiology and psychology of visual and tactual reading.* New York: American Foundation for the Blind.

Mangold, P. (1993). *Teaching the braille slate and stylus.* Castro Valley, CA: Exceptional Teaching Aids.

Mangold, S. S.(1977). *The Mangold developmental program of tactile perception and braille letter recognition.* Castro Valley, CA: Exceptional Teaching Aids.

Miller, W. H. (1993). *Complete reading disabilities handbook.* West Nyack, NY: Center for Applied Research in Education.

Morris, O. F. (1976). Using an experience story approach to teach beginning braille reading. In *Selected papers: Association for Education of the Visually Handicapped, 53rd Biennial Conference, July 1976, Louisville, KY* (pp. 99-105). Philadelphia: Association for Education of the Visually Handicapped.

Rex, E. J., Koenig, A. J., Wormsley, D. P., & Baker, R. L. (1994). *Foundations of braille literacy.* New York: AFB Press.

Routman, R. (1994). *Invitations: Changing as teachers and learners K–12.* Portsmouth, NH: Heinemann.

Samuels, S. J., Schermer, N., & Reinking, D. (1992). Reading fluency: Techniques for making decoding automatic. In Samuels, S. J., and Farstrup, A. E. (Eds.), *What research has to say about reading instruction* (pp. 124–144). Newark, DE: International Reading Association.

Schroder, V. C., & Lovett, A. K. (1993). Modeling the process approach in the early elementary grades. In Cullinan, B. (Ed.), *Pen in hand: Children become writers* (pp. 36–49). Newark, DE: International Reading Association.

Swenson, A. M. (1988). Using an integrated literacy curriculum with beginning braille readers. *Journal of Visual Impairment & Blindness, 82,* 336–338. (Reprinted in this volume.)

Swenson, A. M. (1991). A process approach to teaching braille writing at the primary level. *Journal of Visual Impairment & Blindness, 85,* 217–221. (Reprinted in this volume.)

Tierney, R. J., Readence, J. E., & Dishner, E. K. (1990). *Reading strategies and practices* (3rd ed.). Boston: Allyn & Bacon.

Wormsley, D. P. (1979). *The effects of a hand movement training program on the hand movements and reading rates of young braille readers.* Ann Arbor, MI: University Microfilms International.

MAKING THE TRANSITION FROM PRINT TO BRAILLE

FRANCES MARY D'ANDREA

Ten-year old Angelo was recently diagnosed with Stargardt's disease and has lost his central vision. He can read greatly enlarged print, but reads slowly and becomes fatigued after only 10 minutes. He is beginning to fall behind in his schoolwork and worries about how he will keep up.

Sarah lost her vision suddenly at age 16 as a result of injuries sustained in a car accident. She has recovered from her other injuries and is ready to go back to school. Sarah is concerned about how she will be able to maintain her previously high grades and how she will get ready for college.

Thirteen-year old Jesse's vision had been slowly deteriorating, and a series of operations have been unsuccessful in stemming his vision loss. He has now lost much of the remaining vision in his good eye and can no longer read from large-print books, even with magnification, or play his beloved soccer. An average student, Jesse was never very interested in academics. He says he has no motivation to attend school, especially since he can no longer play on the soccer team.

Amanda, a third grader, was diagnosed with a brain tumor, and although the surgery and necessary treatments destroyed the tumor, she now has only light perception. Previously an avid reader, Amanda misses being able to curl up with a book.

Four different children with four different situations. Yet they have one thing in common: They are all former print readers who are making the transition to braille. Chapters 2 and 3 discussed development of braille skills for children who are congenitally blind or visually impaired and who will have their first experience with reading and writing with the medium of braille. This chapter deals with children who are adventitiously blind—those who lose their vision or whose visual impairment becomes more severe later in childhood or adolescence. These children present special challenges to educators who are responsible for teaching braille reading and writing.

ASSESSING INDIVIDUAL NEEDS

Most children who are adventitiously blind have had some experience reading print before they begin to learn braille. Thus, many of them have some basic literacy skills that young congenitally blind children lack. They usually understand the concept of *symbolic language*—that words and ideas can be expressed in written or embossed symbols. They may also understand the basic concepts of reading a book, such as left-to-right progression across a page and turning one page at a time, and may be familiar with letter-sound relationships and simple grammatical rules. Therefore, it may not be necessary to provide the type of basic experiences described in Chapter 2 to these children.

It is imperative to remember, however, that children who are adventitiously blind or visually impaired are individuals with unique needs, problems, and abilities. Hence, much of what they will need to be taught will depend on several factors, including the following:

- the child's age at onset of vision loss
- suddenness or gradual development of onset of vision loss
- the child's current level of visual functioning and prognosis
- the child's literacy skills prior to starting braille
- the child's motivation to learn braille and his or her attitudes toward braille and vision loss

Teachers need to consider each factor carefully before they begin braille instruction and to assess each child's current level of functioning. All these factors are described in the sections that follow, and suggestions about how they influence braille instruction are offered. Chapter 7 contains a thorough discussion of assessment and lists some assessment tools that can be used to ascertain a student's literacy levels before and during braille instruction.

Age at Onset of Vision Loss

The age at which children lose their vision has great bearing on the braille-reading skills the children have to be taught. The later the loss, the more years of practice children have had with literacy skills in general. In addition, they will have had more experience with reading—or at least examining—a variety of printed materials, including books and magazines; seeing print in its many forms; writing; and observing people reading and writing. Moreover, although children who lose their vision early have additional years to build up speed and accuracy in reading braille, those who lose their vision in childhood or adolescence may have a broader repertoire of visual-cognitive experiences to bring to the reading process. The younger the child, the more the instruction has to emphasize the types of cognitive language experiences mentioned in Chapter 2. The older the child, the more the instruction has to focus on techniques to build up speed and facility in reading braille.

Thus, there is a great difference between the needs of a child who loses his or her vision at age 5 and one who loses it at age 15. The teaching approaches and materials used for children of different ages of onset also differ, as is discussed in greater detail later in this chapter. The following suggestions may be helpful in considering how the age of onset affects the braille teaching process:

- The young child who is preliterate or was just barely starting to read print before vision loss will need more of the basic language and concept development experiences discussed in Chapter 2. Five year olds who have recently lost their vision do not have the depth of experiences that older adventitiously blind students have. Therefore, the use of emergent literacy strategies is essential for young children. However, students who have been facile

It is important to find age-appropriate reading materials at students' reading level to make the process of learning to read braille enjoyable.

readers for many years are more likely to look on braille as a code to decipher and compare to print reading. Hence, the materials and strategies suitable for them may be quite different, as is discussed later in this chapter.

- Finding age-appropriate materials is important. An older student who is learning braille will not enjoy the process if the reading materials are designed for the interests and experiences of a kindergarten child. Some students making the transition from print to braille may enjoy reading high-interest, low-vocabulary books such as those available in braille from the American Printing House for the Blind (APH). Other materials can be transcribed from print books. Also, using a student's own words and experiences as a springboard to reading (as in the language experience approach to reading discussed in Chapter 3) ensures that the vocabulary and subject matter are interesting to the student.

- The usual differences between teaching elementary school and middle school or high school students apply to teaching braille. Although every student has individual needs, the adolescent years present unique challenges. Adolescents find it even more important to fit in and to be one of the crowd than do elementary-school-age students. Self-esteem, which is also a larger issue for adolescents, is discussed at greater length in the section on "Motivation Level and Attitudes." Again, teachers will have to carefully tailor braille instruction to the needs of individual students. Taking the time to find out a student's interests, goals, and concerns is important no matter what the student's age, but it is essential when dealing with adolescents.

Onset of Vision Loss and Level of Visual Functioning

Children who previously had 20/20 vision and, as a result of an illness or accident, abruptly lost their vision, have to contend with many new challenges suddenly: a new mobility method, new ways of accomplishing daily living skills, and a new reading medium.

In contrast, for children with progressive vision loss, whose vision has decreased to the point that print reading is no longer efficient, print reading may have become a chore as they struggle to read print slowly and painstakingly. These children may have developed negative attitudes toward reading in general that may surface when they learn braille.

Students who have always had low vision may also benefit from braille instruction. A teacher may get a new student who has been reading materials in regular or large print and has gotten further and further behind in school. By middle school or high school, these students may be several grade levels below their sighted classmates in reading and writing skills or may be spending considerably more time doing classwork and homework to keep up.

The following are some considerations to keep in mind regarding this factor:

- Although a complete learning media assessment is necessary for every student, it is crucial for students whom the teacher suspects are having difficulty reading print and who would benefit from braille instruction (see Chapter 1). It is also vital for students who have transferred from another school or teacher and have never had a comprehensive learning media assessment. Anytime a change in reading medium is considered—in this case, from print to braille—a full-scale learning media assessment is called for, whether the student had a sudden vision loss, has a progressive loss, or has always had low vision. Determining a student's primary reading medium is an important issue: Students should not be allowed to limp along in print for years, getting further and further behind and more and more frustrated.

- Continuing assessments of literacy media needs are essential for students with low vision who had a learning media assessment earlier in their schooling. As the students' academic tasks change, the visual demands will also change. A student may have done well reading print in the first grade with the short reading tasks and larger type size of primary readers and workbooks. By the third grade, however, reading assignments are longer; the print size of materials is smaller; reading materials are less dependent on pictures to supplement meaning; and other educational materials, such as dictionaries and maps, are introduced. Thus, ongoing assessments are necessary to track students' performance on current educational tasks and to look ahead to future needs (Koenig & Holbrook, 1989). Figure 4-1 summarizes some of the factors involved in continuing assessment of literacy media. Koenig and Holbrook (1995) provide a form for recording data and observations relevant to this process. A separate inventory is available for conducting the suggested review of literacy tools. It includes a list of visual, tactile, and auditory tools traditionally used in literacy instruction (such as low vision devices, bold-lined paper, braille, slates and styli, and cassette books), and a list of frequently used technology and computer applications (for example, large computer monitors, braille notetakers, and synthesized speech). From this list, teachers can evaluate the tools the student is using and, if necessary, select additional tools that will most efficiently meet the student's needs.

- Physical health should be taken into consideration. If a student has been injured or seriously ill, health concerns, stamina, and strength are other factors to consider in planning a literacy program. Some children may still be on medication that makes them feel drowsy or less alert than usual (Harrison, 1987). The teacher needs to be aware of these medical issues. Ask the student's parents or review the student's confidential file for medical informa-

---

STEPS IN A CONTINUING ASSESSMENT OF LITERACY MEDIA

Step 1. Review available information on the student's visual functioning.
a. functional vision evaluations
b. ophthalmological exams
c. clinical low vision evaluations
d. indications of change in visual functioning

Step 2. Evaluate the student's current reading efficiency.
a. results of informal reading inventory
b. reading of content materials at grade placement
c. reading comprehension rates
d. adequacy of reading rate

Step 3. Review and evaluate academic achievement.
a. Does the student accomplish academic tasks with success?
b. Are the student's time requirements reasonable compared to peers?

Step 4. Evaluate handwriting efficiency.
a. Can the student read his or her own handwriting?
b. Is the student's handwriting viable and effective for communicative needs?

Step 5. Review the literacy tools the student now uses.
a. Does the student have a repertoire of tools to use for current needs? for future needs?
b. Does the student have adequate technology skills for current needs? for future needs?

Step 6. Interpret the results of the assessment based on existing information and future needs.

Figure 4-1. Summary of the Steps in a Continuing Assessment of Literacy Media
Source: Adapted from Alan J. Koenig and M. Cay Holbrook, *Learning Media Assessment of Students with Visual Impairments: A Resource Guide for Teachers* (2nd ed.), (Austin: Texas School for the Blind and Visually Impaired, 1995).

tion. The teacher may need to slow the pace of the lessons and schedule more breaks for a student who has decreased stamina and other health concerns.

Prior Literacy Level

Students' level of literacy skills in print before they switched to braille is another important factor to assess. The skill levels of two students of the same age may vary widely. It should not be assumed that a student was performing at grade level as a print reader before he or she lost vision. As mentioned earlier, some students with degenerative visual conditions or low vision may have struggled for a long time to read print comfortably and may be reading slowly with frequent errors and great fatigue.

Thus, even though students with low vision have been print readers for many years, they may not have gained all the literacy skills that most others of their age have acquired. A careful assessment of literacy skills may indicate gaps in knowledge and skills that will have to be addressed. For example, students may have a limited vocabulary because they have not had the direct experiences that everyone assumed they had. Or they may have poor decoding skills (the ability to sound out words), lack dictionary skills, or have difficulty skimming for information in a story or on a page. Chapter 7 discusses in detail assessments that can be used to ascertain a student's reading and writing levels. It is important to address general difficulties with the reading and writing process when a student starts to learn braille because along with the braille code, the student is also learning reading and writing skills. The following are some considerations to keep in mind when assessing students' prior literacy levels:

- Watch students' behavior. Both teachers of visually impaired students and classroom teachers need to be aware of avoidance behaviors and watch for signs that low vision students are having difficulty reading. Students often become adept at hiding their poor reading skills by using various coping strategies that help them avoid detection. For example, they may rely on their listening skills or on friends or neighbors to help them with their work or do the work for them. They may also frequently "forget" to bring books and materials to class or engage in disruptive behavior in class. Another common coping strategy is to avoid making eye contact with teachers during class to avoid being called on (Brozo, 1990), especially for tasks that require reading aloud. Such avoidance behaviors are frequently clues that the students are having trouble reading print and may benefit from a change in reading medium.

- Do a complete records review. School records and interviews with teachers and parents can help the teacher of braille obtain information on a student's level of literacy before the vision loss. The student's permanent record may list scores on standardized tests taken in the past, and his or her previous Individualized Education Plans (IEPs) should document whether tests were taken with adaptations (such as large print or extra time).

- Talk to the student's parents and teachers. Interviewing a student's parents, as well as current and previous teachers, can also give information about the student's reading performance. Ask the teachers and parents if they have samples or portfolios of the student's previous work that they are willing to share. These samples can give information on such matters as handwriting, spelling, grammar, and vocabulary, and will contribute to a more complete picture of the student's current literacy level when compared with the work the student is presently doing.

- Pay particular attention to the student's reading speed, reading stamina (how long he or she can read print before becoming fatigued), and comprehension skill.

- Include recreational reading in the assessment. Anecdotal items, such as the student's interest in reading and how much time the student spent in reading for pleasure before the vision loss, can tell the teacher a great deal about the student's facility (or frustration) with reading, as well as reading habits and interests. Asking parents and teachers such questions as, "How often did Tim pick up a book to read at home?" or "What kinds of books did Jessica take out of the school library?" can give the teacher information about the student's reading preferences and whether reading was an enjoyable leisure activity. Reading-interest inventories, discussed later in this chapter, can also be helpful.

Motivation Level and Attitudes

The most important issues in teaching braille to students who are adventitiously blind are attitudes and motivation (Harrison, 1987; Olson, 1981; Simons, 1995). As Harrison noted, "A girl may have an IQ of 120, sensitivity of touch and an excellent memory, but if she does not want to learn braille, progress will be at a snail's pace and all the modern methods in the world will be of no avail" (p. 45). Thus, a teacher needs to ask some questions: How does the student feel about the vision loss? What experiences has he or she had with braille? How does the student feel about learning to read "all over again?" How does he or she feel about reading and writing in general? What are the student's goals for the future, and what part does literacy play in those goals?

For some students, learning braille is equivalent to admitting that they are going blind (Harley, Truan, & Sanford, 1987; Harrison, 1987)—a profoundly emotional issue. As Perle (1978, p. 256), who lost most of his vision suddenly at age 20 after having low vision most of his life, expressed it:

> Shock and disbelief was a constant companion during the last half of August. What would happen to me? Would I be able to read with the same intensity as I had in the past? Would I be able to handle a career such as law with the vision I now possessed? Above all, would I be able to drive again?

Teachers need to be sympathetic and open with students and spend some time listening to the students' concerns. Again, a positive attitude toward braille and demonstration and modeling of some of its uses may be helpful. But sometimes teachers just have to be patient and start braille instruction at a later time (Harley, Henderson, & Truan, 1979; Harrison, 1987). How long to wait depends entirely on the individual situation. A teacher needs to be sensitive and vigilant to pick up cues that a student is more open and ready to start instruction. By continuing to be enthusiastic about braille and showing the benefits of using braille for some everyday tasks with which the student is having difficulty, the teacher can keep the door open to braille instruction later in the school year or even the next school year.

As noted earlier, reading may have negative associations for some students with low vision, who may feel that they have done poorly at it. It is important for these students to have immediate success in their introductory lessons. If the teacher has done a careful assessment of skills, the teacher can address specific deficits and gaps in learning to help such students catch up to their classmates, which will increase their feelings of success.

Students who have low vision or a degenerative eye condition may be somewhat more difficult to motivate if they have picked up the attitude that braille is not as good as print. To overcome this misconception, teachers have to be enthusiastic and positive in their approach to braille instruction and demonstrate some immediate uses and advantages of braille. In short, teachers should "present braille as a new beginning, rather than the bottom of a long slide down from print" (Fitzsimons, 1993, p. 1). Teachers can also use a number of strategies to create and foster students' motivation to learn braille.

STRATEGIES

CREATING AND FOSTERING MOTIVATION

✛ Keep the student's specific interests, age, and reading levels in mind. Find stories on sports, animals, skateboarding, or whatever interests a student. Locate magazine stories from a variety of sources and transcribe them into braille. (There are many magazines for young people; ask the librarian or media specialist in your school or at the local public library for suggestions.) Choose books that are well below a student's frustration level that the student can read comfortably. It may be a challenge to find such books for older students, but stories that the students have written can be used, such as language experience stories of important events in their lives (see Chapter 3). It is important for new readers to have immediate success.

✛ Conduct a reading-interest inventory—a survey of the topics the student likes and dislikes to read about (for a sample form, see Figure 4-2). The student can fill this out alone, or the teacher and student can do it together orally. The information from this inventory can be used to help the teacher learn what kinds of reading materials the student prefers and his or her attitudes toward reading.

✛ Introduce the student to another braille user. Another student who reads and writes in braille, preferably one who is adventitiously blind and close to the student's age, can serve as a role model for the benefits of using braille. Often, hearing about braille from another student who has gone through a similar experience carries more weight than urging from a teacher. If there are few braille readers in the area of the same age or ability level as the student, contact teachers in neighboring areas to see if their students want to be pen pals or telephone buddies with your student or want to meet him or her. Pen pals can also be from different states or countries and from public or residential schools. The students can be the same age, or an older

READING-INTEREST INVENTORY

Student _____ Date _____

Please fill out this survey to let me know what you think about reading and books.

1. In my free time I like to _____ .

2. The kinds of books I like to read best are _____ .

3. The activity I like to do best at school is _____ .

4. I usually read about _____ times a week.

5. When I go to the library, I _____ .

6. When I read material that is too difficult for me, I _____ .

7. When my teacher reads to the class, I _____ .

8. My reading class is _____ .

9. My teacher helps me the most when _____ .

10. I worry about school when _____ .

11. My least favorite kinds of books are _____ .

12. Here's how I feel about the following kinds of books:

    a. mysteries   love 1 2 3 4 5 6 7 8 9 10 hate

    b. poetry   love 1 2 3 4 5 6 7 8 9 10 hate

    c. plays   love 1 2 3 4 5 6 7 8 9 10 hate

    d. biographies   love 1 2 3 4 5 6 7 8 9 10 hate

    e. sports stories   love 1 2 3 4 5 6 7 8 9 10 hate

    f. comedies   love 1 2 3 4 5 6 7 8 9 10 hate

    g. romances   love 1 2 3 4 5 6 7 8 9 10 hate

    h. essays   love 1 2 3 4 5 6 7 8 9 10 hate

    i. science   love 1 2 3 4 5 6 7 8 9 10 hate

    j. animal stories   love 1 2 3 4 5 6 7 8 9 10 hate

    k. nature stories   love 1 2 3 4 5 6 7 8 9 10 hate

    l. other_____   love 1 2 3 4 5 6 7 8 9 10 hate

Figure 4-2. Sample Reading-Interest Inventory

student, college student, or adult can be paired with a beginning braille reader. The magazines of national consumer organizations such as the American Council of the Blind (ACB) or the National Federation of the Blind (NFB) sometimes print requests for pen pals, as does the newsletter *Awareness* of the National Association for Parents of the Visually Impaired (NAPVI) (see Resources).

✤ Find an adult who reads braille to serve as a mentor to the student. The adult may act as a tutor or just as a friend and role model. The student could visit the mentor at his or her place of work to see how braille is used on the job. Mentors may be found by contacting a local chapter of a blind consumer organization, such as ACB or NFB, or a local blindness agency. The Careers and Technology Information Bank of the American Foundation for the Blind (AFB) is another source for finding adults who can talk to the student, especially about employment issues and the various types of braille access technology (see Resources).

✤ Find functional uses for braille. Introduce immediately functional uses for reading braille, including address books, telephone lists, homework assignments, menus, notes, and shopping lists. If students can see an immediate use for this new skill, they will probably have a greater motivation to learn more. After all, reading and writing may not be students' most pressing concerns after they lose their vision. Initially, they may be more anxious about finding their lockers or organizing and locating their materials. Showing them how braille can help right away with labeling and organizing can be a good introduction to the code. Label personal belongings, such as the doors of lockers, notebooks, audiotapes, and compact discs (CDs). These initial practical experiences could be in grade 1 braille, so students can start using braille as soon as they have learned a few letters. Using students' names to label belongings is also motivating. It gives students an immediate use for braille in organizing their lives and practice in writing skills if a slate and stylus are used. Labelers that braille on plastic tape strips (such as Dymo tape) are available from various commercial sources (see Resources). These labelers have a limited number of braille contractions, but for initial practice with braille labeling, this is not a problem.

✤ Use technology as a motivating factor. Chapter 8 details specific types of technology that may be helpful for students, but it is important to note here that computers, personal notetakers, and other forms of braille access technology may be the hook to get students engaged in braille. Computers are often popular with students, and most young people have had some familiarity with computers at school or at home. The ability to use certain types of assistive technology for braille reading and writing may be an incentive for reluctant students. For example, one student resisted learning braille until his teacher introduced him to a portable braille notetaker. He could carry the notetaker to class, take notes, hear what he had written using the speech in the notetaker, and provide his teacher with a print copy of his homework. As his writing of braille improved, he also became motivated to improve his braille-reading skills. (The uses of technology are discussed later in this chapter in the section "Approaches for Teaching Braille Writing.")

Teachers need to take advantage of the enthusiasm of students who are highly motivated to learn braille and are raring to go, but resist the temptation to overload enthusiastic beginners with too much material at one time (see the section on "Scheduling Braille Instruction" later in this chapter). Short lessons with frequent breaks are helpful to all beginners. These lessons can start with a warm-up activity (such as those described later in this chapter), followed by a short reading passage, a writing exercise, a different reading activity, and so on. The duration of reading activities can be lengthened as students' competence increases. The duration of lessons also depends on the students' ages, since older students have longer attention spans than do younger students. Look for signs of fatigue—students may crane their necks, hunch their shoulders, sigh loudly, start making more errors, or complain of tiredness. Short breaks between activities, during which students get up from the table, stretch, and walk around, can alleviate fatigue and keep them motivated. As Betts (1979) stated, "interest + personal needs + aspirations + attitudes = motivation" and an eagerness to learn that teachers need to cultivate. Other strategies that teachers can use to sustain and increase motivation follow.

STRATEGIES

SUSTAINING AND INCREASING MOTIVATION

✛ Write directions in braille. Give students written directions in braille that they have to follow. With younger children, you might have a treasure hunt in the classroom to find a prize. With older students, you can work with an orientation and mobility instructor to write directions to a special place on a route (such as an ice cream parlor or convenience store).

✛ Encourage students to subscribe to braille magazines. Several braille magazines of interest to older children and young adults are available. Most students enjoy getting mail, and having subscriptions to periodicals will give them practice reading at home. (See Resources for the names and addresses of braille magazines.)

✛ Establish peer tutoring. Peer tutoring can be done in one of two ways. A new braille student can be paired with a more advanced braille student to work on braille together, play games, and the like. The students can reinforce each other's skills and share written communications. Or, an older braille student can serve as a peer tutor to a younger braille student. This form of tutoring builds skills and self-esteem, especially if the older student is a new braille reader who is helping a young child who knows even less.

✢ Write short braille notes to students. Place private notes in braille in unexpected places for students to find—a short, encouraging note in a student's lunch box or a silly riddle in a student's notebook. As the student's parents learn braille, encourage them to do the same. Who doesn't like to receive unexpected notes?

✢ Play games. Games are nonthreatening and enjoyable, and since many games show only one word or letter at a time, they can help build symbol- and word-recognition skills. Commercially produced braille-adapted games, including Scrabble, Monopoly, Password, and Uno, are available from many sources of specialty products (see Resources). Most of these games are in print and braille together, so they can be played with sighted peers. The student or teacher can easily make other word games, such as concentration and hangman. APH manufactures a Game Kit that can be used to make new games. The kit comes with tactile game boards, index cards, tactile and large-print dice, and other items.

✢ Have students teach braille to sighted classmates. Most students like the idea of knowing a secret code they can use to pass notes to classmates. Blind students can start with grade 1 braille and make alphabet cards (some are available from AFB) to give to friends until they learn the letters. This is also a good way to get students to practice their slate-and-stylus skills.

✢ Have students keep logs of books they read. Students find it motivating to see how many books they have finished by the end of the year. They can enter the title and author of each book when they finish reading it, as well as a few short comments about it. This strategy encourages reluctant readers because it helps them establish a list of favorite authors or reading genres so they can find more books they may enjoy.

✢ Encourage students to enter contests. Keep an eye out for essay contests held by magazines for young people that students can enter. Ask the librarian or media specialist in school for suggestions or look in teachers' journals and magazines for announcements. Magazines for adolescents often have poetry and short-story contests as well. In addition, local, state, or regional organizations, such as the Chamber of Commerce or Lions clubs, occasionally sponsor contests, and NFB sponsors an annual, national contest, Braille Readers Are Leaders, that has a special category for older students who are learning braille. The opportunity to write for publication, recognition, or an award may be motivating to students.

✛ Use braille. When students read aloud, use braille texts, rather than print texts, to follow along. Using braille sends a message that the teacher values braille as much as the student does and keeps teachers aware of what the students are reading.

GETTING READY TO TEACH BRAILLE

When teachers begin a braille program for students who are making the transition from print to braille, they need to address many of the same factors mentioned in Chapters 2 and 3, including concept development, finger and hand dexterity, and tactile sensitivity and perception. However, the needs of students in this population differ from those of children who are congenitally blind.

Language and Concept Development

As noted earlier, children who had some sight early in life and have been print readers retain concepts related to literacy that they learned earlier. In addition, these children may have already learned many other concepts that must be carefully and specifically taught to congenitally blind children, and these concepts can be applied to new situations.

However, it should not be assumed that because children once had vision or saw a picture of something that they fully understand the concept being taught. There may still be large gaps in understanding, especially among children who have had low vision all their lives. As with all children, it is important to introduce new vocabulary in a clear and understandable manner. The following are some suggested strategies to help these students with the development of language and concepts.

S T R A T E G I E S

FOSTERING LANGUAGE AND CONCEPT DEVELOPMENT

✛ Use descriptive language and tactile models to introduce new vocabulary. The use of verbal and tactile comparisons (such as "the cilia look like tiny hairs around the edge of the paramecium"), concrete examples, models, and the like is crucial. Unlike congenitally blind students, adventitiously blind students probably understand the concept of a model, but it is up to the teacher to put that model in a context the students can understand. The use of real objects whenever possible is still preferable to the use of models.

✛ Remember the content areas. New vocabulary needs to be introduced in a meaningful fashion, especially in academic subjects such as social studies, science, health, and mathematics. For example, if students in a middle school science class are using microscopes to see the parts of a plant cell, a student who recently lost his or her vision will need assistance in applying these new concepts to those he or she previously learned. By the use of highly descriptive words and three-dimensional models of a cell, the adventitiously blind student can develop a better mental picture of the different structures. The teacher must ensure that the student clearly understands the concepts being taught. One way to ensure comprehension is to ask the student to repeat the information in his or her own words.

✛ Create a vocabulary box or file. Using a file folder similar to the one discussed in Chapter 2 or a file box with index cards can be helpful in keeping track of vocabulary and concepts discussed in class. In the example of the middle school science class, the student could keep the file and add to the list of vocabulary words in a manner meaningful to him or her. The student could also use the file to maintain a spelling list and glossary or personal dictionary.

Finger and Hand Dexterity

Some adventitiously blind children will have no difficulty with hand strength and agility, especially if they had been writing fluently in print or using a keyboard. However, the finger and hand dexterity of children who lost their vision as the result of an accident or brain tumor may be affected. Thus, a thorough assessment of this area is necessary. An occupational therapist may be able to assist the teacher of the visually impaired to assess a student's fine motor skills, if one is available through the school district (see Chapter 2). The teacher can also review the student's medical records for insights in this area. Even if a student's strength and agility are not impaired, a student who is learning braille for the first time still needs to learn the correct mechanics of the position and movement of hands across a page of braille (see Chapter 3).

- Keep initial lessons short. Students may become quite fatigued at first from holding their hands in the unaccustomed manner necessary to read braille. It is a good idea to keep lessons short at first and give frequent breaks to allow them to shift their positions.
- Allow students to experiment with different reading postures. Although, as described in Chapter 3, studies have found how highly effective braille readers position and read their materials (Olson, 1981; Rex, Koenig, Wormsley, & Baker, 1994), encourage students to try new positions that may be effective for them. Adolescents are usually fidgety and need to move around a bit during class periods. Giving them the opportunity to change their positions will lessen fatigue and loosen stiff arm and shoulder muscles (Harrison, 1987).

• Foster positive attitudes by ensuring comfort. Furniture fit (described in Chapter 3) is just as important for older children as for younger children. If a student is not motivated to learn braille, furniture fit may be even more important, since the fatigue and discomfort of working at a desk or table that is not the correct height only makes an unmotivated student even less likely to want to use braille.

Tactile Sensitivity and Perception

It should never be assumed that because children once read print they will be immediately able to discern and discriminate among tactile symbols. Rather, they will need tactile readiness and perceptual activities like those discussed in Chapter 3 before they learn to trust their hands to give them accurate information. The more time a teacher spends ensuring that a student has the appropriate sensitivity and perceptual skills for braille, the faster the student will move when he or she actually starts to read. In addition, the proper hand placement and reading mechanics discussed in Chapters 1 and 3 are equally important for older children.

In addition to the strategies discussed in Chapter 3, teachers can use the following strategies to develop tactile readiness and perception and increase speed and accuracy.

STRATEGIES

DEVELOPING TACTILE SENSITIVITY AND PERCEPTION

✦ Use a warm-up before the lesson. After the student masters tracking across lines of symbols using correct hand positions and techniques, he or she can read lines of simple and familiar words each day before the lesson until a certain criterion is reached (for example, 50 words in a minute). The student can set his or her own criterion for the day or can keep track of his or her progress on braille graph paper or a chart.

✦ Start with double- or triple-spaced lines. As the student becomes more adept at using hands to track across lines and find the next line, he or she can gradually come to use single-spaced lines. At first, the teacher may even want to put two spaces between words on a line until the student builds up speed and accuracy and begins to see each word as one braille unit.

✦ Teach signs that are reversals well apart from each other. Former print readers who are learning braille frequently have trouble with reversals. They sometimes spontaneously state that particular characters are the reverse of others. The teacher should try to discourage this practice, since these students are doing an extra mental step while reading. *Never tell students that certain symbols are reversals.* Instead, if students are having difficulty with certain letters, point out other characteristics of the letters by comparing them to print letters—for example, a braille *j* turns in the same direction as a print *j*.

✛ Students are also much less likely to reverse letters if they read potential "confusers" in context, so give them many opportunities to read actual phrases and sentences.

✛ Encourage a light touch. Beginning braille readers often push down too hard on the dots because they are tense and not familiar with reading braille. Using a light touch actually helps in tactile identification and increases reading speed. In addition to providing short activities and frequent breaks at first, the teacher can try these strategies to encourage students to lighten their touch:

- Use relaxation exercises to alleviate tension. Ask students to close their eyes and take a few deep breaths or to close their eyes, tense up their bodies, and then slowly relax, starting at their toes and working up to their heads.
- Put colored chalk on the dots and encourage students to get as little chalk dust as possible on their fingertips.
- Ask students to practice moving their hands across lines of braille on a single sheet without moving the paper on the table.

✛ To discourage scrubbing (the up-and-down movement across a word or letter) and encourage smooth, rapid movement across lines of braille, have the student go across rows of from 6 to 10 symbols as quickly as possible to find the one that is different in each row. Also, encourage students to use context clues to figure out new words and to identify words as units. Tell them that it is better to skip an unfamiliar word and try to figure it out in context than to scrub the individual letters over and over again. The overlearning technique and the cloze procedure described in Chapter 3 are also helpful for older students.

✛ Strategies described in Chapter 3 to increase fluency, such as repeated readings, are also useful for this population.

✛ To help students increase their reading speeds, use timed drills and repeat them until the students have "overlearned" the materials. A drill can consist of 50 or more Dolch or other vocabulary words that students need to be able to recognize instantly. Start with one-minute drills in which the teacher times students as they read as many words as possible and then count the number of words they have read after the minute is up. Gradually increase drills to two minutes, three minutes, and so on as the students gain more and more proficiency. Having the students read short stories or passages from books, so they are also using context clues, will help them build up speed. Making a game out of timed drills will lessen the anxiety some students feel with them. Students can chart their progress in identifying words or symbols per minute on braille graph paper.

✣ Students can also increase their reading speed by finding two words on a page, going back to the top of the page, and tracking rapidly down the page to find the two words again. Teachers can use this activity for finding new vocabulary words or with words that express the main idea of a paragraph (Olson, 1977).

✣ Vary activities in each lesson. To keep students interested and prevent fatigue, integrate decoding, reading, review, writing, and speed drills in a lesson. As students gain proficiency, the activities can be lengthened. Do not drag out a lesson by focusing on one skill for too long.

A variety of materials are commercially available to use when introducing braille reading to help in developing tactile perception skills and get students to use their tactile sense to gain information (see "Developing Tactile Perception Skills").

MATERIALS

DEVELOPING TACTILE PERCEPTION SKILLS

✣ APH's Tactual Discrimination Worksheets of embossed shapes and lines come in four packets with gradually increasing degrees of difficulty. The student is required to feel the shapes or lines in the row and find the ones that are different or that match, according to the directions in the manual.

✣ *The Mangold Developmental Program of Tactile Perception and Braille Letter Recognition* (Mangold, 1989), described in Chapter 3, although designed for young, congenitally blind students, can be used successfully with older adventitiously blind readers. The precision teaching design allows students to move on to the next lesson if they meet the criterion for the current one, so students can progress at their own pace, practice as much as they need to, and chart their own progress. This program can be used in conjunction with the teacher's own literacy activities.

✣ Teachers can make their own tactile readiness sheets by using the activities developed by the Texas State School for the Blind that are reprinted in "Ideas for Developing Braille Tactile Skills Worksheets" in this chapter from Olson's (1981) *Guidelines and Games for Teaching Efficient Braille Reading*. These activities are perfect for older students who are making the transition to braille because they are more challenging than the Mangold materials, can be converted into competitive games, and can be used to build speed.

PARENTS AS PARTNERS

It is extremely important to involve parents in the transition from print to braille. Parents are often bewildered by their child's sudden vision loss, and have difficulty dealing with their own emotional distress. Many have had little contact with people who are blind or have low vision and thus have numerous questions: What are the options for their child? What do they as parents need to know to ensure that their child gets what is needed? What can be expected of their child now? How will their child complete schoolwork, go to college, and find a job? What if their child has additional special needs? Direct education and counseling may be necessary to help parents understand their own emotions and cope realistically with their child's needs and feelings (Hudson, 1994).

Thus, teachers of visually impaired students often have to deal with the emotional needs not only of students but also of parents. Parents may feel sorrow and pity for their child or conversely may have unrealistically high expectations. It may also take a while for parents to be able to discuss the educational needs of their child with the teacher. Braille may carry a certain stigma or connotation of helplessness for some parents that they will need to overcome. The following suggestions may be useful for supporting the parents of students who are making the transition from print to braille.

STRATEGIES

SUPPORTING PARENTS

✢ Show enthusiasm for braille reading and writing. This is one of the best things that a teacher can do to help parents and should also be the easiest. The teacher needs to emphasize the benefits that students derive from learning braille. Pointing out the usefulness of braille for real-life tasks and demonstrating its importance to the child, now and in the future, will help ease parents' anxiety about their children learning braille (see "Some Uses of Braille Reported by Blind Adults" in this chapter).

✢ Introduce parents to braille-reading adults. It can be as effective for parents to meet successful adults who are blind and use braille as it is for their child. Introducing parents to capable braille-reading adults may lessen their concern that their child will not be able to compete in school or in the workplace.

✢ Show parents new braille access technology. Incorporating technology as quickly as possible with braille instruction will help parents see braille as a "modern" tool of learning (see Chapter 8). It may also relieve some of their concerns about their child's ability to go to college and the jobs their child can get.

IDEAS FOR DEVELOPING BRAILLE TACTILE SKILLS WORKSHEETS

Directions: Students should be given the worksheets prior to any introduction to braille letter recognition. The teacher will initially want to double space between the rows of braille characters on the worksheets. Students who are achieving 100 percent accuracy on a particular worksheet may wish to time themselves and record their rate of progress each day.

FORMAT

1. Horizontal lines of braille dots (2,5) with regular breaks between them.

2. Same as #1 except with irregular breaks.

3. Horizontal dots (1,4) and (3,6).

4. Same as #3 except intermingle several breaks among the braille characters.

5. Horizontal lines of dots (1,4), (2,5), and (3,6).

6. Same as #5 except intermingle several breaks among the braille characters.

7. Rows of braille dots (1,3), (4,6), (1,6), and (3,4).

8. Rows of braille dots (1,3), (4,6), (1,2), (2,3), (4,5), and (5,6).

9. Rows of braille dots (1,3), (4,6), (1,2), (2,3), (4,5), (5,6), (1,6), and (3,4).

DIRECTIONS FOR STUDENT

Track across the lines and verbalize "break" each time a break occurs.

Same as #1.

Track across the lines and tell whether the dots are "high" or "low."

Track across the lines and tell whether there is a "high" symbol, "low" symbol, or a break.

Track across the lines and tell whether dots are "high" dots, "low" dots, or "middle" dots.

Track across the lines and tell whether there is a set of "high," "low" or "middle" dots or a break.

Tell whether the dots are "straight up and down" or "slanted."

Track across the lines and tell whether the dots are "close together" or "far apart."

Track across the braille lines and tell whether the dots are "straight up and down and close together," "straight up and down and far apart," or "slanted."

(continued on next page)

✚ The strategies for involving parents offered in Chapter 1, such as showing them the *Personal Touch* video, teaching parents braille, and introducing parents to other parents and support groups, will be helpful for these parents as well. NAPVI, NFB, and ACB also organize parent support groups and may have local chapters in the area (see Resources for additional information).

✚ If a student became blind because of a particular disease or rare disorder, parents may be able to join support groups sponsored by an organization for that condition. Encourage the parents to contact the National Parent to Parent Support and Information System, a nationwide support group; or the National Information Center for Children and Youth with Disabilities for further information and support (see Resources), or refer to the *AFB Directory of Services* (1997).

IDEAS FOR BRAILLE TACTILE SKILLS WORKSHEETS *(continued)*

10. Rows of braille dots (1,6), (1,5), (3,4), (2,4), (3,5), and (2,6).

    Track across the lines and tell whether the dots are "slanted–close together" or "slanted–far apart."

11. Rows of braille dots (1,6), (2,4), (1,5), (5,6), (1,2), (3,5), (2,6), (1,3), (4,6), (1,3), and (3,4).

    Track across the lines and tell whether the dots are "slanted–close together," "slanted–far apart," "straight up and down–close together," or "straight up and down–far apart."

12. Rows of braille dots (1,3), (1,6), (2,4), (1,5), (5,6), (1,2), (3,5), (2,3), (4,5), and (2,5).

    Track across the lines and tell whether the dots are "slanted," "straight up and down," or "side by side."

13. Rows consisting of two cells followed by a space, with dots 1,2 and 3 in the first cell and some combination of 2 of these 3 dots in the second cell.

    Track across the lines and tell whether the missing dot in the second cell is a "high," "low," or "middle" dot.

14. Rows containing two braille cells followed by a space, in which the first braille cell is a full cell sign, and the second cell contains only 5 dots in various combinations.

    Track across the lines and tell whether the missing dot is on the "right side," "left side," "high," "low" or "middle."

15. Rows of braille cells consisting of various numbers of dots.

    Identify verbally the number of dots in each cell.

16. Rows of braille cells arranged in the following order: Full cell, (4,5,6), (1,2,3), full cell.

    Verbally count the number of cells in each row.

Source: Adapted from M. R. Olson, *Guidelines and Games for Teaching Efficient Braille Reading* (New York: American Foundation for the Blind, 1981), pp. 106–107. Copyright © 1981, American Foundation for the Blind. Originally based on the *Reading Skills Continuum,* Texas State School for the Blind.

TEACHING READING TO OLDER CHILDREN

Former Print Readers

Adventitiously blind teenagers, who may already have mixed or negative feelings about learning braille, may reject braille entirely if they have to read books on the preprimer level ("baby books"). Therefore, it is essential to find an approach to reading that will engage older students. Furthermore, these students may already know *how* to read; what they are concerned with is reading in a different medium. The teacher can assure them that they can "bring their literacy skills with them," so to speak, as they learn a new way to read (Smith, 1978). That is, good phonics skills or the good use of context clues will not change just because the reading medium is different.

SOME USES OF BRAILLE REPORTED BY BLIND ADULTS

- index cards on clothes hangers with braille descriptions of colors, patterns, and so forth to coordinate clothes and accessories

- braille labels on all food containers, with magnetic strips with braille Dymo tape attached to metal cans

- braille books and magazines for recreational reading

- knitting patterns and bus and train schedules in braille

- braille calendar and phone files

- recipe files-binders in braille on washable thermoform paper

- notes on directions for using home appliances in braille

- a slate and stylus near every telephone with 3x5-inch index cards for taking messages

- braille files of contract numbers, medical plans, tax information, bank information, and other personal papers with braille labels for ease of organization

- braille reference materials, tables, mathematical information, and other items frequently referred to at work and home

- braille notes from audiotaped materials for ease of finding and organizing information

- braille notes at meetings and conferences

- braille notes for giving speeches and talking to groups

Source: Adapted from Kathleen M. Huebner, "Daily Uses of Braille as Told by Four Adult Braille Users," *Journal of Visual Impairment & Blindness, 83* (1989), pp. 308–309.

It is important for older children who are learning braille to see an immediate function for braille reading and writing and begin to use braille as soon as possible for personal needs. If they are already feeling the loss of the ability to read and write in print, being able to apply newly learned braille skills immediately will help them regain a sense of control and self-sufficiency.

Any program designed to teach braille to older students has to balance high interest and an initially low braille vocabulary level and be paced carefully to allow for enough practice without being so slow that students get frustrated or lose interest. Teachers often put together their own programs to use with individual students (Erin & Sumranveth, 1995). For example, they may put into braille things that are of immediate use and interest to a student, such as telephone numbers, cafeteria menus, and labels, and use these words as a basis from which to start. Teachers also commonly use the language experience approach or whole language approach (see Chapter 3).

Another approach is to use published curricula to teach braille reading and writing. The materials listed under "Curricula for Older Students" are among the few available for this population of students.

MATERIALS

CURRICULA FOR OLDER STUDENTS

✛ *Braille Too* (Hepker & Coquilette, 1995), produced by the Grant Wood Area Education Agency, was designed by two itinerant teachers specifically for former print readers in middle and high school who are beginning to learn braille. The program does not contain tactile readiness materials, but initial introduction of alphabet letters is designed to match the sequence of letters introduced in the Mangold program (Mangold, 1989). Its over 600 pages of text are divided into 10 units that teach the code gradually, using a wide variety of activities (such as multiple-choice and fill-in-the-blank questions, contraction drills, and practice sentences). The selections are written so that no words that contain contractions or abbreviations are used until the rules for them have been introduced; thus, students are always reading grade 2 braille. The vocabulary and reading passages are aimed at the interests and experiences of adolescents. Writing exercises are also included and are available in large or regular print or on audiocassette.

✛ *Read Again* (Caton, Pester, & Bradley, 1990), published by APH, is designed for adults who have lost their vision, but is often used by teachers of adventitiously blind children, probably because it is readily available (Erin & Sumranveth, 1995). This book starts with tactile readiness exercises and then teaches grade 1 braille, introducing contractions over a series of lessons. Because it was not written for young children, the vocabulary and selections are best suited to older high school or college-age students. The many other curricula designed for adults have the same drawbacks for use with school-age students. It is important for teachers to use materials such as *Read Again* carefully and in an age-appropriate fashion.

✛ The Royal National Institute for the Blind publishes several reading series for middle and high school–aged students who are learning braille. *Spot the Dot* (Fitzsimons, 1993) was designed for students aged 12–16, and *Braille in Easy Steps* (Lorimer, 1988) for students aged 10–14. These books use the British braille code, which is different from the code used in the United States. In addition to British spellings (such as *colour* for *color* and *theatre* for *theater*), the British code does not use the capital dot and has a few different usage rules. However, it may be worthwhile to review these series to see if any lessons and activities can be adapted.

Students Who Use Print

Teaching braille to students who are still using print also requires an individualized approach. The article "Teaching Braille Reading to Students with Low

Vision," by Holbrook and Koenig (1992) (reprinted in full at the end of this book) outlines the major instructional approaches to teaching braille to students who are learning print at the same time ("parallel instruction") or print readers who are adding braille instruction ("nonparallel instruction").

According to Holbrook and Koenig, the language experience and whole language approaches are preferable for nonparallel instruction, although the basal reader approach may have some utility if teachers choose grade levels carefully. *Read Again* can be taught as a stand-alone program for older students if it is supplemented to include reading materials that are of greater interest to older students. *Patterns: The Primary Braille Reading Program* (Caton, Pester, & Bradley, 1980), discussed in Chapter 3, is useful only for its introductory lessons and vocabulary and comprehension skills, since it is geared for students through the third-grade reading level only.

Students with low vision sometimes use their residual vision for certain tasks in braille. For example, they may learn various dot configurations on an enlarged braille cell to gain a "mental picture" of the letters and symbols or use their residual vision to find where the braille is on a page and how long the lines are and then read the braille tactilely. Although some teachers discourage students from using residual vision while reading braille, there is generally no harm in allowing students to do some tasks visually as long as their tactile reading is fluent, their posture is good, and they are not fatigued by trying to use vision for tactile tasks.

Scheduling Braille Instruction

It is often difficult to give older students enough time to practice so they can become fluent in reading braille. Students who start braille instruction after the first or second grade are definitely not following the curriculum presented in the regular classroom. Most of their classmates have advanced beyond such early experiences as learning the alphabet and forming letters, which new braille students have to spend time doing. Therefore, teachers, students, and parents have to decide how much time to allocate to "relearning." Parents and students need to realize that time is required to learn to read braille and that the student's classes will not wait for them to relearn reading and writing before the class goes on to new materials. Students may therefore feel pressure to learn braille as quickly as possible to keep up with their classes. Teachers may be tempted to give a "crash course" in braille, but it is usually not a good idea to do so, since it will frustrate students and may lead teachers to take short cuts in their teaching methods that result in poor braille-reading skills. "If braille is to be learned thoroughly and become a useful tool, the pace of instruction, as far as possible, must be geared to the learning pace of the individual" (Lorimer, 1988, p. 5). Thus, some students may learn braille in a matter of weeks, whereas others may take months.

Students may be anxious to learn braille quickly to keep up with their classmates, but it is important to pace instruction so students learn thoroughly.

Compromises and difficult decisions need to be made. Daily instruction in braille is critical. It is certainly better for students to invest the time to master braille reading and writing as early as possible—even if they have to attend summer school, after-school tutoring sessions, or even an extra year of high school before graduating—than for them to have no literacy skills. The long-term needs of students must be considered when making these decisions: What are a student's future goals for employment, higher education, and independent living? Parents and students who have doubts about the importance of learning braille will probably be interested to know that the vast majority of people who are blind and are employed are braille readers (Kirchner, Johnson, & Harkins, 1997).

So how is the teacher of visually impaired students to schedule braille instruction? With an elementary school student, the teacher may work one-on-one on a student's reading and writing program in the classroom while the other students are at learning centers, engaging in small-group reading instruction, or doing seat work during reading instruction. In this way, the classmates and teacher see the student learning and using braille, get accustomed to the sound of the braillewriter, and can even learn some braille themselves. The pull-out model (in which a student leaves the classroom for instruction in another room) is often used for older students who are learning braille, since the classrooms of middle or high school students are generally not conducive to working with one student separately, and older students may also feel uncomfortable doing lessons and activities that are different from their classmates.' With middle or high school students, teachers may need to schedule one or more periods per day for individual braille instruction in another room. Consult with a student's school to make sure that the student receives credit for the time he or she is with the teacher of visually impaired students.

Although the use of audiotaped books can take up some of the slack for a student who is learning braille, it does not take the place of being able to read and write. Audiotapes, while useful, have some major drawbacks. First, it can be difficult and time consuming to skim through them or to relocate specific information, especially since most textbooks consist of several tapes. Second, students who use audiotaped books still have to take notes on what they hear, as do students who tape class sessions. Since students have to listen to entire tapes to find the information they need to remember, they may have to relisten to six hours of tapes per day if they use audiotapes for all their classes. It is much more efficient to use braille to take notes during class as the other students are doing in print. As students become more proficient in braille, they can do more and more work in braille and use audiotapes only as backups when necessary.

A variety of strategies can be used to increase the reading fluency of middle and high school students and stimulate their interest in practicing braille skills.

STRATEGIES

INCREASING STUDENTS' BRAILLE-READING SKILLS

✛ Get students involved in meaningful, interesting literature as soon as possible. Many excellent braille books are available for young adults, and there are several ways to obtain them. Chapter 1 and the Resources section list such sources as the Library of Congress's National Library Service for the Blind and Physically Handicapped and the American Action Fund for Blind Children and Adults, both of which have lending libraries of braille books. Sources for purchasing books include the National Braille Press, Seedlings, and several religious organizations. In addition, numerous articles, short stories, and even entire books may be found on the Internet, downloaded onto a computer, formatted for braille, and then printed with a braille embosser (see Chapter 8 for further information).

Reading to a student as he follows along can help him improve his braille-reading skills.

✦ Read aloud to a student as he or she follows along. Make sure to pace the reading so the student does not get too far behind and give up. Stop periodically and let the student supply the next word in a sentence. A student can also read along with an audiotape. Use as slow a tape speed as possible without distorting the voice. Then have the student go back and read the passage again without listening to the audiotape. Repeat this process, gradually increasing the tape speed.

✦ Use repeated readings. Choose a short passage and time the student while he or she reads it aloud. Then have the student read it over and time him or her again. Chart the number of words read per minute each time the passage is reread. This strategy is effective for increasing speed and fluency, and students are motivated by seeing their speed increase. The steps for this strategy are described more fully in Chapter 3.

✦ Start with short pieces. Use short, motivating texts such as jokes and riddles that are fun to share with friends and family members and can promote positive attitudes toward braille. Students can also write their own.

✦ Use poems. In addition to being short, poems that rhyme can help a student practice words with the same endings. The predictable rhythm and rhyme scheme help the student identify unfamiliar words. Shel Silverstein's poetry collections, such as *Where the Sidewalk Ends,* are popular with younger students. Older students may enjoy short poems by Robert Frost, Langston Hughes, and Emily Dickinson, among other famous poets.

✤ Use song lyrics. Students are usually familiar with the lyrics of popular songs, so even new words can be introduced in a comfortable manner. Lyrics are often printed in pamphlets that come with CDs or cassettes and can be transcribed into braille. (Just be aware of the vocabulary of some popular songs and avoid offensive lyrics.)

✤ Use predictable texts with a lot of repetition. High-interest, low-vocabulary books may work well with some teenagers. Several series of these books are available.

✤ Have the student devise new endings to familiar stories. Have a student follow along while the story is read aloud; stop before a story ends and ask the student what he or she thinks will happen next. Then read the ending together to see if the student's prediction was correct. This activity builds comprehension. The new endings of stories can be written down and shared with others. The teacher can also start reading a story or book aloud, get to a climactic part, and then encourage the student to finish the story on his or her own.

✤ Read aloud plays from braille anthologies. Middle and high school English classes frequently use anthologies of literature as textbooks that are available in braille. These books often include short plays that the teacher and the student can read aloud. Assign parts beforehand; if the student is a beginner, he or she can take the main part, and the teacher can take the others. If the reading is being tape-recorded, practice a few times first, so the student can hear how good he or she sounds. This is an activity that a student may want to do with his or her classmates.

✤ Suggest that students practice reading familiar stories to their younger brothers and sisters in print with braille overlays, such as the TWIN-VISION books (see Resources for sources). Reading to others will increase their self-esteem, and give them valuable practice with easy-to-read materials to increase their fluency.

APPROACHES FOR TEACHING BRAILLE WRITING

Another key to teaching middle and high school students literacy is to allow them time and opportunities for self-expression (Atwell, 1987; Oldfather, 1995). Such opportunities are beneficial for all adolescents, but are especially valuable for students who are making the transition to braille, for whom opportunities for self-expression may lead to greater feelings of control and acceptance. As Oldfather (1995, p. 422) noted:

> Students are more willing to express themselves in a responsive classroom culture in which the teacher invites them to express their ideas and feelings, listens responsively to what they have to say, celebrates and exhibits their

writings and creative products, and negotiates with them (within certain parameters) about what they might learn and how they might share what they have learned.

Whatever approach they use to teach braille reading and writing to adolescents who are former print readers, teachers should create a climate of acceptance and respect, so students will feel free to express themselves.

Many of the writing approaches and techniques mentioned in Chapter 3 are appropriate for adventitiously blind students. The difference is that most of these older students probably have had some experience putting their thoughts on paper. Thus, although it may sound obvious, the best way for students to learn writing skills is for them *to write*. Give students many opportunities during the day to practice writing—not just for "braille practice" or English assignments that will be graded. Remind the students how often people write for personal reasons and the kinds of things they write: lists, reminders to themselves and others, class notes, and so on. Although it is important for students to learn all the correct mechanics of writing and the uses of various braille contractions and their rules, the major point to stress is the *purpose* of the written message even while they are learning a new medium of expressing it.

Therefore, overstressing correctness from the start will only discourage new braille writers. Choose to focus on one thing at a time—for example, correct letter formation with the slate, the use of punctuation, or run-on sentences, but not all three at once. Also, allow students a great deal of practice and opportunity to explore—whether they start with the slate and stylus, the Perkins brailler, or assistive technology devices. There is a difference between teaching the *method* by which students will write braille and teaching the *process* of writing. Writing should be taught as communication; but to communicate effectively, students have to learn several methods of braille writing: the slate and stylus, the Perkins brailler, and various types of braille access technology.

As with reading braille, technology can be the incentive that students need to get involved in writing braille. And not only is technology motivating, it can help students communicate more effectively. Students who are learning braille still need to be able to turn their papers in to their teachers in print by using many of the available types of technology.

Small personal notetakers are popular in schools for many reasons. Notetakers often give feedback to users in speech, and, in some models, with a refreshable braille display (see Chapter 8). They are easier to carry than the Perkins brailler and quieter to use. They also have features similar to those of computers, such as a calculator and address book. Some notetakers can be connected to computers and printers to print out hard copy in print or braille. Many students find notetakers motivating and fun to use. Since most of the portable notetakers can be used with either grade 1 or grade 2 braille, they can be used in braille instruction as soon as students know the alphabet.

Other important technological devices are various types of software and embossers, the Mountbatten brailler, and refreshable braille displays. Each has its particular strengths for braille students. Students with keyboarding skills will be relieved to know that they can use these skills on computers that have been adapted with synthesized speech, braille translation software, braille printers, and refreshable braille displays (see Chapter 8 for details on using technology in teaching braille).

The importance of the slate and stylus for older students cannot be overstated. Students who have already known the convenience of being able to jot down a note, a telephone number, or directions on paper with a pen or pencil will appreciate the immediacy and convenience of the slate and stylus. Compared to the Perkins brailler, a slate and stylus are easy to carry and practically silent to use. In addition, slates are inexpensive—especially compared to the Perkins brailler or any of the electronic braille methods (such as electronic notetakers and computers with embossers). Although a slate can be used as the only tool for writing braille, students typically use it for personal communication. In other words, they use the slate for quick notes and messages, reminders to themselves, lists, and taking notes in class. It is important that they learn the correct method of using the slate and have enough time to practice using it, but the essential thing is that they can read back what they have written to themselves.

Use of the Perkins brailler is also important. Many students initially write faster on the Perkins brailler than with a slate and stylus, and its one-button control to move the paper down is easier than the method used on the slate. The Perkins brailler is often used for writing long papers and final drafts of reports and stories. (It is important in braille mathematics as well.) Although learning to use the Perkins brailler is essential, it is a heavy piece of equipment, so it is not as portable as a slate and stylus, which can be put in a pocket or purse. The Perkins is sturdy, however, and, with proper care and occasional cleaning, will probably last a lifetime.

After students have learned some of the techniques needed for braille writing, they also need to work on the writing process itself. Older students who had some literacy experiences before they became blind may be aware of the writing process and just need to learn some new strategies for editing, constructing outlines, and the like. They may have some difficulty organizing themselves and their writing in the new medium. Other students may not know the steps of prewriting, composing, revising, editing, and publishing (see Chapter 3), or may need assistance with one or more of them. The following strategies may help students organize their writing.

S T R A T E G I E S

TEACHING WRITING SKILLS

✛ Teach the steps of the writing process to students who are not familiar with it, and, as previously mentioned, make sure the students see a purpose in their writing. If students are having difficulty with the writing process, the teacher may want to consult the reading specialist or language arts teacher at the school for additional strategies. *Foundations of Braille Literacy* (Rex et al., 1994) also contains some useful information applicable to this population, such as descriptions of the various approaches to teaching writing.

✛ Teach tactile editing marks. Swenson's system of tactile editing marks, which teachers can use to give students feedback on their written work, is presented in Chapter 3 along with suggestions about how to use them. Whether the teacher uses these marks or develops another system, it is important to use a set of marks consistently, so students have a clear idea of what changes they need to make.

✛ Teach the use of a braille eraser. Understanding how to use a braille eraser to completely remove any braille dots from a page is an important skill. Several types of braille erasers are available from Howe Press, APH, and the Royal National Institute for the Blind, as well as from commercial suppliers (see Resources). Braille erasers may not always be appropriate, but they may prevent students from having to re-braille their work if there are only a few small mistakes.

✛ Teach students that first drafts in braille should be double or triple spaced. Leaving two or three spaces between lines in the first draft allows more room for editing marks, additions to be inserted later, and sections to be deleted.

✛ Teach students to cut and paste. Students who are used to writing and rewriting in print may be loathe to rewrite braille over and over again to fix errors. One strategy that may be helpful is to teach them to write in "chunks"—braille paragraphs on half sheets of paper or large index cards. These paragraphs can be rearranged, cut apart, and stapled in their final positions.

Students who write using such technology as computer word-processing systems on computers can learn the cut-and-paste features of most programs. With these features, such tasks as moving sentences and paragraphs to other sections of a document or removing sections are much easier on a computer than on a brailler.

✛ Encourage students to keep a journal. Maintaining a diary or personal journal will give students not only practice writing but also a place for self-expression. Make sure students understand that the journal is their private place to write; they are not graded and do not have to be turned in unless the student wants feedback.

SUMMARY

Although students who lose their vision later in childhood or adolescence are a smaller population of braille readers than are students who are congenitally blind (Erin & Sumranveth, 1995), the challenges they pose to teachers are just as great. Students who are making the transition from print to braille have special considerations because of their ages and prior experiences with literacy in print as well as the emotional impact of vision loss. Careful assessment of their past and current literacy levels, coupled with an approach based on needs, motivation, interests, and strengths of individual students, can lead to a successful transition. Above all, new braille readers must have opportunities to read and write braille throughout the day and receive sufficient support and encouragement from teachers and parents to become fully literate in this new medium.

REFERENCES

AFB directory of services for blind and visually impaired persons in the United States and Canada (25th ed.). (1997). New York: AFB Press.

Atwell, N. (1987). *In the middle: Writing, reading, and learning with adolescents.* Portsmouth, NH: Heinemann.

Betts, E. A., (1979). Capture reading motivation. In J. L Thomas & R. M. Loring (Eds.), *Motivating children and young adults to read* (pp. 63–70). Phoenix: Oryx Press.

Brozo, W. G. (1990). Hiding out in secondary classrooms: Coping strategies of unsuccessful readers. *Journal of Reading, 34,* 324–328.

Caton, H., Pester, E., & Bradley, E. J. (1980). *Patterns: The primary braille reading program.* Lexington, KY: American Printing House for the Blind.

Caton, H., Pester, E., & Bradley, E. J. (1990). *Read Again.* Lexington, KY: American Printing House for the Blind.

Erin, J. N., & Sumranveth, P. (1995). Teaching reading to students who are adventitiously blind. *RE:view, 27,* 103–11.

Fitzsimons, S. (1993). *Spot the dot.* London: Royal National Institute for the Blind.

Harley, R. K., Henderson, F. M., & Truan, M. B. (1979). *The teaching of braille reading.* Springfield, IL: Charles C Thomas.

Harley, R. K., Truan, M. B., & Sanford, L. D. (1987). *Communication skills for visually impaired learners.* Springfield, IL: Charles C Thomas.

Harrison, F. (1987). Teaching braille to latecomers in the 12–16 age range. *British Journal of Visual Impairment, 5,* 45–49.

Hepker, N. L., & Coquillette, S. C. (1995). *Braille too.* Cedar Rapids, IA: Grant Wood Area Education Agency.

Holbrook, M. C., & Koenig, A. J. (1992). Teaching braille reading to students with low vision. *Journal of Visual Impairment & Blindness, 86,* 44–48. (Reprinted in this volume.)

Hudson, D. (1994). Causes of emotional and psychological reactions to adventitious blindness. *Journal of Visual Impairment & Blindness, 88,* 498–503.

Kirchner, C., Johnson, G., & Harkins, D. (1997). Research to improve vocational rehabilitation: Employment barriers and strategies for clients who are blind or visually impaired. *Journal of Visual Impairment & Blindness, 91*(4).

Koenig, A. J., & Holbrook, M. C. (1989). Determining the reading medium for students with visual impairments: A diagnostic teaching approach. *Journal of Visual Impairment & Blindness, 83,* 296–302. (Reprinted in this volume.)

Koenig, A. J., & Holbrook, M. C. (1995). *Learning media assessment of students with visual impairments: A resource guide for teachers* (2nd ed.). Austin: Texas School for the Blind and Visually Impaired.

Lorimer, J. (1988). *Braille in easy steps.* London: Royal National Institute for the Blind.

Mangold, S. S. (1989). *The Mangold developmental program of tactile perception and braille letter recognition.* Castro Valley, CA: Exceptional Teaching Aids.

Oldfather, P. (1995). Commentary: What's needed to maintain and extend motivation for literacy in the middle grades. *Journal of Reading, 38,* 420–422.

Olson, M. R. (1977). Teaching faster braille reading in the primary grades. *Journal of Visual Impairment & Blindness, 71,* 122–124.

Olson, M. R. (1981). *Guidelines and games for teaching efficient braille reading.* New York: American Foundation for the Blind.

Perle, T. (1978). A matter of adjustment: A personal reaction to visual loss. *Journal of Visual Impairment & Blindness, 72,* 255–258.

Rex, E. J., Koenig, A. J., Wormsley, D. P., & Baker, R. L. (1994). *Foundations of braille literacy.* New York: American Foundation for the Blind.

Simons, B. (1995, December) *Adolescents in transition between print and braille: An integrated literacy curriculum guide.* Paper presented at the conference Getting in Touch with Literacy, Austin, TX.

Smith, M. M. (1978). *Getting in touch with reading.* Louisville, KY: American Printing House for the Blind.

TEACHING BRAILLE TO STUDENTS WITH SPECIAL NEEDS

FRANCES MARY D'ANDREA

Eight-year-old Peter has been struggling with braille since kindergarten. Although he loves to be read to and is highly verbal, he still cannot consistently tell a d *from an* f, *or a* u *from an* ing *and reverses many other letters. He has a difficult time writing a coherent sentence and spelling many common words. Peter is beginning to get discouraged as he sees his friends tackling harder reading material, when he is still plodding through the same book for weeks.*

Jan was a junior in high school when she had an accident that left her blind and with the use of only one hand. She has good tactile skills and is learning the braille code rapidly, but has difficulty staying on the line of braille and finding the next line and is very slow at writing with an adapted Perkins brailler.

Keisha is an adorable 6 year old in a fully inclusive program who has spastic quadriplegia and light perception only. She has limited use of one hand and poor tactile skills, but is highly verbal and curious about her environment and wants to learn to read just as her friends are doing.

Robert, a 10-year-old boy diagnosed with retinopathy of prematurity, has been slow to develop and attends school in a special class for children with mild to moderate intellectual disabilities. Lately, he has been showing more interest in the braille labels around the room and exploring the print-braille books that his teacher reads to the class. Robert has been asking questions that indicate an increased awareness of braille letters and words. His teacher is beginning to wonder, "Where do I go from here?"

Approximately 60 percent of young children with severe visual impairments have multiple disabilities (Blind Babies Foundation, cited in American Foundation for the Blind, n.d.). Thus, students may have not only a visual impairment, but a physical or intellectual disability (or all three) as well. This chapter discusses the needs of students who, in addition to their visual impairment, have other special needs that have to be considered when teaching braille reading

The author wishes to thank Jay Gense, Therese Rafalowski-Welch, Nancy Godfrey, and Debbie Harlin for their assistance in developing the section on Special Needs of Students Who Are Deaf-Blind.

and writing. Specifically, it suggests strategies for teaching braille to students with learning disabilities, physical disabilities, or mild intellectual disabilities and students who are deaf-blind. Like every other child, these children have the potential to learn and deserve the opportunity to maximize their potential to the best of their ability. Because of the variety of disabling conditions, each student comes with his or her own set of unique needs and special circumstances.

IMPORTANCE OF THE TEAM APPROACH

It can be a challenge to teachers to plan the educational programs of students with multiple disabilities, who often need to receive services from several service providers. For example, a physical therapist (PT) may be indicated for a student who has cerebral palsy or hemiparesis (paralysis on one side of the body), an occupational therapist (OT) may be needed to work on the use of hands or on feeding difficulties, and a speech and language therapist may be required to work on language development and communication skills. The teacher of visually impaired students is a necessary part of the team if a child is also blind or has a visual impairment. And if the child is going to be a braille reader, the teacher definitely has to work closely with the team providing appropriate services. The physical, sensory, and communication needs of the student with multiple disabilities have to be considered. Coordinating all these services, and seeing the child as a whole person, rather than little unconnected bits, is essential.

One approach that has been proved effective in assessing and planning for students with disabilities in a coordinated fashion is the *transdisciplinary team*. Although transdisciplinary teaming is often used for students with severe cognitive disabilities, it has great potential for students who are learning braille and have physical or other disabilities as well. It is important to note that assessment and teaching are closely tied. Everyone who works with a student should be involved in planning the educational program as well. And by middle school and sometimes earlier, the student should be invited to participate in planning meetings, if possible.

An important part of the transdisciplinary team process in teaching is the concept of *role release* (Gallivan-Fenlon, 1994; Smith, 1995), that is, the sharing of roles and skills among team members. Role release ensures that skills are not taught in isolation, but are integrated within a student's day at naturally occurring times—even if a particular specialist is not present. This concept is important for two reasons: It helps the student find meaning in using skills at appropriate times, and it helps specialists, such as teachers of visually impaired children who are often itinerant, by ensuring that skills are reinforced and taught all day long, not just when the specialists are there. Using role release effectively requires a great deal of work by all team members to communicate with each other, to train each other on

Like every other child, children with multiple disabilities deserve the opportunity to maximize their potential, for example, by learning to read and write in braille.

important skills to reinforce with a student, and to maintain communication and the consistent application of skills between the home and school.

Some teachers are uncomfortable with the concept of role release because they think it means that their skills will not be as valued if "just anyone" can do them. However, role release does not mean, for example, that teachers of visually impaired children let classroom teachers or other specialists be the experts on braille literacy. Rather, it means that they can train classroom teachers to use what they have taught their visually impaired students to make sure that braille is used throughout the day. Certified teachers of visually impaired children are the specialists who know how to teach braille reading, writing, and mathematics, as well as other disability-specific skills. They play a crucial role in deciding when certain skills should be taught and in what sequence, assessing the skills, determining the maintenance and application of skills, developing Individualized Educational Plans (IEPs), and so forth. Role release simply means that the team shares knowledge and techniques to ensure that all skills are being applied in meaningful ways throughout the school day (and at home).

The following example illustrates how transdisciplinary teaming works with Keisha, who was introduced at the beginning of this chapter:

> The teacher of visually impaired children works with Keisha two hours a day in the regular kindergarten classroom, helps the classroom teacher and paraprofessional make adaptations for Keisha, and transcribes classroom materials into braille. The classroom teacher and aide use these materials to teach beginning reading and mathematics skills to Keisha throughout the day, even after the teacher of visually impaired children has left.
>
> While working with Keisha, the physical therapist and the teacher of visually impaired children discovered that Keisha has better control of her right arm when she is placed in a prone stander. At these times, Keisha can reach for and explore the embossed shapes in the book on the tray before her. Therefore, the physical therapist has taught all the teachers the proper use of the prone stander, so it can be used at appropriate scheduled times during the day. With the speech and language therapist, the teacher of visually impaired children is working on a communication system for Keisha on the classroom computer. This system is used throughout the day and at home by all Keisha's teachers, family members, and classmates. A log is kept by the team at school and by the parents at home, and frequent visits are made by the parents to school and the teachers to the home, so that Keisha's family can use the same techniques and terminology at home that are used at school. Therefore, each specialist has trained all the others who care for Keisha in specific skills, so the skills are applied consistently in all settings. Keisha's progress is monitored by each teacher collecting data on her activities in their context. With these data, periodic progress reports are written, IEPs are developed, and Keisha's program can be changed if current methods are not working.

Ongoing assessment is especially important with a child who has special needs, so that changes can be made appropriately.

To use this team model effectively, the team members must continuously coordinate their activities—no small feat when some or most of the service providers are itinerant. The following strategies will help to foster communication and coordination among the team members.

STRATEGIES

COMMUNICATION AND COORDINATION OF TEAM MEMBERS' ACTIVITIES

✛ Time must be set aside for regular team meetings, at which progress and problems can be brought up and the team members can brainstorm ideas and work out a plan together. How frequently the team meets depends on the needs of particular students. The team probably has to meet more frequently at the beginning of the school year. Students whose placements or services are changing or who have a variety of special needs may require more meetings than do students who are in established programs. Some teams have found it beneficial to create a fixed schedule of meetings at the beginning of the year (such as the second Tuesday of each month); other teams plan meetings to coincide with quarterly progress reports.

✛ It is essential for all team members to be notified of meetings in a timely manner, so each individual's busy schedule can be accommodated as much as possible. It is frustrating to hear about an important meeting after it has taken place. If the school does not provide a mailbox for all its itinerant staff members in the faculty lounge or office, perhaps a message box consisting of large manila envelopes with the specialists' names on them could be put in a prominent place in a student's classroom. Notes between the various teachers and between parents and teachers could be placed in these envelopes so that teachers could check them when they arrive to work with the student. Space on a bulletin board in the classroom could also be reserved for announcements for the various service providers about upcoming meetings.

✛ It is helpful if a team member takes a few notes at a meeting to share with members who could not attend. In any case, it is a good idea to document what is discussed at meetings, so the team can remember the decisions that have been made. And it is gratifying to look back over the notes at the end of the school year to see how far a student has come.

✛ A notebook shared between school and home can be a useful tool for keeping lines of communication open. Each team member can jot down a few lines after each session with a student to share the student's progress with the other members and the parents. The message does not have to be long and elaborate; it can be something as simple as, "Keisha's new adaptive chair seems to improve her posture quite a bit" or "Brett wrote a wonderful story today on the brailler. Ask him to read it to you."

✛ If permission is granted by the parents and school administrators, videotaping a student can be a helpful way of sharing ideas and strategies with other members of the team. For example, if the speech and language therapist and the physical therapist can rarely meet together with the student because of scheduling problems, the physical therapist can videotape the student doing activities in several positions. Viewing the videotape may provide helpful information for the speech and language therapist to use in designing a communication system that allows the student the best range of motion. Or, teachers can videotape the student doing activities that the parents can replicate at home.

✛ Another helpful strategy for dealing with hectic schedules is for the classroom teacher to place a large chart on a bulletin board or in an individual folder for each student that shows the weekly or monthly schedules of when each specialist comes to the classroom, as well as scheduled activities, such as lunch, physical education, and field trips. For working with a student with multiple disabilities, scheduling usually revolves around many specialists, all of whom need to see the student and to work together, so a detailed schedule is necessary.

Some students with physical disabilities, such as Keisha, have more obvious needs that must be considered before a braille program is started. Other students, such as Peter, introduced at the beginning of the chapter, have difficulties that show up only after they have undergone some training in the braille code—another good reason for ongoing assessment and transdisciplinary discussions. But once the team has met, what then? Team members will look to the teacher of visually impaired children as the expert on specific strategies and techniques that are effective for students who are learning braille and have additional learning needs. The next sections discuss specific disabilities that visually impaired students may have and suggest some strategies for teaching braille reading and writing for each. Since little specific research has been conducted in this area, many of the ideas presented here are tried-and-true suggestions from practicing teachers in the field. These strategies may need to be adapted further to fit the needs of particular students, so it is important to be especially flexible and try new approaches and strategies when teaching braille to students who are blind or visually impaired and have additional disabilities.

STUDENTS WITH LEARNING DISABILITIES

There are some children who have good verbal skills, an enriching home and school environment, and caring parents and teachers who pay a great deal of attention to the children's education, but who nevertheless have reading and writing difficulties. These students may not be able to remember common and often-used contractions, frequently reverse braille symbols, or have poor word-attack skills. Other students may have difficulty with comprehension; even though they can read with some fluency, they cannot tell teachers anything they have just read or answer questions related to comprehension.

These students may or may not be labeled learning disabled. It is sometimes difficult to formally identify learning disabilities in a child who is blind or severely visually impaired, especially given the lack of standardized tests that are normed for children with visual impairments (see Chapter 7 for a more thorough discussion of this issue). In some states, a child's visual impairment is seen as the cause of the learning problem, and it is up to the teacher of visually impaired children to remediate and teach the student strategies. However, the National Committee on Learning Disabilities (cited in Turnbull, Turnbull, Shank, & Leal, 1995) acknowledged that in children with sensory impairments, learning disabilities may be due to a dysfunction of the central nervous system, and are not the result of sensory impairments. In any case, what a child is "officially" labeled may be the least important consideration. In some states, children who are blind can be served in a program for learning disabled children and still receive services from teachers of visually impaired children, but in other states, services for blind children who may also have learning disabilities are difficult to come by. What is most important is that teachers *recognize when students are having difficulty reading and writing.* Teachers need to be able to diagnose learning problems that are preventing students from learning to read and write effectively, help the students recognize their strengths, and teach the students strategies that can remediate these difficulties. Some students have hidden learning problems that show up only after their reading and writing programs have begun. These students usually are excited about learning to read at first, but get frustrated and discouraged when they struggle through their reading lessons. In addition, there are some students with low vision who still have great difficulty reading even after they have switched from print to braille.

Assessment

The first step in addressing a student's difficulty in learning is to conduct a careful assessment of the student's reading and writing problems. Is the student having difficulty with certain contractions (for example, *e* versus *en*) or reversing certain letters? Look for patterns of errors that he or she may be making. Or is the student able to read aloud with no errors, but not able to tell anything about what he or she just read? A miscue analysis, a test for phonological errors (letter-sound relationships), and a test of reading comprehension will give a better picture of the student's strengths and weaknesses (see Chapter 7 for detailed information on tests, techniques, and forms for assessing specific areas of possible difficulty). The teaching strategies used will depend on the student's specific problems and whether they relate to braille mechanics, braille reading and writing, comprehension, or all three.

The assessment may reveal a problem with the braille code per se (including mechanical problems such as hand-movement patterns and recognition of symbols) or with the reading *process* (such as the meaning of words, syntax [sentence structure], and the use of context). For example, the student may reverse many letters and contractions, miss lower signs while reading, be unable to remember any contractions while writing simple sentences, and have great difficulty identifying common words and contractions. However, the assessment may indicate that the student can identify letters, contractions, and short-form words in isolation or even in sentences, but has difficulty comprehending what he or she just read. Since the strategies a teacher uses will differ, depending on whether the difficulty lies in recognition of the braille code itself or in the child's perception and understanding of what he or she is reading, they should be used only after the assessment process, outlined in Chapter 7, is completed.

STRATEGIES

TEACHING BRAILLE TO STUDENTS WITH LEARNING DIFFICULTIES

Addressing Braille Reading Deficiencies

✛ Check the size and fit of furniture (see Chapter 3). Physical factors such as these should always be considered first when looking for underlying causes of reading difficulties, since it is easy to rule them out quickly.

✛ For students with poor tracking skills (difficulty finding the next line, staying on the line, and the like) and slow reading speed, use some of the strategies mentioned in Chapters 3 and 4, such as using the *Mangold Developmental Program for Tactile Discrimination and Letter Recognition* (Mangold, 1989; see Chapter 3). The teacher's manual that comes with the Mangold program gives excellent directions on how to do mastery learning and precision teaching in tracking lines, using hands correctly, and other skills that foster good braille-reading habits. Use these tracking exercises as warm-ups before the reading task. Even if a student has finished the entire Mangold program, he or she can still use specific pages before a lesson to get ready for reading. Also, many of the strategies for increasing reading fluency presented in Chapter 3 may be appropriate for students with learning difficulties.

✛ For students who have problems with braille reversals, the following strategies are useful:

 • Use mnemonics. Mnemonics are memory strategies that help people learn and remember, such as rhymes and songs. They can be used with children of all ages. For example, if a young student consistently confuses *e* and *i*, use enlarged braille cells to show how *e* and *i* are like a slide (make sure the student has had experience with a slide). Show the student how the letters slant in different directions, and teach this rhyme: "For *i* we go up high, for *e* we come down 'wheee'!" This rhyme reminds the student that *i* starts low on dot 2 and goes up to dot 4, and *e* slants downward from dot 1 to dot 5. With older students or those who are making the transition from print to braille, try other mnemonics, such as "The letter *e* comes first in the alphabet before *i,* so remember it includes the dot 1," or "The letter *e* is the fifth letter of the alphabet, so it includes the dot 5." Just remember which mnemonic has been taught, so the student does not get confused. Encourage students to come up with their own tricks to remember letter formations, rules of usage, and so forth. Students are more likely to remember rules they develop on their own.

• Use enlarged braille cells, such as the Swing Cell produced by the American Printing House for the Blind (APH) or a facsimile of a large cell (like half an egg carton) that teachers can make themselves to show the dots used in the letter (see Chapter 3).

• Use overlearning techniques, such as those described in Chapter 3. If a student is having trouble with *o* and *ow*, for example, make worksheets on which the student must go across rows of full cells and circle all the *o's* he or she can find. Then add other symbols—except *ow*—and ask the student again to find the *o's*. It is important to introduce symbols that are reversals at different times. Repeat this exercise until the student can quickly find all the *o's* with at least 90 percent accuracy. Then do the same with the *ow*. Once the student is at 90 percent accuracy with that symbol, the teacher can begin to show the two symbols together (Olson, 1981). Make these types of drills fun and interesting for students and have the students chart their progress on tactile graph paper.

• Use color coding for students with low vision. A student with low vision who was learning braille benefited from having large-cell representations in which dots 1,2,3 were one color and dots 4,5,6 were another. The teacher who devised this system called it "Color Me Braille" (Frankel-Mislinski, 1995).

• Use the Voxcom (also known as the Language Master) and flash cards with the words on them. These machines give feedback tactilely with braille words and auditorally as a student puts the cards through the machine. (This is discussed in more detail in Chapter 3.) The student can also keep a word box of problem words that can be pulled out for extra practice.

• Use visualization. Students who had some vision before they began braille instruction and are having great difficulty reading braille may find it helpful to picture the braille dots mentally as they read. A student who is reversing *f* and *d*, for example, may be helped by pointing out that a braille *f* points in the same direction as a print *f*.

• Teach students to use context clues. As was discussed in Chapter 4, reversals are less likely to occur when students use the context to figure out unknown words.

✛ Make sure that students know letter sounds and have phonics skills and can tell words apart by sound. Some research suggests that one of the strongest predictors of reading achievement is phonemic awareness (Lerner, Cousin & Richek, 1992; Mather, 1992; Spear-Swerling & Sternberg, 1994). Specific instruction in phonics is often indicated for children who have reading difficulties. If students are having trouble differentiating among the sounds of words, they will have difficulty reading or sounding words out. Phonics instruction is discussed in Chapter 3, but it is especially important for students with learning disabilities. Teachers can use several activities to expand students' phonemic awareness. Many of them start with auditory activities that increase students' awareness of the sounds of different words. For example, the teacher can play a game in which he or she says two words, such as *pat* and *bat,* and asks the student to tell whether the words are the same or not. Or a student can be asked to listen for short words embedded in longer words. For example, ask the student to listen for the word *can* and tell if it is found in the words *candle, castle, can't,* or *camp.* An excellent source of auditory experiences and games such as these is *The Green Readiness Book* (Rosner, 1986).

✦ Teach phonics skills in context with predictable books or stories. A helpful strategy for students who have great difficulty remembering vocabulary words is to teach word families (such as the *at* family: *bat, cat, fat, hat,* and *mat*) and then use them in short stories. As the students learn more word families, the teacher can add these words to subsequent stories. Sometimes these stories are just what students need to begin to see the relationship between sounds and symbols. Some commercially available books, such as Dr. Seuss books, have enough predictability and repetition to be used in this manner.

✦ Teach students to use context clues as well as phonics. If a student comes across a word that he or she does not know immediately, teach the student to skip it and finish the rest of the sentence, rather than scrubbing up and down across each letter of the word (see Chapters 3 and 4). Some authors, however, suggest that this strategy should be used only by students who have had some background in phonemic instruction, or else students will constantly skip words and guess at their meaning (Mather, 1992). Often, students can use a clue from the first letter of the unknown word and then read the rest of the sentence to identify the problem word. If this word continues to give trouble, put it on a flash card (like the ones described in Chapter 3) or Voxcom card for extra practice.

✦ If a student is having difficulty with grade 2 braille, consider using grade 1. There is some evidence that instruction in grade 1 (uncontracted) braille is useful for students with learning disabilities (see, for example, Troughton, 1992). Other students may find grade 2 easier because some contractions stand for whole words.

✦ Teach students to use an electronic braille notetaker. Several teachers have had success teaching students with learning disabilities using a portable notetaker, such as Braille 'n Speak or Braille Lite (see the Resources section at the end of this book). These devices give extra feedback to students in the form of speech on the braille that is entered.

Increasing Comprehension

✦ Set a purpose prior to reading. The teacher can tell students certain specific facts about a selection that may be helpful, and set a goal for reading as well. For example, the teacher may say, "In this story, Gerald wants a pet, but his parents say he can't have one. Let's read to find out what Gerald decides to do." This strategy may help a student who has difficulty finding the main idea; he or she can then find details to support it.

✛ Help students make predictions about the content. For example, ask a student to read the title of the selection and make informed guesses as to what the story is about, whom it is about, whether it is a true story or a make-believe one, and other pertinent issues. If the title of the story is "The Dog Who Sang for the King," the student may be able to guess that the story is about a dog and that it is probably a make-believe story because dogs don't ordinarily sing. This is a good strategy for getting students to attend to meaning. The teacher may have to model it for students because some are at a loss as to how to predict what may happen. They may feel afraid to guess for fear they may be wrong. The teacher will need to make this a low-risk activity for students who are afraid to try by providing some ideas to start with and asking them to help think of alternative ideas. Then they can continue reading to see which of their predictions are correct.

✛ Help students activate prior knowledge (Miller, 1993)—that is, help them use their own experiences to bring meaning to the text. This strategy is especially important for congenitally blind children who may have had fewer experiences or difficulty developing concepts (see Chapter 2) and may require the teacher to arrange for the student to have certain experiences that he or she has missed. For example, a student was having difficulty understanding a short story about children putting on a play because he had never been to a play and was unfamiliar with the word *play* as a noun. He only knew it as a verb, as in "to play a game." He needed more experiences and examples before he could understand the story.

✛ Introduce new vocabulary before students read stories. The teacher may wish to make a list of words that could be unfamiliar or troublesome to a student before he or she reads a selection. These words can be put on flash cards and used in sentences and kept in a word box to go over again and again, if necessary. Another activity that children may enjoy is "Go up the word ladder." Affix a tactile ladder shape on a file folder or stiff card (by gluing yarn or creating this shape and making it tactile on a thermoform machine). Every time students read a word from their word-bank box correctly, they can move their markers up one rung of the ladder. If they reach the top of the ladder, they get a little card to take home that states how many words they read on the word ladder that day (Kaye, 1984).

✛ Encourage students to reread a section that they had trouble understanding. For example, if a student is asked, "What happened after the queen heard the dog singing?" and the student cannot answer, allow him or her to go back to that section, reread it silently, and then tell in his or her own words what happened next. Some students seem to think that it is "cheating" to go back and reread. However, this strategy is helpful for making sure a passage is understood, and it develops a student's ability to skim for information (an extremely important skill for braille readers).

✛ Use the cloze procedure. This procedure, in which a passage is given to a student with words missing, is described in detail in Chapters 3 and 7. It is an excellent strategy for students who have difficulty with comprehension because they must pay attention to meaning to fill in the missing words. Students who have done poorly in reading may need to be reassured that sometimes there can be more than one "correct" answer; they can fill in any word that makes sense to the whole passage.

✛ Play the question game. In this game, students earn points for asking appropriate questions about the passage just read, not for supplying the answers. This game can be played in teams, between two students, or with the teacher and the student. Predetermined categories are established, such as factual, inferential, vocabulary, and grammar. The student who goes first asks a question that falls into one of these categories. If the question is actually something that can be answered from the text, he or she gets a point. For example, the student may say, "This is a factual question: What day of the week did this story take place?" If the opposing student can answer the question from the text, the student *who asked the question* gets a point. The student who goes first keeps asking questions from the passage until he or she cannot think of any more. Then the opposing student tries to think of some to gain points. After the next passage is read silently, the opposing student gets to go first to ask questions. This game forces students to pay attention to the meaning of the passage, but because students have to supply questions, rather than answers, the format is less threatening and more fun for students who have difficulty with comprehension. In addition, it teaches students about the different things to look for in a passage and helps build vocabulary.

✛ Teach students about metaphors and figures of speech. Children who are blind and have learning disabilities are often very literal and have difficulty understanding common idioms and figures of speech, perhaps because they lack experience with the concept being illustrated or because the metaphor is a visual comparison. For example, a blind child may have difficulty comprehending the sentence, *"When I tripped in the cafeteria with my tray, it rained milk all over the floor."* The student may say, "This doesn't make sense! It can't rain milk!" Specific instruction in common figures of speech may help blind students understand figurative language. One teacher focuses on an Expression of the Week with her blind students who are learning disabled. Each week they choose an expression, such as "Money always burns a hole in my pocket" or "He has a skeleton in his closet" to discuss and write about.

✛ Use students' interests to guide teaching. As mentioned earlier, if teachers find topics of great interest to students, students with learning disabilities will push themselves to read the content because they are motivated by the subjects (Fink, 1996). The teacher can then build on the texts and use them to teach new vocabulary words and concepts.

Sources of Problems

In addition to trying various strategies to address students' specific reading problems, teachers can also consider whether some problems stem from certain sources that can be eliminated or altered. For example, one source of reading and writing problems that should be considered first is *inconsistent braille instruction.* If a student has had infrequent lessons, has few opportunities to use braille during the day, and has not received books and other educational materials in braille, he or she may not have a reading disability, but may just need more direct instruction in the code and more practice using it. An assessment instrument, such as the Minnesota Braille Skills Inventory (Godwin et al., 1995), may provide information on how well the student knows the braille code.

The second point to consider is whether the *method of reading instruction* used in the classroom is the best for the individual student. Mather (1992, p. 93) concludes that "One best method does not exist for teaching reading to children. . . . All children do not learn to read by the same method, and . . . different children require different reading methods at different times in their development." If a student seems to be having difficulty with a particular approach, one solution may be simply to try a different program or approach (see Chapter 3 for a discussion of different approaches). Perhaps the student needs a more structured approach, with more time spent on the development of specific skills. For example, there is some evidence that the whole language approach is difficult for students with learning disabilities (Lerner et al., 1992; Mather, 1992; Spear-Swerling & Sternberg, 1994) and that it should be supplemented with specific instruction in phonics and word recognition. If a careful assessment reveals that the new approach has led to an increase in the student's reading speed, comprehension, and enjoyment, then perhaps a new approach was what the student needed.

A third consideration is the classroom environment (Silberman & Sowell, 1987). An evaluation of this environment fosters a teacher's awareness of the many influences on students with learning difficulties in regular classrooms. A crowded classroom, with many activities going on at one time and a noisy, cluttered instructional area, may be too distracting for much learning to take place. Minimize distractions as much as possible by clearing the student's desk or table of anything that is not being used during a lesson. Also, have all necessary materials near enough at hand, so the lesson is not interrupted by a search for braille paper, for instance. Try to find as quiet a space as possible or to schedule lessons while a compatible activity is going on. Different classroom teachers have different styles and create different classroom climates. What is chaos to one teacher is stimulating to another. Thus, work with the classroom teacher as much as possible to create the best climate possible for the student to learn, or work with the student in a quieter room with fewer distractions.

Teaching Students to Apply Strategies

If a student is taught specific strategies or practices the same skills over and over and does not make progress, he or she may not know which strategies to apply to figure out unfamiliar words while reading independently. For example, the student may not be monitoring what he or she is reading or may not be aware that he or she is making errors while reading. Students need to apply what they have learned to a specific task and to regulate the use of specific strategies. The process of selecting, monitoring, deciding on strategies, and revising strategies when necessary is called *metacognition* (Borkowski, 1992; Van Reusen & Head, 1994). Students develop these skills over time and need a great deal of practice to become truly independent. At first, teachers may need to prompt students to use a particular strategy. A list of steps to follow in certain situations may be helpful so that the students can refer to them. The students may be asked to name each step in an appropriate situation and eventually to review all the steps silently before starting the task. Metacognition is also a powerful motivator because students regulate their own learning and make their own decisions in problem solving, rather than helplessly depending on the teacher to always tell them what to do next. The following are several metacognitive strategies that can be used to help students learn.

STRATEGIES

TEACHING METACOGNITIVE STATEGIES

✛ Teach students to be aware of text structures. It is important to teach students to identify how a chapter or story is organized (Muth, 1987). Pointing out the different ways a text can be organized can help students discover the author's intent and framework for the text and how the ideas are arranged (Collins, 1994). For example, a story may be told as a flashback, and a social studies chapter may be written chronologically or in a manner that compares different cultures. The teacher can instruct students about different ways that text can be structured and teach them clues to identifying which approach an author is using. These strategies include looking for and listing subheadings; looking for key words, such as *because* and *if . . . then;*

and making a conceptual map of the text with the title in the middle and ideas from the text around it (Muth, 1987). The use of these strategies will also help students make more efficient use of their study time because they can approach the reading task with a better plan of how to read it for understanding.

✤ Teach students to identify the main idea and then the supporting details. Students need to learn that not all information in a paragraph is of equal importance. This is a difficult concept for students with reading problems, who have a hard time sorting out a main idea from ideas that are of lesser importance. To teach this concept, start with simple paragraphs of a few sentences and help the students to rank them in order of importance (Stewart & Tei, 1983).

✤ Teach students to ask themselves questions as they read. To get students to focus on the most important elements in a chapter or story while they are reading, suggest that they try to predict what will happen next (Collins, 1994; Sanacore, 1984; Stewart & Tei, 1983) or what the comprehension questions will be at the end.

✤ Teach students to vary how they read, depending on what they are reading. Many students with learning disabilities approach all reading tasks the same way. They read a story for enjoyment the same way they approach a social studies textbook or a recipe for baking a cake. They need to learn what experienced readers know without being aware of it: Different types of reading tasks require different types of reading skills. For example, students can learn to read instructions through once to make sure all the needed equipment is available and they have a general idea of the task involved. Then they can go back and reread each step as they are performing it. A teacher can model this concept for a student by saying, for instance, "OK, let's read this through to make sure we understand how to put this new equipment together. . . . Now, let's go back and decide what the first step is . . . . OK, we did this first step, now let's reread the directions to see what the second step is. . . . Now we've got this done, let's go on to the next step to make sure we do it correctly." Students should learn to vary the speed at which they read, depending on the task; to stop periodically to check for comprehension; and to reread sections that are important.

✤ Teach students to recognize when the text is difficult or confusing. Students need to know that sometimes the text does not make sense or is written in a confusing way (Stewart & Tei, 1983). Students with learning disabilities are apt to think that their lack of understanding is always the result of their own poor skills, not possibly an author's failure to present ideas clearly. The teacher can demonstrate for the student that it is all right to admit when he or she does not understand and that sometimes a text does not clearly present the author's purpose by saying, for example, "I don't think this makes sense because . . ." or "I need to look this word up in the dictionary because I don't understand how it's used here." Learning to read critically is an important skill.

✛ Teach students the difference between "fix-up" strategies and "study" strategies. Collins (1994) noted that two types of strategies should be taught specifically to students: strategies to resolve the failure of comprehension (fix-up strategies) and strategies that enhance the storage and retrieval of information (study strategies). Examples of the former strategies are some of those listed earlier, such as rereading, adjusting the rate of reading different texts, and predicting what will happen next. Examples of study strategies include summarizing in one's own words, taking notes, making outlines, and underlining key words and concepts (braille students can use Wikki Stix [see Chapter 2] for this purpose). Some of these strategies are complex and will need to be taught over time.

✛ Observe students when reading and writing and point out their effective use of strategies. For example, the teacher can say to a student, "I noticed that when you were reading and you got to that word you didn't know, you read the rest of the sentence to get the context. Then you went back and read the sentence correctly. That seemed to work better than when you used to just guess at the word without knowing what the sentence was about. What do you think?" Such statements help students realize that they have used an effective strategy that is an improvement over their past reading behavior. The next time they come across an unfamiliar word, they will be more likely to remember the strategy they used successfully and be able to use it again.

Fostering the Love of Reading

Although the development of skills is important, that is not all there is to reading. Drilling on certain skills over and over may help students read more fluently and with better understanding, but it is also imperative for students to have material that is worth reading. The provision of high-quality literature that is of great interest to students is an effective means of stimulating students with reading deficiencies to read successfully (Fink, 1996; Miller, 1993; Roswell & Natchez, 1989). Students who have difficulty reading may have never developed the love of reading or may never read for information, simply because it has always been too difficult. Finding appropriate reading material based on a student's skills, interests, and knowledge is an integral part of teaching any student, but it is especially important for students with learning disabilities. The use of reading-interest inventories (described in Chapter 4) is one way to discover students' interests. Another way is to ask the student or classroom teacher about recent activities or lessons that piqued the student's interest. For example, if a student found a science experiment on the life cycle of frogs fascinating, the student and teacher of visually impaired students could find and read books about frogs in general, which could lead to interest in poison frogs of the Amazon, and finally about disappearing habitats and endangered species. High interest in a subject leads to greater motivation to read and a greater willingness to tackle more difficult reading assignments.

Consulting Other Professionals

Sometimes a teacher of visually impaired children will run through an entire repertoire of strategies with a particular student to no avail. These strategies should not take the place of appropriate referrals or consulting professionals who are trained to work with children with specific disabilities. The teacher may need to enlist the help of a teacher of children with learning disabilities in the school or district. If the teacher suspects that a student is having difficulties that go beyond his or her visual impairment, the help of the school's reading specialist or other curriculum specialist can be enlisted to discuss possible strategies that can be adapted to work with the student who uses braille. If a school does not have a reading specialist, ask the supervisor for advice on finding a reading specialist who is trained to work with specific reading and writing disabilities. Similarly, a speech and language therapist can provide strategies that work with print-reading children, which can be adapted for use in reading braille (for example, by using real objects instead of pictures). Since there is a dearth of research on children with severe visual impairments and additional learning disabilities, a teacher may have to try techniques that work with sighted children and adapt them for braille, such as those used with Tony:

> Tony is a 7-year-old student who had surgery to remove a brain tumor at age 5. The surgery damaged his optic nerves, causing him to become blind. Tony is quite verbal and highly motivated to read braille and has excellent tactile perception. However, because of his short attention span and poor memory, numerous attempts to teach him to read braille had failed. Ms. Watkins, the teacher of visually impaired children, taught Tony the braille alphabet by using the Mangold program (Mangold, 1989), although it took a great deal of time. She tried using the *Patterns* series (Caton, Pester, & Bradley, 1980), which was commonly used in that school district, but Tony could never remember the vocabulary words from one day to the next, or even from one hour to the next. After practicing the words in sentences, on flash cards, on the Voxcom (see Chapter 3), and so on, Tony still had difficulty recalling the words he had been introduced to, and because he was concentrating so hard on remembering the words, his comprehension suffered. Ms. Watkins felt at a loss; she had never had to teach braille to a student with Tony's learning difficulties, and she could see that Tony was getting more and more frustrated. She did not know what to try next.
>
> Finally, she approached Mr. Montez, the learning disabilities teacher at the school. Mr. Montez had never taught a student who was visually impaired, but listened sympathetically to Ms. Watkins. He suggested that she do an assessment to see if Tony's specific reading problems could be identified. After Ms. Watkins did a thorough assessment (using the tools and methods dis-

cussed in Chapter 7), she and Mr. Montez reviewed the results together and discussed what Tony's strengths and needs appeared to be. The results indicated that Tony had poor word-recognition and reading comprehension skills but excellent auditory-processing and phonics skills.

Mr. Montez suggested that Ms. Watkins try a linguistic approach and gave her some guidance in using word families, such as the *at* family (*fat, sat, cat,* and *mat*), to create stories that Tony could read. Ms. Watkins decided to use grade 1 braille to teach Tony to read this way. She wrote Tony a short story about his cat that included as many of the same word-family words as possible. Tony enjoyed reading a story about his pet and was excited that he could read all the words. With Mr. Montez's help, Ms. Watkins added more word families and wrote more small stories and books for Tony using these words. She and Tony also played games that reinforced word identification and comprehension (such as cloze passages that used the words he was learning). After a year of mastering the consonant and short and long vowel sounds, with a few other nondecodable words (such as *said* and *the*), Tony was reading more fluently and with greater comprehension. Equally important, he felt successful and had higher self-esteem. The next year, more contracted words were introduced, and by the end of fourth grade, Tony had jumped three grade levels in reading and was almost up to his peers. Talking to an expert and working together to use a different approach were the first steps in the long process of teaching Tony to read.

SPECIAL NEEDS OF STUDENTS WITH PHYSICAL DISABILITIES

Physical disabilities, such as cerebral palsy, juvenile rheumatoid arthritis, and conditions that may be the result of injuries or accidents, such as hemiparesis (paralysis on one side of the body) or missing limbs, certainly need to be factored into the decision to use braille as a communication mode. Rogow (1988) mentioned several factors that should be considered in choosing a symbol system:

- Communication needs of the student;
- The sense modalities the child actively employs;
- Level of comprehension of verbal language;
- Child's ability to read print or braille;
- Child's ability to make use of visual symbols, including those capable of being highlighted with color, contrast, or increased size;
- Child's ability to utilize touch as an input modality;
- Degree of hand control needed to read tactile symbols and ability of child to discern such symbols;
- Amount of training required for symbol interpretation;
- Versatility and flexibility of system. (p. 102)

The Braille Assessment Checklist for Persons with Multiple Disabilities (reprinted as an Appendix to this chapter) is designed to guide teachers of individuals with visual impairments and additional disabilities in choosing the appropriate literacy media for their students. It can be used as an information-gathering tool to summarize information about the student from various sources and can also suggest areas in which adaptations would be useful. The checklist covers five categories: general visual information, physical considerations, cognitive considerations, language, and auditory functioning. (A blank version of this form appears at the end of the Resources section of this book.) In addition, *Learning Media Assessment of Students with Visual Impairments* (Koenig and Holbrook, 1995) also includes forms and guidelines for assessing students who have physical disabilities in addition to blindness or low vision. If, after these factors are considered, braille is still judged to be the most appropriate system for a particular student, four basic physical factors need to be evaluated to know how best to meet that student's needs: range of motion, where the student has most motor control, tactile sensitivity, and stamina.

Evaluation

First, *range of motion* must be evaluated. If a student has a physical disability to the extent that he or she will never be able to hold a book independently, turn a page, or move his or her hands and arms across a full page, then a communication medium other than braille should probably be viewed as the primary medium. The student's braille reading may be limited to identifying braille labels on objects placed before him or her or using braille on some sort of electronic communication device that may have speech or print output. If a student has a larger range of motion—even if only for one hand—then the possibility of braille usage increases; he or she may be able to read words and phrases and use technology to produce braille with a device adapted for one-hand usage, such as an adapted Perkins brailler or Braille 'n Speak. Creative uses of braille, combined with speech on an electronic communication board, may be in order for a student who has a limited range of motion. Another strategy is to put the braille in a narrow column that the student can reach. This strategy is useful for, say, a student with juvenile rheumatoid arthritis who, because of damage to joints, has a limited range of motion and can comfortably track across only six inches of braille text.

The second important factor to evaluate is where a student has the most motor control. Some students may have more control on one side of the body than on the other. For example, a student who has a right-side hemiparesis may need to have reading materials positioned to his or her left. In rare cases, individuals with multiple disabilities who lack hand mobility but are strongly motivated may be able to learn braille using another part of the body, such as a foot. The teacher of visually impaired children and the transdisciplinary team have to weigh the pros and cons of each strategy and communication method.

In the case of a student with a severely limited range of motion and no light perception, a teacher can design a communication board. Comunication boards can be as simple as a board with squares containing braille words or tactile symbols to which an individual can point or as complex as an electronic device that "speaks" for the user (see Huebner, Prickett, Welch, & Joffee, 1995, for a more detailed discussion of ways to create communication boards and other types of augmentative and alternative communication devices). The teacher will need to think creatively about where to put the board. Sometimes right at midline at waist height on a lap tray is not the best place for the student. Perhaps the board will have to be placed to the left side of the body, up against the chest, or down to one side at hip level. Working closely with a physical therapist, occupational therapist, and speech-language therapist, a teacher can help the student with severe physical disabilities to communicate in a functional manner.

The third important factor is the careful evaluation of a student's *tactile sensitivity*. Certain physical disabilities, such as high spinal cord injuries, can lead to decreased tactile awareness. For students with poor sensitivity, many tactile readiness activities may be necessary, such as those described in Chapter 2.

Another option for students with poor tactile sensitivity is to use jumbo or large-cell braille. Jumbo braille is larger than regular braille and can be written with a jumbo brailler or jumbo slate and stylus (both available from Howe Press; see Resources). Large-cell braille uses dots the same size as regular braille, but that are more spread out, as in jumbo braille. Both variations can be useful, but their use limits the amount of reading material available; teachers may have to make many of the materials themselves. Making these materials may be worth the effort if it gets students to start reading.

The *Fishburne alphabet*, a special code based on larger lines and dots, may have some use with students who have poor tactile skills because of physical disabilities. It is generally used with older people who lose their vision and wish to have a large-size tactile method of marking and identifying items. No texts or commercially available materials are written in Fishburne. At this point, it can only be written one letter at a time on a small strip of plastic label tape. This may be adequate for labeling teacher-made and electronic communication boards, but students would need an alternate method for written communication.

Moon code, another tactile code that is sometimes used with older adventitiously blind people, is based on the appearance of the print alphabet and is larger than conventional braille. More widely used in England than in the United States, its disadvantages are similar to those of the Fishburne alphabet in that there is no simple way to write more than a letter at a time, especially for a student with physical disabilities. As with the Fishburne alphabet, there may some benefits to trying the Moon code with a student who cannot use braille, such as for labeling. Research is being conducted in England on teaching the Moon code, instead of braille, to students with multiple disabilities, but no results have yet been published.

The fourth factor to keep in mind is *stamina and fatigue*. Children with physical disabilities often have to expend a great deal of energy to keep themselves positioned correctly in chairs and in managing their bodies and their belongings. It is exhausting for some students to sit for long periods trying to pay attention to lessons and to keep up with the demands of reading and writing. (Other students need to shift their positions frequently to prevent pressure sores.) Frequent breaks may be necessary for these students, as may supplementing braille with audiotapes, readers, tape-recorded lectures, and so forth.

Other Adaptations

Other adaptations may be necessary for students with physical disabilities. For example, students who have missing limbs or digits may have to use different fingers to read braille. The video *Understanding Braille Literacy* (1993) introduces a young boy who, because of a deformity in his hands, uses his thumbs to read braille quite successfully. Again, creativity is necessary along with a certain amount of trial and error. Experiment with having a student use other fingers if the standard methods of braille reading and writing (especially on some electronic braille devices) are unsuccessful.

Students with physical disabilities may need special setups for keeping materials within reach and more space to keep their materials. It is important for these students to be well organized and to keep materials within easy reach. They may need a larger work space (as well as more storage space, a common need for many braille readers) to make sure that they can position themselves in the most efficient way.

Whether students have limited use of their hands because of cerebral palsy, accidents, or other physical disabilities, special strategies can help them learn to read braille fluently, keep their place on the page (and find it again), and write braille with various devices. The following strategies may be helpful to students with physical disabilities, including those who can use only one hand.

STRATEGIES

BRAILLE READING AND WRITING FOR STUDENTS WITH PHYSICAL DISABILITIES

Reading Braille

✦ To prevent a piece of paper or a book from slipping while it is being read, place it on a nonslip surface. Several products can be used for this purpose, including rubber pads (such as those sold by Exceptional Teaching Aids) or rubber mesh or sheeting (sold in rolls at discount stores); Dycem (available from Flaghouse, Maxi-Aids, and other educational supply companies; see also Chapter 3 and Resources); Permatex Blue RTV, a silicone gasket maker used for repairing tires (available from auto-supply stores) can be squeezed from a tube between two pieces of wax paper, flattened (or rolled with a rolling pin), and left to dry overnight to form a nonslip pad (K. Heller, personal communication, 1994).

✤ Single pages of braille material can also be held in place with a clipboard or a push-pin board (available from Exceptional Teaching Aids), or by putting them in a three-ring binder. A push-pin board can also be made by covering a cork tile (available at hardware stores) with contact paper.

✤ There are several strategies for keeping one's place when reading braille with one hand:

- The Stokes Braille Place Holder, a sheet of metal that slips under the braille page, with a strip of magnetic plastic placed on top of the page at the last line read, can be purchased from APH (see Resources). Yarn stores also sell small magnets with magnetic backing that can be used to mark the place. Make sure not to squish the braille dots.
- Small magnetic bookmarks, consisting of a folded strip of cardboard with magnets on each end, are available in some bookstores. The page is placed between the bookmark, and the magnets hold it in place.
- A small Post-it note can be used to mark a place temporarily if a student is interrupted while reading. Make sure the student has a consistent procedure, such as always placing it above or below the last word read.
- A large paper clip can mark the line on which the student left off.
- Place Wikki Stix (available from Exceptional Teaching Aids) below the line where the student left off reading.

✤ To teach students to find the next line of braille while reading, show them how to quickly retrace the line just read or trace along the bottom of the line of cells to the beginning of the line and then drop their fingers down to the next line.

✤ Arranging materials in the work space for ease and convenience of use is important for students to make the best use of limited range of motion. An *L*-shaped space may work best, with the materials placed on the student's best side and at midline.

✤ Braille on narrow paper or columns for students who have a limited range of motion and cannot cross to midline.

✤ Make sure to provide enough "wait time" for students to respond. Sometimes, students with physical disabilities need extra time to respond motorically, so braille reading may be slow—especially at first—depending on the nature of the disability. Students may also need extra time to arrange their environments, get out books and materials, and put materials away.

✤ Use adapted braille materials, such as TACK-TILES (available from Los Olvidados; see Resources), which are similar to Lego building blocks except that each tile has a braille symbol on top. The tiles fasten to a base and can be used to make words and sentences in braille. They are difficult to dislodge because they stick to the base and are larger than a regular braille cell, so they are especially useful for students who have poor tactile discrimination and poor fine motor skills.

Writing Braille

✛ Use adapted equipment that requires less physical effort to use. Some students with physical disabilities may not have the strength necessary to push down the keys on a regular Perkins brailler, so an electric Perkins brailler (available from Howe Press) may be easier for them to use. The Mountbatten Brailler (available from HumanWare) is another type of electronic brailler whose keys are easy to push down; it can print out in braille or print or it can be hooked up to a computer. Key extenders are available for the Perkins brailler; the Howe Press catalog reports that pressing them requires 30 percent less effort than on a regular brailler.

✛ Find adaptations for students who can use only one hand. A one-handed student may need to rely on the Perkins brailler with the extender keys just mentioned, which bring the keys out toward the student, so they are closer together. Howe Press also sells a unimanual brailler, designed for one-handed use; a student pushes key combinations of dots 1, 2, or 3, but the brailler will not advance to the next cell until either the space bar or key 4, 5, or 6 is pressed. For example, if the student wanted to write the letter *t*, he or she would first press down keys 2 and 3; the brailler would "hold" these keys until keys 4 and 5 were pressed and then would advance to the next cell. To key the letter *a*, the student would push key 1 and then the space bar to go on to the next letter. Electronic braillers are also useful. Braille 'n Speak has a one-handed mode that can be used to input braille. For students who prefer to use a regular keyboard, several models of adapted one-handed keyboards are available from LS&S. Sticky Keys (a computer program that comes with Macintosh computers and is available in accessibility programs designed for IBM-compatible versions) allows a one-handed person to do keyboard commands necessitating two key strokes.

✛ For students who prefer to type input into a computer rather than use braille input, adapted keyboards for one hand are available. Keyboards, such as the BAT (available from Infogrip) and the Maltron single-handed keyboards, may be useful, and software is available for them as well. In addition, there are alternate input devices such as the PowerPad (available from Dunamis)—a tactile overlay that can be configured to work with a computer (see Chapter 8 and Resources).

✛ Adapt slate-and-stylus techniques for students who can use them. Teaching slate skills may be difficult if a student does not have the full use of both hands, but if possible, students should be taught some skills for taking short notes, labeling, and so forth on a slate. The following are some strategies for teaching slate skills to students with physical disabilities:

- One teacher had success teaching a student to use a modified stylus grip that allowed the student to use her thumb to locate the next cell on the slate. Instead of holding the stylus as usual with the index finger over the top and the thumb and third finger down on the shank, the student held the stylus with the index and third finger over the top, so the tip of the thumb was free to feel for the next cell.
- A slate can also be anchored with a rubber pad or by gluing foam-rubber strips to the back of it to prevent it from sliding on the table surface.
- A heavy board slate (such as the one sold by APH) may also be easier for the student to use. It can be backed by rubber or Dycem if sliding is a problem.
- Howe Press also sells a small plastic notebook with a built-in eight-line slate attached to the cover. Braille paper is inserted and held in place by three rings, so it is easily accessible until a fresh piece is needed.
- Yet another option is to use the Marburg Braille Writing Slate, a full-page plastic slate (available from Maxi-Aids; see Resources). The advantage of this slate is that the paper does not have to be moved down; the rows are numbered in braille to help the student keep his or her place on the page. Wikki Stix could also be used for this purpose. It should be noted, however, that the Marburg is manufactured in Germany and so holds braille paper that is slightly longer than paper found in this country; thus, the bottom row will be empty unless longer paper is used.
- Use a stylus that has a flat side or is otherwise "anti-roll" and attach it with a string to the slate, if possible. The saddle-type stylus, available from APH, is flat and has a hole in it that could be used to attach it to a slate.

SPECIAL NEEDS OF CHILDREN WITH INTELLECTUAL DISABILITIES

The question frequently arises as to the minimum IQ score a child can have and still be able to learn braille. This is not the most relevant question to ask, however. First, it is difficult to ascertain some children's IQ scores because of the lack of standardized tests available for blind children (see Chapter 7, Assessment, for a full discussion of this issue). Second, some students with severe physical disabilities that affect speech and movement may test much lower than their actual cognitive functioning. Third, all students deserve a chance to learn and become literate to the fullest extent possible. A standard based on an artificial score may lead teachers to limit what students learn and deter them from trying various activities that may be of value to the students. Thus, the more relevant question is, What communication skills does this student need, and how can I help him or her to learn them?

A good resource for evaluating a student's readiness for a functional braille-reading program is Koenig and Holbrook's *Learning Media Assessment* (1995), which includes a section on "Selecting Media for Students with Additional

Disabilities." Koenig and Holbrook devised a Functional Learning Media Checklist and Indicators of Readiness for a Functional Literacy Program, both of which are useful for teachers. These forms enable teachers to record and analyze a student's behavior systematically and to use the information to decide on appropriate learning media.

Little research has been done on students with cognitive disabilities who are blind or have low vision and may learn enough braille for it to be functional. Many methods used for sighted children with cognitive disabilities are based on visual cues and pictures that are not appropriate for these students. Therefore, other strategies and methods have to be used that are based on developing tactile skills, basic concepts, and experiences.

Students may be slow learners and need a good deal more exposure to braille labels, braille books, and the like before braille begins to make sense to them. They may need repeated exposure to their names in braille, the days of the week on a calendar, and so forth before it dawns on them that the bumps mean something and are in a consistent pattern. In this author's experience, some students who have been labeled developmentally delayed or intellectually disabled may be in upper elementary school or even middle school before something "clicks" and formal braille teaching can begin in earnest. In the *Personal Touch* video (Mangold & Pesavento, 1994), a young man who learned braille only after age 10 states that even though he was slow to learn braille, "it opened up a whole new world for me." Hence, braille reading and writing skills may not only be functional but can improve the quality of students' lives in other ways, such as by providing an enjoyable leisure activity.

Some students have many obstacles to overcome before they can start formal braille training, but once they start, they can catch on, and at least learn enough braille for it to be functional. The key is to make the environment as enriching as possible, with braille clearly evident in the classroom and home. The many uses of braille for functional and recreational purposes must be constantly demonstrated and modeled for the students.

This is not to say that "readiness" activities alone should be taught for years without any connection to functional activities. Students may never be able to identify six embossed shapes with 95 percent accuracy, for example, but may be able to identify their names in braille to find their own belongings. By presenting braille reading materials in the actual environments in which they will be used, providing enough practice, and carefully choosing which reading-related goals they want students to master, teachers may be surprised at just how much braille their students actually learn.

Many of the same activities discussed in Chapter 2 are important for students with mild cognitive disabilities who are blind or visually impaired as well; the difference is they may need to be carried on for a longer time and in more and varied environments, as in the following strategies.

TEACHING BRAILLE TO STUDENTS WITH MILD INTELLECTUAL DISABILITIES

✛ Consider a student's future uses of braille and goals. If the student has learned enough braille that he or she can read a shopping list or follow simple directions, then braille has a definite functional use for the student. Instruction is considered successful if the student can learn as much braille as possible to be independent.

✛ Teach the functional uses of braille. The "Functional Uses of Braille" in this chapter lists some uses of braille that can improve a student's independence and quality of life. Choose age-appropriate activities for students that demonstrate the functional uses of braille.

✛ Give students a great deal of practice in many different contexts. Students need to be exposed to the material many times before they learn it. Seeing the material (such as braille vocabulary words) in the context in which it will be used and with greater frequency will help students learn it and generalize it. For example, if specific vocabulary words are being taught, such as *milk* and *banana,* use those words to make a shopping list one day, write a recipe the next day, and point them out on the school menu the third day. Make sure that parents also have a list of what the students are working on, so they can reinforce what the students have learned at home. Some students may require years of exposure to braille before it starts to make sense to them.

✛ Give lots of praise and encouragement. Reinforce a student for using braille and for showing an interest and attempting to use it. Reading is inherently rewarding in itself, but a word of praise and a "high five" can give recognition to the student's effort to accomplish a difficult task.

✛ Consider using grade 1 braille. Students with mild cognitive disabilities may do better starting with grade 1 braille and then either going on to grade 2 braille or continuing with grade 1 (Troughton, 1992), especially if they are using a phonetics approach and have difficulty understanding why *fan* is spelled out, but *can* only uses the letter *c.* By teaching grade 1 first, the teacher is opening the door to further literacy experiences in which grade 2 braille may be considered. If a student does not progress beyond grade 1 braille, at least he or she has acquired a functional communication method.

✛ Provide students with many and varied language and experiential activities, such as the ones described in Chapter 2. Although tactile awareness and readiness activities, tracking, and so forth still need to be taught, show students how the readiness activities are connected to actual braille reading. Some students can learn enough braille for it to be functional without extensive readiness.

✛ Keep reading to students in braille and let their fingers feel as you read. Model correct braille-reading techniques and show the use of braille by reading braille often to students. Sit behind the students and take their hands in yours, so their fingers are touching the braille. As you read, move their hands smoothly and lightly over the characters to develop their kinesthetic sense of what it feels like to read.

✛ Label everything in the classroom and home that would ordinarily be in print, including a calendar, weekly cafeteria menu, work folders, coat hooks or cubbyholes, and personal belongings. Also point out objects that are brailled in public places, such as rest rooms, elevators, and forms of public transportation, so the students learn that braille has meaning outside school.

✛ Use technology to help motivate students and give them extra practice. Computer programs and technology that have both braille and speech output can give needed reinforcement to students. And computer games that are in both braille and speech are fun for everyone.

✛ Use a slow pace and introduce small pieces at a time. Make sure that lessons are structured, so as not to overload the students with too much information at one time.

✛ Use language experience stories to motivate students and to allow them to see the connection between what was said and done and what was written. These stories are also an excellent way of introducing new vocabulary.

✛ Expose the student to the *Patterns* series (Caton et al., 1980), but give extra help with worksheets and activities. The teacher may decide to use the series just for the vocabulary words, experience activities, and stories and not use the worksheets or use the worksheets with adaptations (such as doing them with the students, rather than asking the students to do them independently or using only one or two examples on each page). Use *Patterns* in conjunction with language experience activities and good-quality short books that have familiar or repetitive stories.

Motivation is another key consideration. Some students are highly motivated to learn braille because their classmates are doing so, or because they want to read books, or because they have had some success that was highly praised by their teachers and parents. These students may certainly be more than willing to put forth the effort to learn as much braille as they can. This is true for all students, and it is certainly true of students with intellectual disabilities.

FUNCTIONAL USES OF BRAILLE

- grocery lists
- recipes
- automatic teller machines
- bills (utility and telephone companies often supply braille bills on request)
- standard check-off forms
- job application forms
- forms for purchasing merchandise from catalogs
- menus
- watches and clocks

- raised-line drawings
- maps, charts, and graphs
- interpreting diagrams using a braille key
- magazines
- elevator markings
- braille signage
- address books or Rolodex files
- personal telephone lists—create a sample braille page of how they are arranged
- personal filing systems
- keeping track of printed materials

Some programs have been successful in using tactile symbols as a bridge to braille reading. For example, the Texas School for the Blind and Visually Impaired uses a standardized set of tactile symbols with students who have low language skills. These symbols are used throughout the students' school and home programs as a way of communicating needs and wants, activities, and requests. Once these symbols are consistently understood, braille can be added to them. Then the symbols can be slowly phased out until students recognize and use the braille words. Some students continue to use this tactile symbol system without making the transition to braille. A great deal more research is needed in this area to develop "best practice" strategies for using tactile symbols as a precursor to braille with children who have cognitive disabilities.

For some students with moderate to severe cognitive disabilities, the first task is to understand symbols. Calendar boxes are often a way to start. By using real objects associated with activities a child will engage in, the child can begin to make this association, which can lead to the use of a more abstract tactile symbol system as just described. The use of these types of alternative communication systems is best discussed by the educational team. For more detailed discussions of these types of systems, see the *Augmentative and Alternative Communication* quarterly professional journal. The discussion in *Hand in Hand* (Huebner, Prickett, Welch, & Joffee, 1995) on the use of calendar boxes and communication boards by students who are deaf-blind may be applicable to students with cognitive disabilities.

The use of real objects as tactile symbols to represent a student's activities can lead the student to understand more abstract symbols.

Developing some sort of communication system—both receptive and expressive—is an important goal for all students. Take the students as far as they can go. If they learn to use objects or tactile symbols to communicate needs and desires, it can only add to the quality of their lives. If they get to grade 1 braille, fantastic! If they learn only enough braille to locate their names to find their lockers and time cards on the job, that is good, too. If they progress to the point that they are using braille efficiently for functional tasks, then their options for employment and leisure activities will continue to expand.

SPECIAL NEEDS OF STUDENTS WHO ARE DEAF-BLIND

Although the incidence of deaf-blindness among students is very low, this group presents unique challenges to teachers of braille reading and writing. (See the Resources section for the names of organizations that work on issues relating to deaf-blindness and may be able to provide additional information and support.) Although they may share the label deaf-blind, these students are a diverse group, and their receptive and expressive language needs (see Chapter 2) are highly individualistic. There is little research about teaching braille skills to these students and much of what is known is based on the experience of individual teachers.

It is beyond the scope of this book to describe in detail all the special communication needs of students who are deaf-blind. For a comprehensive source of information about communication and orientation and mobility (O&M) with students who are deaf-blind, see *Hand in Hand* (Huebner et al., 1995). This section discusses some overall issues that may be helpful in working with a student who is deaf-blind and learning braille.

It is important for teachers to realize that deaf-blindness is a unique disability. It is not simply being deaf and also being blind. A child who is deaf-blind requires specialized instruction to learn to be as independent as possible in all areas: O&M, daily living skills, and communication (including reading and writing). A child's success in learning depends on many factors, such as the ages of onset of blindness and deafness; degrees of residual hearing and residual vision; and, most important, the language base of the child. In short, each child who is deaf-blind brings a unique set of circumstances to a teacher. For the most part, teachers need to use an individualized approach and a great deal of one-on-one instruction.

Thus, although the transdisciplinary team approach is important for all children with special needs, it is absolutely essential in the education of deaf-blind children. Members of the team should probably include an occupational therapist and physical therapist, since the child will be learning a great deal motorically, and these systems need to be intact and fully functional. An augmentative and alternative communication (AAC) specialist should be involved, as well as a speech and language therapist who understands deafness and language development in deaf children. A deaf-blind specialist will be an important part of the team, or, since so few are available, a teacher of visually impaired children working with a teacher of hearing impaired children. And it should go without saying that the parents will have a primary role on the team.

Students Who Are Born with Deaf-Blindness

Some students are born with deaf-blindness. For a child who is congenitally deaf-blind, the key is language development. From the very first, the child will need to be immersed in a language-rich environment in which there is a great deal of interaction between the child and his or her caregivers. If the child is going to be using sign language, then the parents need to learn it thoroughly—not just commands and simple questions. Emotions, likes and dislikes, and the general day-to-day conversation found in any home are important. A sign-language vocabulary of just a few dozen words will not be enough to express everything and will not expose the child to the rich array of language he or she will need to know.

Early intervention is crucial. Most parents need help from specially trained teachers who have experience in teaching infants and toddlers who are deaf-blind. These special teachers can help the parents learn to communicate with their child and support the child's development of concepts. Many of the early emergent literacy experiences listed in Chapter 2 are appropriate for deaf-blind children as well. The difference is that they may need to be repeated many times and that the activities will probably take longer to complete to allow time for explanation and comprehension, as in the following helpful strategies for building the use of language and early braille experiences with congenitally deaf-blind children.

STRATEGIES

DEVELOPING A LANGUAGE FOUNDATION WITH CONGENITALLY DEAF-BLIND CHILDREN

✛ Building receptive language is the first step. No one can learn to read and write in any medium until he or she has a foundation in language. The young deaf-blind child must have intervenors (individuals who assist the child by acting as his and her eyes and ears and facilitating the child's interactions with the environment) and early experiences with language to learn its importance. This is where braille instruction starts.

✛ Depending on the amount of residual hearing, the child's first language may be some form of sign language. American Sign Language (ASL) is not English; it has its own grammar and syntax. It is also highly visual with subtle nuances that are missed by a person who cannot see them—body language and facial expression are major parts of it. When presenting ASL tactilely it may be necessary to sign at a slower pace and add more information that may be missed by the student with a visual impairment; additional signs may be needed to supplement facial expression. For example, when a question may be indicated visually in ASL by raising the eyebrows, a question sign or manual marker can be provided to the deaf-blind individual for this purpose. The educational team may use other forms of sign language, such as Signed Exact English, that are based on English word order and syntax, for students who will be using braille (Prickett, 1995). Whatever communication system is used, it must be started early and used consistently by all caregivers and in different situations.

✛ Build from signing skills to braille. Braille labels can be a good place to start in teaching deaf-blind children the uses of written communication. For example, the teacher and parents can sign the name of an object and then present the braille label on that object—such as the sign for the child's favorite type of cereal and the braille label on the box—as the bridge to understanding.

✛ Start with labeling in grade 1 braille. Associate these labels with name signs with which the child is already familiar. Eventually, the child will learn fingerspelling of people and place names for which there are no standard signs. Fingerspelling will

GOOD CANDIDATES FOR LEARNING BRAILLE

A student who is deaf-blind may be a good candidate for learning to read in braille if he or she can:

- share ideas or converse about simple topics, follow simple directions, and express what he or she wants.

- think about and communicate not only immediate daily experiences, but nonroutine experiences—what others are doing, his or her family life, and what he or she plans to do in the future.

- remember sequences.

- make fine tactile discriminations. (For example, Roberto likes to study the teacher's key ring with her home and school keys; he can identify by touch the keys for her car and for the classroom door; and he likes to be allowed to lock the door at night.)

- handle and work with items or materials by touch in an organized fashion, because braille must be followed from left to right and top to bottom.

- do detailed work and pay attention for prolonged periods. Learning to read requires patience!

Source: Reprinted from Kathleen Mary Huebner, Jeanne Glidden Prickett, Therese Rafalowski Welch, and Elga Joffee, Eds. *Hand in Hand: Essentials of Orientation and Mobility for Your Students Who Are Deaf-Blind* (New York: AFB Press 1995), p. 291.

eventually be associated with separate braille letters, although it will take the child a long time to realize that fingerspelling is made up of separate letters that correspond to the "bumps" he or she feels.

✛ Use language experience stories. Taking vocabulary from the student's direct experiences is often the best way to tie those experiences into meaningful literacy for the student. A child will probably not have a great deal of motivation to read regular storybooks if he or she has no functional vision or hearing. Whereas sighted children are bombarded with print in the environment, children who are blind rarely encounter braille in their homes, and deaf-blind children may encounter even less evidence of written communication in their environment. Make books about the child's experiences that are sequential and use tactile "pictures" that include real objects the child encounters. For example, a book could be made called "Celia's Bath Time," whose pages contain braille (and print) text and real objects in the order Celia would experience them. Thus, page 1 could feature the washcloth, page 2 might present a favorite bath toy, page 3 could include the soap, and subsequent pages could include a piece of towel, a powder puff, and so forth. Appropriate yet simple text using the child's name and some of the key words would accompany the pictures. The text would be signed as it is read.

✛ Allow a great deal of time for these experiences. As mentioned earlier, many of the emergent literacy activities discussed in Chapter 2 can be adapted for deaf-blind children, but they may need to be done much more slowly and with abundant explanation. If the student and teacher go to a pumpkin patch to pick out a Halloween pumpkin to carve, the teacher will need to spend a great deal of time explaining what they are doing and for what reason. The activities cannot be hurried and must be presented from beginning to end. The child will not learn the in-between steps without direct instruction. If a cooking experience is being presented, the child must be physically involved in each step of the process. This is good teaching practice under any circumstances, especially when working with children who are blind or visually impaired, but it is essential for children with dual sensory impairments to develop language and basic concepts.

✛ The use of a tactile symbol system, as discussed earlier in regard to children with cognitive disabilities, may be necessary with some deaf-blind students. Use object boxes to symbolize the activity that will be done next, and make sure the object is what the child will encounter. For example, if you are going to the playground as the next activity and the child likes to swing, use a piece of the chain that the child is used to holding onto as the object representing the experience. Using a miniature swing set will confuse the child, who has never experienced the swing in that form.

✛ Build from concrete to abstract. If the teacher gradually builds to a more abstract symbol system, this will offer a clue to how well the student does with symbolic information. This could be a gateway to braille as well. Watch the student to see how concrete he or she needs the information to be. Does just signing a word the first time lead to comprehension? If so, perhaps the child does not need to use an object system and can go right into more abstract symbology, such as tactile symbols or braille. Additional guidelines to help the team make decisions about the most appropriate symbol system to choose are presented in "Good Candidates for Learning Braille."

Deaf Students Who Become Visually Impaired

Some students develop a hearing impairment first and acquire a visual impairment later. Students with Usher I syndrome, for example, have a severe congenital hearing impairment that affects their ability to use oral and written language, and acquire a visual impairment later in life, often during adolescence. These students face a double challenge in learning braille literacy skills, because braille is in English, which may be a second language for a student who is born deaf, whose first language is often ASL (which has no written equivalent). Some of the common contractions in braille, such as *rather* and *quite*, have no direct equivalents in ASL, and the vocabulary in some of the texts commonly used with individuals who learn braille as adolescents or young adults is difficult to understand and has little or no meaning for students who are deaf-blind. Again, using an in-

---

COMPONENTS OF A MODIFIED GRADE 1 BRAILLE PROGRAM FOR DEAF-BLIND STUDENTS

SUBSKILL CHECKLIST: MODIFIED GRADE 1 BRAILLE, RECEPTIVE AND EXPRESSIVE

A modified Grade 1 braille program must be tailored to individual needs. An individual may or may not receive training or achieve complete competence in all the skills listed.

1. Student reads/comprehends/writes letters of the alphabet
2. Student reads/comprehends/writes simple punctuation and composition signs
3. Student reads/comprehends/writes simple (cardinal) numbers
4. Student reads/comprehends/writes mixed numbers
5. Student reads/comprehends/writes familiar vocabulary words based on individual needs
6. Student reads/comprehends/writes simple phrases and/or sentences using this vocabulary

FUNCTIONAL SKILLS

These are skills and vocabulary that are functional for everyday use.

- the alphabet
- capital and number signs
- period, question mark, (and possibly) exclamation mark
- colon for telling time
- dollar and decimal signs for functional money skills
- fractions (maybe) for recipes

Source: Adapted with permission from Michelle Smithdas and Nancy W. Godfrey, personal communications, Helen Keller National Center, Sands Point, New York, 1996.

dividualized approach with words of immediate use and high interest to the student will be helpful.

A modified system of braille—shorter and simplified—is used with older students at the Helen Keller National Center for Deaf-Blind Youths and Adults (M. Smithdas and N. Godfrey, personal communications, December 1996 and March 1997). The components of this system (see "Components of a Modified Grade 1 Braille Program for Deaf-Blind Students" in this chapter) may be useful to keep in mind for students who have grown up using ASL and are learning braille in late adolescence or young adulthood.

It should noted, however, that this approach was not designed to be used indiscriminately with all students but rather is a suggestion of where to start. The individual student may need more or fewer vocabulary words than are offered in this program. Only a full assessment of language and tactile skills, along with other skills discussed in Chapter 8, conducted by qualified members of the transdisciplinary team, can truly point the way to the full program that the student needs.

A modified grade 2 braille program can also be developed to use with students who need to go on beyond grade 1 braille; however, an individual's training may not include all grade 2 contractions. Each student's program is individualized, depending on his or her reading comprehension skills, language skills, and everyday functional needs. It is essential for a teacher of visually impaired children to work closely with parents, the speech and language therapist, and others on the transdisciplinary team to create a program that is right for each student. Some students may learn the entire braille code in grade 2, and some may learn just enough to have functional literacy. It is important to keep a record of the braille vocabulary and grade 2 contractions the student learns so that they can be used in all settings.

In addition to the difficulties that students who were born deaf face in having to learn English, emotional issues relating to vision loss can affect them greatly. Students who grew up in deaf culture and are now losing vision may often feel isolated and frustrated in trying to communicate with others. Their teachers will need to give a great deal of emotional support to these students, be patient and persistent, and be prepared to listen to and reassure them. Some students may benefit from counseling or participation in a support group. The strategies suggested here will be helpful for both teaching braille reading and writing and helping students with the emotional effects of this process.

STRATEGIES

WORKING WITH STUDENTS WHO ARE CONGENITALLY DEAF AND ACQUIRE A VISUAL IMPAIRMENT

✛ Use a modified braille approach such as that used at the Helen Keller National Center (see "Components of a Modified Grade 1 Braille Program for Deaf-Blind Students" in this chapter), based on the student's needs and experiences. As noted, English reading and writing assessment is necessary to determine if a modified braille approach is appropriate. Remember, as discussed in Chapter 4, the best way to teach braille to students learning it later in life is to make it immediately useful and relevant.

✛ Use strategies for teaching braille to students who learn English as a second language, such as the ones listed in Chapter 6.

✛ Make sure that the student clearly understands the braille instruction. If the student has been using ASL—a visual medium—his or her entire life, and now has to learn to sign tactilely, there may be some misunderstandings at first. The ASL will have to be modified to take into account the student's new visual impairment: Signs may need to be made smaller, closer to the body, or further away depending on the student's vision and field loss. Until the student is used to these changes, the teacher may have to describe and explain things several times and in several different ways. Check for understanding by asking questions and asking the student to apply the braille skills in appropriate contexts. The teacher can do this by brailling simple directions for the student to follow and by asking the student to match labels to objects, or to write the braille himself or herself.

✛ Introduce the student to others who are deaf-blind. Deaf-blindness can be an isolating disability, so meeting and talking to others who have similar life situations can be empowering and reassuring. The organization the Foundation Fighting Blindness (formerly the National Retinitis Pigmentosa Foundation) may have information about support groups in the area (see Resources).

Visually Impaired Students Who Become Hearing Impaired

Other students may be visually impaired and acquire a hearing impairment later on. If these students are already braille readers, their braille reading and writing per se may not be affected. However, whether they can continue to use speech or need guidance in other aspects of communication will depend on the amount of residual hearing they have. They may need direct instruction in sign language (ASL or Signed English) and other modes of communication (such as print on palm).

These students will find assistive technology to be of great help to them. If they have a strong background in braille reading, the use of refreshable braille displays on computers and portable braille notetakers (see Chapter 8) will enable them to continue to use computers without speech input. There are also devices that enable braille readers to use the telephone communication systems designed for people who are deaf. Those systems, known as Teletype for the Deaf (TTY) or Telecommunications (or Telephone) Device for the Deaf (TDD), consist of a keyboard and computer that are able to transmit print over the telephone lines for reception by telephones with the same equipment. Devices such as the TeleBraille from TeleSensory Corporation and the Lite Touch from Blazie Engineering attach to the telephone or modem and display refreshable braille instead of print (see Resources).

Deaf-Blind Students with Cognitive Disabilities

Some students who are deaf-blind have cognitive disabilities, too. The strategies for teaching braille to students with cognitive disabilities mentioned earlier in this chapter may be relevant for these students, but may have to be taught differently because of the dual sensory impairment. Teachers may need to do many of these

Some TDD systems use braille input and display refreshable braille, allowing braille readers who are deaf to communicate over telephone lines using a computer and a modem.

activities hand over hand (or hand *under* hand), rather than just describing them verbally, and use a type of gesture system, rather than ASL. Communication boards and object boxes and calendars are also useful. *Hand in Hand* (Huebner et al., 1995) presents excellent guidelines and strategies for setting up communication systems with students who are deaf-blind and have additional disabilities.

THE CHALLENGE OF TEACHING STUDENTS WITH MULTIPLE DISABILITIES

Students with visual impairments and additional disabilities are often a large part of the caseload of teachers of visually impaired children. These teachers must be able to teach a wide variety of students, ranging in age from 3 to 21, ranging in grade from preschool (or younger in a home program) through high school, and ranging in ability level from profoundly intellectually disabled to academically gifted—and everything in between. Braille students who have additional disabilities, such as learning disabilities, physical disabilities, intellectual disabilities, or some combination of conditions, can be a real challenge for teachers of visually impaired children, since each child has his or her own unique needs and strengths. Many teachers find the variety stimulating and rewarding.

One of the most important lessons about teaching braille to students with multiple disabilities is, Don't give up; try another way. It takes some students a very long time to catch on to braille—beyond what is normally considered the time necessary for emergent literacy. Many factors can contribute to this delay, including the lack of experiences, lack of internal organization systems, or even lack of consistent instruction. Students whose physical disabilities prevent them from actively exploring their environment need many concrete experiences such as those described in Chapter 1, so that the world is more meaningful to them, as well as specific instruction in tactile skills, depending on their disabilities. Other students may be born with premature nervous systems, and it may simply take longer to get their internal learning systems in place. Some students need to learn specific strategies to teach them how to learn better.

It takes repetition, patience, flexibility, and creativity on the part of the teacher of visually impaired children and the other members of the transdisciplinary team to work out a system that will work for the individual student. But teachers should not sell these children short. If teachers try to maximize each student's potential, that will enable them to become as literate as they possibly can.

REFERENCES

American Foundation for the Blind (n.d.). *Facts about the teaching of children who are blind or visually impaired.* Washington, DC: Governmental Relations.

Borkowski, J. G. (1992). Metacognitive theory: A framework for teaching literacy, writing, and math skills. *Journal of Learning Disabilities, 25,* 253–257.

Caton, H. R., Pester, E., & Bradley, E. J. (1980). *Patterns: The primary braille reading program.* Louisville, KY: American Printing House for the Blind.

Collins, N. D. (1994). *Metacognition and reading to learn* (ERIC digest). Bloomington, IN: ERIC Clearinghouse on Reading, English, and Communication.

Fink, R. P. (1996). Successful dyslexics: A constructivist study of passionate interest in reading. *Journal of Adolescent and Adult Literacy, 39,* 268–280.

Frankel-Mislinski, K. (1995). *Color me braille.* Paper presented at the Getting in Touch with Literacy conference, Austin, TX.

Gallivan-Fenlon, A. (1994, Spring). Integrated transdisciplinary teams. *Teaching Exceptional Children,* 16–20.

Godwin, A., Grafsgaard, K., Hanson, N., Hooey, P., Martin, J., McNear D., Rieber, C., Tillmans, E. (1995). *Minnesota braille skills inventory: A resource manual.* St. Paul, MN: Minnesota Department of Education, Minnesota Educational Services.

Huebner, K. M., Prickett, J. G., Welch, T. R., Joffee, E. (Eds.). (1995). *Hand in hand: Essentials of communication and orientation and mobility for your students who are deaf-blind.* New York: AFB Press.

Kaye, P. (1984). *Games for reading.* New York: Pantheon.

Koenig, A. J., & Holbrook, M. C. (1995). *Learning media assessment of students with visual impairments* (2nd ed.). Austin: Texas School for the Blind and Visually Impaired.

Lerner, J. W., Cousin, P. T., & Richeck, M. (1992). Critical issues in learning disabilities: Whole language learning. *Learning Disabilities Research and Practice, 7,* 226–230.

Mangold, S. S. (1989). *The Mangold developmental program of tactile perception and braille letter recognition.* Castro Valley, CA: Exceptional Teaching Aids.

Mangold, S. S., & Pesavento, M. E., *Personal touch: Braille for lifelong enrichment* [videotape]. Winnetka, IL: Hadley School for the Blind.

Mather, N. (1992). Whole language reading instruction for students with learning disabilities: Caught in the cross fire. *Learning Disabilities Research and Practice, 7,* 87–95.

Miller, W. H. (1993). *The complete reading disabilities handbook.* West Nyack, NY: Center for Applied Research in Education.

Muth, K. D. (1987). Structure strategies for comprehending expository text. *Reading Research and Instruction, 27,*(1), 66–72.

Olson, M. R. (1981). *Guidelines and games for teaching efficient braille reading.* New York: American Foundation for the Blind.

Prickett, J. G. (1995). Manual and spoken communication. In Huebner, K. M., Prickett, J. G., Welch, T. R., & Joffee, E. (Eds.). *Hand in hand: Essentials of communication and orientation and mobility for your students who are deaf-blind* (pp. 261–287).

Rogow, S. M. (1988). *Helping the visually impaired child with developmental problems.* New York: Teachers College Press.

Rosner, J. (1986). *The green readiness book: Auditory and general readiness activities for reading and arithmetic.* New York: Walker.

Roswell, F. G., & Natchez, G. (1989). *Reading disability: A human approach to evaluation and treatment of reading and writing difficulties.* New York: Basic Books.

Sanacore, J. (1984). Metacognition and the improvement of reading: Some important links. *Journal of Reading, 27,* 706–712.

Silberman, R. K., & Sowell V. (1987). The visually impaired student with learning disabilities: Strategies for success in language arts. *RE:view, 18,* 139–150.

Smith, M. (1995). Providing itinerant services to students with visual and multiple impairments. *The Driving Force* [newsletter of Association of Education and Rehabilitation of the Blind and Visually Impaired, Division 16], *3*(2) 1, 6–8.

Spear-Swerling, L., & Sternberg, R. J. (1994). The road not taken: An integrative theoretical model of reading disability. *Journal of Learning Disabilities, 27,* 91–103.

Stewart, O., & Tei, E. (1983). Some implications of metacognition for reading instruction. *Journal of Reading, 27*(1), 36–43.

Troughton, M. (1992). *One is fun.* Unpublished manuscript. Brantford, Ontario.

Turnbull, A. P., Turnbull, H. R., Shank, M., & Leal, D. (1995). *Special education in today's schools.* Englewood Cliffs, NJ: Prentice Hall.

Understanding Braille Literacy [videotape]. (1993). New York: AFB Press.

Van Reusen, A. K., & Head, D. (1994). Cognitive and metacognitive interventions: Important trends for teachers of students who are visually impaired. *RE:view, 25,* 153–162.

BRAILLE ASSESSMENT CHECKLIST
FOR PERSONS WITH MULTIPLE DISABILITIES

Directions

In the *general visual information* category, information from the learning media assessment is noted. Information from the eye report should be listed, including the eye condition (if known), and whether it is stable, unstable, or deteriorating. Distance and near acuities should be noted, as well as visual field information (note any central or peripheral field losses, as well as blind spots). Also in this area the teacher should report results of the functional vision assessment, including use of current vision for reading print or seeing small objects. Environmental modifications such as lighting preferences, use of color and contrast, etc. are important and can be listed on the form. Use of low vision devices (if any) such as hand-held magnifiers, monocular telescopes, CCTVs, or others the student may have had prescribed should be listed, including how well they are used. The teacher should also add information about the individual's use of tactile channels, especially if he or she has already been a braille reader. Current literacy skills should be noted, as should efficiency in current media, such as reading rate, accuracy, fatigue, distance from page (if using print), and ability to read own handwriting. The teacher can then list academic and vocational requirements of literacy (how will the student use reading and writing?), as well as recreational and personal requirements (functional literacy). It should be noted that the teacher may not have all the information already at his or her fingertips and will need to do the standard assessment procedures first. Other areas may not seem to be immediately applicable for a student but by having them on the form, the teacher can be reminded to consider their importance.

The second area to consider is *physical considerations* for reading and writing braille. The individual's medical records will be helpful to you, if you have access to them, as well as reports from an occupational and physical therapist (OT and PT). Is there a medical diagnosis of the physical condition? Note the student's body posture: is she able to sit up straight, or is she positioned in a different way? Consider the student's endurance and stamina. Does the student have use of two hands, or is hand movement restricted? Can the student maintain a relaxed, curved hand and finger position? Can the student maintain a consistent light touch on the braille dots? Assess the learner's arm/hand movements: does she have a full range of motion up/down and right/left? Can she cross midline? How is the learner's muscle strength? Is coordination affected? Is the student's tactile sensitivity affected? Other useful information could include whether the learner is taking any medications that may effect general health, alertness, or fatigue.

The third area of consideration is *cognitive abilities.* There may be some evidence in the student's records that the cognitive disability is congenital or acquired (for example, from a brain injury). Some factors that may affect the individual's braille reading ability are memory, perception and attention, organization, abstract thinking skills, and generalization. If the learner has a current psychological report, you may be able to find some of this information there. Some of these areas may be more difficult for you as a teacher to assess, but a staff psychologist or psychometrist may be able to assist you. Also observe the learner's behaviors, and note signs of confusion, short attention span, etc. These will not necessarily preclude teaching braille to this individual, but may help you plan your lessons and suggest strategies that will help your student learn. For example, this individual may need shorter lessons, more frequent breaks, extra practice on certain skills, and suggestions for organizing materials.

Language is the fourth area to consider. In this space, the teacher can record information from a Speech/Language Pathologist (SLP) report, or results of any testing the teacher may have done. If the learner speaks English as a Second Language, this information can also be recorded here, as well as the learner's primary language, and literacy level in both the primary language and English.

The last area that should be considered is the category of *auditory skills.* Does the learner have a hearing impairment? There are several combinations to consider. Does your student have a congenital visual impairment (VI) and an acquired hearing impairment (HI) (perhaps from the effects of aging, or a syndrome)? Does your student have a congenital hearing impairment (such as a person with Usher's syndrome)? Perhaps your student has both a congenital hearing and visual impairment, or perhaps your student has acquired both a hearing and visual impairment (for example, from an accident, reaction to medication, or effects of aging). Each of these scenarios will have an effect on learning to read and write braille, and should be noted in your assessment. An audiologist's report will be helpful to you, if available.

Appendix. An Assessment Form for Students with Multiple Disabilities

BRAILLE ASSESSMENT CHECKLIST
FOR PERSONS WITH MULTIPLE DISABILITIES

Name _____ Date of Birth _____

Address _____ School/Facility _____

City _____ State _____ Zip _____ Completed by _____ Date _____

Key:　I　=　Impairment/difficulty
　　　OK　=　No impairment
　　　NA　=　Not applicable

I. General Category	I	OK	NA	Comments (including assessment dates)
Eye condition: _____				Eye report information:
Stable	☐	☐	☐	
Unstable	☐	☐	☐	
Deteriorating	☐	☐	☐	
Acuity	☐	☐	☐	
Central loss	☐	☐	☐	
Use of current vision: Reading print/ Seeing small objects	☐	☐	☐	Functional vision assessment:
				Environmental modifications:
Use of low vision devices: Type & competency:	☐	☐	☐	Low vision evaluation:

Appendix. *(Continued)*

Source: Adapted from Kathryn Wolff Heller, Lisa-Anne Soucy, Frances Mary D'Andrea, and Mary Beth Caruso, *AFB Braille Literacy Mentors in Training: The Next Generation* (Atlanta: American Foundation for the Blind, 1997).

| Use of tactile channel: | ☐ | ☐ | ☐ | Sensory channel assessment: |

Affective status: ☐ ☐ ☐ Interview:

Current literacy skills: Learning media assessment:
   Conventional ☐ ☐ ☐
   Functional ☐ ☐ ☐
   Literacy readiness

Efficiency in current media:
   Distance from page ☐ ☐ ☐
   Reading rate ☐ ☐ ☐
   Accuracy ☐ ☐ ☐
   Fatigue ☐ ☐ ☐
   Able to read own handwriting ☐ ☐ ☐

Literacy requirements across
   environments: ☐ ☐ ☐ Ecological assessment for braille literacy:

Other information: ☐ ☐ ☐

II. Physical Category	I	OK	NA	Comments
Physical condition:	☐	☐	☐	Medical report:

Appendix. *(Continued)*

Endurance/stamina: ☐ ☐ ☐

Body posture/position: ☐ ☐ ☐   PT report:

Use of two hands: ☐ ☐ ☐   OT report:

Finger/hand position: ☐ ☐ ☐

Light touch on braille: ☐ ☐ ☐

Arm/hand movement:
   Range of motion   ☐ ☐ ☐
   Muscle strength   ☐ ☐ ☐
   Coordination   ☐ ☐ ☐

Tactile perception: ☐ ☐ ☐

Other information: ☐ ☐ ☐

Appendix. *(Continued)*

III. Cognitive Category	I	OK	NA	Comments
Intellectual status: Type of impairment: _____ _____ ☐ Congenital ☐ Acquired	☐	☐	☐	Psychological report:
Memory	☐	☐	☐	
Perception/attention	☐	☐	☐	
Organization	☐	☐	☐	
Abstract thinking	☐	☐	☐	
Generalization	☐	☐	☐	
Other information:	☐	☐	☐	

IV. Language Category	I	OK	NA	Comments
Language & communication:	☐	☐	☐	SLP report:
Other information:	☐	☐	☐	

V. Auditory Category	I	OK	NA	Comments
Hearing impairment:				Audiological & medical report:
Congenital VI & acquired HI	☐	☐	☐	
Congenital HI & acquired VI	☐	☐	☐	
Congenital VI & HI	☐	☐	☐	
Acquired VI & HI	☐	☐	☐	
Other information:	☐	☐	☐	

Appendix. *(Continued)*

TEACHING BRAILLE READING AND WRITING TO STUDENTS WHO SPEAK ENGLISH AS A SECOND LANGUAGE

MADELINE MILIAN

Carmen, aged 3, recently came to the United States with her family from Mexico and is now enrolled in an early intervention program. Although the program specializes in educating children who are blind or visually impaired, Carmen presents a new challenge for teachers and other staff members. She communicates only in Spanish, and the teachers and staff members speak only English. This situation has raised some questions about the type of changes needed in the program to provide appropriate and meaningful services to Carmen and her family.

Soua, a 7-year-old Hmong student, spent most of her life in a refugee camp in Thailand before her family recently moved to the United States to join other members of their extended family. Soua, who is totally blind, is now receiving educational services to meet the needs related to her visual impairment. However, this is the first time her vision teacher and orientation and mobility instructor are working with a student who speaks a language other than English and who is part of a culture unknown to them.

Fifteen-year-old Dieudonne came to the United States two years ago from Haiti to live with his older sister and her family. Shortly after his arrival, he suffered a head injury that resulted in the loss of most of his vision. He started receiving educational services as soon as he returned to school from the hospital. However, because of his limited knowledge of English and the absence of professionals who can effectively communicate with Dieudonne and understand his culture, the process has been frustrating for him and for the educators who are working with him and his family.

This chapter discusses issues relevant to the education of many students like Carmen, Soua, and Dieudonne who are blind or visually impaired and are in the process of learning English. Professionals in the field of vision who work with these students have to make instructional decisions and plan programs to address both their vision and language needs.

Teaching a second language in a school setting requires equal attention to the development of speaking, listening, reading, and writing skills, so that students develop literacy skills that will help them gain access to all academic areas. Consequently, for students who use braille as their means of using written language, the teaching of English as a second language (ESL) and the teaching of braille are inseparable.

No national data are available on the number of students who are blind or visually impaired who come from homes where a language other than English is spoken or who have been identified as having limited English proficiency. Furthermore, little is known about which languages these students speak. However, given that the number of all students in the United States who have been identified as having limited proficiency in English has increased dramatically since 1980, it is feasible to suggest that the proportion of students with limited English proficiency who are blind or visually impaired has increased as well. According to the National Center for Education Statistics (NCES, 1995), whereas 1.9 million students aged 5 to 17 in U.S. schools were classified as having difficulty with English in 1980, there were 2.4 million such students in 1990. In addition, although 5.3 percent of all students nationwide had difficulty speaking English in 1990, the percentage of such students was higher in a number of states, including California (14.9 percent), Texas (11.3 percent), New Mexico (10.5 percent), Arizona (8.9 percent), New York (8.2 percent), New Jersey (6.0 percent), Hawaii (5.7 percent), Rhode Island (5.6 percent), Florida (5.6 percent), and Massachusetts (5.4 percent)(NCES, 1995).

The literature on language in the field of visual impairments has focused primarily on the development of children's first language (see, for example, Bigelow, 1986; Dunlea, 1989; Kekelis & Andersen, 1984; Landau & Gleitman, 1985). Therefore, an understanding of the acquisition of a second language is required before one can explore the language and concept development of children who are blind or visually impaired and are learning a second language. The next section presents an overview of the factors that affect success of students in learning a second language (Cummins, 1981; Larsen-Freeman & Long, 1991)—both those relating to the individual student and those relating to the educational program—and the implications for teaching students who are blind or visually impaired. Subsequent sections present specific approaches and strategies for teaching braille reading and writing to these students.

At the outset, it should be noted that ESL students are a diverse group whose only commonality frequently is that they are learning English. Therefore, it is difficult to suggest programs or strategies that will work with all ESL students, and many of the descriptions and suggestions in this chapter may apply only to some ESL students. As with any other group of students, understanding and providing for the learning needs of individuals is the key to ensuring the educational success of students who are learning English.

FACTORS THAT AFFECT THE LEARNING OF A SECOND LANGUAGE

Individual Factors

Important factors related to individual students include the ages at which students are exposed to a second language, students' literacy skills in their native languages, and students' aptitude for languages.

Age of Exposure to a Second Language

There has been considerable discussion of whether the age at which one is first exposed to a second language affects the acquisition of that language. Although the "ideal age" for learning a second language is not known, there is some general agreement on how age contributes to the learning of a second language (Bialystok & Hakuta, 1994; Ellis, 1994). Young children have the advantage of learning a second language with native-like pronunciation, but adults and older children initially make more rapid progress than do young children. However, since adults may reach a plateau earlier than young learners and young learners have more time to develop proficiency in a second language, the ultimate attainment of young learners is likely to surpass that of adults.

Since students who are blind or visually impaired enter school anywhere from infancy to age 21, instructional decisions for ESL students need to be based on age, language proficiency, and visual needs. For example, for preschool children who are still in the process of acquiring their first language and need to learn the basic concepts for the development of braille literacy and orientation and mobility (O&M) skills, the issue of teaching English and also fostering cognitive growth needs to be examined.

For young children, language and cognitive development are interdependent. This is especially true for children who are blind or visually impaired, for whom rich and sufficient sensory experiences are essential to learning about the environment and enhancing their later understanding of the connections between what they learned in the past and what they are currently learning (see Chapter 2). Therefore, professionals in instructional programs that provide services to students who are blind or visually impaired and speak a language other than English have to recognize the need to communicate in ways that contribute to the student's overall cognitive development. In other words, teaching English may be one objective, but ensuring that the instruction leads to cognitive growth needs to be a fundamental goal for the young child. Toward this end, early intervention educators working with young children need to create programmatic and instructional changes that may include the use of the children's first language. The following are useful strategies that teachers can use for including young children's native language in instructional programs.

INCLUDING CHILDREN'S NATIVE LANGUAGE IN INSTRUCTION

✤ Read books with children or listen to songs in their native languages. Teachers who are not familiar with the children's native language can play recorded stories and songs in these languages to the students. Once children have become familiar with the themes of books and songs, these books and songs can be introduced in English.

✤ Lend family members stories that have been published in their native languages so they can read them at home with their children. The same stories, or similar versions, can be read in English at school.

✤ Develop a list of words that are frequently used at school, including functional words and those that are needed for introducing new concepts. Translate the list of words into a student's native language, give copies to all who have contact with the student, and encourage everyone to use words to facilitate communication with the student.

✤ Contact the foreign language departments of local colleges or universities and explore the possibility of asking college students who speak the languages of the young students to volunteer to translate books, read stories to young children in their native languages, audiotape books in these languages, and assist with a number of other activities.

✤ Ask family members to share children's stories and poetry that are popular in their cultures, so they can be incorporated into the language and readiness components of the early intervention program.

✤ Employ bilingual teachers or paraprofessionals who can introduce and reinforce new concepts in the children's native languages.

If a student enters a school program at age 14 with a proven record of academic success, teaching ESL should become one of the central components of his or her program. However, the practice of providing a program that only emphasizes language instruction should be avoided. Instead, learning English should take place throughout the instructional day. The use of modified instruction in the various content areas to introduce specific vocabulary and academic concepts facilitates growth in the English language in a more meaningful way than does teaching English in isolated lessons. With this approach, all teachers need to consult with each other about the modifications that are required in the instructional program, so that the student can master both English and academic subjects. (The steps in developing lessons that integrate content and language are presented later in this chapter in the section on "A Model Lesson Plan.")

Literacy Skills in the Native Language

Since students who have received substantial educational preparation in their native language find it easier to learn a second language (Cummins, 1981), it is critical for a teacher to know the number of years a student attended school in his or her country, if the student received consistent instruction, and if the student is able to read and write in the native language. This information often reveals gaps in education that may otherwise be attributed to the student's lack of ability. Obtaining information on the quality of instruction a student received is more difficult to determine, given the different educational systems and pedagogical practices of various countries.

Teachers of students who are visually impaired may want to find out if or when the braille code was introduced to the students, the consistency of its use, and if the students had sufficient materials available to reinforce the skills they learned. Because ESL students frequently enter the United States without records from schools in their native countries, the only ways to obtain this information are to interview the students or their parents or to try to contact the schools.

Students who were introduced to the braille code but received limited instruction or opportunities to practice may need to be exposed to activities that foster tactile sensitivity and perceptual skills to improve their knowledge of braille. It will also be important to be able to determine whether problems that arise in braille reading and writing result from difficulties with perceptual skills, such as reversals or insertions, from lack of literacy skills, or from lack of knowledge of English. Therefore, a "meaningful assessment" (see Rex, Koenig, Wormsley, & Baker, 1994, and Chapter 7 of this book), information on a student's educational history, and the provision of opportunities for the student to demonstrate his or her knowledge of content areas and the braille code in the student's native language are necessary to determine whether a student is familiar with the techniques of reading and writing in braille. Assessment of ESL students who are blind or visually impaired is discussed in more detail later in this section.

Students who attended school in their native countries and became proficient in using the braille code will mainly require a program to enhance their English skills and to introduce braille contractions and rules in English. A teacher may want to review the braille code used in a student's native language to identify signs that may be used differently than in English (for example, signs used for accented vowels in Spanish have different meanings in English). The teacher may also want to learn if the braille code in the student's native language has a contracted form; if not, the concept of contractions may have to be explained. It is important to remember that the foreign language braille code used in the United States is different from the braille codes used in the native languages of other countries; for example, the accent sign (dot 4) is used in a foreign word in front of the accented letter in English text, but the accent sign is not used when the text is written in the native language. A useful guide to the braille codes of other countries is *World Braille Usage* (1990), and a guide to the braille system used in Mexico is *Manual de Enseñanza de Escritura y Lectura Braille* (n.d.), published by Editorial Braille del Comite Internacional Pro Ciegos (see Resources).

Students with low levels of literacy skills and those who did not attend school in their native countries present a challenge to teachers. They need experiences that will enhance their tactile sensitivity and perception (see Chapter 2 for strategies), as well as early literacy activities and language development (sometimes both in English and in the students' native language). They may also need special assistance to learn basic concepts related to the school setting and routine that are usually taken for granted with students of school age, such as:

- the names and functions of instructional tools and materials used in the classroom, such as the braillewriter, braille paper, slate and stylus, audiotape recorder, and audiocassette
- daily school routines, including the class schedule; location of important places in school; and the names of their teachers (since many English names may be new to the students and difficult for them to pronounce)
- the names of foods commonly served at school and samples of these foods to taste
- descriptions of the concepts of size, shape, touch, and taste and experiences to facilitate their understanding and use of the words
- all body parts
- the days of the week and the months and seasons of the year
- concepts of space, quantity, and time, taught in ways that involve body actions and the manipulation of tangible objects

To determine if a student has the necessary prior knowledge to understand a new concept, the teacher can either question the student in his or her native language or demonstrate the concept in English by using concrete objects, hands-on activities, and communication strategies that are typically used when teaching English in content areas and provide opportunities for the student to show that he or she understands the concept. Teachers who are not familiar with their students' native languages may request assistance from bilingual paraprofessionals, teachers, or other students.

Young children who enter preschool and kindergarten speaking a language other than English also need to be taught basic concepts (space, time, quantity, and body concepts) that are essential for the subsequent mastery of braille and O&M skills. Because it will be difficult for these non-English-speaking children to learn new concepts in English, teachers may want to design programs that use a combination of the children's native languages, when possible; easily understood phrases in English; and activities that require movement and handling tangible objects.

For preschool children who are blind or visually impaired and speak a language other than English at home, language assessment should concentrate on the children's language skills in their native language. Interviews with parents and other family members about the expressive and receptive use of language at home and observations of the children's interactions with family members and play activities with other children who speak the same native languages are essential parts of these evaluations. The assistance of bilingual professionals who can provide feedback on the children's use of language will be helpful to early intervention teachers who do not speak these languages.

Aptitude for Learning Languages

Students learn new skills at different rates, and learning a second language is no exception. One variable that accounts for this differential learning is aptitude. According to Carroll (1981), language aptitude consists of the ability to (1) identify distinct sounds, form associations between sounds and symbols, and retain these associations; (2) recognize the grammatical functions of words in sentences; (3) learn associations between sounds and meaning; and (4) infer the rules governing language. Consequently, a student who can code the sounds of language, recognize grammatical structures, identify similarities and differences in grammar and meaning, and use rote memory will have an easier time learning a second language.

Instruments for measuring individuals' aptitude for learning languages were developed in the 1950s and 1960s (Ellis, 1994). The two best known aptitude tests are the Modern Language Aptitude Test (MLAT) (Carroll & Sapon, 1959) and the Pimsleur Language Aptitude Battery (PLAB) (Pimsleur, 1966). The MLAT was initially developed to screen candidates for foreign language instruction at the U.S. Foreign Service Institute, but a number of different forms of this test have since been developed, including the MLAT-Elementary, which was designed to select elementary school students to participate in foreign language programs. One disadvantage of these aptitude tests is that they were designed to test the aptitude of persons whose first language is English for learning another language, so their use with ESL learners may not be appropriate. Furthermore, the practicality of using aptitude tests has been questioned (Bialystok & Hakuta, 1994), since teachers would still encourage students to learn English even if it was found that they had little aptitude for learning a second language. A more practical solution would be to incorporate the skills that have been identified as being part of language aptitude into the language programs of all students.

Other individual factors, such as motivation, personality, attitude, and cognitive styles, have received considerable attention in the field of second-language acquisition. For further information on these factors, see Larsen-Freeman and Long (1991) and Ramírez (1995).

Program Factors

Several factors relating to the instructional program also contribute to the language and academic achievement of all ESL students, particularly those who enter school with low levels of proficiency in English. Among these are the teaching styles of and strategies used by ESL teachers, collaboration among professionals, and assessments.

Teaching Styles of and Strategies Used by ESL Teachers

The availability of qualified ESL teachers is crucial when teachers for visually impaired children and O&M instructors begin to address students' language, academic, and mobility needs. ESL teachers can serve as a resource to

- explain the normal process of acquiring a second language.
- suggest ways to adapt the curriculum.
- suggest ways to incorporate English through content-area instruction.
- locate appropriate materials.

Although ESL teachers are essential, their preparation frequently emphasizes the use of visual cues in teaching English. Since the visual approach has limited or no utility for students who are blind or visually impaired, ESL teachers need to develop new ways of teaching that include the use of other modalities and activities that

- substitute real objects or models of objects for pictures.
- concentrate on the use of physical actions and three-dimensional models of objects when the real objects are not available.
- use appropriate tactile representations of objects or concepts.
- use written materials in braille.
- encourage students to use braille to complete assignments, rather than to rely on their oral skills.

In addition, initially, ESL teachers may not be familiar with the methods of educating students who are blind or visually impaired, so teachers need to refer them to relevant general publications, such as *When You Have a Visually Handicapped Child in Your Classroom* by Torres and Corn (1990). Although ESL teachers will not replace teachers of visually impaired students, they need to know about students' learning needs to provide appropriate instruction. The following suggestions point out some ways that teachers of visually impaired students and O&M instructors can assist ESL instructors.

STRATEGIES

ASSISTING THE ESL TEACHER

✛ Provide specific information on how visual impairments affect the way students learn.

✛ Share the objectives being worked on with students, so there is some connection and reinforcement of skills across programs.

✛ Observe an ESL lesson and offer suggestions for teaching techniques that are appropriate for students with visual impairments.

✛ Invite the ESL teacher to observe some lessons to become familiar with the techniques, descriptive language, and specialized equipment commonly used by teachers of visually impaired children and O&M instructors.

✛ Assist the ESL teacher in modifying lesson plans and materials so lessons are more appropriate to the students' learning needs.

✛ Share specialized materials with the ESL teacher so he or she can make them available to be used by students during ESL lessons.

✛ Help the ESL teacher locate written materials in braille, so students have access to these materials during ESL lessons.

Collaboration Among Professionals

It is imperative for all professionals who work with ESL students who are blind or visually impaired to be informed about the overall goals of students' programs and to collaborate in the development and support of the programs. Such collaboration is essential for students who have limited proficiency in English because fragmented educational programs limit the students' success in learning English and academic subjects. Following are some strategies for professionals to use to collaborate with each other.

STRATEGIES

COLLABORATING WITH OTHER PROFESSIONALS

✛ Ask the ESL teachers to explain the progression of second-language development and the ESL students' levels of English-language proficiency (see "Stages of Second Language Development," later in this chapter) and share information with colleagues about the students' progress.

✛ Communicate strategies that are effective and ineffective with the ESL students.

✤ Share materials that have been successful with the students so others can incorporate them into their programs.

✤ Discuss problems regarding students and ask for suggestions that will lead to possible solutions or improvements.

✤ Inform colleagues about conferences or publications on working with students who are learning English.

Assessment

Before school personnel can determine appropriate placements and instructional goals for students, they need information on the students' proficiency in English and their native languages and knowledge in academic areas. However, the shortage of qualified bilingual educational evaluators and school psychologists who can assess students in their native language, together with the lack of published materials in braille in languages other than English, have severely hampered the ability to apply best assessment practices. Consequently, school personnel may need to rely on alternative nonstandardized and informal assessments, rather than standardized assessment tools, when making decisions about initial placements or types of instruction. They may also need to question the validity of whatever procedures they select and realize that the information they gather from students of diverse cultural, linguistic, and educational backgrounds may be only estimates of what students actually know.

Many formal instruments for measuring the language proficiency of ESL students are not appropriate for students who are blind or visually impaired or are of limited use, since their administration depends, for the most part, on the use of visual information, and they have not been transcribed into braille. (For a list of language proficiency tests, see the Resources section.) Therefore, teachers either can use parts of a test, transcribe other parts into braille, and conduct informal assessments with the assistance of bilingual paraprofessionals or translators, or they can obtain information only on students' oral proficiency in English. Frequently, no information on the students' primary languages is gathered for assessment purposes, which leaves teachers with a limited view of what their students know.

Teachers can use the Student Profile form presented as an appendix to this chapter as a guide for determining what they need to know about the language needs of ESL students. Other ideas, such as the use of the cloze procedure to determine a student's comprehension in English, are presented in Chapter 7. The procedures for using the cloze test in English can be followed for using it in a student's native language, assuming that a fluent speaker of the student's native language is available to select an appropriate passage and assess the student's performance on it. (For a discussion of different ways of assessing students, see Chapter 7; for details on assessing linguistically diverse students, see Hamayan & Damico, 1991; and for language proficiency tests and academic achievement tests in languages other than English, see the Resources section.)

Assessments of students' proficiency in their native languages should include listening and speaking for young children and reading and writing for older children. However, since it may not be possible to conduct formal assessments in all areas because of the limitations just mentioned, school personnel should at least use informal measures to gather such information. This process may require them to locate individuals outside the school who can help the assessment team evaluate the students and communicate with the students and their families until appropriate school personnel can be hired, particularly when students speak languages that no one in the school speaks. Sources of such short-term help include community agencies, the school district's bilingual division, foreign language departments at local colleges or universities, and local translating agencies.

PARENTS AS PARTNERS

In addition to the individual and program factors just discussed, working in collaboration with parents and other family members of students who are blind or visually impaired and whose primary language is not English is another critical area teachers need to consider. There is general agreement in the field of education that school personnel and families need to work together to create better learning environments for students. However, involving families in activities that satisfy their needs and the needs of schools can be complex, especially when family members do not speak English or do not share the culture of school personnel. There may be numerous problems to overcome: language barriers; different verbal and nonverbal communication styles, perceptions of the role of the schools and parents' responsibilities in education, and expectations for children who are blind or visually impaired; ignorance of the special education system in the United States; inaccessible transportation; and limited or no exposure to braille.

These difficulties should not discourage teachers from establishing connections with family members and attempting to create successful partnerships with them. A desire to understand non-English-speaking families and learn more about their cultures is the first step in this process. Learning about the following characteristics of such families, some of which were noted by Lynch and Hanson, 1992, and Ortiz and Garcia, 1988, will help teachers and other school personnel understand and work with them. It should be emphasized, however, that each family's experiences are unique, so that it should not be assumed that families who speak the same language and come from the same culture are all alike.

- *Length of time the family has lived in the United States.* Knowing how long a family has lived in this country may be one indication of the parents' understanding of the U.S. educational system. If a family has recently immigrated to the United States, school personnel may want to arrange for an orientation meeting to explain the important aspects of the educational system. A translator will be needed to facilitate communication.

- *Child's schooling in the native country.* This information is particularly important for students who enter U.S. schools in middle school or high school. Parents whose children never attended school in their native country probably participated only in informal ways of teaching the children and may have limited experiences with more formal activities such as supervising homework or helping with spelling or math. They may not know about such specialized equipment as the braillewriter and slate and stylus or even about the braille system as a way to communicate. Thus, they may feel inadequate or unprepared to help with school-related activities at home.

- *Culturally based expectations for children with disabilities.* Since social, cultural, and economic factors influence the treatment of and opportunities for people with disabilities around the world, it may be helpful for school personnel to know the expectations that families have for their blind or visually impaired child. Knowledge of families' expectations will help teachers and other professionals develop goals that will be acceptable to family members and establish trust between them and the family. Culturally conflicting goals should be avoided until a good communication system exists, so that family members and professionals can express their views on the value or irrelevance of goals and activities.

- *Religious beliefs and medical practices.* It is important for teachers to have an idea of the families' understanding of the cause of the child's blindness or visual impairment, whether their medical practices are different from Western medical practices, and the comfort they may find through religious practices that may help them accept and cope with the child's disabilities. This information will guide teachers when communicating with family members and help them develop activities for students that are not forbidden by different religions or cultures.

- *Reasons for moving to the United States and expected length of stay.* Families come to this country for many reasons, including political, economic, and professional opportunities, or employment transfers. In addition, a child's disability may be another reason why a family moved to this country. The family's expected length of stay may also influence the student's motivation to learn English and braille.

- *School-related activities in which families may participate.* The level and type of involvement can range from visible activities, such as joining school-wide committees, to less visible, but nevertheless important activities like helping children organize their time at home so they can complete their homework assignments more quickly. Families' perceptions of their roles and responsibilities related to school may differ according to their countries of origin. For example, in some countries, schools and families have distinct responsibilities that do not always overlap. Therefore, families' failure to participate in school activities should not be viewed as a sign of uninvolvement or lack of interest; rather, it may indicate that family members do not view themselves as having the right to tell teachers and administrators how to conduct business at school.

Increasing the involvement of family members of students who speak a language other than English requires school personnel to rethink their strategies and approaches, reconceptualize their views of family involvement, and be willing to create new ways to make families part of the school community. The following are some suggestions that teachers can use to encourage participation of parents and other family members in school. In addition, "Resources for Working with Families of ESL Students" lists sources of useful materials and resources.

STRATEGIES

ENCOURAGING FAMILY PARTICIPATION IN SCHOOL

✛ Review the informational handbooks or program guidelines that families often receive when their children are enrolled in school to ensure that they are written in terms that families will understand. It is particularly important that these handbooks and guidelines clearly explain the rights of parents and families in the special education system and are translated into the languages spoken in the local ethnic communities.

✛ Produce a welcoming videotape to show to families whose children are entering school. This video can feature the different professionals and their roles, available programs, the history of the school, activities in which family members can participate at the school level, and other special features of the school. It should not only provide general information, but also transmit the message that families are a crucial part of the children's education and are welcome at school. In addition, teachers could produce a classroom video that explains the typical activities of the classroom; introduces the students, teachers, and other service providers; and shows some of the specialized equipment that the students use. If possible, these videos should be made in the languages that the students' families speak.

MATERIALS

RESOURCES FOR WORKING WITH FAMILIES OF ESL STUDENTS

✛ *Reach Out and Teach: Meeting the Training Needs of Parents of Visually and Multiply Handicapped Young Children* (Ferrell, 1985), a book that provides practical guidance, strategies, and resources for parents of infants, toddlers, and preschool children who are visually impaired, has been translated into a number of other languages, including Hebrew (by the Association for the Development and Improvement of Services for People with Disabilities and Mental Retardation in Israel [Almog], P. O. Box 3489, Jerusalem, Israel) and Italian (by the Servizio di Consulenza di Trento, Via Druso, 7-38100, Trento, Italy [0461] 39595). Publishers of these and other versions might be located by consulting catalogs of books in print that are published for most countries by R. R. Bowker (see Resources).

✛ *Building Blocks: Foundations for Learning for Young Blind and Visually Impaired Children/Peldaños del Crecimiento: Bases para el Aprendizaje de Niños Ciegos y Disminuidos Visuales* (Dominguez & Dominguez, 1991) is a bilingual English-Spanish book available from the American Foundation for the Blind (AFB) that also covers early learning from infancy through preschool and provides guidance, activities, and resources for parents as well as professionals.

✛ Braille alphabet cards are often available from organizations such as AFB. *The Burns Braille Transcription Dictionary* (Burns, 1992), provides the essential alphabet, contractions, punctuation, signs and symbols, and brief descriptions of rules for their use in print-to-braille and braille-to-print sections.

✛ The Blind Childrens Center in Los Angeles (see Resources) publishes a number of useful pamphlets in English and Spanish for family members of young children who are blind or visually impaired. Topics covered in the pamphlets include language and motor development and playing with young children.

✛ *Reaching all Families: Creating Family-Friendly Schools,* a booklet published by the U.S. Department of Education (Office of Educational Research and Improvement, 1996), provides information and ideas on strengthening connections between schools and families.

✛ AT&T's Language Line Services (800-528-5888) offers over-the-phone translations from English into more than 100 languages. Schools and agencies can use this service to communicate by telephone with family members when no translator is available at school.

✤ Invite family members to visit the classroom. The first time they visit, they can observe the class routine and their child. Later, they can be invited to share aspects of their culture with the class, which can enhance the classroom's multicultural curriculum, as well as reaffirm the school's commitment to family involvement.

✤ Conduct small, informal workshops on specific topics, such as Helping Your Child with Homework or Understanding the Way Your Child Reads, in which family members and teachers can share helpful tips. Small, informal workshops conducted by individual teachers are much less intimidating to family members with limited proficiency in English than are large, formal ones and tend to be much more efficient in getting parents to ask questions and solicit help. Furthermore, since many ESL students live with extended families, it is important to invite all the members of a family, not just the mother and father.

✤ Establish a family center at the school. The center can be a place where families can meet other families or teachers; relevant magazines and pamphlets are available for family members; and school nurses, social workers, school psychologists, O&M specialists, and other service providers conduct workshops that are relevant to families' needs. At the center, ESL teachers and others can formally tutor family members in English, and family members can share their languages with teachers and other staff members. The establishment of such a center will send the message to families that they have their own place in the school.

✤ Send home print copies of the braille books the children are using. It is much easier for non-English-speaking parents to help their children when they have print copies because they can look up words in dual-language dictionaries and explain the meaning of the words to their children.

✤ Develop bilingual forms to inform family members of their children's progress or of events at school. Bilingual forms can be created with the help of bilingual school personnel, bilingual parents or friends, or language-translating computer programs; forms can be duplicated and distributed when necessary. Forms created with language-translating computer programs should be read by fluent speakers of the languages before they are finalized. Language-translation programs are often advertised in software catalogs and business magazines and may be purchased in computer-equipment stores.

✤ Visit the students' ethnic communities. Visits to such places as restaurants, grocery stores, cultural centers, bookstores, music shops, and community events can provide some important cultural information about the students' families. Information learned or materials bought during visits can be incorporated into a multicultural or daily living skills program curriculum.

✤ Send home copies of the braille code with an explanation on how to use it (see "Resources for Working with Families of ESL Students" in this chapter) so family members can answer questions the children may have about it while completing their homework assignments or doing independent activities, such as writing letters to friends or relatives.

✛ Pair families who are experienced with the educational system with those families whose children have recently entered the school district or program to serve as mentors in dealing with the special education procedures. Both sets of families should speak the same language.

✛ Videotape individual lessons with a student and send a copy home. The video will show some of the techniques used at school to teach specific strategies for using braille, so family members can try to incorporate the strategies when helping the child at home.

✛ Arrange for the program to offer an ESL class for family members at school. By holding the class at school, families will feel that there is a place for them at school and will have greater access to school personnel. The ESL curriculum may include vocabulary on and topics related to special education, disability, and medical issues in addition to the usual topics covered in ESL programs.

APPROACHES TO TEACHING READING TO ESL STUDENTS WHO USE BRAILLE

The importance of helping students who are blind or visually impaired attain literacy skills and the complexity of the issues involved in doing so were covered extensively in *Foundations of Braille Literacy* (Rex et al., 1994). One important issue revolves around the models of reading instruction and specific approaches to teaching reading used in the classroom and their implications for students who learn braille. The models of reading instruction presented by Rex et al. and summarized in Chapter 3 of this book are the meaning-centered, skills-centered, and interactive models; the reading approaches are the basal reader, language experience, literature-based, and whole language approaches.

Reading models and approaches have also received considerable attention in the fields of ESL and bilingual education. The following summary presents implications of some of the various reading approaches for students who are learning English as a second language and is a synthesis of the writings of Carrasquillo and Rodriguez (1995), Chamot and O'Malley (1994), Garibaldi (1994), and Taylor (1993).

Basal Reader Approach

Basal readers are designed for students whose first language is English, so there are disadvantages to using only basal readers with ESL students without paying attention to their reading needs. In particular, such readers are based on the assumption that all students have the same information and have had similar experiences that allow them to understand the stories—obviously not the case with

ESL students. When reading many stories, students need to have basic knowledge about common events and celebrations in the United States or an understanding of cultural values to arrive at the same conclusions as other students.

Phonics Instruction

Two problems have been identified with using the phonics approach with ESL students. First, even if ESL students can sound out words accurately, they may not recognize the words if the words are not part of their oral vocabularies. Second, if ESL students use the sounds of their native languages to sound out English words, teachers may pay greater attention to their pronunciation than to their comprehension. In addition, the use of words that have phonic regularity but lack connection to students' lives and are not part of their oral vocabularies may reduce ESL students' interest in reading.

Whole Language Approach

The whole language approach focuses on teaching language as an entire system of communication in which listening, speaking, reading, and writing are integrated into the language arts curriculum. When using this approach to reading, teachers provide experiences that are meaningful and centered on the literacy needs of the students. Another aspect of the whole language approach is the rich variety of materials that are frequently available to students in classrooms. The following is a summary of the advantages to using this approach with ESL students:

- Teachers have flexibility in choosing topics that students can relate to and that take advantage of what the students already know.
- Students can learn comprehension, pronunciation, and spelling while enjoying literature that is culturally sensitive or that introduces them to the new culture.
- Collaborative learning, often used in whole language classroom, provides opportunities for all ESL students to contribute to activities.
- The individual pace allows ESL students to take the extra time they sometimes need to complete assignments.

Although the whole language approach offers a balanced language environment for ESL students, modifications are necessary to address the needs of individual students.

Language Experience Approach

The language experience approach allows ESL students to use their own oral language to create stories that teachers will write and share with them or their classmates. This approach has been used successfully with ESL students of all ages and can be used with one student to construct a personal experience story or with a group of students to construct a group experience story. A recommended sequence of activities using this approach involves the following steps:

1. Choose the experience.
2. Organize the experience.
3. Conduct the experience.
4. Discuss the experience.
5. Compose the story.
6. Read the story.
7. Conduct follow-up activities.

Field trips, science experiments, cooking activities, and other school events can generate themes for developing stories.

When using the language experience approach with ESL students, teachers need to decide if and how they will correct the students' oral language when they transcribe the stories into writing. Teachers may decide to write the students' language verbatim the first time and then follow an editing process with them to develop corrected products.

An additional issue to consider when using this approach with ESL students who use braille is how to introduce new braille contractions. As when correcting students' oral language, teachers can introduce new contractions gradually during the editing process.

Readers can review the general strategies for each approach provided in Chapter 3. The following are some suggestions of how to adapt the various approaches to teaching reading when working with ESL students who are learning braille.

STRATEGIES

ADAPTING DIFFERENT APPROACHES TO READING INSTRUCTION TO ESL STUDENTS

Basal Reader Approach

✛ Analyze the cultural assumptions inherent in the stories and explain them to the ESL students. When teachers take the time to discuss such information, the students can gain an understanding of the new culture from these stories.

Phonics Instruction

✛ Select the names of tangible objects or concepts that can be easily demonstrated to the students when teaching specific sounds and then have students use these words in sentences, so that comprehension and pronunciation are combined.

✛ Incorporate phonics instruction into other reading approaches; for example, when students write stories using the language experience approach, conduct phonics activities with some of the words the students have used and that therefore already have meaning to them.

Whole Language Approach

✦ Provide storybooks written in grade 1 braille, since ESL students may not be familiar with all the English braille contractions they need to read new words.

✦ Make sure that direct instruction is also included in the whole language approach. For example, Reyes (1992) investigated the use of dialogue journals with Hispanic students. (In the dialogue journal approach, students write in their journal about a topic or a personal concern, and the teacher responds in writing in the journal; see Chapter 7.) She observed that most of the students simply did not notice the corrections their teachers made and were not aware that they were making spelling and grammar mistakes. She concluded that teachers may need to explicitly show ESL students their errors and explain how to correct them so the students can improve their writing.

Language Experience Approach

✦ Be sensitive to students' feelings when correcting their errors. For example, model correct language, and ask students questions such as "Is there another way we could say this?" or "Let's try saying it this way," that make it easier for students to accept corrections.

✦ When transcribing the first draft of a story, include only the braille contractions the student already knows, and write words containing new contractions in grade 1 braille. Introduce the new contractions in subsequent versions of the story.

✦ Use the language experience approach as a supplemental activity to reading instruction, rather than as the main reading program. ESL students also need exposure to stories written in different styles to increase their knowledge of English.

Teaching and reinforcing reading skills is an important role for teachers of students with visual impairments. Consequently, knowing the benefits and limitations of each reading approach for teaching ESL students who are blind or visually impaired is an important competence that teachers can share with their colleagues. An excellent source of information related to reading and ESL students is the textbook *Kids Come in All Languages* (Spangenberg-Urbschat & Pritchard, 1994). Specific instructional strategies are discussed under "Planning Braille Lessons for ESL Students" and "A Model Lesson Plan," later in this chapter.

TEACHING WRITING TO ESL STUDENTS WHO USE BRAILLE

Students whose first language is English are often expected to enter school with adequate listening and oral skills and to have a developmentally appropriate understanding of the grammatical structure of English. Although students without disabilities typically have these skills, students with disabilities, including those who are blind or visually impaired, may not. Moreover, students whose first language is not English enter U.S. schools with a variety of levels of listening and oral skills, ranging from low to adequate, and have limited vocabularies, knowledge of the new culture, and understanding of the grammatical structures of the English language. Therefore, given the interaction among listening, speaking, reading, and writing, the success of students with limited English proficiency in attaining literacy depends on the degree to which programs incorporate and intertwine all four of these language areas into their curricula.

The key, therefore, is to provide multiple writing opportunities for students who are learning English. These writing opportunities will support the oral-language fluency of students as well as their ability to read in English.

It is important to emphasize that writing is defined here as composing and creating written work for a variety of reasons and purposes, rather than simply copying materials or practicing spelling words. In addition, prewriting skills in braille, such as inserting braille paper, learning how to operate a braillewriter, learning the keys of the braillewriter, and writing the alphabet are prerequisites to creating and composing written work.

A discussion on creating original written work via braille needs to include the use of braille contractions and the rules for using them, particularly for students who are not native speakers of English and who are likely to experience difficulty with spelling when expressing their ideas in writing. Unfortunately, there is little information on the development of written language in ESL students who use braille. However, the abundant body of research on the literacy development of ESL students who use print can at least provide some preliminary guidelines for teachers of students who use braille. The following suggestions are based on the findings of Hudelson (1986) and their implications for ESL students who are blind or visually impaired. Other instructional strategies appear in the sections that follow.

STRATEGIES

TEACHING WRITING TO ESL STUDENTS WHO USE BRAILLE

✢ Engage ESL students in the process of writing as early as possible. Students who are learning English as a second language can compose written work in English before they have mastered the sound system or rules of the language such as spelling, segmentation, capitalization, and punctuation. For example, they may use their knowledge of their native language and apply it to English, as in the case of a Spanish-speaking student who writes *da* instead of *the*, indicating his unfamiliarity with the English sound *th* and his ability to hypothesize how to write in English by using a sound from Spanish that may sound similar to him. ESL students make use of whatever they know about English to create written work. Likewise, ESL students who use braille should also be able to write before mastering grade 2 braille and need to be given opportunities to write in English without having to remember grade 2 contractions and their rules. Once they develop consistent vocabularies and sentence patterns, contractions can be introduced when they use those words in writing.

✛ Tailor instruction to the individual student and be flexible about allowing students to use grade 1 braille. Introduce grade 2 braille sequentially, depending on the progress of individual students. Some students may need to spend more time with grade 1 braille and then progressively make the transition into grade 2, as in the case of students who did not attend school before they entered the United States, while others can be introduced quickly to grade 2 braille.

✛ Get ESL students involved in writing in all areas of the curriculum. Students can use writing to express their feelings and opinions, create poems or stories, report, explain, summarize, or draw conclusions. Incorporating the language used in different content areas into their written work helps them understand the functions of writing and provides opportunities to use language. Students who are blind or visually impaired must be given opportunities to participate actively in content-area activities, such as science experiments, physical education, art, music, and health education. Through such active participation, they will learn vocabulary and the concepts related to it concurrently and use words in meaningful ways.

✛ Encourage ESL students to make changes in their written work on the basis of suggestions from readers. Although they may still have difficulty communicating their ideas, these students are capable of using readers' comments from teacher-student or student-student conferences to revise and edit their work. Changes that teachers may recommend include adding more information to stories and working on the order of words in sentences (for students with emerging language abilities); or editing the text for clarity (for students with intermediate or advanced levels of fluency). For students who use braille, teachers need to decide how and when to introduce contractions in the process of writing. As was discussed in the section on the language experience approach, teachers may want to teach new contractions and the use of contractions after students have edited their work for content.

✛ Be aware of the views on writing and the writing tools that are being communicated to students. ESL students' writing reflects their teachers' assumptions. When students believe that their teachers value writing that contains proper spelling and grammar, they limit their writing to those words they know how to spell and to the grammatical structures they know how to use. When teachers encourage students to concentrate on planning and developing ideas to write about and provide opportunities for revising and editing, students will view writing as a process that includes writing and correcting a number of drafts until the final product is achieved. The context in which writing is taught has an impact on the writing students produce, the progress students make over time, and students' views of the writing process. For students who use braille, the context of writing instruction includes the teacher's views of the tools used for writing (the braillewriter, slate and stylus, and computer) as well as the writing process. Depending on the audience they write for and the function of their writing, students may need to have access to tools that produce both braille and print (see Chapter 8).

It is important to stress that because ESL students speak a variety of languages and come from different countries and cultures, individual differences in their writing development can be expected, depending on the cultural traditions and literacy events these students experienced at home and in their communities. ESL students who are blind or visually impaired are also a diverse group with different ages of onset of their visual problems, degree of exposure to braille and to print, presence of other disabilities, level of education, and community and family expectations for them. Thus, it is common to find differences in the development of these students' oral and written languages.

STAGES OF SECOND LANGUAGE DEVELOPMENT

In order for teachers to plan lessons that are appropriate to their particular students, it is helpful to be aware of the sequence in which ESL students develop oral language. According to Krashen and Terrell (1983), there are four stages of oral language development:

- *Preproduction:* The student begins to develop receptive (comprehension) language skills in English.
- *Early production:* The student begins to develop expressive communication in English by using single words, phrases, and short sentences.
- *Emergence of speech:* The student answers questions and expresses himself or herself using more complex phrases and sentences.
- *Intermediate fluency:* The student participates in conversations but still lacks academic language to function at the level of native speakers.

It is important to note that during preproduction—also known as the "silent period"—students do not produce language; the length of this period varies among students, but it is a normal part of the process of acquiring a second language and needs to be respected.

It is not known whether students who are blind or visually impaired develop a second language at the same rate as sighted students because of the dearth of research in this area. However, based on what is known about the process that sighted students undergo, the following activities are suggested as appropriate at the different stages.

STRATEGIES

ACTIVITIES FOR TEACHING BRAILLE READING IN DIFFERENT STAGES OF DEVELOPING ENGLISH AS A SECOND LANGUAGE

Preproduction

✚ Select a few objects (nouns) typically found in the classroom. Pair verbs with the selected nouns and make action phrases, such as "Open [or close] the book," "Turn the computer on [or off]," "Sit on the chair," and "Place the book on the table." The phrases can vary according to the new vocabulary introduced to the student. Repeat each phrase and guide the student through the action. Then repeat each phrase and have the student demonstrate the action.

✚ Select parts of the body and appropriate verbs to make action phrases like "Touch your head," "Bend your knees," "Point to your nose," and "Lift your right [or left] foot." Demonstrate each phrase and guide the student through the action. Repeat each phrase and have the student act out the phrase.

✚ Select several basic concepts and pair them with nouns to make action phrases, for example, "Stand behind the chair," "Place the ball under the table," and "Take the pencil out of the box." Demonstrate each phrase and guide the student through the action. Repeat each phrase and have the student act out the phrases.

Early Production

✚ Select nouns that belong to the same category, such as apples, grapes, and bananas, and bring the items to class. Have the student practice naming the items. Pair the nouns with adjectives to create short sentences such as, "The apple is round" and "The grapes are small," and then have the student repeat them. Have the student create his or her own short sentences. Give the student a braille copy of the nouns and short sentences to practice reading them.

✚ Create a list of classroom labels (such as door, closet, sink, desk, and table) and braille each noun on an index card. Read each noun and have the student repeat it, then place the card on the appropriate place. Give the student a copy of each label.

✚ Read and have the student listen to simple rhymes, poems, songs, and short stories with repetitive language patterns. Have the student repeat parts of the rhymes, songs, or short stories, first with assistance and later independently. Give the student a copy of the important language patterns introduced in the oral activity.

Emergence of Speech

✛ Using the language experience approach, have the student contribute to the development of a class story based on a field trip, play, or other common class experience. Elicit verbal contributions from the student by using open-ended questions, such as "Tell me about the ————." Write the class story in braille and print using the comments made by the group, and then have all the students copy it.

✛ Read a story that is appropriate to the student's age level. Give the student an audiotape and braille copy of the story. Have the student read the braille copy while listening to the audiotape. After the student has listened to the story a few times, have him or her write a number of phrases or sentences related to the story.

✛ After the student participates in a daily living skills or O&M lesson, have the student audiotape the activities completed in the lesson. Have the student listen to the audiotape and write key words related to the lesson.

Intermediate Fluency

✛ Have the student create a story and write a "book." After the student finishes, have the student share it with the class during a storytelling time.

✛ Foster the student's development of specific content-area vocabulary by making sure that the student actively participates in experiments and activities related to content-area instruction. Have the student keep a vocabulary notebook and journal for each content area to help him or her master vocabulary and concepts. Vocabulary notebooks and journals in braille can be kept in three-ring binders. In the case of vocabulary notebooks, have the student write one letter of the alphabet on the top of each page and enter new words as he or she encounters them in reading, writing, or oral practice.

✛ Create activities that engage students in all areas of language: listening, speaking, reading, and writing. Students who are literate in their native language in either print or braille can use most of their literacy skills when they are learning English. For example, if a student learned to write words in alphabetical order and locate words in the dictionary in the native language, he or she will be able to use these skills in English without much difficulty. The following activities will help teachers incorporate all four areas of language:

  ▪ Engage the student in a lesson in which the student acts out verbal commands, such as "Stand up," "Sit down," "Clap your hands," and "Touch your head." Provide the student with a written version of each command and read it to the student again; then have the student read the commands and act them out again. Have the student copy the commands, at first using grade 1 braille to make sure he or she notices all the letters found within each word, and then introducing the contractions.

- Practice with the student acting out a number of action words such as stand, run, walk, hop, and jump. Present the written words to the student on index cards and read them to the student again. Then have the student read the words and act them out again. Have the student place the words in alphabetical order and then copy them.

- Give the student a number of simple written sentences that use personal pronouns, such as "My name is Wan Mei," "I am a girl," "I am 11 years old," "I have two brothers," and "I like to read." Read the sentences to the student, and then have the student read the sentences. Suggest ways of creating new sentences by changing the personal and possessive pronouns. For example, the student can change the previous sentences to "Her name is Wan Mei," "She is a girl," "She is 11 years old," and so forth.

PLANNING BRAILLE LESSONS FOR ESL STUDENTS

To date, no curriculum exists that is specifically designed to teach English as a second language to students who are blind or visually impaired. Consequently, teachers of students with visual impairments and ESL instructors need to be creative when using available materials and district-sponsored programs. The suggestions that follow, although general, can provide some assistance to teachers and ESL instructors who work with these students.

In addition, to assist teachers in understanding characteristics of students' native languages and recognizing some typical errors that ESL students may make in English, Table 6-1 summarizes some of the common difficulties of ESL students when speaking, reading, or writing in English. This information will help teachers focus on areas that may be particularly troublesome for students. It must be emphasized, however, that given individual differences, these errors are not always present in speakers of the same language and that some of the reading and writing difficulties may be more evident, depending on the students' reading media.

S T R A T E G I E S

TEACHING BRAILLE TO ESL STUDENTS

✛ Obtain a copy of the school district's ESL curriculum and follow the suggested sequence of language activities. Although modifications may be needed in the presentation of lessons and the use of materials, the language sequence should provide a structure that can be used with ESL students who are blind or visually impaired.

Table 6-1. Phonological, Reading, and Writing Difficulties of ESL Students When Using English

Language	Phonology	Reading and Writing
Arabic	• Short vowel sounds, particularly /i/, /e/, and /o/, are confused. • Consonant sounds are overemphasized. • The sounds of consonants /p/ and /b/ are confused. • The consonant /v/ is usually pronounced as /f/. • The /th/ sound is often pronounced as either /t/ or /d/. • When initial two- or three-consonant clusters occur in words, students tend to insert short vowels to help pronunciation. • The /ng/ sound is usually pronounced as /n/ or /nk/.	• Arabic is written from right to left, but numbers are written from left to right. Only consonants and long vowels are written. There is no distinction between upper- and lower-case letters. When writing in English, students tend to omit capital letters and have difficulty forming letters. • Students typically misread /p/ and /q/, and /d/ and /b/. • In Arabic there is no equivalent to the English auxiliary *do;* instead, questions are indicated by rising intonation. Students tend to form questions in English such as *You like to play?* or *When you went to school?.* • In Arabic, the verb *to be* is not used in the present tense. Students frequently omit this form in English, saying, for example, *The girl happy* or *She going home.*
Chinese	• The sound of /ea/ is often confused with the short sound of /i/, so *eat* may sound like *it,* and *seat* may sound like *sit.* • The sound of /oo/ as in *fool* and /u/ as in *full* may be confused. • The sound of /v/ is absent in most dialects; thus, /v/ is sometimes pronounced as /w/ or /f/. • Speakers of many Chinese dialects have difficulty distinguishing the sound of /n/, since it is absent from their dialects. • The sound of /th/ is absent in Chinese, so it is usually replaced with the sound of /t/, /f/, /s/, /d/, or /z/. • Students from the southern region of China have difficulty distinguishing the sounds of /l/ and /r/. • Students tend to either add an extra vowel to the final consonant or drop it altogether.	• English spelling patterns present difficulties for native Chinese speakers, since they use a nonalphabetic writing system. • Information is compacted when using Chinese ideograms. At first, Chinese students have slow reading rates in English because of the "spread-out" format of the alphabetic script. • English tenses are a problem, since verbs in Chinese are not conjugated to reflect time tenses. • Auxiliaries to form questions and negatives are not used in Chinese, so the use of *do* and *don't* require practice. • The spoken form of Chinese does not use gender distinctions; the pronouns *he, she,* and *it* share the same sound. Hence, it is common for students to confuse pronouns in English. • Articles are sometimes omitted or inserted when they are not needed, since articles are not used in Chinese.

Table 6-1. *(Continued)*

Language	Phonology	Reading and Writing
Farsi	• The short sound of /i/ and the sound of /ee/ are often confused, as are /a/ and /e/, and /u/ and the sound of /oo/. • The /th/ sound is often pronounced /t/. • The /ng/ sound is pronounced as two separate sounds: /n/ and /g/. • The /w/ and /v/ sounds tend to be confused. • The /r/ sound is difficult to pronounce. • Two- and three-consonant clusters are difficult to pronounce; students tend to add an /e/ to help pronounce them.	• Farsi is written using Arabic script. As in Arabic, it is written from right to left, but numbers are written from left to right. Since no capital letters are used, students have difficulty mastering the distinction between upper- and lower-case letters. • Initially, because of differences in the direction of reading and writing, students tend to confuse such letters as /b/ and /d/, /p/ and /q/, and words like *from* and *form* and *tow* and *two*. • In Farsi, adjectives always follow nouns, and verbs are usually placed at the end of sentences. In the initial stages of learning English, word order is difficult for students. • Questions are created by using a special question word or by intonation. In English, students tend to overuse intonation and frequently omit the auxiliary *do* when forming questions. • Since articles are not used in Farsi, students have difficulty with them in English. • In Farsi, no gender distinctions are made in using pronouns, so confusion between *he* and *she* is common in English. • When numerical determiners are used in Farsi, nouns do not take the plural form. Thus, it is common to hear students say *two book* or *five pencil*.
Japanese	• The sounds of /au/ and /oa/, are confused, so *coat* and *boat* could sound like *caught* and *bought*. • The sound of /u/ is often pronounced /a/, which makes it difficult for words like *much*, *such*, and *luck* to be understood. • The /th/ sound may be pronounced /s/ or /z/. • The letter /v/ may be pronounced /b/. • Students have difficulty with the sounds /h/ and /f/, depending on the vowel that follows. • The /n/ sound may disappear if it occurs after a vowel or may become /m/ or /ng/. • The letters /l/ and /r/ are pronounced like the Japanese /r/, which sounds like /d/.	• Consonant clusters are difficult for Japanese students, so they often insert extra vowels. • Students tend to forget to use the third-person singular -*s* in English. • Mastering the correct usage of articles and plurals is difficult. • Personal pronouns in Japanese imply age, relationship, and status. Since personal pronouns in English are not as exact, Japanese students are often embarrassed by the lack of choice. • Pairs of quantifiers, such as *whole-all, all-every, much-a lot of,* and *much-many,* are difficult for students to use.

(continued)

Table 6-1. (*Continued*)

Language	Phonology	Reading and Writing
Russian	• Distinguishing short and long sounds of English vowels is difficult for students who speak Russian, since pairs like *sat* and *set*, *seat* and *sit*, and *field* and *filled* often sound similar. • The /*th*/ sound is often replaced by /*s*/ or /*z*/. • The /*ng*/ sound is usually replaced by /*g*/ or /*n*/. • The sounds /*w*/ and /*v*/ are not clearly pronounced. • Final voiced consonants are devoiced in Russian, causing students to mispronounce words that end in voiced consonants, such as /*b*/, /*d*/, or /*g*/. • The combined sounds of /*th*/ and /*s*/, as in *three-fourths*, are difficult to pronounce. • The initial consonant clusters /*tw*/, /*tr*/, /*pr*/, /*dr*/, and /*br*/ are difficult to pronounce.	• The Cyrillic alphabet used by Russians contains some of the same letters used in English, but a number of letters used in English are not present in the Cyrillic alphabet. Students need to learn how to form the new letters. • Since auxiliaries, such as *do, have, will,* and *be* do not exist in Russian, students have difficulty with questions and responses that require their use. Typical errors include: *I no want it* or *What you want?* • Russian uses only a simple past tense, leading to errors in using the perfect and progressive tenses in English. • Russian uses only a simple present tense, leading to errors in using the present perfect or present progressive forms in English. • Future perfect or progressive tenses are not used in Russian, so students sometimes use the simple present tense to refer to the future. • Because Russian does not use articles, students have difficulty with them when they are introduced in English. • Nouns in Russian are masculine, feminine, or neuter, so English personal pronouns are difficult for students to use.
Spanish	• Vowel sounds in English often cause difficulties for Spanish-speaking students, so *seat* and *sit*, *sheep* and *ship*, and *pool* and *pull* are often confused. • Spanish has only one sound for /*b*/ and /*v*/, so words containing the /*v*/ sound may be mispronounced. • The sounds /*ch*/ and /*sh*/ are often confused, so pairs like *cheap* and *sheep* may be pronounced similarly. • The sound of /*y*/ is often pronounced /*j*/, causing confusion with such pairs as *yellow* and *jello*. • English consonant clusters are difficult for Spanish speakers to pronounce. • The combination of /*s*/ plus another consonant sound never appears at the beginning of a word in Spanish. When it occurs in English, the *s* is often pronounced *es*, so *Spanish* becomes *Espanish,* and *school* becomes *eschool*.	• All letters are pronounced in Spanish, a practice that carries over when students begin to read English. • Since Spanish has sound-spelling correspondence, English spelling presents difficulties, particularly with words containing double letters. • Word-order rules are not strict in Spanish, which leads to difficulties in following the stricter rules for statements and questions in English. • Since adjectives are typically placed after the noun in Spanish, it is common to hear students use the same word order in English, as in *house white* or *dress purple*. • Auxiliaries are not used for questions or negatives in Spanish, which causes errors in English, such as *When you came?* or *I no want*. • The use of double negatives is standard in Spanish, leading to errors like *I don't see nothing*. • Many English phrases that use forms of the verb *to be* use the verb *to have* in Spanish. For example, *I am hungry* may be expressed *I have hunger*. • Spanish nouns, articles, and adjectives have grammatical gender. Beginning students tend to follow this concept in English and produce errors like *The house is dirty; I will clean her.* • Because the *-s* to create plurals is also added to articles, adjectives, and possessives, students may carry this practice over into English as well.

Table 6-1. *(Continued)*

Language	Phonology	Reading and Writing
Vietnamese	• Vietnamese contains a highly complex vowel system with many more sounds than English. • The sounds of /f/, /th/, /g/, /z/, /ch/, and /sh/ are particularly difficult for Vietnamese students to pronounce. • The initial sound of /t/ could be pronounced /d/. • Consonant clusters are difficult, and letters are often omitted; for example, *abstract* may be *pronounced* abtrak.	• Spelling in Vietnamese is phonetic, so students find English spelling much more difficult. • Vietnamese is a monosyllabic, noninflecting, and entirely phonetic language, whereas English is a polysyllabic inflecting language. Students may require a period of adjustment to those novel features of English, particularly when they are not familiar with languages that share these features. • Forms of the verb *to be* are rarely used in Vietnamese, leading to such errors as *This book not good.* • English tenses are particularly difficult for Vietnamese students to understand, so they frequently use the present tense.

Sources: Adapted with permission from B. Smith, "Arabic Speakers" (pp. 142–157), J. Chang, "Chinese Speakers" (pp. 224–237), L. Wilson and M. Wilson, "Farsi Speakers" (pp. 129–141), I. Thompson, "Japanese Speakers" (pp. 212–223), B. Monk and A. Burak, "Russian Speakers" (pp. 117–128), N. Coe, "Speakers of Spanish and Catalan" (pp. 72–89), and P. J. Honey, "Vietnamese Speakers" (pp. 238–251), in M. Swan and B. Smith, Eds., *Learner English: A Teacher's Guide to Interference and Other Problems,* (Cambridge, England: Cambridge University Press, 1987). Copyright © 1987, Cambridge University Press.

Modifications might include changing visual examples to tangible examples, transcribing the reading and writing exercises into braille, and providing opportunities for students to use objects that may be new to them.

✛ The teacher of students who are visually impaired, the O&M instructor, the ESL teacher, and others who are involved in instruction should get together as soon as the student enters the program to design an Individualized Education Program that takes the student's vision and language needs into consideration.

✛ Use what are known in the field of education of second language students as "sheltered English" techniques when teaching in content areas. That is, use short, simple sentences; use familiar vocabulary and idioms; repeat and paraphrase ideas often; include hands-on activities; speak clearly and naturally, paying attention to the rate of speech and pronunciation; and check frequently to see if the student understands what is being said.

✛ Use instruction that integrates language in the content areas. The use of thematic units facilitates teaching English in the content areas (Milian, 1997). A detailed example of how to plan lessons that combine content and language instruction is presented in the next section.

✛ Use technology to supplement the language program. Although most available bilingual and ESL software requires some vision, students can work with peers and benefit from listening to language patterns (see Resources for a list of companies that supply bilingual and ESL software and Chapter 8 for information about using technology with students).

✛ Create units of "nouns," according to students' interests, language levels, and ages, by bringing objects to class every week. Discuss the uses and qualities of the objects and have the students talk and write about them. Possible units can be "Things We Play With," "Things We Cook With," and "Things We Find in a Garden."

✛ Use music to facilitate language learning. Songs that include repetition and bilingual versions of songs help students increase their vocabularies and reinforce language concepts.

✛ Provide stories that represent the cultures of the students. These stories can be included in reading instruction if the literature-based approach is used, for leisure reading, or as part of a multicultural program. They can be used as a tool to tap into students' previous knowledge and to help them make connections with new information that is being taught.

✛ Have students demonstrate their understanding of a concept by showing the action or providing answers that show it. Asking students "Do you understand?" will not provide a true picture of what they understand, but saying "Show me" or "Explain to me" will.

✛ Involve students in recording favorite books or plays. Students with lower levels of language fluency can play smaller roles and provide sound effects.

✛ Compile lists of terms in the students' native languages and keep them in an accessible place. Include terms for giving directions or instructions, for asking if the students need more information, and for preventing accidents. Since each situation is different, develop your own lists and then ask speakers of the selected languages for advice.

✛ Use the Voxcom (also known as the Language Master) to have students practice and review new vocabulary words, phrases, or sentences in English (see Chapter 3).

✛ Allow sufficient time for students to respond to questions and to create their own sentences.

✛ Avoid the use of idioms and colloquialisms until students have sufficient understanding of English to understand explanations of such expressions.

✛ Purchase an ESL activity book and use the activities that are appropriate for a student's age, level of English fluency, and cognitive ability (see Resources for companies that publish ESL and bilingual instructional materials).

✛ Teach students how to use the dictionary and have one accessible so they can practice using it and learn its value for reading, writing, and finding the meaning of new words.

✛ Value the students' ability to speak languages other than English and encourage them to use and share their native languages with others in class. Bilingualism should be viewed as an ability, rather than a disability.

✛ Have the school or agency join one or more of the ESL and bilingual national professional organizations. The journals published by these professional organizations can be placed in the school's library and articles can be shared with teachers who work with nonnative speakers of English. Two important professional organizations in the United States are Teachers of English to Speakers of Other Languages and the National Association for Bilingual Education (see Resources for their addresses).

✛ Use the Internet to gain access to information about teaching ESL and other topics related to students who come from culturally and linguistically diverse populations. For example, through Yahoo, search for Education: Languages. From there, select the site for English as a Second Language, where there is information on materials, lessons, and relevant articles.

✛ Contact vendors who specialize in hardware and software for individuals with visual impairments (see Resources) and ask about the availability of products with speech or braille in languages other than English.

As an example of how thematic lessons can be developed for ESL students, a model lesson plan that combines content from a particular academic area with language instruction is presented in the next section. This model was adapted from lessons presented by King, Fagan, Bratt, and Baer (1995) and Short (1991).

A MODEL LESSON PLAN

Developing the Theme

As noted earlier, lessons that are connected to a global theme are more successful in reinforcing language than are isolated lessons. The following is an example of a goal for a unit using a thematic approach:

> Students will become familiar with the characteristics of the solar system and its individual planets.

Identifying Objectives

Content Objective

The content objective is developed by answering the following question: What new content-area knowledge is the student expected to learn in this lesson? Typically, objectives are written using "observable" or "measurable" words, such as *list, summarize, describe, compare,* or *discuss.* Content objectives for ESL students need to match the levels of the students' receptive and expressive languages. For example, a student who is at the early production level may be able to achieve an objective that involves "listing" or "naming," but will not be successful with an objective that requires "discussing" or "analyzing." For the purpose of the unit on the solar system, the following science, math, and art objectives can be used:

1. The student will verbally provide the names of the planets in the solar system.
2. The student will place the planets in the correct location within the solar system, demonstrating their distances from the sun and different sizes.
3. The student will orally explain the basic concepts of the Impressionistic style used by Vincent Van Gogh in his painting *Starry Night*.

Language Objective

To develop language objectives, teachers need to concentrate on questions such as the following:

- What speaking, listening, reading, and writing skills is the student expected to achieve?
- What language structures should be introduced or reviewed?
- What braille contractions may be new to the student when working on reading and writing skills?
- What sounds may be new to the student when working on speaking and listening skills?

Some language objectives appropriate for the content objectives of this lesson include the following:

1. The student will demonstrate the use of *than* to make comparison statements by orally constructing sentences such as "Mercury is closer to the sun than Jupiter."
2. The student will learn or indicate his or her knowledge of the use of the capital sign and braille contractions (for example, *ar, er, th,* and *en*) by writing the names of the planets.
3. The student will learn the concept of ordinal numbers to orally construct sentences, such as "Mercury is the first planet from the sun," "Venus is the second planet from the sun."

Identifying and Defining a Target Vocabulary

A target vocabulary can be identified by answering the following question: What words are included in this lesson that the student needs to know to achieve the content and language objectives? Identifying vocabulary words and developing appropriate examples for introducing them are critical steps in fostering a student's understanding of the lesson. Based on the stated goal and objectives, some target vocabulary words for this unit are *solar system, planet, orbit, sun, moon, stars, distance, diameter, rotation, brush, stroke, landscape,* and *texture.*

Before starting a lesson, teachers can read the written materials, including textbook pages, workbook pages, or handouts, that will be used to cover the content area, select vocabulary words that are essential for understanding the academic concepts introduced in the lesson, and identify any new braille contractions in the vocabulary words. Then the teacher can present the target vocabulary to the student using the following suggestions.

STRATEGIES

INTRODUCING NEW VOCABULARY WORDS

✢ Explain the meaning of the selected target vocabulary words and provide examples of the use of these words before introducing the academic concepts.

✢ Provide the student with a brailled list of words and terms that he or she will need to master to understand the concepts covered in the unit or lesson.

✢ Summarize the content covered in the written materials in a way that is appropriate to the student's level of language proficiency by selecting the critical ideas or concepts and listing them using written language that is familiar to the student.

✢ Introduce new vocabulary words without contractions first to give students opportunities to practice specific sounds and spelling patterns and then introduce the braille contractions. The approach typically used for introducing spelling words can work well for teaching vocabulary words in braille to ESL students. That is, a new word is introduced in grade 1 braille so the students can practice its spelling, and it is also introduced in grade 2 braille so the students learn the contractions included in the word. Students can then demonstrate knowledge of one or both written forms of the word.

✢ Pay special attention to clarifying vocabulary words that are specific to subjects such as math, science, and social studies. For example, words frequently used in math, such as *plus, minus, equal,* and *sum* may require explanation and demonstration for ESL students at all age levels. Although an ESL student in the fifth grade may be able to solve written mathematical operations using the mathematical symbols $+$, $-$, x, and $\div$, the student may not be able to solve the same mathematical operations when they are presented orally or in a word problem because he or she may not be familiar with the English names for the symbols.

Selecting Materials

The best materials to use would be any type of concrete objects related to the topic of the lesson. However, teachers need to pay special attention to materials that students may not be familiar with, given their geographic or economic backgrounds. For example, in a cooking unit, many students may not be familiar with some of the ingredients included in a typical recipe or with the types of appliances found in the kitchen. Therefore, it will be necessary to spend time on the names of ingredients and the function of kitchen appliances so the students can benefit from the lesson.

In line with the goals and objectives of the unit on the solar system, some appropriate materials might include a three-dimensional model of the solar system, and books and videos on the solar system, such as the book and video versions of *Magic School Bus Lost in the Solar System* (Cole, 1992) and *Van Gogh: Getting to Know the World's Greatest Artists* (Venezia, 1988).

Developing Procedures for Teaching

Motivation

Planning activities that will generate interest and motivate students to learn about the topic are key to this step. It is important to design motivational activities that can provide information on the students' prior knowledge on the topic to guide teachers about the activities and specific content that needs to be included in the lesson. Motivational activities can be conducted in a variety of ways, but typically include discussions, listening to a poem or song, listening to an invited speaker, or taking a field trip to a specific site. Motivational activities need to be presented using language that is understandable to the ESL students; otherwise, the student may miss important connections between the activity and the lesson's objectives. A motivational activity appropriate for the unit on the solar system could include a trip to a local science museum and a discussion of what was learned on the trip about the solar system.

Information

The teacher connects the information generated by the motivational activities to the content objective by expanding on what the students already know about the topic. The activities included under "Identifying and Defining a Target Vocabulary" and "Motivation" expose students to the topic so they can better comprehend the new information.

Practice

Practice activities give students opportunities to demonstrate their understanding of both the content and language objectives by participating in activities that are directly related to the objectives. A variety of practice activities should be provided, so ESL students are not restricted only to writing and reading activities, where they may be at a disadvantage, particularly activities that involve reading from a textbook written for a specific grade level and answering questions based on what was read. In addition, ESL students need opportunities to practice their listening, speaking, reading, and writing skills and to demonstrate what they have learned through the language area with which they feel most comfortable. Practice activities have a connection to the overall theme of the unit and can take a variety of forms, such as the following:

- working with classmates to develop and implement a project
- getting involved with a community organization
- creating three-dimensional models
- inviting speakers to the classroom
- participating in class debates
- preparing written or oral reports

After the students complete the practice activities, teachers will determine if more practice and review are needed, or if they can move on to the evaluation part of the lesson.

Evaluation

The evaluation component of the lesson includes an activity that allows the students to demonstrate how well they have achieved the objectives of the lesson. Frequently, the term *evaluation* is associated with tests; however, it is not always necessary or desirable to limit the evaluation to a test-taking activity.

When designing evaluation activities, teachers should keep in mind that they may need to make some adaptations to the activities to allow ESL students to demonstrate what they have learned. The following are some suggestions for adaptations.

STRATEGIES

ADAPTING EVALUATION ACTIVITIES FOR ESL STUDENTS

✢ Have the student work with another student who is more fluent in English.

✢ Design assignments that can be completed in groups.

✢ Allow the student to use a dictionary while completing the assignment.

✢ Provide both audiotaped and written versions of the assignment.

✢ Allow the student to complete the assignment either orally or in writing.

✢ Modify the requirements of the assignment so they are appropriate to the student's language level.

✢ If necessary, have the student complete the assignment in his or her native language, provided that someone in the program can understand that language.

Teachers may also want to evaluate their presentation of the lesson to make sure that the students' difficulties with the objectives are not the result of the way the content was introduced and covered. They may use the following questions as a guide for such evaluations:

- Did I spend adequate time covering the content?
- Were the materials used appropriate, given the student's visual impairment and cognitive and language levels?
- Did I spend adequate time covering the target vocabulary?
- Were the modifications of the assignments adequate to allow the student to demonstrate his or her knowledge?

Extension or Follow-up

Enrichment activities to enhance students' recently acquired knowledge can be conducted either before or after the evaluation. For example, if students learned about American political parties in social studies, they can interview people who have come from other countries about the political parties in their countries and compare those parties with parties in the United States.

SUMMARY

Teaching students who have visual impairments requires specialized skills that will facilitate the students' educational success. When a student who is blind or visually impaired enters school with limited knowledge of English, teachers may feel unprepared to teach him or her. However, following a few simple guidelines makes the process much easier, such as asking ESL teachers for advice; involving the student's family; trying new ways of teaching; integrating language instruction with content-area instruction; being open to the new learning opportunities that working with non-English-speaking students provides; and asking people who have learned a second language, particularly those who are blind or visually impaired, to share their experiences.

Teachers need to be patient with themselves and with their ESL students. For a teacher, creating changes in a program to accommodate the learning needs of students who are learning English requires time, reflection, and new skills. For a student, learning a new language and adapting to a new culture and lifestyle is a slow process that requires time and understanding from the members of the new culture. Teachers of students who are blind or visually impaired and are learning English as a second language will be successful when they learn about how a second language is acquired and give themselves and their students time to adjust to the new educational and cultural situation.

REFERENCES

Bialystok, E., & Hakuta, K. (1994). *In other words: The science and psychology of second-language acquisition.* New York: Basic Books.

Bigelow, A. (1986). Early words of blind children. *Journal of Child Language, 14,* 47–56.

Burns, M. F. (1992). *The Burns braille transcription dictionary.* New York: American Foundation for the Blind.

Carrasquillo, A. L., & Rodriguez, V. (1995). *Language minority students in the mainstream classroom.* Bristol, PA: Multilingual Matters.

Carrol, J. (1981). Twenty-five years of research on foreign language aptitude. In K. Diller (Ed.), *Individual differences in language ability and language behaviors* (pp. 83–118). Rowley, MA: Newbury House.

Carroll, J., & Sapon, S. (1959). *Modern language aptitude test.* New York: Psychological Corporation.

Chamot, A. U., & O'Malley, J. M. (1994). Instructional approaches and teaching procedures. In K. Spangenberg-Urbschat & R. Pritchard (Eds.), *Kids come in all languages: Reading instruction for ESL students.* (pp. 82–107). Newark, DE: International Reading Association.

Cole, J. (1992). *Magic school bus lost in the solar system.* New York: Scholastic.

Cummins, J. (1981). The role of primary language development in promoting educational success for language minority students. In California State Department of Education (Ed.), *Schooling and language minority student: A Theoretical rationale* (pp. 3–49). Los Angeles: California State University.

Dominguez, B., & Dominguez, J. (1991). *Building blocks: Foundations for learning for young blind and visually impaired children/Peldaños del crecimiento: Bases para el aprendizaje de niños ciegos y disminuidos visuales.* New York: American Foundation for the Blind.

Dunlea, A. (1989). *Vision and the emergence of meaning: Blind and sighted children's early language.* New York: Cambridge University Press.

Ellis, R. (1994). *The study of second language acquisition.* New York: Oxford University Press.

Ferrell, K. A. (1985). *Reach out and teach: Meeting the training needs of parents of visually and multiply handicapped young children.* New York: American Foundation for the Blind.

Garibaldi, V. A. (1994). Selecting materials for the reading instruction of ESL children. In K. Spangenberg-Urbschat & R. Pritchard (Eds.), *Kids come in all languages: Reading instruction for ESL students.* (pp. 108–131). Newark, DE: International Reading Association.

Hamayan, E., & Damico, J. (Eds.). (1991). *Limiting bias in the assessment of bilingual students.* Austin, TX: Pro-Ed.

Honey, P. J. (1987). Vietnamese speakers. In M. Swan & B. Smith (Eds.), *Learner English: A teacher's guide to interference and other problems* (pp. 238–251). New York: Cambridge University Press.

Hudelson, S. (1986). ESL children's writing: What we've learned, and what we're learning. In P. Rigg & D. S. Enright (Eds.), *Children and ESL: Integrating perspectives* (pp. 25–54). Washington, DC: Teachers of English to Speakers of Other Languages.

Kekelis, S. L. & Andersen, E. (1984). Family communication styles and language development. *Journal of Visual Impairment & Blindness, 78,* 54–56.

King, M., Fagan, B., Bratt, T., & Baer, R. (1995). ESL and social studies instruction. In J. Crandall (Ed.), *ESL through content-area instruction* (pp. 85–114). McHenry, IL: Delta Systems.

Krashen, S., & Terrell, T. D. (1983). *The natural approach: Language acquisition in the classroom.* Hayward, CA: Alemany Press.

Landau, B., & Gleitman, L. R. (1985). *Language and experience: Evidence from the blind child.* Cambridge, MA: Harvard University Press.

Larsen-Freeman, D., & Long, M. H. (1991). *An introduction to second language acquisition research* (pp. 153-218). New York: Longman.

Lynch, E. W., & Hanson, M. J. (1992). *Developing cross-cultural competence: A guide for working with young children and their families.* Baltimore: Paul E. Brookes.

Manual de enseñanza de escritura y lectura braille. (n.d.). [Available from Editorial Braille del Comite Internacional Pro Ciegos, Mariano Azuela 218, Colonia Santa Maria la Ribera, 06400 Mexico, D.F., Mexico].

Milian, M. (1997). Using interdisciplinary thematic units with second language learners: Part I. *The Colorado Communicator, 20,*(2) 47–52.

National Center for Education Statistics. (1995). *The condition of education.* (NCES No. 95-273). Washington, DC: Department of Education, Office of Educational Research and Improvement.

Office of Educational Research and Improvement. (1996). *Reaching all families: Creating family-friendly schools.* Washington, DC: U.S. Department of Education.

Ortiz, A., & Garcia, S. (1988). A prereferral process for preventing inappropriate referrals of Hispanic students to special education. In A. Ortiz & B. Ramirez (Eds.), *Schools and the culturally diverse exceptional student: Promising practices and future directions* (pp. 6–18). Reston, VA: Council for Exceptional Children.

Pimsleur, P. (1966). *Pimsleur language aptitude battery (PLAB).* New York: Harcourt Brace Jovanovich.

Ramírez, R. G. (1995). *Creating contexts for second language acquisition: Theory and methods.* White Plains, NY: Longman.

Reyes, M. L. (1992). Challenging venerable assumptions: Literacy instruction for linguistically different students. *Harvard Educational Review, 62,* 427–446.

Rex, E. J., Koenig, A. J., Wormsley, D. P., & Baker, R. L. (Eds.). (1994). *Foundations of braille literacy.* New York: American Foundation for the Blind.

Short, D. J. (1991). *How to integrate language and content instruction: A training manual* (2nd ed.). Washington, DC: Center for Applied Linguistics.

Spangenberg-Urbschat, K., & Pritchard, R. (Eds.). (1994). *Kids come in all languages: Reading instruction for ESL students.* Newark, DE: International Reading Association.

Taylor, M. L. (1993). The language experience approach. In J. Crandall & K. Peyton (Eds.), *Approaches to adult ESL literacy instruction* (pp. 47–58). McHenry, IL: Delta Systems.

Torres, I., & Corn, A. L. (1990). *When you have a visually handicapped child in your classroom: Suggestions for teachers.* New York: American Foundation for the Blind.

Venezia, M. (1988). *Van Gogh: Getting to know the world's greatest artists.* Chicago: Children's Press.

World braille usage. (1990). Washington, DC: National Library Service for the Blind and Physically Handicapped.

STUDENT PROFILE
Students with Limited English Proficiency Who Are Blind or Visually Impaired

1. General Information

Student's name _____

Age _____ School _____ Grade _____

Name and title of person completing form _____

Date completing form _____

Date student entered program _____

Date student first entered U.S. school system_____

Did student attend school in another country before entering school in the United States?

☐ Yes ☐ No   If Yes, how long? _____

Language(s) spoken at home _____

Language(s) understood by the student (answer even if the student is not verbal) _____

_____

Language(s) spoken by the student _____

Type of instruction the student has received in the United States related to his or her native language and English-language development:

Type of Service	Length of Service	
☐ Native language instruction	from _____	to _____
☐ English as a second language	from _____	to _____
☐ Content-area ESL	from _____	to _____
☐ Speech/language therapy	from _____	to _____
☐ Other _____	from _____	to _____

Type of instruction currently provided to the student related to his or her native language and English language development:

Type of Service	How Frequently?
☐ Native language instruction	_____
☐ English as a second language	_____
☐ Content-area ESL	_____
☐ Speech/language therapy	_____
☐ Other _____	_____

Appendix. Form for Gathering Information about the Language Needs of ESL Students Who Are Blind or Visually Impaired

2. Language Skills: Listening, Speaking, Reading, and Writing

The student receives information through   ☐ Voice   ☐ Signs

What strategies do school personnel use to ensure understanding?

_____

_____

_____

_____

The student communicates expressively through

☐ Voice   ☐ Signs   ☐ Communication board   ☐ Other

If the student uses voice, what is known about the phonology and grammar structure of the student's primary language that may influence the clarity and quality of the student's oral communication?

_____

_____

_____

_____

_____

The student writes information in
☐ Regular print   ☐ Large print   ☐ Braille   ☐ Both print and braille

Did the student learn to write in the primary language?
☐ Yes   ☐ No

If the student writes in print (regular or large), what specific information is known about the student's primary language that may influence the quality and clarity of the student's writing? (directionality, type of alphabet, and so forth.)

_____

_____

_____

_____

_____

The student gains access to written information through
☐ Regular print   ☐ Large print   ☐ Braille   ☐ Both print and braille

If the student uses braille, did he or she learn it in the primary language?

☐ Yes   ☐ No

If yes, what are some differences between the braille code in the student's primary language and the braille code taught at school?

_____

_____

Appendix. (*Continued*)

_____

_____

_____

_____

(To answer questions about the braille code of the student's primary language, teachers may want to consult *World Braille Usage,* 1990, published by the Library of Congress.)

What else is known about the educational history of the student that will facilitate understanding of student's current functioning? (Some important factors may be past educational experiences, history of the ethnic group in the community, medical problems, school attendance, family's educational and social levels, and siblings' contributions to the student's education.)

_____

_____

_____

_____

_____

_____

_____

_____

_____

_____

_____

_____

3. Language Proficiency Levels: Listening, Speaking, Reading, and Writing

Proficiency Levels in Language Other than English			
Date	*Instrument*	*Area*	*Results*

Appendix. (*Continued*)

Proficiency Levels in English			
Date	Instrument	Area	Results

4. Instructional Goals for the Primary Language and English

Goals for Language Other than English		
Date	Area	Goals

Goals for English		
Date	Area	Goals

Appendix. (*Continued*)

ASSESSING THE LITERACY SKILLS OF STUDENTS WHO ARE BLIND OR VISUALLY IMPAIRED

CAROL ANN LAYTON

Carlos, an 8-year-old second grader, was adventitiously blinded at age 5 and has received services from an itinerant vision teacher in a mainstream setting for the past three years. He struggles to finish his classroom work and spends many hours at home laboring over homework. The Individualized Education Program (IEP) team has requested an additional assessment of Carlos.

Mia, a high school junior, was blinded as a result of a car accident. She has received braille instruction daily for one semester. The IEP team must determine her progress in braille and request another assessment.

Jacob entered seventh grade this year. Blind since birth, he has received consistent instruction since early childhood from a teacher of visually impaired students. Jacob's braille reading speed is unusually slow, and braille writing is difficult for him. An assessment of his current level of literacy is needed to determine accurate IEP goals for the coming school year.

Amanda, a fourth-grade student, is in a daily pull-out program for braille literacy skills and receives daily instruction from an itinerant teacher of visually impaired students. Amanda's regular classroom and vision teachers contemplate placing her in the regular classroom for all subjects, with some additional support from the vision teacher. Amanda is academically competitive with her classmates in all subjects, but are her braille literacy skills advanced enough to concentrate on or emphasize general academics? An assessment is needed to make the best decision for Amanda.

Assessment is the process of gathering information to determine what a student knows and can do (Hart, 1994). Instruction and assessment are not separate processes; assessment is a dynamic, ongoing process that guides instruction over an extended period. Because the intellectual, visual, and perceptual functioning of students and their achievement may vary over time and according to their ability, environment, and others' expectations for them, instruction in braille literacy skills must be based on the unique needs of each student. Assessment determines what those needs are and answers the following essential questions:

- At what level is the student functioning?
- What is the next step in instruction?
- What method will best expedite the student's mastery of the next step?

In practice, it is not enough for a student to master the techniques of using a brailler and to learn the braille code. Students must gain proficiency in reading and writing—a combination of knowing the braille code and expanding their cognitive and perceptual skills to learn to read and write. This chapter focuses on the student who is already learning to read and write braille and presents practical guidelines and resources for teachers for conducting accurate assessments and developing a repertoire of basic problem-solving techniques to facilitate literacy learning in the classroom. The initial assessment of a student's literacy media is discussed in Chapters 1 and 4.

During an assessment of a student's literacy skills, information is collected from many sources, including

- standardized tests
- direct observation
- classroom work
- portfolios
- interviews
- diaries
- checklists
- informal reading inventories
- miscue analysis
- criterion-referenced tests
- curriculum-based assessment
- diagnostic teaching

All this information is combined to plan and guide literacy instruction. The sections that follow discuss each of these sources of information and techniques for collecting the data (see the Resources section for information on where to obtain various assessment tools referred to in this chapter).

STANDARDIZED TESTS

Standardized tests have been normed on samples of students that are usually reflective of the most recent U. S. census before the date of the test. That is, the expected outcomes used to determine how the raw scores are ranked are based on the performance of a group of students considered to be representative of the national population. The instructions for administering these tests and methods of scoring are detailed to such an extent that the tests are administered in a consistent manner, and the tests generally have adequate reliability (that is, they can be depended on to obtain similar results each time they are used for the same student) and validity (they actually measure what they purport to measure). Standardized tests should be used with caution on students who are blind or visually impaired because they often measure the impact of impairments on students, rather than the knowledge or concepts that students have acquired.

Few tests have been normed on samples of students with visual impairments. The development of such tests is difficult because making comparisons among students who are blind or visually impaired or creating a homogeneous sample of students with similar impairments are complex tasks. Blind students are generally not a homogeneous group, owing to such differences among students as age of onset of vision loss, type of loss, and amount of residual vision (Bradley-Johnson, 1994). However, some usable information can be obtained from tests that have been normed on sighted students. Although the tests lose some of their validity when they are transcribed into braille, a comparison of students who read braille with students who read print gives excellent information for placing braille-reading students in mainstream settings. It should be noted that information from any standardized test must be weighed against other forms of assessment, such as observations or interviews, to verify students' strengths and weaknesses.

Standardized Tests for Assessing Literacy Skills

Few standardized tests that measure academic achievement are available in braille or large type. One such test, the Stanford Achievement Test (1989), measures word-study skills, vocabulary and comprehension. When the test was modified for students who are blind or visually impaired (Duckworth, n.d.), inappropriate items were omitted, and the results were renormed on the basis of the chosen items. Consequently, the normative data are still based on the performance of sighted students, but all the items used are appropriate for students with visual impairments. Another standardized test that is available in braille or large type is the Diagnostic Reading Scale (1981; Duckworth & Caton, 1992), which assesses word analysis, comprehension, and oral and silent reading levels.

Intelligence and Aptitude Tests

The Blind Learning Aptitude Test (BLAT) (Newland, 1971), a nonverbal test that was standardized on students who are blind or visually impaired, purports to measure some problem-solving abilities. However, the age of the instrument and the technical aspects of the standardization process limit its usefulness. Although the BLAT is an aptitude test, not an intelligence test, it can offer some information on a student's problem-solving ability. Furthermore, since it was developed for blind or visually impaired students, it can be administered with less caution than can standardized intelligence tests normed on sighted students.

The results from a commonly used measure of intelligence—the verbal scale of the Wechsler Intelligence Scale for Children–III (WISC–III) (Wechsler, 1991)—should be interpreted with caution. One practice that is helpful is to report the intelligence score as a range, saying, for example, "On January 25, 1996, John performed within the average range on the verbal scale of the WISC–III." When using an intelligence test like this, which was normed on a sighted population, examiners should note that comparisons are being made to sighted students, since with students who are blind or visually impaired, conceptual information often emerges more slowly after extensive experiences (see Chapter 2).

Standardized intelligence tests have several valid uses for students who are blind or visually impaired. Because literacy and literacy-related tasks are cognitive in nature, students' limited experiences or the lack of conceptual information may hinder their ability to use their cognitive potential effectively and hence have a direct impact on reading comprehension and written communication. Qualitative information about students' conceptual development and problem-solving ability that is gleaned from intelligence and aptitude tests can guide teachers in providing basic and enriched programs of general experiences that are designed to enhance students' understanding of the environment. Thus, the scores on these tests are used not to evaluate students, but to plan programs.

Occasionally, because of federal regulations, it is necessary to administer intelligence tests when informal cognitive measures indicate that a student may have mental retardation or a learning disability that will be a factor in planning his or her education. If a child with a visual impairment has had broad exposure to conceptual information through intervention but is unable to use this information effectively, these tests can give a measure of the student's ability to generalize and to solve problems. This type of qualitative information can help teachers document the specific needs of individual students, so they can plan effective programs for the students.

It is important to reiterate that measures of intelligence and cognition are uniquely integrated with conceptual information. Blindness or a visual impairment often limits or alters the conceptual information a student gains from an experience to a tactile-auditory part of the whole experience. Without the vicarious information obtained from vision, a student's potential may be significantly underestimated.

DIRECT OBSERVATION

Direct observation of reading and reading-related tasks involves viewing and recording students' activities in and reactions to their environment. Observations are usually recorded as notes or anecdotal records. After observing students during reading lessons, teachers often pinpoint behaviors that merit further investigation and think of new ways to teach their students. Unless teachers take the time to record what they have observed and plan for further observations, they may overlook important data that could guide instruction. Keeping pads readily available on which to jot down ideas and observations to be placed in students' records is a practical way to record informal observations and areas for which further assessments will be helpful. A generic observation sheet (see Figure 7-1 for a sample) is a convenient way to organize information (a blank copy of this form appears in the Resources section). The sample observations recorded in Figure 7-1 report that Matthew is not pausing at periods, commas, and question marks and is rereading several sentences on each page of text. The notes indicate that his comprehension is affected by his omission of punctuation. These observations will help the teacher remember to include instruction and practice for Matthew on attending to punctuation in reading. Future assessment will entail monitoring Matthew's reading to see if the instruction was effective: Is Matthew pausing at punctuation appropriately? Is he still rereading sentences, or has his problem been successfully remediated?

OBSERVATION RECORD

Student _____Matthew_____ Date _____9-15_____

Location _____Resource Room_____ Observer _____Carol_____

Time	Observations	Notes
9:10	- not pausing at periods - rereading several sentences	hurting comprehension

Figure 7-1. Sample Observation Record

CLASSROOM WORK

By looking for recurring errors in students' classroom work, collected informally over a certain period, teachers can gain insights into problem areas and the skills students have mastered. A beneficial way to use this information is to review the work with the student. Asking about the errors and the skills that the student has mastered gives the teacher worthwhile data and allows the student an opportunity to learn from his or her own mistakes by listening to the teacher explain and demonstrate corrections. This type of "thinking aloud" with a student can be an effective teaching and diagnostic strategy.

PORTFOLIOS

Portfolio assessment is a better developed and more elaborate system of reviewing students' classroom work. Portfolios are collections of work that demonstrate what students are capable of doing and are organized to show the depth and range of students' skills (Salvia & Ysseldyke, 1995). Portfolios are mirrors of learning in that they reflect students' continuous progress. Most portfolio assessments require students to be involved with the teacher in evaluating their own work. As teachers collaborate with students to produce evidence of students' advancing skills, in addition to guiding their instructional progress, the students can become much more involved and motivated in their work. The contents of *literacy portfolios* (a term coined by Cooper, 1993) may include samples of classroom work, records of independent reading and writing, checklists and surveys, and self-assessments. Portfolios are excellent ways to involve parents in the educational planning of their students by inviting them to read the portfolios and make comments about their children's progress.

Using a Portfolio to Document Progress in Writing

Writing portfolios are powerful instructional and assessment tools that allow students to learn from their own work. General purposes of writing portfolios (Hart, 1994) are to

- demonstrate growth
- encourage self-assessment
- document creative processes from the beginning to the end
- document the range of work the student produced.

These examples of braille writing document not only students' progress in braille, but their progress as writers. Some types of work that might be included in a writing portfolio, according to Hart (1994), are

- an important piece of writing with the student's written rationale of why he or she chose it

- a writing inventory, listing stories and reports that the student has written
- the evolution of a work, including the first draft, succeeding drafts, and the final product
- the student's free pick from his or her writing, along with the rationale for its selection
- the student's final reflections about the selections chosen for the portfolio, as well as the student's reflections about his or her growth as a writer.

Journals are another type of work that may be included in students' literacy portfolios (if the entries are intended for an audience). Journals can be effective tools for monitoring students' ability to communicate purposefully in writing. A variety of types of journals can be used effectively in the classroom (Cooper, 1993):

- *diaries*—private records; students should be informed if they will be read by others
- *response journals*—students' reactions to and questions about material they read; these can be personal records or read by teachers
- *dialogue journals*—conversations between individual students and teachers about what the students have read
- *double-entry journals*—entries made before, during, and after reading assignments; they may be read by teachers
- *learning logs*—daily lists of what students have learned during reading that may also be treated like dialogue or response journals

Dialogue journals are particularly enjoyable because they efficiently integrate reading and writing in a natural setting. Looseleaf binders make excellent journals and allow teachers to insert their responses in braille when appropriate.

Self-Assessments

Figures 7-2, 7-3, and 7-4, respectively, are examples of forms on which students can assess their own reading and writing and record the books or selections they have read independently. (Blank copies of these forms appear in the Resources section.) Figures 7-2 and 7-3 are forms that may be attached to particular pieces of work that have been selected to be part of a literacy portfolio.

INTERVIEWS

The content of interviews can range from a structured set of questions to a casual conversation. Parents, content-area teachers, the school librarian, and the student who is being assessed often have astute observations regarding the student's reading habits and literacy skills. Allowing them to participate in the assessment process enhances and enlightens the information that is collected. The information can be obtained directly during the interview or indirectly by having the

SELF-ASSESSMENT OF READING

Name _____ Date _____

The following piece of work demonstrates my strengths in reading. These strengths are _____

_____

_____

_____

_____

I will work to improve my reading by _____

_____

_____

_____

_____

Figure 7-2. Sample Form for Students to Assess Their Own Reading

SELF-ASSESSMENT OF WRITING

Name _____ Date _____

The following piece of work demonstrates my strengths in writing. These strengths are _____

_____

_____

I will work to improve my writing by _____

_____

_____

_____

_____

Figure 7-3. Sample Form for Students to Assess Their Own Writing

RECORD OF INDEPENDENT READING

Student _____

Date	Title of Book	Notes

Figure 7-4. Sample Form for Recording Books Read Independently

teachers, parents, and student record their answers on the forms presented in Figures 7-5, 7-6, and 7-7, respectively. (Blank versions of these forms appear in the Resources section.)

Asking simple, direct questions can often pinpoint simple and direct solutions to problems with schoolwork. For example, if a student is having difficulty turning in homework assignments, it would be helpful to interview the student, teachers, and parents about the reasons for his or her failure to complete homework. The interviews might reveal that the student simply needs help labeling homework in his or her notetaker, so it can be easily retrieved in class.

The questionnaire for the student's teachers can be expanded or modified to include specific areas of concern that have been raised during periods of observation and collaborative team teaching. It will also elicit additional thoughts from the teachers as they incorporate literacy skills throughout the curriculum and school day. The questionnaire for the student's parents (Figure 7-6) contains open-ended questions that give the parents an opportunity to offer insightful comments about their child's educational program. Questions on the student's form (Figure 7-7) should be modified according to the age and level of the student.

QUESTIONNAIRE FOR TEACHERS

Directions: The following questions are an essential part of the assessment of [student's name]. You have had [student's name] in your classes and have observed him [or her] in many settings at school. To help meet his/her educational needs, the IEP team would like to have some input from each of his/her teachers. As teachers, you know that each part of the student's day at school is important when assessing the educational needs of students. Please take the time to jot down some thoughts on each of the following questions. [Student's name] will benefit from the time you took to help ensure that his/her educational needs are addressed to maximize his/her strengths. Please regard this written questionnaire as a confidential part of the assessment report. Feel free to write additional thoughts and comments on the back of these pages. After you complete this form, please return it in the enclosed self-addressed envelope. Thank you for your time and interest.

Teacher's name _____ Subject _____

Student's name _____ Date _____

1. What are this student's learning strengths?

2. What learning strategies work best for this student?

3. What kinds of materials are most effective with this student?

4. What types of learning situations are most beneficial for this student?

5. What type of reading material does this student prefer?

6. Are there any specific observations that you can make regarding the student's current literacy needs?

7. What kind of literacy tasks does this student need to complete during the daily school routine?

Figure 7-5. Sample Assessment Interview Form for Teachers

PARENT INTERVIEW

Directions: The following questions are an essential part of the assessment of your child, [student's name]. To help meet his/her educational needs, the IEP team would like to have some input from you as a parent. Each part of the student's day is important when assessing the educational needs of students. Your observations are extremely valuable to the overall planning for your child. Please take the time to jot down some thoughts on each of the following questions. If you prefer to give your comments in person, contact your child's vision teacher or counselor, who will record your comments for you. [Student's name] will benefit from the time you take to help ensure that his/her educational needs are addressed to maximize his/her strengths. Feel free to write additional thoughts and comments on the back of these pages. After you complete this form, please return it in the enclosed self-addressed envelope. We value your comments. Thank you for your time.

Parent's Name _____ Interviewer _____

Student's Name _____ Date _____

1. How well do you think your child is doing in school?

2. Please describe your concerns about your child's work in school.

3. Does your child engage in leisure activities?
   If so, what kind?

   Does he or she do these activities independently or with other children?

4. Does your child participate in household responsibilities and chores?

5. What social activities interest your child?

6. Does your child require help with homework?
   If so, what is the best way to help your child?

7. What type of leisure reading materials does your child prefer?

8. Are there any specific observations you can make regarding your child's current literacy needs?

9. Do you have any comments or suggestions about additional support that is needed to help your child succeed in school or in daily living?

Figure 7-6. Sample Assessment Interview Form for Parents

STUDENT INTERVIEW

Directions: Your answers to the following questions will play an essential part in planning your instruction and schedule at school and determining educational goals that you think are the most important. Please take the time to jot down some thoughts on each question. After you complete this form, please return it to your vision teacher.

Name _____ Date _____

1. How well do you think you are doing in school?

2. Please describe your concerns about your schedule and the subjects you are taking.

3. Do you like to read during your free time?
   What kind of material do you like to read?

4. Do you enjoy doing schoolwork that involves reading and writing?

5. Are you able to finish your work in a reasonable amount of time?
   If your answer is no, what do you think is the problem?

6. What kind of help do you think you need?

7. Do you think your braille skills are adequately developed?

8. Do you require help with your homework?
   If so, what is the best way to get this help?

9. What are your plans when you graduate from high school?

Figure 7-7. Sample Assessment Interview Form for Students

DIARIES

Diaries serve as a link between school and home. Teachers may want to ask a student's parents to keep a diary of the child's activities. This type of information provides valuable insights into the parents' expectations for the student. Diaries are also useful for determining literacy goals and needs. Consider the following scenario: A third-grade student who receives daily instruction from a teacher of students who are visually impaired is struggling with reading. The teacher has noted that the student's progress is slow, so she asks the parents for information regarding the student's reading-related activities at home. The parents keep an informal diary or journal for three weeks detailing the time the student spent on homework and literacy tasks. After reading the diary, the teacher discovers several helpful bits of information:

- The parent is reading all the reading assignments aloud to the student.
- The student chooses books on audiotape for leisure reading.

In light of this information, the teacher makes the following changes in the student's schedule and instruction:

1. The student attends an afternoon study hall to help him or her finish homework that requires reading. The teacher encourages the student to read independently and uses paired reading (taking turns reading with a more advanced reader) to reinforce his or her reading skills.
2. The teacher helps the student locate leisure reading materials on an easy, independent level to encourage the student to practice reading skills.
3. The teacher and student begin a literacy portfolio that will include a record of independent reading.

CHECKLISTS

Checklists, in which items are grouped according to skill level, are a method of recording behaviors systematically. An advantage of checklists is that information can be recorded on an ongoing basis. Some checklists instruct a teacher to use a differently colored pencil for each observation of a student and to record the date of the specific observation in the same color at the top of the checklist. For example, both the date April 15, 1996, and all entries on April 15, 1996, would be recorded in red; at the next assessment, say, on May 5, 1997, both that date and the entries recorded on it would be in blue. This procedure enables the teacher to track when certain behaviors and consequential assessments have occurred.

One of the more comprehensive checklists of braille reading and writing skills is the Assessment of Braille Literacy Skills (ABLS) by Koenig and Farrenkopf (1995). The convenient and easy-to-use format of this checklist provides a thorough, systematic way for teachers to keep track of students' literacy skills. The ABLS is comprehensive; it covers unique features of braille reading, such as hand movements and tracking patterns, and advanced functional skills like writing term papers and taking notes in class. When a specific skill has been mastered, the date of the assessment is recorded.

The Minnesota Braille Skills Inventory (MBSI) (Godwin et al., 1995) addresses all the braille codes and most of the braille symbols that a student might encounter throughout school. It is organized into six sections addressing different areas of braille code knowledge: literary code, basic Nemeth (mathematics) code, advanced Nemeth code, computer code, music code, and dictionary/foreign language symbols. The teacher can choose the appropriate sections to offer to a given student. The symbols are presented in isolation to test knowledge of the code; it is not a reading comprehension test.

The Braille Assessment Inventory (Sharpe, McNear, & McGraw, 1996) assists teachers of visually impaired students to make appropriate choices in determining literacy media. It can be used as a comprehensive and objective checklist to document and monitor students' performance. The technical manual is easy to read, and the instrument is extremely helpful in planning instructional interventions.

The *Informal Assessment of Developmental Skills* by Swallow, Mangold, and Mangold (1978) consists of a collection of checklists for assessing a student's braille writing, scriptwriting, and typing. These checklists are extremely useful in formulating IEP goals.

INFORMAL READING INVENTORIES

Informal reading inventories are powerful assessment and instructional tools that are designed to be used by teachers. More usable information is acquired from them than from any other reading-assessment tool. The manuals are written in clear and concise language. Typically, they provide graded word lists and passages to match students with appropriate reading materials and to help teachers gain insight into the reading behavior of individual students.

These inventories give a teacher a wealth of information on a student's word identification and recognition, oral reading rate, silent reading rate, listening level, and comprehension. Most include a section on miscue analysis (discussed in depth in the next section) which gives detailed information about the types of reading errors that an individual student is making.

A number of excellent reading inventories are available only in print, including the Analytic Reading Inventory (Woods & Moe, 1989), Basic Reading Inventory (Johns, 1994), and the Burns/Roe Informal Reading Inventory (Burns & Roe, 1993). Thus, graded word lists and reading passages must be translated into braille format. However, the Diagnostic Reading Scale (Spache, 1981) is available ready-to-use in braille from the American Printing House for the Blind (APH) (Duckworth & Caton, 1992).

Informal reading inventories can produce key information for determining the goals of a student's reading instruction, as the following examples illustrate:

- If a student is reading on a grade level below his or her placement, the student may be having difficulty comprehending his or her textbooks. The instructional implication is to place the student at a more appropriate level or to provide remediation at the current reading level by providing more instruction and practice to enhance the student's skills.
- If a student's listening comprehension is below his or her grade placement, then the student may have difficulty comprehending books on audiotape. Extra support is indicated. Perhaps, a reader can explain the text in simpler terms as it is read to the student.
- If a student is unable to use phonetic clues, then he or she will be dependent on sight-word vocabulary and contextual clues to determine new vocabulary. Phonetic decoding skills can be taught at any age. The teacher can help by going over new vocabulary before the student reads a chapter and checking to make sure the student has well-developed concepts associated with the vocabulary.
- If a student is reading at a lower level than his or her placement, the student may require additional practice at his or her independent or leisure reading level. Many students who do not initially choose to read in their leisure time develop this pastime when they are given books that are easy and enjoyable to read.

MISCUE ANALYSIS

Analysis of a student's miscues is an instrumental part of any informal reading inventory. A miscue is a reading of a text that differs from the original. Miscue analysis enables a teacher to determine which cognitive strategies the student is using to read. This information is important because the goal of reading is to glean meaning from text, and teachers of visually impaired students need to focus on reading as a process, not simply braille as a code.

Readers use three types of clues to help them gain meaning from a text: graphic clues, syntactic clues, and semantic clues. With a *graphic clue,* the reader uses the configuration of the word (for a braille reader, tactile information) to determine the choice of a word and its meaning. In the following example, the reader substituted *cut* for *cat.* These two words have graphic similarity but no syntactic or semantic similarity.

> *cut*
> The dog chased the cat up the tree.

With a syntactic clue, the reader uses the sentence structure to help decide on a word and its meaning. In the next example, the reader substituted *cat* for *dog.*

These two words have no graphic or semantic similarity, but they have some syntactic similarity (both words are nouns).

> *cat*
> The dog chased the cat up the tree.

With a semantic clue, the reader uses the context of the sentence to identify a word and its meaning. In the following example, the reader substituted *kitty* for *cat.* These two words have no graphic similarity, but they do have semantic and syntactic similarity.

> *kitty*
> The dog chased the cat up the tree.

For a word to be *acceptable* in context, it must have *both semantic and syntactic similarity.* In other words, the substituted word makes sense and is grammatically correct. Acceptable miscues are made by good readers on a consistent basis and indicate that the reader is comprehending the text and probably has a good idea of the word that was in the original text.

The qualitative analysis system, developed by Christie (1981), is an easy-to-use system of miscue analysis for print readers. The method of miscue analysis described here has been adapted from that system for braille readers and offers a viable method of gathering important assessment information in five easy steps.

STRATEGIES

A FIVE-STEP MISCUE ANALYSIS FOR BRAILLE READERS

Step 1. Select miscues for analysis.

Choose material on the student's independent or instructional reading level (determined using the cloze procedure described later in this chapter). Ask the student to read the story aloud while you audiotape what he or she is reading. Record the following types of errors on a print copy of the story, using the notation shown in the examples.

✚ substitutions

> *mowed*
> Jack showed his new pet to Jill.

✚ omissions

> He named his (cat) Rufus.

✚ insertions

> *very*
> Rufus was ʌ long and skinny.

✛ word-order reversals

        for Rufus everywhere
Jack and Jill searched everywhere for Rufus.

Do *not* record the following errors on the analysis sheet.

✛ hesitations

✛ variations in pronunciation involving dialect

✛ repetitions

✛ prompts (the teacher providing clues to the student)

✛ omissions of entire lines of text

✛ disregard of punctuation

Step 2. Transfer the errors to the Miscue Analysis Chart (see Figure 7-8; the full chart appears in Figure 7-11, and a blank version appears in the Resources section).

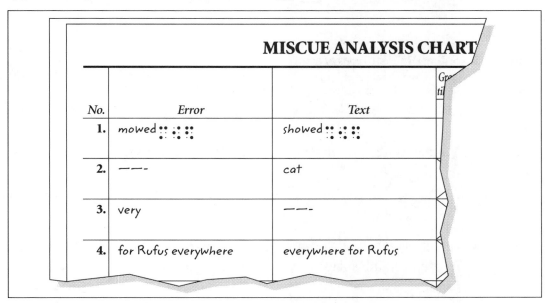

Figure 7-8. Recording Reading Errors on the Miscue Analysis Chart
Source: Adapted with permission from James F. Christie, "The Effect of Grade Level and Reading Ability on Children's Miscue Patterns," *Journal of Educational Research, 74* (1981), pp. 419–423.

The following rules govern the recording of errors (see Figure 7-9):

1. Record identical substitutions only once.

    John   John
Jack showed his new pet to Jill, but Jack did not let Jill hold the cat.

2. If the student makes several attempts to identify a word, record the first *complete* word or nonword substituted.

       2 mowed
       1.mo
Jack showed his new pet to Jill.

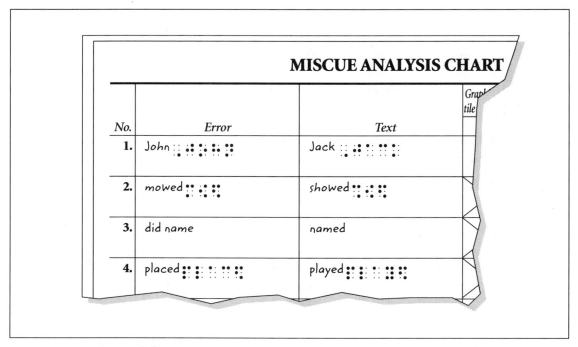

Figure 7-9. Recording Different Types of Errors
Source: Adapted with permission from James F. Christie, "The Effect of Grade Level and Reading Ability on Children's Miscue Patterns," *Journal of Educational Research, 74* (1981), pp. 419–423.

3. If one miscue causes the student immediately to make another miscue, record the miscue as one error.

   did name
   He ⌃ named his cat Rufus.

4. Note self-correction on the print copy with the symbol © (it is recorded in the self-correction column shown later in Figure 7-11).

   placed©
   Jack and Jill played with Rufus.

Step 3. Analyze the miscues.

Graphic/Tactile Similarity

The substitution of an individual word or nonword for an individual text word should be analyzed for graphic-tactile similarity and recorded in the Graphic/Tactile Similarity column on the Miscue Analysis Chart (see Figure 7-10). Do not analyze omissions, insertions, reversals, substitutions, prompts, disregard of punctuation, omissions of entire lines of text, or miscues that consist of more than one word for graphic/tactile similarity. (In the previous example, error number 3, *did name*, would not be analyzed for graphic/tactile similarity.) Record these situations by

MISCUE ANALYSIS CHART

No.	Error	Text	Graphic/Tactile Similarity — Yes
1.	that	the	✔
2.	was	just	✔
3.	walks	walked	✔
4.	find	finished	✔
5.	now	no	✔
6.	started	stated	✔
7.	now	was	
8.	up	down	

Figure 7-10. Recording Errors that Are Graphically/Tactilely Similar on the Miscue Analysis Chart

Source: Adapted with permission from James F. Christie, "The Effect of Grade Level and Reading Ability on Children's Miscue Patterns," *Journal of Educational Research, 74* (1981), pp. 419–423.

drawing an *X* through the box under Graphic/Tactile Similarity on the Miscue Analysis Chart. To determine graphic/tactile similarity, do the following:

✛ Compare the braille cell configuration. Graphic/tactile similarity is determined by the number and position of dots in the braille cell, rather than by the sequence and shape of the print letters.

✛ Applying the system devised by Sowell and Sledge (1986), use the following criteria to judge graphic/tactile similarity in miscues. The following types of mistakes are considered graphically or tactilely similar and should be marked yes in the Graphic/Tactile Similarity box of the Miscue Analysis Chart (see Figure 7-10).

1. One- or two-dot differences and/or a similar configuration:

that dots 2,3,4,5

the dots 2,3,4,6

2. A change in the position of dots in the braille cell:

   was   dots 3,5,6

   just   dots 2,4,5

3. Changes of inflectional endings:

   (walk)s

   (walk)ed

4. A three or more cell similarity in a word:

   f/in/d

   f/in/i/sh/ed

5. A reversal:

   n/ow   dots 2,4,6

   n/o   dots 1,3,5

6. A one-letter difference in a word:

   st/ar/t/ed

   st/a/t/ed

Acceptability in Context

Judge all errors recorded on the Miscue Analysis Chart for their acceptability in context, taking the following two factors into account:

1. Syntax: Is the error grammatically acceptable in the context of the entire sentence?
2. Semantics: Does the error make sense in the context of the sentence and the preceding portion of the paragraph?

If the error is *both* syntactically and semantically acceptable, check the box in the Acceptable column. If the error is not both syntactically or semantically similar, check the box in the Unacceptable column (see Figure 7-11). Only unacceptable miscues are further analyzed. To call attention to an acceptable miscue would disrupt the flow of the story. Since compehension is the goal of all reading, it is better if the reader does not stop to self-correct acceptable miscues.

Step 4. Determine the totals and percentages.

Graphic/Tactile Similarity

1. Count the number of checks in the Yes column for graphic/tactile similarity. Place the total in the box marked Column Total (see Figure 7-11).
2. Count the number of boxes that do not have *X*s in them. Place each total in the box marked Number of Errors Analyzed.
3. Determine the percentage of errors that were graphically or tactilely similar by dividing the column total by the number of errors analyzed (see Figure 7-12) and record.

MISCUE ANALYSIS CHART

No.	*Error*	*Text*	*Graphic/Tactile Similarity*	*Context*		*Self-Correction*
			Yes	*Acceptable*	*Unacceptable*	
1.	mowed ⠍⠪⠫	showed ⠩⠪⠫	✔		✔	
2.	——-	cat	☒		✔	
3.	very	——-	☒	✔		
4.	for Rufus everywhere	everywhere for Rufus	☒	✔		
5.	placed ⠏⠇⠁⠉⠫	played ⠏⠇⠁⠽⠫	✔		✔	✔
6.						
7.						
8.						
9.						
10.						
11.						
12.						
13.						
14.						
15.						
		Column Total				
		Number of Errors Analyzed				
		Percentage				

Figure 7-11. Recording Errors that Are Syntactically and Semantically Acceptable or Unacceptable

Source: Adapted from James F. Christie, "The Effect of Grade Level and Reading Ability on Children's Miscue Patterns," *Journal of Educational Research, 74* (1981), pp. 419–423.

Acceptability in Context

1. Count the number of checks in the Acceptable and Unacceptable columns. Enter each total in the appropriate column total box:

2. In the Acceptable column only:

✛ enter the total number of errors analyzed for acceptability in context in the box marked Number of Errors Analyzed. (This number should equal the total number of errors recorded on the analysis sheet.)

✛ determine the percentage of errors that were acceptable in context by dividing the column total by the total number of errors analyzed (see Figure 7-12).

Unacceptability in Context

1. Count the number of errors in the Unacceptable column only that were self-corrected.

2. Determine the percentage of unacceptable errors that the student corrected him- or herself by dividing the column total for unacceptable self-corrected errors by the column total for unacceptable errors in context (see Figure 7-12).

Profile Sheet

1. Transfer the percentages from the Miscue Analysis Chart to the blanks below the appropriate bar graphs in the Profile Sheet (see Figure 7-13). (A blank version of this form appears in the Resources section.)

A HANDY GUIDE TO CALCULATING TOTALS AND PERCENTAGES

Graphic/tactile similarity

a. Column total (number of checks in the Yes column) _____

b. Number of errors analyzed (total boxes without *X*s) _____

c. Percentage of miscues with graphic similarity (a ÷ b) _____ %

Acceptability in context

a. Column total (number of checks in the Acceptable column) _____

b. Number of errors analyzed (total number of errors analyzed) _____

c. Percentage of miscues acceptable in context (a ÷ b) _____ %

Correction strategy

a. Column total (number of unacceptable miscues self-corrected) _____

b. Number of errors analyzed (total unacceptable miscues) _____

c. Percentage of unacceptable miscues self-corrected (a ÷ b) _____ %

Figure 7-12. Form for Calculating Totals and Percentages
Source: Adapted with permission from *Learning Media Assessment* by Alan J. Koenig and M. Cay Holbrook. Copyright © 1993, by the Texas School for the Blind.

PROFILE

PREDICTION STRATEGY		CORRECTION STRATEGY
_____		_____

Graphic/Tactile Similarity	*Errors Acceptable in Context*	*Unacceptable Errors, Self-Corrected*
100 % _____	100 % _____	100 % _____
90 % _____	90 % _____	90 % _____
80 % _____	80 % _____	80 % _____
70 % _____	70 % _____	70 % _____
60 % _____	60 % _____	60 % _____
50 % _____	50 % _____	50 % _____
40 % _____	40 % _____	40 % _____
30 % _____	30 % _____	30 % _____
20 % _____	20 % _____	20 % _____
10 % _____	10 % _____	10 % _____
0 % _____	0 % _____	0 % _____
_____	_____	_____

Figure 7-13. Sample Miscue Analysis Profile Sheet
Source: Adapted from James F. Christie, "The Effect of Grade Level and Reading Ability on Children's Miscue Patterns," *Journal of Educational Research, 74* (1981), pp. 419–423.

2. Fill in the bar graphs.

A sample exercise to give practice in miscue analysis appears as an appendix to this chapter.

Step 5. Apply the results to reading instruction.

The profile sheet can give the teacher valuable information that can be applied to the devleopment of instructional strategies. The following are some examples of how a teacher might apply the results of a miscue analysis to problem solving.

✛ If the percentages for both graphic/tactile similarity and the number of acceptable miscues are high, a teacher can assume that the strategies the student uses allow him or her to understand (gain meaning from) the text. However, the student still needs to become more proficient in the braille code. To measure the student's skills in reading the braille code, the teacher needs to apply the ABLS Checklist (Koenig & Farrenkopf, 1995) or a similar checklist.

✛ If the percentage for graphic similarity is high and errors acceptable in context is low, the student may not be relying on contextual clues. The student may be focusing too much attention on word identification instead of comprehending the text.

✛ If the percentages for both graphic similarity and errors acceptable in context are low, the student may be placing too much emphasis on the context of the story. When a problem exists in one of these areas, strategies to remediate either decoding difficulties or practice using contextual clues can be implemented. If both problems exist, the student may require easier reading material. Students should read material and gain experience with vocabulary that is easily decoded and comprehended.

✛ If the correction strategy shows that the student has a low percentage of self-correcting unacceptable miscues, the student's understanding of the text is being disrupted. The student may need some assistance in developing the ability to monitor his or her own reading. A low percentage of self-correcting miscues might also indicate problems with comprehension. The student may need some instruction in strategies to improve his or her comprehension (including practice with semantic and syntactic cues) and may require help with his or her braille skills. By examining the miscues, the teacher will be able to determine the specific areas that need remediation.

After analyzing the results from a miscue analysis, the teacher has to decide on and apply a variety of strategies that will enable the student to learn the braille code and engage in the cognitive process of comprehending the text.

CRITERION-REFERENCED TESTS

Criterion-referenced tests provide information about a student's level of skills by comparing the student's knowledge against a standard. No normative data are acquired from this type of test—that is, the student is not compared with a normative sample; the test simply establishes which skills the student has mastered. Criterion-referenced tests are easily adapted for braille readers because there are no standardized directions to violate and their validity is focused on the criterion used to measure the particular skills. To ensure that the modifications for braille readers are appropriate, the examiner must determine if each adapted item still assesses what the original item assessed. If so, the validity of the instrument has not been compromised.

Some of the most frequently used criterion-referenced tests are the comprehensive, multilevel Brigance Diagnostic Inventories. The Brigance Diagnostic Comprehensive Inventory of Basic Skills (Brigance, 1983) and the revised Brigance Diagnostic Inventory of Early Development (Brigance, 1991), both of which are available from APH (see Resources), come with tactile supplements that include braille reading passages. The basic-skills inventory measures detailed word analysis, word recognition, spelling, punctuation, capitalization, and writing letters and envelopes. The early-development inventory measures readiness, phonics, and word recognition. Not all of the Brigance tests can be used effectively with students who are blind or visually impaired; teachers of students who are visually impaired have to choose appropriate sections for individual students. Teachers can link assessment to instruction by using the behavioral objectives in these tests, which provide a good overview of each domain (for example, letter recognition). Pinpointing areas in which mastery is not indicated leads teachers to develop instructional objectives in an appropriate next-step format.

Other criterion-referenced tests include the Braille Unit Recognition Battery (Caton, Duckworth, & Rankin, 1985), which measures the identification of braille units by students in Grades 3–12; the Diagnostic Reading Scales (Spache, 1981), a norm-referenced test that can be used as a criterion-referenced test; and the Basic Reading Rate Scale (Duckworth & Caton, 1986) (available in both braille and large-type editions), which measures reading rate. All are available from APH.

CURRICULUM-BASED ASSESSMENT

Curriculum-based assessment evaluates which reading skills students have retained and are able to apply, using chapter tests from textbooks and teacher-prepared tests, which are often more valid than are individually administered achievement tests because they cover the actual instruction in which students have participated. When this type of assessment is used, the teachers can modify assessments in the same way that they modify instruction. For students who consistently do poorly on chapter tests, teachers must determine if the problems are the result of content that is too difficult for the students or inadequate reading or writing skills. For further information on curriculum-based assessment, see Salvia and Hughes (1990).

DIAGNOSTIC TEACHING

Diagnostic teaching is one of the most dynamic ways to assess and modify instruction. In simple terms, it involves monitoring a student's responses and making changes in methods and materials, if necessary, while presenting a lesson. If instructional strategies are not leading to progress, the instruction needs to be modified to suit the needs of the individual student. Thus, diagnostic teaching is problem solving in action. During diagnostic teaching, it is often advantageous to include the student in the assessment process by giving immediate feedback and allowing the student to set his or her own goals. Coupling diagnostic teaching with goal setting gives a teacher a powerful motivational tool.

Oral Retellings

Oral retellings, a strategy that is used as a measure of reading comprehension, is a good example of how diagnostic teaching may be used as an assessment and instructional tool. As the name suggests, in oral retelling, students are asked to describe in their own words what happens in a story they have just read. Oral retelling is an informal comprehension measure whose efficacy was established by Fuchs, Fuchs, and Maxwell (1988). It is commonly a part of miscue analysis (Goodman, Watson, & Burke, 1987), but can be used independently as well. The approach focuses the student on recall and getting meaning from text and increases the student's reading skills. A teacher may use oral retellings to pinpoint a student's difficulty comprehending a textbook, for example, and, at the same time, guide the student through the instruction by asking prompting questions. The following are appropriate prompts to use:

1. "Tell about the story as you would to someone who never heard it before."
2. If the student hesitates, say "What comes next?"
3. If the student is unable to start the retelling, prompt him or her with a few of these questions:
   - "What happened in the story?"
   - "Who was the story about?"
   - "When did the story take place?"
   - "Where did the story occur?"
   - "Was there a problem in the story?"
   - "How did the story end?"

Retellings can be used to compare reading comprehension and listening comprehension. They can also be used to compare a student's comprehension with material at different reading levels. For example, give the student easy reading materials and ask for a retelling. Record the retelling on audiotape. The next day, read from some of the student's instructional materials and record the retelling. It is common for comprehension to drop when many new vocabulary words are introduced. Since science and social studies textbooks are often written at levels higher than a student's achievement level, the material is often difficult to read. All the student's attention is focused on reading the words, and little is left for comprehension. Retellings easily establish a student's ability to comprehend material. Therefore, it is good practice to monitor the student's comprehension of all his or her textbooks. Although books on audiotape may be used when the text is well above the student's reading level, the student's listening comprehension level should also be checked.

Many of the strategies listed in other chapters can be easily used in diagnostic teaching. For example, the technique of repeated readings (see Chapter 3) has a built-in assessment component that enables a teacher to modify instruction and assess its effect on a daily basis. Some other examples of instructional strategies that can be used for diagnostic teaching, such as those involving word identification, reading rate, and comprehension, follow.

Word Identification

Word identification refers to the ability to use phonetic clues (sounding out words), semantic-syntactic clues (deriving meaning from the context), and structural clues (examining prefixes and suffixes) to identify unknown words. It also refers to the ability to recall words that were previously encountered; thus, word recognition and memory are inseparable. The following assessment strategies can help teachers understand the word-identification approaches used by students.

S T R A T E G I E S

ASSESSING STUDENTS' WORD-IDENTIFICATION APPROACHES

✛ Use flash cards with braille characters to assess students' recognition of both letters and the specific sounds that each letter represents (see Chapter 3). Flash cards become part of daily drills that students can easily monitor. Here are a few variations on the limitless questions a teacher can ask to make assessment a game using these cards:

- "How quickly can you name all the letters in the stack of flash cards?"
- "Can you name a word that begins with this letter?"
- "Can you recall a word that ends with this letter?"

The teacher can simply record the information gained from this activity or help students record it in a meaningful way using a tactile chart or graph. The objective is to help students acquire more words in their automatic reading vocabulary.

✛ Use a basic sight-word list (words most commonly used in written English), such as the Dolch Basic Sight Word List (Dolch, 1936), to assess word recognition. The Dolch word list is available on word cards printed in braille from APH. Arranging the words in consecutive levels will give the teacher an idea of how many commonly used words are in a student's automatic repertoire. A checklist constructed from these basic sight words can be used to teach a few new words each week. Students should be encouraged to make these words part of a bank of words that they recall automatically without having to use word-identification clues such as phonetics.

Students can keep track of their own assessments in this area by graphing the number of words from the checklist that they automatically recall, a strategy that motivates them to learn more words. Teachers can introduce goal setting by discussing with students the number of words that should be added to the list in a given week. These frequently used words can be drilled daily for added practice. After the students have mastered their entire lists, teachers can add a time element to see how quickly the students read their entire list. Students can then graph the time it takes; as they read more quickly, they will note that the decreasing time it is taking to read the list indicates their progress.

✤ The cloze procedure, developed by Taylor (1953), is based on the theory that people want to complete unfinished patterns. It relies on the ability to predict unknown words in a reading passage using both semantic and structural clues (see Chapter 3). In creating cloze activities, it is generally preferable to use paragraphs of about 250 words at a student's approximate instructional level. The first and last sentences of a paragraph are reproduced without deletions, and in the other sentences, every *n*th word is replaced with a blank to be filled in. No proper nouns or unusually difficult vocabulary words are deleted. The younger or more inexperienced a reader, the greater the intervals between deletions. For example, many teachers recommend that for beginning readers, every 10th word should be deleted, compared to every fifth word for experienced readers. Young, inexperienced readers may also benefit from a "word bank," from which they can make appropriate choices.

The commonly accepted way to score a traditional cloze procedure is to omit every fifth word in a passage of 250 words (Miller, 1993). The number of blanks that are correctly filled in with the omitted word is divided by the total number of blanks to derive a percentage. Students are not penalized for spelling errors. Thus, if there were 40 blanks and a student supplied correct answers for 20 blanks, his or her score would be 50 percent. To get a rough estimate of a student's reading level, use the following guide (Miller, 1993):

- 60 percent or more of the correct words provided = *independent reading level* (material can be read fluently with high comprehension; the level at which the reader has little or no problem decoding or comprehending)
- 40 percent or more of the correct words provided = *instructional reading level* (material is challenging with few new words and good comprehension; the level at which the reader benefits from instruction)
- 40 percent or less of the correct words provided = *frustration reading level* (text with many unknown words and poor comprehension; the point at which the reader experiences extreme difficulty with decoding or comprehension)

To ensure that a student's reading level is not overestimated, it may be a good idea to raise the criterion for each level to a higher percentage; for example, making 70 percent the independent reading level.

The cloze technique is often used as a measure of comprehension as well. The teacher can easily braille a passage and omit words that are key to understanding the passage. Using the cloze method, along with retellings, can give the teacher ample information regarding the student's comprehension.

✛ The analytic method, which encourages students to find a common generalization among several words, is another strategy that can be used to teach and assess word-identification skills (Tierney, Readence, & Dishner, 1990). Letter sounds are never learned in isolation. For braille readers, this method stresses auditory discrimination, tactile discrimination, word blending, and contextual application. The steps in the procedure are as follows:

1. First, the teacher writes a sentence on the brailler that includes the target word (in this case, *cat*): "The cat ran from the boy."

2. The teacher writes additional words on the brailler for the student to read. In this example, the teacher might select words such as *cat, cup, can, cake,* and *car,* all of which begin with the letter *c.* The student then discovers that all the words begin with the same braille character and that they all sound alike.

3. The teacher reads a new group of words, such as *cape, cookie, dog, Doug,* and *Carl,* several of which begin with *c,* and asks the student to identify those that begin with *c.*

4. Next, the student analyzes a *c* word and a rhyming word, such as *cat* and *bat,* and should discover that the words sound alike at the end and differ at the beginning. The teacher then adds more pairs of words.

5. Finally, the student reads the new words in a short sentence.

In this procedure, the teacher has not only helped the student learn to identify words, but has assessed the student's ability to use auditory discrimination, tactile discrimination, word blending, and contextual application. The teacher records the success of the procedure and the new words learned, so that this information will be readily available for use in making future lesson plans. This strategy also can be used for building vocabulary.

Reading Rate

Knowledge of a student's average reading rate is useful in determining appropriate reading media for the student. However, this information should be collected only after a period of sustained instruction. Measuring reading rates in both braille and print is valid, but only if a student has been consistently instructed in both media over a period of time. For example, if a student with low vision is not able to read print accurately and rapidly, a teacher may decide that braille may be a more efficient medium for the student. To compare the efficiency of the two media, braille instruction would need to be consistently and effectively delivered over a period of time.

The choice of reading materials to be used in these assessments depends on the purposes for which the data are to be collected. For example, if the purpose is to determine how well a student can read his or her social studies textbook, then the reading passages should be taken from this book. If the purpose is to compare the efficiency of braille and print, then different braille and print passages at the student's instructional or leisure reading level should be selected from the same source. Both paragraphs should be at the same level of difficulty and include roughly the same number of new words at the same level. The following is an effective and easy method of measuring a student's reading rate.

STRATEGIES

MEASURING A STUDENT'S ORAL READING RATE

✢ Choose several short passages of approximately the same complexity that will require the student to read for about three to five minutes.

✢ For two or three days, ask the student to read a passage out loud while he or she is timed with a stopwatch.

✢ Record the number of seconds the student needed to read the passage. To determine the student's oral reading rate, divide the number of words in the passage by the number of seconds needed to read each selection; then multiply the quotient by 60 to get the number of words read per minute. Average the rates collected each day over a two- or three-day period.

Two strategies that can be used to increase reading rates as well as for assessment are repeated readings and Reading Recovery, which are discussed in Chapter 3.

Comprehension: The K-W-L Method

Constructing meaning from reading to achieve comprehension is a complex task. It can be even more challenging for students who are blind or visually impaired, who often have a limited range of previous experiences to which to refer while reading. The K-W-L method is an informal assessment strategy that can be used to determine a student's level of comprehension.

The K-W-L method (which stands for "know, want, learn") is a simple method developed by Ogle (1986) that determines how much prior knowledge a student has about a particular subject and also serves as a way to measure comprehension after reading. It can be used with emerging readers by allowing them to dictate their answers (Miller, 1993). The steps in the K-W-L method, along with a helpful variation, are presented next.

STRATEGIES

STEPS IN THE K-W-L METHOD

✛ What do I know? The teacher begins by reading the title of the story to the student and asks the student to predict what he or she thinks the story is about. The student's brailled answers are an indication of his or her prior knowledge. (Younger students may need the teacher to braille their ideas.) The teacher may need to supplement the concepts the student has listed and to provide an experience or field trip to fill in missing conceptual information.

✛ What do I want to learn? The teacher encourages the student to determine what other information about the concept is needed and to braille his or her questions. Again, the teacher may need to braille these questions for a young student as the student dictates them.

✛ What have I learned? After reading the story, the student records the concepts or information he or she has learned.

✛ What more do I want to learn? An additional step (not in the original K-W-L strategy) is this: After the teacher and student have assessed the student's prior knowledge and reading comprehension, it may be evident that the student needs more experiences about the subject to improve his or her ability to comprehend and hence to make reading meaningful. In this case, the teacher tries to provide as many experiences as possible.

The K-W-L pages can serve as part of the student's reading portfolio, which documents conceptual growth and enables the teacher to ascertain the student's level of conceptual knowledge about a variety of subjects.

TYING ASSESSMENT TO INSTRUCTION

Assessment and instruction complement each other; instruction without assessment becomes haphazard. Good educational goals are the result of ongoing instructional assessment. Record keeping and assessment of skills, two critical activities, can lead to progress and motivation to succeed. Whenever possible, the student should be involved in the assessment process, because learning to self-evaluate work is key in developing personal goals and independence. Personalizing instruction and assessment are critical to helping students acquire the skills needed to be successful in school and life.

REFERENCES

Bradley-Johnson, S. (1994). *Psychoeducational assessment of students who are visually impaired or blind.* Austin, TX: Pro-Ed.

Brigance, A. H. (1983). *Brigance diagnostic comprehensive inventory of basic skills.* North Billerica, MA: Curriculum Associates.

Brigance, A. H. (1991). *Diagnostic inventory of early development—Revised.* North Billerica, MA: Curriculum Associates.

Burns, P. C. & Roe, B. (1993). *Burns/Roe informal reading inventory.* Boston, MA: Houghton Mifflin.

Caton, H., Duckworth, B., & Rankin, E. (1985). *Braille unit recognition battery: Diagnostic test of grade 2 literary braille.* Louisville, KY: American Printing House for the Blind.

Christie, J. F. (1981). The effect of grade level and reading ability on children's miscue patterns. *Journal of Educational Research, 74,* 419–423.

Cooper, J. D. (1993). *Literacy* (2nd ed.). Boston: Houghton Mifflin.

Dolch, E. W. (1936). A basic sight vocabulary. *Elementary School Journal, 36,* 456–460.

Duckworth, B. J. (n.d.). *Braille edition of the Stanford Achievement Test.* Louisville, KY: American Printing House for the Blind.

Duckworth, B., & Caton, H. (1986). *Basic reading rate scale—Braille edition.* Louisville, KY: American Printing House for the Blind.

Duckworth, B., & Caton, H. (1992). *Diagnostic reading scale.* Louisville, KY: American Printing House for the Blind.

Fuchs, L. S., Fuchs, D., & Maxwell, L. (1988). The validity of informal reading comprehension measure. *Remedial and Special Education, 9,* 20–28.

Goodman, Y. M., Watson, D. J., & Burke, C. L. (1987). *Reading miscue inventory: Alternative procedures.* Katonah, NY: Richard C. Owen.

Godwin, A., Grafsgaard, K., Hanson, N., Hooey, P., Martin, J., McNear, D., Rieber, C., & Tillmans, E. (1995). *Minnesota braille skills inventory: A resource manual.* St. Paul, MN: Minnesota Department of Education, Minnesota Educational Services.

Hart, D. (1994). *Authentic assessment: A handbook for educators.* Menlo Park, CA: Addison-Wesley.

Johns, J. L. (1994). *Basic reading inventory* (6th ed.). Dubuque, IA: Kendall/Hunt Publishing.

Koenig, A. J., & Farrenkopf, C. (1995). *Assessment of braille literacy skills.* Houston, TX: Region IV Education Service Center.

Miller, W. H. (1993). *Complete reading disabilities handbook.* West Nyack, NY: Center for Applied Research in Education.

Newland, J. E. (1971). *Blind learning aptitude test.* Urbana, IL: University of Illinois Press.

Ogle, D. (1986). K-W-L: A teaching model that develops active reading of expository text. *The Reading Teacher, 39,* 564–570.

Salvia, J., & Hughes, C. (1990). *Curriculum-based assessment.* New York: Macmillan.

Salvia, J., & Ysseldyke, J. E. (1995). *Assessment* (6th ed.). Boston: Houghton Mifflin.

Sharpe, M. N., McNear, D., McGraw, K. S. (1996). *Braille assessment inventory.* Colombia, MD: Hawthorne Educational Services, Inc.

Sowell, V., & Sledge, A. (1986). Miscue analysis of braille readers. *Journal of Visual Impairment & Blindness, 80,* 989–992.

Spache, G. D. (1981). *Diagnostic reading scale.* Monterey, CA: CTB/McGraw-Hill.

Stanford achievement test—Form G. (1989). San Antonio, TX: Psychological Corporation.

Swallow, R. M., Mangold, S. S., & Mangold, P. (Eds.). (1978). *Informal assessment of developmental skills for visually handicapped students.* New York: American Foundation for the Blind.

Taylor, W. L. (1953). Cloze procedure: A new tool for measuring readability. *Journalism Quarterly, 30,* 415–433.

Wechsler, D. (1991). *Wechsler intelligence scale for children* (3rd ed.). San Antonio, TX: Psychological Corporation.

Tierney, R. J., Readence, J. E., & Dishner, G. K. (1990). *Reading strategies and practices* (3rd ed.). Boston: Allyn & Bacon.

Woods, M. L., & Moe, A. J. (1989). *Analytic reading inventory.* Columbus, OH: Merrill Publishing.

PRACTICE EXERCISE IN ANALYZING MISCUES IN BRAILLE

The following passage shows 15 coded miscues marked on this print copy, made by a student reading braille aloud. The first 5 miscues were transferred to the Miscue Analysis Chart and have been analyzed as examples. Transfer the remaining 10 coded miscues to the chart and complete the analyses. Calculate the percentages and complete the Profile Sheet. To check your answers, see the answer keys that follow.

Prairie Dog Pete lives in Prairie Dog Town among (his) family and friends.

He has sharp/claws [marp ©], stubby legs and a short, flat tail. He is quite handsome, with

light brown fur and deep dark eyes. Prairie Dog Pete has a ∧ [very] loud bark that he

uses when an enemy approaches [animal]. That wonderful barking is how prairie dogs got

their name! They are really rodents that belong to the squirrel family.

Pete likes living in Prairie Dog Town. Prairie Dog Town has over 500 members.

All prairie dogs love the town. There/are [These ©] rules in Prairie Dog Town. Most prairie

dogs live in family groups known [know] as coteries. These coteries inhabit a specific

territory. The territory may have as many as 50 to 100 burrows. Each burrow

has at least two entrances for protection (and ventilation) [last] [loves] Pete lives with his family

in his burrows and surfaces during the day to socialize with other prairie dogs.

Eating is ∧ [not] done above ground. Pete and all prairie dogs love to eat green [golf]

plants, especially grass. Occasionally, Pete finds a delicacy like a grasshopper to eat.

Those [Through] are really special meals.

Pete's family has several baby prairie dogs. These babies will remain in the

burrow until they are about six weeks old. They will then be (old) [en] enough to come

above ground for food and fun. [fun and food]

MISCUE ANALYSIS CHART

No.	Error	Text	Graphic/Tactile Similarity Yes	Context Acceptable	Context Unacceptable	Self-Correction
1.	——	his	✗	✔		
2.	marp ⠿	sharp ⠿	✔		✔	✔
3.	very	——-	✗	✔		
4.	animal ⠿	enemy ⠿		✔		
5.	these ⠿	there ⠿	✔		✔	✔
6.						
7.						
8.						
9.						
10.						
11.						
12.						
13.						
14.						
15.						
	Column Total					
	Number of Errors Analyzed					
	Percentage					

Appendix. Practice Exercise *(Continued)*

A HANDY GUIDE TO CALCULATING TOTALS AND PERCENTAGES

Graphic/tactile similarity

a. Column total (number of checks in the Yes column)   _____

b. Number of errors analyzed (total boxes without *X*s)   _____

c. Percentage of miscues with graphic similarity (a ÷ b)   _____ %

Acceptability in context

a. Column total (number of checks in the Acceptable column)   _____

b. Number of errors analyzed (total number of errors analyzed)   _____

c. Percentage of miscues acceptable in context (a ÷ b)   _____ %

Correction strategy

a. Column total (number of unacceptable miscues self-corrected)   _____

b. Number of errors analyzed (total unacceptable miscues)   _____

c. Percentage of unacceptable miscues self-corrected (a ÷ b)   _____ %

Appendix. Practice Exercise *(Continued)*

PROFILE

	PREDICTION STRATEGY	CORRECTION STRATEGY
	_____	_____

Graphic/Tactile Similarity	Errors Acceptable in Context	Unacceptable Errors, Self-Corrected
100 % _____	100 % _____	100 % _____
90 % _____	90 % _____	90 % _____
80 % _____	80 % _____	80 % _____
70 % _____	70 % _____	70 % _____
60 % _____	60 % _____	60 % _____
50 % _____	50 % _____	50 % _____
40 % _____	40 % _____	40 % _____
30 % _____	30 % _____	30 % _____
20 % _____	20 % _____	20 % _____
10 % _____	10 % _____	10 % _____
0 % _____	0 % _____	0 % _____

Appendix. Practice Exercise *(Continued)*

MISCUE ANALYSIS CHART

No.	Error	Text	Graphic/Tactile Similarity — Yes	Context — Acceptable	Context — Unacceptable	Self-Correction
1.	——	his	✗	✔		
2.	marp	sharp	✔		✔	✔
3.	very	——-	✗	✔		
4.	animal	enemy		✔		
5.	these	there	✔		✔	✔
6.	know	known	✔		✔	
7.	last	least	✔		✔	
8.	——	and ventilation	✗		✔	
9.	loves	lives	✔		✔	
10.	not	——	✗		✔	
11.	golf	green			✔	
12.	through	those	✔		✔	
13.	——	old	✗		✔	
14.	en	enough	✔		✔	
15.	fun and food	food and fun	✗	✔		
Column Total			7	4	11	2
Number of Errors Analyzed			9	15		11
Percentage			78%	27%		18%

Appendix. Practice Exercise Answer Key

A HANDY GUIDE TO CALCULATING TOTALS AND PERCENTAGES

Graphic/tactile similarity

a. Column total (number of checks in the Yes column) _____ 7 _____

b. Number of errors analyzed (total boxes without *Xs*) _____ 9 _____

c. Percentage of miscues with graphic similarity (a ÷ b) _____ 78 _____ %

Acceptability in context

a. Column total (number of checks in the Acceptable column) _____ 4 _____

b. Number of errors analyzed (total number of errors analyzed) _____ 15 _____

c. Percentage of miscues acceptable in context (a ÷ b) _____ 27 _____ %

Correction strategy

a. Column total (number of unacceptable miscues self-corrected) _____ 2 _____

b. Number of errors analyzed (total unacceptable miscues) _____ 11 _____

c. Percentage of unacceptable miscues self-corrected (a ÷ b) _____ 18 _____ %

Appendix. Practice Exercise Answer Key

PROFILE

PREDICTION STRATEGY		CORRECTION STRATEGY
_____		_____

Graphic/Tactile Similarity	*Errors Acceptable in Context*	*Unacceptable Errors, Self-Corrected*
100 %	100 %	100 %
90 %	90 %	90 %
80 %	80 %	80 %
70 %	70 %	70 %
60 %	60 %	60 %
50 %	50 %	50 %
40 %	40 %	40 %
30 %	30 %	30 %
20 %	20 %	20 %
10 %	10 %	10 %
0 %	0 %	0 %
_78%_	_27%_	_18%_

Appendix. Practice Exercise Answer Key

ACCESS TO INFORMATION: TECHNOLOGY AND BRAILLE

FRANCES MARY D'ANDREA AND KITCH BARNICLE

Judy D, a consumer relations officer at a large governmental agency in Washington, DC, just discovered the New York Times *Classified section on the Internet. Judy, who is an avid braille reader, "surfs" the Internet daily, with one of three refreshable braille devices connected to computers. "If I had had access to the* New York Times *when I was growing up," she said, "I might be in an entirely different profession today. I never knew there were so many different types of jobs!" In the demonstrations on braille users' access to the Internet that Judy gives around the country, she uses a portable laptop computer with a refreshable braille display and an overhead projector to allow sighted participants to see the screen that she is reading using the braille display. Judy does not use speech to access anything on the Internet because she thinks it limits her ability to scan and read different parts of the screen and slows her down when she is on-line.*

Another avid braille reader, Penny Z, a private consultant in Atlanta, has recently become a technology user. For years, she used only a slate and stylus, and did not even own a Perkins brailler. She became involved with technology when she volunteered in a technology resource room at a private agency for blind people. She began teaching herself to use the available technology so she could demonstrate it to visitors. Her husband purchased her first piece of high-tech equipment—a portable notetaker—as a Christmas gift. From that point on, she became a "techie." From the notetaker, she expanded to using a personal computer for word processing and linked it to the notetaker for saving files. She then learned to use two different types of scanners to access print information and how to download the information scanned into the computer. By this time, she was also using a speech-synthesis program to read what was on the computer screen. Next, Penny learned how to use braille-translation software and a braille printer to print hard braille (paper) copies of the materials she had scanned. As she earned money from private consulting, she purchased the technology she had learned at work for use at home. She discovered how to access the Internet using a speech synthesis program she purchased, along with the modem and some on-line software. A new world of information has now found its way into her home.

The authors wish to thank Ike Presley, Betsy Presley, Paul Schroeder, and Barbara Paton for their contributions to this chapter.

269

Cassilda is a fifth-grade student in a progressive school district in which her teacher has the students searching the Internet to participate in a multimedia archaeological site "adventure." Cassilda likes to hear the audio clips that the other students have accessed, but she has no way to read the screen on her own and is dependent on her computer "buddy" to read the screen. This buddy does all the keyboarding, while Cassilda listens passively to his explanations. She is itching to get her hands on the computer. Ms. Johnson, Cassilda's teacher of students who are visually impaired, is exploring what kind of computer station to purchase for Cassilda so she can be more independent. Ms. Johnson is concerned that she will not be able to figure out how to use the equipment herself, much less teach Cassilda to use it.

The rapid development of assistive technology in recent years has given people who are blind or visually impaired access to nearly all the functions and capabilities of personal computers. At the same time, the quantity of information available through advances in computer technologies, such as CD-ROM, and telecommunications—electronic mail (e-mail) and the Internet—as well as the ability to manipulate information, has increased exponentially. In general, computer technology has been a tremendous benefit to students who are blind or visually impaired, who are now able to gather and manipulate information as quickly and effectively as all other students.

For example, using computers equipped with special-access technology, such as programs that translate print into braille, braille displays, braille printers, speech synthesizers, and braille notetakers (mini-computers with braille keyboards for inputting and storing documents), blind or visually impaired students can:

- quickly note ideas, thoughts, or outlines
- compose documents with relative ease using the regular keyboard
- monitor and review writing by using speech output or other types of access
- revise work by adding, deleting, or rearranging large blocks of text
- output drafts in braille through grade 2 braille-translation software for careful review and more revision if desired
- edit documents with ease, using insertions, deletion, and other functions of the word-processing program, including spell checking and grammar checking in a few programs
- print out final clean copies of their work in print and braille. (Rex, Koenig, Wormsley, & Baker, 1994, p. 97)

These capabilities greatly facilitate students' ability to learn to write and to complete their written work in all subjects.

Technology is thus an essential tool for literacy for people who are blind or visually impaired. Just as today's students must be *computer* literate, students who are blind or visually impaired must also be *technologically* literate. It is crucial, therefore, that teachers of students who are visually impaired help students to learn the value of information technology in general, to become comfortable with different forms of technology, and to remain flexible in adapting to the different forms technology will take as it continues to develop.

The job of a teacher of visually impaired students in today's highly technical information age is a challenging one. Not only do teachers need to be knowledgeable about blindness and low vision, but they must keep up with the fast-paced, constantly changing world of information access. Sometimes it is difficult even to know where to start with technology. Teachers have a multitude of questions. "When should I introduce students to the braille notetaker?" "When should I teach them how to use the computer?" "Should I teach them to use refreshable braille displays or stick with speech?" "What kind of technology should I be introducing students to, and how much?" For some teachers, just the mention of a computer with many software and hardware adaptations is intimidating. To teach students to use technology efficiently, teachers need to be intimately acquainted with that technology.

This chapter presents an overview of the main types of computer-based technology that give people who are blind or visually impaired access to information, with particular emphasis on the specialized assistive technology that uses or provides access to braille and the issues involved in using it. It then suggests strategies and resources to help teachers familiarize themselves and their students with various types of technology.

TECHNOLOGY FOR BRAILLE USERS

Over the course of their education and into adulthood, students who are blind or visually impaired will use many types of technology, both inexpensive low-tech devices and costly high-tech devices. Despite the emphasis on high-tech devices in this chapter, the ability to use inexpensive, low-tech equipment is just as important as knowing how to operate the computer-related devices discussed here. Although it may seem that electronic devices have supplanted traditional tools, such as the slate and stylus, children who are adept at using multiple devices will be able to function in a wide range of situations (for further information on the Perkins brailler and the slate and stylus, see Chapters 3 and 4). No device is infallible or unbreakable, so the more options a student has, the better he or she will be able to cope with the unexpected.

This section provides brief descriptions of many types of assistive technology that are commonly used by students and adults who are blind or visually impaired, including braille notetakers, computers with braille-translation software and braille printers, refreshable (sometimes known as "dynamic") braille displays, alternative input devices, speech synthesizers, and scanners. Specialized assistive technology is essential for the independence and productivity of all people

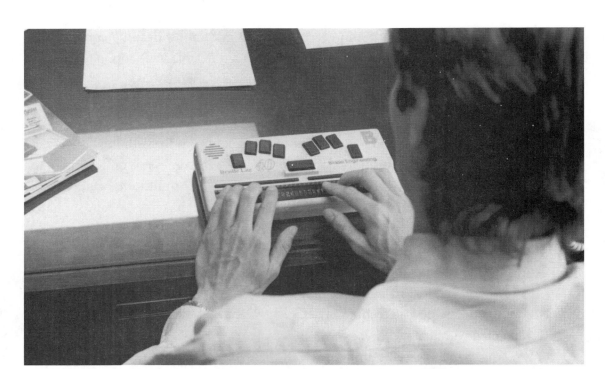

Electronic braille notetakers are widely used because they are small, portable, and convenient. This one has a refreshable braille display.

who are blind or visually impaired. This equipment is increasingly found in schools and the workplace.

Portable notetakers. An electronic braille notetaker is a small, portable device with a braille keyboard used to enter information. The information stored in the notetaker can be accessed immediately using the notetaker's speech-output capabilities. Some models also include a small, refreshable braille display (described under "Refreshable Braille Displays") to access information stored in the notetaker. A notetaker can be connected by a cable to a computer or printer, so the information stored in it can be transferred into the computer or printed directly. A system can be designed to print in standard or large print, or braille, or both, depending on the equipment one buys. Two popular brands of these devices are the Braille Lite and Braille 'n Speak (see Resources). Because of their portability and relative affordability, notetakers are widely used in homes, communities, and workplaces.

Braille-translation software. Before a standard computer file can be printed in grade 2 braille using a braille printer, the document must be translated into braille using translation software. Braille-translation software reformats a computer text file and inserts the necessary contractions and other formatting information needed to print in grade 2 braille. There are many brands of translation software, including the Duxbury Braille Translator, MegaDots, BEX, and others. Most are designed for IBM and compatible computers, although there are a few that work with Apple products, including the Macintosh (see Resources). Many braille-translation programs handle files created with popular word-processor software, as well as the HTML (hypertext markup language) files found on the World Wide Web.

Some programs also allow direct braille input by converting the keyboard into a brailler. Thus, an experienced brailler can use six designated keys to input braille and edit documents. Pokadot is one such program, and other translation software programs also have this capability.

Braille printers. Braille printers (also known as embossers) are electromechanical devices that emboss braille documents from computer files. Unlike an ink jet or laser printer, a braille printer has many mechanical pins that are controlled by the computer. These pins "punch" heavyweight paper to create documents embossed in braille. Interpoint braille printers can produce braille on both sides of pieces of heavyweight paper. Among the common braille printers are Blazer, Juliet, Romeo, Thiel, and Versa Point (see Resources). Different models have different features, such as speed (number of characters printed per minute), size, weight and portability, and price.

Refreshable braille displays. There are other ways of getting output from a computer screen besides printing everything out in braille. As an alternative output device, a refreshable braille display (electronic braille) provides access to text that is normally displayed on a computer screen. The braille display generally consists of a series of plastic pins that move up and down to form a line of braille characters and symbols. After reading a line, the user pushes a button, and the next line of braille appears. Braille displays usually have 40 or 80 individual braille cells that are electronically controlled. Hence, depending on the model, users can access 40 or 80 screen characters at a time. Normally, 80 characters of text appear on each line of the screen, so an 80-character refreshable display would allow the user to read one line of text at a time. Refreshable braille displays are rectangular and are usually placed under the computer's standard keyboard so the user can move quickly from typing to reading. Again, there are many brands, including Alva, INKA, and PowerBraille (see Resources).

Other electronic braille options. A few electronic options combine features. The Mountbatten Brailler (available from HumanWare) is similar to an electric brailler but can be hooked up to a computer; it also prints out hard copy in print or braille, or both. The David is similar to a laptop computer; it can be used as a notetaker but also has the features of a full-size computer. Other brands of electronic braille options also combine several features (see Resources).

Speech synthesizer and screen-reading software. The combination of a computer, speech synthesizer, and screen-reading software provides access to text-based information from a computer. A speech synthesizer can be a circuit board (often referred to as a card) that is placed permanently inside the computer's case, or a portable device that is attached to the computer externally with a cable. Some speech synthesizers are specially made for laptop computers; these credit-card-size synthesizers are inserted into a special slot on laptop computers.

Like the refreshable braille display, a computer fitted with speech-access equipment provides the user with access to the information that would normally appear on a monitor. Special software (known as a screen reader) translates the computer's text so that it can be spoken by the synthesizer. The user sends commands to the screen-reading software, using the keyboard, that tells the speech synthesizer what information on the screen (such as a paragraph, a page, or a menu of options) should be spoken. The screen reader also tells the synthesizer how to speak. For example, the user can send commands that tell the synthesizer to speak slowly or quickly or to speak highlighted text in a high tone and standard text in a low tone. Using screen-reader commands, the user has many options for customizing his or her speech-adapted computer. Some common brands of computer speech-access systems are Artic, JAWS, outSPOKEN, and Vocal-Eyes. Brands of speech synthesizers include Accent, DECtalk, and Double Talk.

Although speech access may seem far removed from braille literacy, it is, in fact, a powerful tool that can be even more powerful when used in conjunction with braille-access devices. Many successful blind adults use various combinations of braille displays, speech, hard-copy braille (braille that has been printed out on a braille printer), and braille input devices such as notetakers. It is included in this discussion because it is frequently integrated with and enhances braille technology in providing access to print materials as well as communication and literacy in general.

Scanners and optical character recognition software. The combination of a computer, scanner, and optical character recognition (OCR) software allows a user to scan printed text into the computer, translate the print through OCR software, and access the information using alternative output methods such as speech or braille. The user places a document, such as a book, newspaper, or utility bill, on the glass face of the scanner and activates the scanning process. After the scanner finishes scanning the document, the OCR software converts the scanned information into recognizable text that can be read using speech or braille output or saved to a file for later use. Some brands of scanners found in school or work settings are Open Book, Omni 1000, and Reading Edge. (For factors that influence which type of scanner to purchase, see "Choosing the Right Scanner" in this chapter.)

Adaptive keyboards. Most people think of the keyboard as the only way to input information into a computer, but there are other input devices that can be useful for children who have not yet learned to type or individuals who have physical

---

CHOOSING THE RIGHT SCANNER

A school district can use a scanner to create braille materials from printed text. If this is the sole reason for purchasing a scanner (and not to teach students to use one), it will be less expensive to purchase a generic scanner that is not designed specifically for blind users. Any commercially available scanner (such as those manufactured by Hewlett-Packard) and OCR software (such as Omni Page Pro) can be used to input text instead of rekeying it. Many popular scanners include OCR software, but the quality is variable. Thus, a school system that wants a scanner only to translate print into braille may want to buy a separate OCR program that has a higher accuracy rate, to save time in the editing or proofreading process.

If a school wants a scanner for blind or visually impaired students, it would be more practical to buy a system specifically designed for blind users. Products such as Reading AdvantEdge and OpenBook Unbound, with scanners and software, are designed to be accessible to blind users and can be used with a computer and speech synthesizer and/or refreshable braille display.

Scanners are also available as stand-alone dedicated reading machines (such as the Reading Edge) that do not connect to computers, but just read print text aloud. These reading machines may be useful in libraries, for example, where users may simply wish to read text but not necessarily to save the contents.

---

disabilities that prevent them from using a standard keyboard. Most computers accept input from adaptive keyboards. These include keyboards that do not have individual keys but instead have a smooth surface. These adaptive keyboards use paper or plastic overlays that can represent user-defined keystrokes. For example, this type of keyboard can be programmed, so that when a student touches the left side of the keyboard he or she is indicating yes, and when the student touches the right side of the keyboard, he or she is indicating no. The overlays can be designed and customized using any number of configurations. These keyboards can then be outfitted with tactile overlays that have braille words or letters on them or can be equipped with other tactile symbols (see Chapter 5 for a discussion of tactile symbols and alternate communication boards and devices). These keyboards (including Intellikeys by Intellitool; PowerPad, available from Dunamis, and Unicorn Board from Unicorn Engineering; see Resources) are frequently used to access educational software that does not require students to type in letters or numbers, but they can often be used with many programs.

SELECTING APPROPRIATE TECHNOLOGY

Student Assessment

The process of incorporating technology into a student's educational program begins with an assessment of the student's current and future needs as well as an assessment of available technology. Decisions on technology are influenced by a student's individual needs, such as visual status, past exposure to technology, goals for the future, and academic needs. Determining how technologically literate a student already is can also be a good way to start incorporating technology into his or her educational plan. For example, a young congenitally blind student who knows nothing about computers or braille notetakers will have to start from scratch. In contrast, a high school student who had good computer skills and has just recently lost his or her sight will need mainly to learn adaptations such as screen-reading programs at the same time that he or she is learning braille reading and writing and how to use a braille notetaker.

A documented, systematic assessment of the student will help to ensure that all key factors have been taken into consideration. The Assistive Technology Assessment for Visually Impaired Students, which appears as Appendix A to this chapter, is a comprehensive assessment form that will help ensure that all important issues are considered during the assessment process.

There are many variables and factors to consider. What are the student's goals—academic, vocational, and for independent living? What equipment does the school have that can be adapted? In what settings will the student need to use this equipment: a resource room, a classroom, or the community? To what technology does the student have access at home, if any? What is the most portable, versatile, and useful technology for the many tasks the student must do?

Making the Selection

As the assessment is being completed, the next task is to select technology that is appropriate for the student. Successful use of assistive technology depends on a careful match between the needs of the student and the performance characteristics of the assistive technology. Because most students who are blind or visually impaired use more than one type of assistive device, ensuring compatibility among the various devices that must interface with each other is one of the most important considerations. For example, a student may need to move information between a braille notetaker and a personal computer or may require access to a computer through speech and braille or speech and screen magnification.

In a school setting the type of technology that is chosen is frequently influenced by the teacher's experience and the technology already available in the school, as well as the needs of all students. It is important to establish priorities among the student's needs. Competing issues, such as the number or type of features desired, the cost of a device, available funding, and the compatibility of the device with other devices, strongly influence purchasing decisions. Clear priorities among essential and optional features of a device that the student needs are helpful when the inevitable trade-offs must be made.

The process of choosing the assistive technology devices that will meet a student's current and near-future technology needs may seem overwhelming, since many factors must be considered and there sometimes appears to be no obvious choice. A thorough discussion of the process of choosing and purchasing adaptive technology is beyond the scope of this chapter, but the following are several strategies that may minimize potential problems. The accompanying list of questions to consider when selecting a computer system may also assist in the decision-making process.

STRATEGIES

DECIDING ON APPROPRIATE TECHNOLOGY

✢ Review objective information on products from several sources, including current users, other teachers, product suppliers, journal articles and reviews, and third-party sources that may have evaluated the devices. One such source is the American Foundation for the Blind (AFB)'s National Technology Center, which regularly reviews new products and prepares lists of available products, their manufacturers, current prices, and strengths and weaknesses (for other sources, see Resources).

✢ Request a trial period, so that the teacher and the student can test the product before purchase. Renting a device for a few months is one way to make sure that it is appropriate. Some software manufacturers distribute demonstration disks of their products that work for a short time (for instance, 30 minutes a day or a set number of days), so that prospective buyers can try them out.

✢ Test any software or equipment being considered for purchase to make sure that it is compatible with the existing system and any other devices whose purchase is planned. Conflicts among systems often arise when multiple devices or software are run from the same computer, especially if the products are made by different manufacturers.

✢ If a computer system and several assistive devices are being purchased at the same time, consider buying the products from a single local supplier who will install each device and make sure the complete system runs smoothly. Since a product supplier (or distributor) is not always the manufacturer, also contact the manufacturer, who may have more information about the product's compatibility with the system.

✢ Do not underestimate the importance of technical support, documentation, and warranties. When multiple devices and software are hooked up to a computer, it is often difficult to tell who is responsible for providing technical support. Find out what type of support the supplier will provide and in which situations you will be referred to the manufacturer. Fill out the warranty and registration cards and send

FACTORS TO CONSIDER WHEN SELECTING A COMPUTER SYSTEM

Many factors need to be considered before a computer system is chosen for a student or a school. The situation is compounded by the fact that many adaptive devices are not readily available at local computer super-stores and must be ordered specially from the manufacturers or suppliers. Here are some questions to ask while shopping for a computer system:

- Is this product designed to work with a computer, or is it a stand-alone piece of equipment that needs no further attachments?

- Is the product compatible with the IBM-compatible or Macintosh computer to which it will be attached?

- What are the system requirements for this piece of hardware or software?

- Does the computer have the resources—RAM (random-access memory), memory, slots—to support this device?

- Are cables included, or are separate cables necessary?

- Is the software compatible with other software and hardware that will be used on this machine?

- How long has the device been on the market?

- How do current users rate the device?

- Does the device have the features the student needs now or will need soon?

- Which features are essential, and which are not?

- Is the device noisy? Will it disrupt others in the classroom? If so, can it be adapted somehow? (For example, a computer with speech will probably work with an earphone, and a braille printer may need to be put in a separate room or run before and after school.)

- Is the size, shape, and weight of the device appropriate for the classroom?

- Is the device portable?

- Will more than one person be able to use the device?

- Does the device use standard batteries that can be purchased anywhere? What is the battery's lifetime?

- What is the initial purchase price of the device?

- How long is the device expected to last?

- How much do supplies cost?

- What are the estimated lifetime costs of the device?

- Will parts eventually have to be replaced?

- Are there labor costs?

- Is the service contract reasonably priced?

- Does the manufacturer or supplier provide a loaner device while the device is being repaired?

- Is the device easy to use?

- What are assembly and installation requirements?

- What are the training requirements?

- Who will provide training?

- Will the student be able to perform all necessary functions, including loading paper, changing batteries, and connecting cables?

- Can the device (hardware or software) be upgraded?

- Are upgrades included in the initial purchase price?

- How quickly might the product become obsolete?

them in, so you will be informed about upgrades, new products, and recalls. Find out the school district's policy on purchasing extended warranties; some districts require them, but others do not.

✛ Ask vendors for the names of other customers who would be willing to share their experiences in using a particular device. There may even be a user group in your area; some user groups have special-interest groups (known as SIGs) for people with disabilities. Local consumer organizations, such as the American Council of the Blind and the National Federation of the Blind, may have members who are technology users and may be willing to speak with you about various products. AFB's Careers and Technology Information Bank is another way to contact technology users (see Resources). Discussing the device with other users can give a better perspective on day-to-day use of the product. Keep in mind, however, that their situation may be different from that of the student.

✛ New computers typically include a sound card designed to produce sounds, music, and speech. When adding a speech synthesizer and screen-reading software, make sure that the sound card and speech synthesizer are compatible. Certain applications, especially multimedia programs found on the Internet and CD-ROMs, may not work well with both the sound card and the speech synthesizer (for example, if the student wants to do an activity on a CD-ROM that makes sounds and then type in words with the speech synthesizer spelling out the words).

TEACHING INFORMATION ACCESS THROUGH ASSISTIVE TECHNOLOGY

It is virtually impossible to give detailed strategies for each of the vast number of different programs and equipment available because technology is changing at such a rapid pace, and any specific software package or piece of equipment is likely to be upgraded or discontinued in the near future. Therefore, this section provides a general discussion about the various kinds of technology, and offers suggestions about how to give students the training they need to use them. It is designed to offer some assistance for beginning teachers who have never taught students to use assistive technology and to suggest resources for obtaining more sophisticated information once teachers have acquired some basic familiarity with the field. However, teachers will need to do their own research and seek assistance from local sources to discover the appropriate systems for individual students, because so much depends on the students' needs, the equipment available in the school system, and the budget for additional equipment.

When to Begin?

The best answer to the question of when to begin teaching students to use assistive technology is "as early as possible." Students should be exposed to braille technology well before they need to rely on it. For example, if teachers wait until it is time for students to write papers to teach them word-processing skills, the energy the students should devote to writing papers will be spent on learning to use a word processor and adaptive technology. If students have already had experience with word-processing skills for simple tasks, such as writing short stories and paragraphs, and have used the adapted equipment available to them, they will have a head start on learning the more complex tasks involved in writing research papers. Teachers need to think ahead and build up skills from the simple to the complex.

Students can often learn to use braillers, slates and styli, and braille notetakers simultaneously. Young children, in particular, have little difficulty learning many different things at the same time. As students develop proficiency, they can move more readily from one piece of technology to another. The key is to get them familiar and comfortable with a wide range of devices. Once students are proficient in simpler types of technology, teachers may seek funding to purchase more sophisticated technology that the students need. Teachers need to keep good records of students' progress through the school year and from one grade to the next. The form shown in Appendix B of this chapter can be used to track a student's progress in learning a variety of devices, such as notetakers, computers, and specific software applications.

The strategies for teaching technology offered here are presented within a suggested timeline for introducing these braille technology skills. However, the grade levels mentioned are a general guideline only. Teachers may not have the opportunity to purchase technology for a specific child or the resources to buy all the devices that are discussed. Nevertheless, this should not delay the students' introduction to technology. Use equipment that is available and adapt the ideas to match a child's abilities and curricular needs.

Primary Grades (K–3)

For younger children, having the experience of seeing and spending time trying out a wide variety of equipment will be an important beginning to later success in using it. Children who are sighted are probably aware of some types of technology; they see computers in stores, scanners in grocery stores, and people using various types of technology in movies and on television. However, children who are blind or visually impaired may miss this incidental vicarious instruction on the types of technology that exist and what they can be used for. Even if there is a computer at home, it is not likely to have speech or a braille display if the parents are sighted. Thus, direct instruction in the different types of technology and what they are used for is necessary. It is becoming more common for computers to be present in preschools and elementary schools, and children who are blind or visually impaired should have the opportunity to use them.

S T R A T E G I E S

TEACHING TECHNOLOGY IN THE PRIMARY GRADES (K–3)

✛ Teach awareness of technology. Depending on a student's age and experience, training in braille technology may begin with physical exploration. Try to make a game out of naming the parts of a device or hooking up the components of a device or computer system. Familiarize the student with the layout of the equipment. Show a student who is learning to use the computer how the keyboard, braille display, and monitor are all connected to the computer with cables.

✛ Teach the basic "rules" of computer use. In the primary grades, students should learn such basics as how to turn a computer on and off correctly, and to treat it carefully (not to bang on the keyboard and to keep food and drinks away from it). This is a lesson that all the children in the class will be learning.

✛ Teach how to navigate on the screen. One of the first and most important things a student who is blind or visually impaired needs to learn about a computer is how to read and manipulate the text and images that are displayed on the screen. Since so much of the information is visual, one of the major adaptations for students who are blind or visually impaired is the use of software programs (such as screen readers) and hardware add-ons (such as refreshable braille displays) that let them know what is displayed on the screen, what computer programs or applications are open, and so forth. This ability will be the basis of computer use throughout their lives. Students need to learn specific skills for navigating systems that utilize pictures for their operation (see "The Sticky Problem of GUI" in this chapter).

Specific strategies for teaching screen-navigation skills will depend on the exact type of software or hardware adaptation that is installed, but these are some good general strategies:

- Learn to use the adaptation the way the student will—with speech or a braille display. Turning off the monitor will help the teacher understand how to navigate around and read the screen using the same options the students will.
- Make a tactile graphic of what the monitor is showing. This may be one way of illustrating for the student what information is on the screen. The American Printing House for the Blind (APH) sells tactile graphics of a Windows 3.1 layout called Opening Windows for this purpose (see Resources).

✛ Teach prekeyboarding activities. Young children can be introduced to computer technology using touch tablets and multimedia software. Many commercial software packages, though not specifically designed for students who are blind or visually impaired, have significant audio components that make them at least partially accessible to these students. Many of the packages are normally operated with a

THE STICKY PROBLEM OF GUI

Most new computers now rely on some sort of "graphical user interface" (GUI, pronounced "gooey") to access information and execute commands, such as the Windows or Macintosh operating systems. (An operating system is the set of instructions to a computer's brain that "defines the scope of its universe"—for example, how much memory it has, what languages it understands, and how it interacts with the user [Espinola & Croft, 1992].) This means that the screen shows pictures (called icons), instead of just text as in the older text-based systems such as DOS (disk operating system). GUI systems also rely heavily on the use of a "mouse" or similar device to move a pointer on the screen to highlight and execute choices.

Because of their visual nature, GUI operating systems make the task of accessing what is on the monitor a tremendous challenge for people who are blind or visually impaired. GUI systems are designed to provide sighted users with a vast amount of information at a glance; however, accessing the same information can be much more difficult for blind and visually impaired users (Leventhal, 1995).

The process of learning to operate in a GUI environment parallels what takes place when learning to operate in a text-based environment. Students still need to learn the keyboard layout, how to navigate through the information on the screen, the screen-reader commands, and the software application commands.

Access to GUI systems continues to improve as publishers of software and developers of screen readers introduce new products that work better together. However, as always, it will be important to ensure that a software product's features are fully accessible to the student using a particular computer setup before purchasing a particular application. More and more users of adaptive technology are switching to the GUI environment, which, despite its drawbacks, does offer some advantages. One key advantage of GUI systems is the ability to operate more than one software application at a time, called multitasking. Multitasking would allow one to operate, for example, a word processor and an Internet browser simultaneously. Another advantage of GUI systems is the ability to customize the colors and font sizes, allowing some users with visual impairments access to a computer without using a separate screen-magnifying program (Shragai, 1995; Shragai & Uslan, 1995).

It appears as though computer systems will be dominated by graphical user interfaces for some time to come. It will be essential for students to master this environment.

computer mouse or other pointing device. However, membrane keyboards such as Intellikeys by Intellitools (see Resources) can simulate mouse activation. Therefore, with a tactile overlay, a blind or visually impaired student can use the software with his or her classmates.

✛ Teach keyboarding skills. Keyboarding skills are generally introduced when students have developed both the motor and academic skills for the task, usually around the third or fourth grade, although instruction may start earlier with students who have excellent motor skills. Students should be able to reach all keys from the home row comfortably, and to strike different keys independently. Before teach-

An adaptive keyboard or input device, such as this membrane keyboard, can be adapted for blind children with the addition of braille letters, words, and/or tactile symbols.

ing keyboarding skills, some teachers also require students to be able to read grade 1 braille. These are some specific points to keep in mind:

- Use drill and practice techniques to teach keyboarding skills. The teacher can read lessons to the student from a typing instruction book, or the student can listen to audiotaped drills for practicing keystrokes, words, sentences, and paragraphs.
- Keyboarding software programs, which can be used with speech output, are available for both IBM-compatible and Macintosh computers. These programs can be customized to match the students' abilities.
- Teach students to input information from hard copy.
- Save printouts of practice sessions to monitor students' progress and share with parents, teachers, and classmates.

✛ Teach early word-processing skills. Basic word-processing skills, such as naming, saving, and printing files can be introduced during keyboarding and screen-reading instruction. However, the formal process of learning how to use a word-processing program should begin when students are comfortable using the keyboard and screen-reading software and can demonstrate basic computer skills—

for example, starting a program. It is important to choose a word-processing package that is appropriate for a student's reading level. Early keyboarding practice can also be used to teach simple word processing, such as typing spelling words or simple sentences and stories.

- Begin instruction in word processing with assignments that give students practice inserting and deleting text. Use familiar quotes or jokes that have extra letters to be deleted and others that have missing letters to be inserted. Such assignments stress the importance of knowing how to maneuver the cursor with the screen-reading program and should require students to maneuver by words and characters, spell words, and use the phonetic spell features.

- Next, have students use the word processor to complete short, simple assignments that are meaningful to them. For example, students can keep journals or complete academic assignments that will reinforce the need to open, save, and print documents.

- Consider using audiotaped tutorials. These are available primarily for adults. However, the teacher may wish to use these tutorials as the basis for creating appropriate lessons for students.

✛ Teach the use of screen-reading programs. Basic screen-reading commands can be introduced before or during keyboarding lessons.

- Begin by creating a file in a word-processing program that contains information with a high degree of interest to the student and adjusting the rate, pitch, tone, and other voice settings for the student. At this stage, the purpose is for the student to learn to use the screen reader, not to do anything with the text that is in the file.

- Teach the student to read sentences first and then words and characters. Have the student spell out the words with speech and progress to reading paragraphs.

- After the student has mastered these skills, teach him or her to adjust the voice settings independently, modify the amount of punctuation spoken, control the speaking of numbers, and use the pronunciation dictionary and the keyboard echoing of characters or words.

- If the screen-reading package has audiotaped instructions, the teacher can utilize these tapes to learn to use the program, in order to teach it to the students. However, these tapes are usually intended for adults and are often not appropriate for young students.

✛ Teach refreshable braille displays. Instruction in the use of refreshable braille displays can begin as soon as a student is proficient in grade 1 braille and can be taught in conjunction with training in speech access. Although refreshable braille displays tend to be expensive, they are an excellent addition to primary-grade classrooms, as well as to later grades, because they reinforce braille reading skills and provide extra feedback when combined with speech. As mentioned earlier, refreshable braille displays can also help with screen navigation and are useful for many of the applications the students will be using.

Upper Elementary (Grades 4–5) and Middle School (Grades 6–8)

As students move into the upper elementary grades and on into middle school, they will begin to learn more advanced skills. This is also the time to begin introducing them to all the resources of the Internet and "surfing the Web."

S T R A T E G I E S

TEACHING TECHNOLOGY TO UPPER ELEMENTARY (GRADES 4–5) AND MIDDLE SCHOOL STUDENTS (GRADES 6–8)

✛ Teach more advanced word processing skills.

- Give additional practice in using features learned in earlier sessions: saving files, naming files, retrieving files, and so forth.

- Introduce advanced activities such as cutting and pasting text during this phase. A word processor's spell-checking feature is a useful tool that students should master early. Additional formatting features such as centering, underlining, and page numbering can be taught when they are needed to complete assignments, as can more sophisticated skills, such as search and replace and the creation of tables. Another feature that is common on many word-processing programs is the dictionary. Braille readers certainly need to learn to use a braille dictionary (see Chapter 3), but the electronic dictionaries (and thesaurus) that are available are useful tools for students to learn.

- As students learn the writing process outlined in Chapter 3, use lessons on the word processor to reinforce these skills.

✛ Teach more advanced screen-reading skills. Once a student is comfortable using the screen-reading commands, he or she should spend time using different software applications. However, the emphasis should be on learning the screen reader, not the application.

- Have students first use applications for which customized screen-reading settings exist. Manufacturers of screen-reading software often distribute these customized settings as "set files" that optimize the use of the screen-reading program for a particular application. These customized settings are frequently available for popular applications such as word processors. After gaining experience using applications with set files, the student can be taught to create his or her own customized settings.

- Teach students to skim through long documents on the word processor using speech. One technique for doing this is to use the search or find feature of the word processor along with speech. For example, if a student is reading a long document about the drafting of the Declaration of Independence and wants to find just the section on Thomas Jefferson, he or she can skim through the document using the key word *Jefferson*.

✛ Teach the use of portable notetakers. Some teachers do not recommend introducing braille notetakers until after a student has mastered the use of braille. However, for some students, notetakers, especially those that include refreshable braille displays, reinforce what they have learned about braille. Some teachers teach the use of notetakers before they teach the use of computers. At any rate, by the sixth or seventh grade, students should be proficient in using braille notetakers.

- Begin instruction with simple applications, such as calendar and calculator functions, opening, closing, and reading files, "chording" (giving instructions to the notetaker by pressing several keys at once); retrieving files; and, of course, taking notes. Students also need to learn how to hook the notetaker up to the computer and the printer.
- Blazie Engineering, manufacturer of the Braille 'n Speak and the Braille Lite, publishes booklets for teachers and students on how to use these notetakers and provides this information on audiotape.

✛ Teach the use of Internet applications. Teaching about the Internet serves a variety of functions. These activities encourage computer use, allow students to practice computer and adaptive skills, and teach efficient use of the rich but sometimes elusive resources on the Internet (see "Accessing the Internet" in this chapter).

- Work with a teacher of visually impaired students in another part of the district or state and connect two students of similar age, ability, and interests and have them correspond with each other electronically.
- Have each student join an electronic mailing list related to a current classroom topic. The students could follow the discussions for several weeks and periodically report to the class what they have learned. Before allowing students to join mailing lists, teachers should monitor them to make sure that the discussions are appropriate for the students. Some mailing lists have moderators who screen the lists for inappropriate messages. Several electronic mailing lists have members who are users of adaptive technology.
- Design activities that slowly introduce students to the Web, rather than giving students free rein, since that could result in a lot of wasted time. Select accessible Web sites that have information of interest and "bookmark" them—that is,

ACCESSING THE INTERNET

The Internet is a vast global network of computers containing a huge variety of electronic information. The World Wide Web (also referred to as the Web or WWW) is the best-known part of the Internet. The power of the Web lies in the ability of users to view and download documents containing text, images, sound, animation, and video, and to follow links (called hyperlinks) within these documents to other information. Computer applications called browsers allow Internet users to "surf" the Web and take advantage of the wealth of information stored there.

Entire books have been written about using the Internet and the World Wide Web and the information that is available on it. It would be easy to spend hours a day just perusing information on almost every subject one can think of. As the vignette about Judy at the beginning of this chapter illustrates, the ability to access the Internet has opened up a new world of information access to people who are blind or visually impaired.

Access to the Internet has opened up new opportunities for teachers as well as students. Internet users can be information gatherers and information distributors. From a teacher's perspective, designing Internet-related activities for students who are blind or visually impaired may seem daunting. However, the structure of the Internet allows teachers and students to get involved in small, manageable steps. Once connected to the Internet a teacher will find a tremendous amount of resources to help design activities for students. Although much of the information on the Internet is designed for visual effect, a great deal of information is accessible to users of adaptive equipment. Learning to use the Internet will become increasingly important when students enter high school. Students should eventually be taught to access it independently, but first they should simply become aware of what the Internet is and what kinds of information are available on it.

Accessing the Internet requires a computer equipped with a modem (a device that enables the computer to send information over a telephone line), telecommunications software, a telephone line, and a way to connect to other computers (usually provided by an Internet service provider, or ISP). One activity that middle school students can learn is to send electronic mail, or e-mail. Once they obtain an e-mail address, they can correspond via messages typed into the computer with other students or classrooms in different parts of the country or the world.

Students can also join electronic mailing lists (these include "newsgroups" and "listserves")—electronic discussion groups of individuals who post messages about particular subjects that everyone who subscribes to the list receives automatically via e-mail. Today there are thousands of such lists on a variety of topics. Although these are too numerous and, frequently, too transient to enumerate, AFB refers to a list of electronic mailing lists of interest to people who are blind or visually impaired on its Website (www.afb.org).

The World Wide Web is part of the Internet that is generally picture-based or at least contains some graphical information. More and more students are using it to find information for research papers and class projects.

Numerous books are available about the Internet and how to use it and it would probably be worthwhile to read some general information before trying to teach students to use the Internet. An excellent resource is Project VISION (Kapperman, Heinze, Hahn, & Dalton, 1997), a booklet of methods and strategies for teaching Internet skills to students who are blind or visually impaired.

store the addresses of these sites in a special list. This list functions like a bookmark because it enables the user to open directly to the specified site. Eventually, the students will need to learn how to type in the Web addresses (called URLs) to find specific sites and students can learn to use the search engines on the Web to find sites on specific topics that interest them. Depending on the software being used to access the Web, there will be different features for students to learn.

• Save time and money by having students save information from the Web and read it off-line (after they sign off from the Internet access service). Although this process requires some additional effort, it prevents students from wandering aimlessly through cyberspace. Viewing information off-line may avoid long-distance telephone charges or fees charged by Internet service providers. In addition, it eliminates the frustration of trying to connect to the service during busy times of the day. In many schools, access to the Internet is limited, so students' activities should include a combination of off-line and efficient on-line activities. For example, if students are corresponding via e-mail, they can prepare messages on a word processor or e-mail program and then connect to the Internet via "flash sessions" and send them in a matter of seconds. Likewise, depending on the setup, incoming e-mail can be collected once a day and read at any time; even Web pages can be created off-line.

• Teach students to use the Internet to search for particular information, such as sports scores and national news. When doing research, they need to search for information using the software installed in the computer, download the information, read it on the screen, and print it out in hard-copy braille. Information sources like the *New York Times, Wall Street Journal,* and Cable News Network all provide on-line news coverage. Until recently, students who are blind or visually impaired had limited access to timely print-based information.

• Give students an imaginary budget and have them "shop" for a set of items appropriate to topics covered in class (such as technology, food, furniture, trips, and books). The teacher can control the complexity of the task through the instructions. For example, one teacher may have students compare only computer A and computer B, providing them with Web or e-mail addresses of these companies. A teacher with more advanced students might lift the restrictions and ask them to find the "best" computer by comparison shopping via the Web, and e-mailing companies to ask follow-up questions. Students will have to be able to hook up a modem and use whatever telecommunications package is available at the school. Their skill in navigating the screen will be useful, especially when accessing the World Wide Web, which has a lot of graphics.

✛ Teach braille-translation software and braille embossing. Older elementary and middle school students need to learn this technology so they can print documents in hard-copy braille, such as items from the Internet or a CD-ROM. Braille translation and printing may be tricky at first, so it is important for students to have a good grasp of braille as well as printing from notetakers, software applications such as word processors, the Internet, or CD-ROM. The classroom teacher or the teacher of visually impaired students will probably continue to translate such documents as homework assignments and tests (see "Using Translation Software" in this chapter).

High School (Grades 9–12)

By the time students start high school, they should be using the skills they learned in the earlier grades with increasing independence and applying these skills to new programs and applications. By the time they graduate, they should have the skills needed to go on to college or to work: the ability to access print in a variety of ways (such as with a screen reader or refreshable braille), to write using a word processor and produce documents in both print and braille, and to use a portable notetaker. They can also continue their education in using the Internet. Once students are comfortable searching for information and specific topics and using e-mail, they can go on to more advanced topics. The following strategies may be useful in teaching technology applications to high school students.

STRATEGIES

TEACHING TECHNOLOGY TO HIGH SCHOOL STUDENTS (GRADES 9–12)

✛ Teach advanced functions of applications.

✛ Teach the more detailed use of the Internet and Web.

 • Have students correspond with mentors. There are programs that match students and classrooms with people in a wide variety of jobs, including scientists, engineers, and health care professionals. Students can e-mail these mentors for assistance on class projects. One such program is AFB's Career and Technology Information Bank, with about 2,000 members who use technology at home and at work. Another program of interest is the DO-IT (Disabilities, Opportunities, Internetworking, and Technology) program of the University of Washington, Seattle, which teaches students to use adaptive technology in addition to providing mentors. (See the Resources section for contact information.)

 • Students can use the Web to advocate for themselves. One common complaint of braille and speech-technology users is that the majority of Web sites are difficult to navigate or inaccessible because of the large number of graphics. However, many Web designers are simply unaware of the needs of users with

USING TRANSLATION SOFTWARE

Braille translation software and embossing are especially useful for persons who do not know the braille code. For example, a classroom teacher could type out a class test or handout into the computer and prepare a braille copy by using translation software and a braille printer. The braille reader could then receive the braille copy at the same time that his or her sighted classmates are receiving the print version. Since braille-translation software is not infallible, the teacher of visually impaired students should proofread documents often to make sure that students are getting correct documents in braille. For example, acronyms in all capital letters, such as ABLE, may be incorrectly translated to include the *ble* contraction, or the format of the braille document may have been changed.

Just as the preponderance of desktop publishing in print has made it easier to create newsletters of poor visual quality, so the reliance on braille-translation software has led to some poor braille. Make sure that the computer-generated braille given to students is correct.

disabilities. Students can e-mail tips to site designers on making the sites more accessible.

• When students have had a great deal of experience using the Internet, they can learn to create their own Web pages, following instructions on the Internet or from the Internet service provider. Creating a Web site is becoming easier as new software tools are introduced. However, it still requires considerable time. An alternative approach would be to pair students in the class with students in a computer class. The blind or visually impaired students could teach the computer students about the accessibility of Web pages and adaptive equipment, and the computer students could help them design Web pages. Likewise a parent, sibling, or volunteer may have the skills and inclination to get involved in such a project.

• Another activity for developing critical-thinking and technology skills is to have students review Web sites. Many magazines publish lists of the Top 100 Web sites, but the criteria they use to judge sites may not include those the students would choose. Students can adapt a published set of criteria to meet their own needs. Encourage them to evaluate the accessibility as well as the content of sites.

✛ Teach the use of OCR scanners. High school is a good time for students to learn how to use scanners and OCR software to create their own braille documents from scanned print materials. Learning how to edit texts that have been scanned is an important skill.

✛ Teach higher-level functions. Students who are interested in mathematics, science, and computer programming can learn the computer braille code (CBC)—the official code for doing programming or entering commands and file names. It is extremely precise. It uses grade 1 braille and special symbols to indicate exactly what programming language is on the screen. Students who are seriously interested in computers and programming will need to learn CBC. Two good resources are *The Computer Braille Code Made Easy* (Dixon & Gray, 1993), and *Code for Computer Braille Notation* (1987). In addition, most refreshable braille displays have a setting to use eight-dot braille. The extra two dots are used to indicate capitalization and the location of the cursor. They give users flexibility to represent more characters than just the alphabet.

✛ Teach electronic braillers and other alternate types of equipment. If all this is not enough, students can also investigate some of the other types of technology mentioned earlier in this chapter, such as small portable computers with braille displays. There is always much to learn.

USING TECHNOLOGY AT HOME

Once students gain access to technology, the issue of using the technology at home usually arises. When students are first learning, the priority is to have the equipment in the classroom where the teacher can provide instruction and monitor their performance. By the fourth or fifth grade, students need to have greater access to the equipment to complete their assignments. Ideally, they will have duplicate computer systems at home and at school, but it is not always feasible to have two systems. Computers are generally expensive, as is the adaptive technology that students need to add. However, the section on "Funding the Purchase of Equipment" offers useful advice on ways to obtain equipment for families who cannot afford it.

Students who are lucky enough to have systems at home as well as at school may need to be trained in the home systems. Teachers may want to go to the students' homes to work with them. One advantage is that they will become acquainted with the families. If a student does not have the same system at home as at school, it is more difficult to teach the home system, but an advantage is that the student is exposed to a wider variety of technology.

TEACHER TRAINING

Developing Expertise

Developing expertise in the use of adaptive computer technology is time consuming. If teachers of visually impaired students do not use the equipment on a daily basis, they may not have confidence in their skills. Often teachers receive only a few hours of training, develop a certain level of proficiency, and then never have the time to practice or increase their skills. Thus, they may be hesitant to recommend the purchase of new devices once they become comfortable with a few pieces of technology because of the time it takes to learn the new equipment.

To assist their students, teachers need to maintain and expand their own adaptive computer skills. The following are several strategies for developing and maintaining these skills.

STRATEGIES

DEVELOPING TEACHERS' SKILLS WITH ADAPTIVE COMPUTERS

✛ Take a continuing education course on basic computer usage. If teachers are unsure of their computer skills, taking a course on the basics of using computers and applications they will be teaching will help them gain confidence. Many school systems offer such courses to teachers, as do community colleges and universities.

✛ Take a university course on adaptive technology. If teachers live near a university that offers such a course, it will give them the opportunity to see a wide variety of devices and what they are used for.

✛ Attend training sessions held at conferences, by the school system, or by equipment suppliers on a particular device you plan to buy. Vendors frequently offer free training if a certain number of people request it.

✛ Read the manual. This advice is a joke of sorts in the computer world, since it is one of the first comments technical support people will make when someone telephones with a question. The manual should be the first source of information for learning how a piece of equipment or software works. Many computers have a built-in help file to turn to.

✛ Choose one location to store all manuals and original software disks. Keep organized by putting the manuals and original disks together in a safe place, preferably in the same room where the equipment is being used.

✛ Observe how the system is installed. If a technology specialist or vendor is installing a piece of equipment (such as an external speech synthesizer or a refreshable braille display), be present and ask questions to make sure you understand what is being added and how. It is worthwhile to keep notes on what is being done in case you ever need to add the same equipment to another computer.

✛ Label cable connections to the computer. Tape a slip of paper to each cable to label it and label the place where it is plugged into the computer. It is often necessary to move a computer to another room, and the cables will have to be put back in their correct places.

✤ If possible, take home small pieces of equipment, such as a braille notetaker, to practice on before attempting to teach them to students.

✤ Test the strategies planned for the students. Teachers can put themselves in the students' place and try the same strategies they ask the students to use.

✤ Use adaptive equipment to complete tasks that would otherwise be done without it. For example, a teacher may not usually use a screen-reading program, but could try it out to create a test or write a report or use a notetaker to make a shopping list or take notes at a faculty meeting.

✤ Create a "cheat sheet" of the most frequently used commands (if one is not supplied by the manufacturer) and keep it with the equipment or in a folder. Create such sheets in braille for students as well.

✤ Choose an activity that is done periodically, like writing a quarterly report, and perform it on the equipment. Doing so will give teachers a chance to practice, as well as to perform complex functions that they may forget how to do if they do not practice them.

Keeping Up to Date

Once the hurdle of learning how to use adaptive technology is overcome, teachers need to develop strategies to keep themselves up to date. As mentioned earlier, technology changes rapidly; new versions of old favorites are introduced with added features. One need not acquire the newest technology immediately if existing equipment is doing the job well. But after a few years, old programs tend to become incompatible with new equipment and hence obsolete. Keeping an eye on trends and new equipment will keep teachers and students up to date with what is being used in colleges and in the job market. Some of the following tips on keeping up to date can be used even before technology is purchased.

STRATEGIES

KEEPING UP TO DATE

✤ Subscribe to technology newsletters and magazines. These can be periodicals specific to people with disabilities (such as those listed in Resources) or about computers in general.

✛ Obtain access to the Internet, in order to be able to obtain up-to-date information on technology, communicate with others in the field, and design activities for students using the Internet.

✛ Attend local, regional, and national conferences when feasible. Closing the Gap, held annually in Minnesota, and C-SUN, sponsored by California State University at Northridge and held in Los Angeles, are excellent national conferences at which the latest technology is displayed and demonstrated (see Resources).

✛ Periodically plan to give demonstrations of specific pieces of equipment to other teachers or parents. This will also force the teacher to learn how to use them. (It makes an even greater impression if students demonstrate the equipment with the teacher.)

✛ Develop a relationship with the school's computer teacher. Pool expertise to make as many machines as possible accessible to students.

✛ Develop a relationship with local equipment suppliers.

✛ Invite suppliers to give demonstrations to groups of teachers, students, and parents.

✛ Get to know the staff that offers technical support. Over time, they will become familiar with the teacher's system.

✛ Create a list of local technology users who can be called upon for assistance.

✛ Develop contacts with teachers and technology users at other schools and universities in your area.

✛ Talk with the Tech Act representatives in your state. The RESNA (Rehabilitation Engineering and Assistive Technology Society of America) Tech Act Project is a program funded by the National Institute on Disability and Rehabilitation Research to provide assistance with technology in every state. To find the address of the Tech Act office in a particular area, call the RESNA Technical Assistance Project (see Resources).

FUNDING THE PURCHASE OF EQUIPMENT

As noted earlier, technology is expensive, and neither the student's family nor the school system may have sufficient funds to purchase all the equipment a student needs. The teacher may then have to switch hats and become a fund raiser. No matter what the source from which funding is being sought, the more convincing the teacher's argument about the functional reasons for using equipment, the more likely he or she is to succeed. Having a student use equipment, even equipment which is at a more elementary level, allows the teacher to indicate that a student is ready to move on, which can be a selling point to the parents and the student him- or herself. The parents and school will see that the students are making progress and need more sophisticated technology to continue to advance. The following are strategies for obtaining funds for technology.

STRATEGIES

OBTAINING FUNDS FOR TECHNOLOGY

✛ Go to local service organizations. Groups, such as the Lions, Delta Gamma, Junior League, and the Optimists Club—even scout troops—may be willing to help. Be specific about what equipment is needed and why.

✛ Demonstrate what the students can do with the equipment. Be specific about how the students will benefit. With permission from the parents and the school, teachers can take pictures, slides, or videos of students using technology and demonstrate how they will benefit from the specific pieces being asked for. Teachers can ask the students to come with them when they give a presentation or invite the group from whom funds are being requested to visit the classroom.

✛ Ask for matching funds, rather than the whole amount. If the school district will agree to supply part of the money, the teacher can ask local service organizations or the Parents Association to buy the rest. These groups may also be willing to fund a small portion of what is needed, such as software.

✛ Use every possible vehicle—the school district, parents, insurance, service organizations, grants, church bake sales, and even garage sales. Be flexible, persistent, and creative. Do not limit the search to only one source of funds.

✛ Contact businesses that are upgrading their systems. From time to time, large companies get rid of old computers with less processing power and purchase new ones. These old computers may be useful for students to start with and gain proficiency on; then it is easier to make a case for upgrading them.

✛ Teachers in rural areas may want to discuss the possibility of setting up consortia of several counties to purchase materials that can be shared. This strategy does not always work, but it may prevent one county from purchasing an expensive item or computer setup and then have students move away. No school district wants to have expensive and valuable equipment gathering dust.

✛ Show appreciation to donors of money or equipment. Have the students write thank-you letters. Write a story and put a picture in the local newspaper. Present a certificate or plaque to the organization to thank them.

✛ When writing grant proposals for funds from agencies or organizations, be sure to follow the directions exactly. Proposals that ask for more money than is offered or do not fit the purpose of the grant will usually not be considered.

✦ Be prepared to do a lot of work. Unfortunately, doing the leg work necessary to write a grant proposal or do a presentation at a local service organization can take a lot of time. The teacher will have to research vendors, prices, and possible sources of funds. However, the results will make all the hard work well worth the time.

SUMMARY

This chapter has just scratched the surface of the enormous topic of access to technology for students who use braille. There is a tremendous amount for both teachers and students to learn. The most important points to keep in mind are these:

- Consider students' needs and abilities first.
- Look ahead to predict as best possible what students will need in the future.
- Start teaching a variety of technology from the beginning.
- Break down instruction into small, manageable steps, slowly building skills in each of the adaptive techniques and equipment the students need to learn.
- Be persistent and flexible in seeking the equipment students need.

With these points in mind, consider again the vignette about Cassilda, introduced at the beginning of this chapter, to see what *could* be:

Cassilda is a fifth-grade student in a progressive school district. The students in her class know how to sign on to the Internet and are participating in a multimedia archaeological site "adventure." Cassilda reads and writes braille and has been using a screen-reading program since the third grade. Ms. Johnson, Cassilda's teacher of students who are visually impaired, started teaching her in the fourth grade to use speech access to obtain information from CD-ROMs and the Internet. Cassilda likes to hear the audio clips that she has accessed and can get more information by reading the text with the external speech synthesizer on her computer. When she finds information she needs for a report, she downloads it and saves it into a file. Later, Ms. Johnson helps her put some of the information into hardcopy braille, a skill Cassilda is just starting to learn, so she can refer to it when making an oral presentation. Cassilda is also learning to use her braille notetaker to take some notes on the information she has just heard. She and her computer buddy compare their notes to make sure they have all the information they need for their project; each has a few details the other missed. Ms. Johnson has spent a great deal of time over the past few years researching the various types of technology that can help Cassilda access print and work more independently and is generally satisfied with the equipment that is available in the school. Cassilda wants to learn to use the notetaker more efficiently and is excited about taking part in the computer activities with her classmates.

REFERENCES

Code for computer braille notation. (1987). Louisville, KY: American Printing House for the Blind.

Dixon, J., & Gray, C. (1993). *The computer braille code made easy.* Boston: National Braille Press.

Espinola, O., & Croft, D. (1992). *Solutions: Access technologies for people who are blind.* Boston: National Braille Press.

Kapperman, G., Heinze, T., Hahn, S., & Dalton, S. (1997). *Project VISION: Visually impaired students and Internet opportunities now.* Sycamore, IL: Research and Development Institute.

Leventhal, J. (1995, May–June). Accessing Microsoft Windows with synthetic speech: An overview. *Journal of Visual Impairment & Blindness, JVIB News Service, 89*(3), 14–18.

Rex, E. J., Koenig, A. J., Wormsley, D. P., & Baker, R. L. (1994). *Foundations of braille literacy.* New York: AFB Press.

Shragai, Y. (1995, November–December). Access to Microsoft Windows 95 for persons with low vision: An overview. *Journal of Visual Impairment & Blindness, JVIB News Service, 89*(6), 5–9.

Shragai, Y., & Uslan, M. M. (1995, September–October). Access to Microsoft Windows for persons with low vision: An overview. *Journal of Visual Impairment & Blindness, JVIB News Service, 89*(5), 13–17.

ASSISTIVE TECHNOLOGY ASSESSMENT
FOR VISUALLY IMPAIRED STUDENTS
Background Referral Information

Identifying Information: Please type or print

Student's name _____ Date of birth _____ Age ____

School system _____ School _____

Classroom teacher _____ Grade level _____

Vision teacher _____ Telephone No. _____

Educational Information

Primary Disability

☐ Orthopedically impaired   ☐ Hearing impaired

☐ Mildly intellectually disabled   ☐ Deaf

☐ Moderately intellectually disabled   ☐ Vision impaired

☐ Severely intellectually disabled   ☐ Blind

☐ Profoundly intellectually disabled   ☐ Other health impaired

☐ Speech-language impaired   ☐ Severely emotionally disturbed

☐ Learning disabled   ☐ Has a behavior disorder

☐ Autistic

Secondary Disability

☐ Orthopedically impaired   ☐ Hearing impaired

☐ Mildly intellectually disabled   ☐ Deaf

☐ Moderately intellectually disabled   ☐ Vision impaired

☐ Severely intellectually disabled   ☐ Blind

☐ Profoundly intellectually disabled   ☐ Other health impaired

☐ Speech-language impaired   ☐ Severely emotionally disturbed

☐ Learning disabled   ☐ Has a behavior disorder

☐ Autistic

Time in Regular Education Class (hours per week)

☐ 0–5   ☐ 6–10   ☐ 11–15

☐ 16–20   ☐ 21–25   ☐ 26–30

Medical Diagnosis

☐ Cerebral palsy   ☐ Closed head injury

☐ Down's syndrome   ☐ Neurological disease (specify)_____

☐ Other syndrome (specify) _____

☐ Unknown

Vision: Please complete with input from vision teacher if appropriate

Date of most recent eye exam _____

Visual status: Right/OD - _____ Left/OS - _____

Field loss (please describe in detail) _____

Appendix A. Form for Assessing a Student's Needs for Technology

Source: Adapted with permission from the Georgia Project for Assistive Technology, Forest Park, GA, August 1996.

Optimal placement of stimuli _____

Age/date of onset _____

Cause of visual impairment (etiology) _____

Is visual condition stable? _____

Describe any deficiencies in color vision _____

Date of most recent low vision exam _____

Was a low vision aid prescribed? Specify _____

Vision concerns

| _____ Acuity | _____ Tracking | _____ Visual field |
| _____ Nystagmus | _____ Scanning | _____ Strabismus |

Date of most recent learning media assessment _____

Results _____

_____

Accessing Print

How does the student access printed information?

☐ Acetate overlays for "dittos": Specify color(s) _____

☐ Materials produced with felt-tip pen on bold-line paper

☐ Materials enlarged on photocopying machine: Specify (i.e., 130%, 3 times) _____

☐ Large-print books   Optimal point size _____

☐ Large-print materials   Preferred point size/viewing distance _____

☐ Others (size/distance) _____

☐ Optical aids

    ☐ Eyeglasses   ☐ Contact lens

    ☐ Handheld/stand magnifier—power _____

    ☐ Telescope—power _____

    ☐ Large-print

    ☐ Closed-circuit television (CCTV)

☐ Braille books and materials. Briefly describe student's braille skills: _____

_____

☐ Books on tape and other recorded materials

☐ Tactile graphics: maps, graphs, charts, geometry figures

☐ Large print/talking calculator

☐ Talking dictionary

How does student gain access to information presented on a chalkboard or overhead projector?

☐ Gets copy from teacher   ☐ Gets copy from other students

☐ Uses handheld or spectacle-mounted telescope   ☐ Sits close enough to read from the chalkboard

☐ Computerized materials when provided with adaptations

    ☐ Computer networks   ☐ Books on disk

    ☐ CD-ROM   ☐ Optical scanner

    ☐ Online information provided via telephone lines

Does the student experience reading fatigue? (Describe conditions under which fatigue occurs.) _____

_____

Appendix A. *(Continued)*

Producing Written Communication

How does the student produce written communications?

☐ Bold-line paper   ☐ Raised-line paper

☐ Felt-tip pens   ☐ White boards

☐ Braillewriter   ☐ Slate and stylus

☐ Mountbatten brailler   ☐ Typewriter

☐ Computer

     ☐ Apple (specify) _____   ☐ Macintosh (specify) _____

     ☐ IBM-compatible (specify) _____

     ☐ How is computer accessed?

         ☐ Regular print   ☐ Large print

         ☐ Speech   ☐ Braille display

Note Taking

How does the student take notes in class?

☐ Bold-line paper and felt-tip pen (Can student read his/her handwritten notes?)

☐ Braillewriter   ☐ Slate and stylus

☐ Tape recorder   ☐ Notebook computer

☐ Braille 'n Speak   ☐ Braille Mate

☐ Type 'n Speak   ☐ Keynote Companion

☐ Mountbatten brailler   ☐ Other (specify) _____

Background information provided by

Name _____   Position _____

Computer-Access Evaluation

Computer Functions

Specify the activities for which the student will use the computer.

☐ Vocational (specify) _____

☐ Writing (specify) _____

☐ Reading (specify) _____

☐ Mathematics (specify) _____

☐ Communication (specify) _____

☐ Recreation/leisure activities (specify) _____

☐ Other (specify) _____

Input

Standard Keyboard

☐ Student can use the standard keyboard without adaptations.

☐ Student can use the standard computer keyboard with adaptations.

     ☐ Keyguard   ☐ Finger guard/pointer

     ☐ Keylatch   ☐ Wrist/arm support _____

     ☐ Moisture guard   ☐ Tactile locator dots _____

Appendix A. *(Continued)*

☐ Braille keyboard

☐ Other (specify) _____

☐ Student cannot use the standard keyboard (with or without adaptations).

If the student can use the keyboard (with or without adaptations), please provide the following information:

☐ Student can identify alphanumeric keys.

☐ Student can identify function keys.

☐ Student can activate two keys simultaneously.

☐ Student can activate/deactivate keys without causing key repeats.

    Method of access

    ☐ Right hand   Fingers used _____

    ☐ Left hand   Fingers used _____

Typing speed (specify) _____ words per minute

☐ Student can touch type without looking at keys.

Specify appropriate keyboard utilities for this student:

☐ Sticky keys   ☐ Repeat keys   ☐ Slow keys   ☐ Toggle keys   ☐ Mouse keys

Alternative Keyboards

If the student cannot use the standard keyboard effectively with or without the above adaptations, please indicate which type of keyboard(s) the student can use to access the computer independently.

☐ Break-apart keyboard

☐ Expanded keyboard (specify) _____

☐ Miniature keyboard (specify) _____

☐ One-handed keyboard

☐ On-screen keyboard with a mouse. Indicate type of mouse: _____

☐ TouchTablet (e.g., Power Pad)

☐ Braille input device (keyboard)

Standard Mouse and Mouse Alternatives

☐ Student can use the standard computer mouse.

☐ Student cannot use the standard computer mouse.

Output

☐ Student can see information on the standard computer monitor without adaptations.

☐ Student can see information on the standard computer monitor with adaptations.

    ☐ Screen-enlarging hardware (specify) _____

    ☐ Flexible-arm monitor stand

    ☐ Enlarged font   ☐ Double spacing

    ☐ Screen-enlarging software (specify): _____

    Magnification _____ Viewing distance _____

    Preferred color combination _____

    Preferred viewing mode (e.g., full screen, line, area) _____

If the student cannot use the standard computer monitor with adaptations, indicate which hardware/software the student can use:

☐ Screen-reading/access software (specify) _____

Appendix A. *(Continued)*

- ☐ Talking word processing (specify) _____
- ☐ Speech synthesizer (specify) _____
- ☐ Student can understand speech produced by speech synthesizer.
- ☐ Braille display
- ☐ Student prefers to read print from a standard computer printer, with other adaptations, such as a CCTV or magnifier.

If the student cannot read the print from a standard computer printer, please specify the following:

- ☐ Student can read the print when enlarged. (Specify preferred font size): _____
- ☐ Student requires a braille printer.

Computer Operations

Indicate which computer operations the student can do:

- ☐ Turn central processing unit on and off
- ☐ Turn monitor on and off
- ☐ Insert disk in disk drive
- ☐ Eject disk from disk drive
- ☐ Turn printer on and off
- ☐ Retrieve desired program for on-screen menu

Software Applications

Specify the software applications the student requires:

Vocational

- ☐ Word processing
- ☐ Database   ☐ Spreadsheet
- ☐ Desktop publishing
- ☐ Computer-assisted design
- ☐ Other (specify) _____

Writing

- ☐ Word processing
- ☐ Grammar checker   ☐ Spell checker
- ☐ Outlining software
- ☐ Word prediction
- ☐ Other (specify) _____

Mathematics

- ☐ Access to Math—Apple IIe
- ☐ Math Scratch Pad—Apple IIc
- ☐ Math CAD—IBM
- ☐ Other (specify) _____
- ☐ On-screen calculator

Cognitive and language

- ☐ Cause and effect (specify) _____
- ☐ Language development (specify) _____

Communication

- ☐ Write OutLoud—Macintosh
- ☐ Speaking Dynamically—Macintosh
- ☐ EZ Keys—IBM
- ☐ Handiword—IBM
- ☐ Other (specify) _____

Recreation/Leisure

- ☐ Cause-and-effect games
- ☐ Other (specify) _____

Appendix A. *(Continued)*

☐ *Other (specify)* _____

Computer Access Recommendations

Input mode

☐ Standard keyboard

☐ Standard keyboard with adaptations (specify) _____

☐ Alternative keyboard (specify) _____

☐ Switch input (specify) _____

☐ Mouse or mouse alternative (specify) _____

☐ Voice recognition (specify) _____

Output mode

☐ Standard computer monitor—optimal size _____

☐ Standard computer monitor with adaptations (specify) _____

☐ Screen enlarging software/hardware (specify) _____

☐ Talking word processing (specify) _____

☐ Screen-reading/access software (specify) _____

☐ Speech synthesizer/sound card (specify) _____

☐ Braille display (specify)_____

Software needs

Specify any software the student needs: _____

_____

_____

_____

Additional comments/recommendations:

_____

_____

_____

_____

_____

_____

_____

_____

Computer Access Evaluation conducted by

Name _____   Position _____

SKILLS NEEDED TO OPERATE EQUIPMENT

Student's name _____

Instructor's name _____

Training date(s) _____

Name and version of device _____

The following checklist will serve as an indicator of the tasks
that this student has learned:

* I - independently performs the task
* N - uses notes ( )% of the time to complete tasks
* V - needs verbal coaching ( )% of the time to complete task
* U - unable to consistently perform the task assigned
* — student has not been shown that particular feature of the device

	Pretest Date						Posttest Date
Major Components							
The student can							
—identify and locate all the alpha keys							
—identify and locate all the number keys							
—identify and locate the special function keys such as help							
—identify and connect the power charger							
—describe and perform the charging procedure							
—state name and manufacturer of device							
—find information in the manual							
—get technical support							
Operating the Menus							
The student can							
—select menu choices							
—exit menus and return to document							
Creating and Writing a File							
The student knows the procedures for							
—creating a new file							
—opening an existing file							
—describing the cursor and its function							
—moving the cursor to the top or bottom of a file							
—quitting and saving a file							

Appendix B. Sample Form for Tracking a Student's Progress in Equipment-Operating Skills

Source: Adapted with permission by Betsy Presley from "Assistive Technology Assessment for the Visually Impaired," by Jay Stiteley and Jim Alan, Texas School for the Blind and Visually Impaired, Austin (n.d.).

	Pretest Date					Posttest Date	
Editing Commands							
The student knows the procedures for							
—positioning the cursor for properly inserting letters, words, and sentences							
—deleting the current word							
—deleting the current character							
—deleting the previous character							
—deleting to the end of a sentence							
—deleting to the end of a paragraph							
—deleting from the cursor to the end of a file							
New Pages, Search Procedures, and Place Markers							
The student knows the procedures for							
—starting a new page							
—searching forward for a specific string of text							
—searching backward for a specific string of text							
—searching and replacing text forward							
—searching and replacing text backwards							
Operating the Disk Drive							
The student knows the procedures for							
—touching the disk properly without affecting its storage capability							
—positioning and inserting a disk							
—formatting a disk							
—removing the disk safely from the disk drive							
—setting the write-protect tab on the diskette							
—transferring files between the device and the disk drive							
File Commands							
The student knows the procedures for							
—reading the disk directory							
—reading subdirectories on disks							
—spelling file names or directory names							
—copying from disk to memory							
—erasing files from memory or disk							
—renaming files							

Appendix B. (*Continued*)

	Pretest Date					Posttest Date	

Printing a File

The student knows the procedure for

—loading the paper into the printer

—connecting the printer cables to the device and the printer

—selecting a specific print driver (if appropriate)

—printing a single page

—printing multiple pages

—printing a single file

—printing groups of files

Calculator Functions

The student knows the procedures for

—entering and exiting the calculator mode

—entering calculations

—operating adding, subtraction, multiplying, and dividing functions

—operating negation, percentages, and parentheses

—operating trigonometric functions (if available)

—operating the square and square-root functions (if available)

—operating the logarithmic functions (if available)

—operating the power and root functions (if available)

Advanced Editing Features

The student knows the procedures for

—moving a block of text

—copying a block of text

—deleting a block of text

—merging documents

—centering text

—underlining text

—making a line right justified

—moving to the start of the next line

—moving to the next tab setting

—inserting the time and date into a file

—inserting the calculated result

Appendix B. *(Continued)*

	Pretest Date					Posttest Date	
—editing directly from disk							
—exiting a file without saving text							
Other Features							
The student knows the procedures for							
—using spell checking, if available							
—adding, deleting, and changing a word in the dictionary							
—saving and retrieving a dictionary file to disk							
—deleting the current dictionary							
—running another application program							
—setting the time and date							
—formatting disks							
—renaming disks							
—copying disks							
Using the Help Key							
The student knows the procedures for							
—entering and exiting the help mode							
Miscellaneous							
The student knows the procedures for							
—reinitializing, resetting, warm-booting the device							
—installing new application programs							
—updating software							

Appendix B. *(Continued)*

DETERMINING THE READING MEDIUM FOR STUDENTS WITH VISUAL IMPAIRMENTS: A DIAGNOSTIC TEACHING APPROACH

ALAN J. KOENIG AND M. CAY HOLBROOK

There are perhaps few decisions made on behalf of students with visual impairments that are more crucial, yet subject to more confusion and controversy, than the decision regarding an appropriate reading medium. Making an initial determination of the appropriate reading medium is not a concern for those who have no visual impairment (i.e., they will learn to read print), nor is it a concern for those who are totally blind (i.e., they will learn to read braille). Difficulties may arise, however, in making decisions for those students who are visually impaired but not totally blind. The purpose of this article is to address these difficulties and propose guidelines for appropriate decision making.

Few published procedures have been available to teachers and parents for assistance in making decisions concerning selection of a reading medium for students with visual impairments. Perhaps the lack of attention in the literature addressing this difficult problem has led to a sense of confusion that has fueled the controversy between teaching print reading or teaching braille reading. While common guidelines for such decisions may be used by professionals throughout the country, these have not been thoroughly documented.

In the past, professionals believed that use of vision could impair sight even further (Irwin, 1920). It was common practice to blindfold, and teach braille reading to all students who were visually impaired and, therefore, "save their sight" for other tasks. The decision to teach braille reading was made without consideration of visual functioning. Today, best professional practice and federal legislation specify that educational decisions must be made by a multidisciplinary team according to the individual needs and abilities of each student. These decisions must be based on information obtained from systematic procedures. Such procedures must be used to determine the most appropriate reading medium for each child.

Reprinted from Alan J. Koenig & M. Cay Holbrook, "Determining the Reading Medium for Students with Visual Impairments: A Diagnostic Teaching Approach," *Journal of Visual Impairment & Blindness,* 83(6) (June 1989), pp. 296–302. Copyright © 1989, American Foundation for the Blind.

This article will focus on students who are entering a developmental reading program, i.e., students who are learning to read for the first time. Students with adventitious visual impairments present separate concerns that, while important, will not be considered within the scope of this paper. This article will: (a) explore the need for, and use of, a diagnostic teaching approach to help in the determination of the initial decision on the appropriate reading medium for students with visual impairments; (b) discuss four areas of importance for educators and parents to consider in making initial decisions; and (c) describe continued evaluation of the initial medium in a number of specific areas.

The early years of a student's life represent a critical period for development of skills that will provide the foundation for all future learning and living. An essential part of this critical period is the role that professionals and parents have in assuring that a solid foundation is provided for each student. No one can predict the future with absolute certainty. However, professionals and parents are called upon to make informed decisions as a team in order to assure an appropriate education for each student with a visual impairment; one essential team decision will involve the primary reading medium.

Diagnostic teaching in the decision-making process

Decisions on the appropriate reading medium cannot be made on the basis of arbitrary information, such as the legal definition of blindness, since students with visual impairments use their vision with differing degrees of efficiency. The early years of a student's education should be used as a diagnostic teaching phase during which different options for reading and writing can be explored. The period of reading readiness presents an ideal time for implementation of a diagnostic teaching approach, since readiness activities seek to stimulate all the senses in preparation for formal reading. By using a diagnostic teaching approach to early reading instruction, teachers and parents can collect information about a student's preference for gathering sensory information. Support for the need for one reading medium or another can be derived from these data. The key element is collecting information that will provide a basis for informed decision making, a process that is undeniably superior to decisions based on arbitrary or superficial information.

Characteristics of diagnostic teaching

Diagnostic teaching combines the two essential educational practices of instruction and assessment and may be characterized by the following principles:
- instruction and assessment cannot be separated in effective teaching;
- students learn and develop as individuals, not as a group;
- information gathered from assessment should be used immediately to change instruction in order to make learning more efficient; and
- systematic problem-solving techniques can be employed to explore areas in a child's development that are unknown.

The use of diagnostic teaching practices is by no means new. Although such an approach is typically associated with the diagnosis and remediation of learning problems, the case can be made that it has value for other applications in which a problem-solving approach is needed. The diagnostic teaching approach provides an excellent means of putting together pieces of a puzzle when one piece is missing or unknown.

The determination of the appropriate reading medium for young children with visual impairments who are beginning to read can be achieved through the use of these strategies.

The process of collecting information

The process of diagnostic teaching uses incidental and structured observations, indirect and direct teaching, and ongoing assessment as a basis for guiding subsequent instruction. By collecting information on visual and tactual efficiency over several months or years of careful diagnostic teaching, a student's learning style will undoubtedly begin to emerge.

At this point, educators should have acquired some preliminary indication of whether a student is primarily a visual learner or primarily a tactual learner, as well as information on the rate of learning with the preferred sensory modality. For some students, a decision on the appropriate reading medium may be made relatively early in the readiness phase, but additional information may be needed for others.

Readiness for formal reading instruction is signaled by the establishment of a number of skills, such as showing interest in books; showing interest in, and telling stories from, pictures; discriminating likenesses and differences in abstract symbols, geometric shapes, letters, and simple words; copying letters and words; identifying one's own name; and identifying letter names and simple sight words.

As these skills are being established, a wealth of information can be collected to support the decision for a specific reading medium. For students whose primary reading medium was not established earlier, scrutiny of the more "formal" readiness skills will be necessary. As students enter the stage in which they are learning prerequisite skills for reading, the educator should provide exposure to printed materials and braille materials, either concurrently or sequentially, in order to determine the level of sustained interest and the rate of learning of specific skills in each medium. For example, a student learning to recognize his/her name could be presented with both the printed version and a superimposed braille version as labels for personal items. After a period of instruction and time to eliminate any novelty effect, the student's use of either the print or braille labels could be determined through observation or direct assessment.

For a student who has not demonstrated a consistent pattern of visual or tactual learning, the data collected during this period of time will be most crucial for consideration by the multidisciplinary team in determining the reading medium. It is possible for a student with a visual impairment at this stage in reading development to show nearly equal preference for visual and tactual information, and additional consideration will need to be made by the team, such as prognosis of the visual impairment and future applicability of each medium.

It is important to allow sufficient time to collect information to support the crucial decision on the reading medium. Team members should not feel compelled to follow the common practice that a child should begin to read at a certain age, but should wait until readiness skills are established; students with visual impairments may require an extended readiness period prior to formal reading instruction. If parents or other team members are reluctant to extend the readiness period, the teacher of the visually impaired must be prepared to discuss the negative consequences of moving a child into formal reading instruction before adequate readiness is established.

Initial evaluation and considerations for determining the reading medium

The initial evaluation phase provides the multidisciplinary team with the early information needed to make a decision on a student's reading medium. This section will discuss the areas to consider in collecting pertinent information through diagnostic teaching and the process of synthesizing these data in a manner that will lead to an informed team decision. Four areas are important to consider during the diagnostic teaching phase in early reading development: 1) visual efficiency and potential, 2) tactual efficiency and potential, 3) prognosis of the visual impairment, and 4) presence of additional handicaps. While factors such as reading rate and reading comprehension are important to consider, such information is difficult to obtain at the readiness/beginning reading level and, therefore, will be discussed later as areas for continued evaluation.

Visual efficiency

A period of diagnostic teaching is ideal and essential for accurately assessing the degree of efficiency with which a student uses vision to gather information about the environment. While educators want to have a total view of visual functioning in students with visual impairments, this discussion will relate to areas that will gain information contributing to a decision on the primary reading medium. Members of the multidisciplinary team will want to systematically collect objective and qualitative information on questions such as:

- Does the student use vision to explore the environment?
- Does the student visually recognize the presence of significant persons in the environment prior to verbal interaction?
- Do objects in the environment stimulate a motor response in the student (e.g., reaching toward objects, crawling toward objects)?
- Does the student use vision to locate objects in the environment? At near distances (within 12-16 inches)? At intermediate distances (within 16-24 inches)? At far distances (beyond 24 inches)?
- Does the student verbally label objects prior to tactual exploration, thereby using vision as a confirming sense?
- Does the student visually identify objects? What are the sizes of objects and at what distances?
- Does the student show interest in pictures? Can the student identify pictures? Of what size? With what level of accuracy? With what level of extraneous background information? At what distances?
- Does the student show an interest in scribbling/writing with a pencil or Magic Marker? Painting? Cutting?
- Does the student discriminate likenesses and differences in objects and geometric shapes? At what distances? Of what size?

- Does the student visually discriminate and match simple words? At what distance and of what size? With what level of accuracy?
- Does the student identify his/her name in print? Of what size? At what distance?
- At what rate does the student success fully complete visual tasks?

There are a number of excellent observation scales and assessment instruments that provide a comprehensive functional vision evaluation, such as those developed by American Printing House for the Blind (APH) (Barraga & Morris, 1980), Florida Department of Education (1983), Smith and Cote (1982), and Roessing (1982). Over a period of time, those involved in the student's program should summarize and compare observations in order to determine whether the student is primarily using his/her visual sense or tactual sense to collect sensory information in the environment. For students who are found to be "visual learners," particular attention must be focused on visual efficiency at near point. Visual efficiency for distant tasks does not guarantee or even imply efficiency at near point and vice versa.

In addition, a student with a central field loss may be able to complete distant tasks with high efficiency, but near tasks with little or no efficiency; because of difficulties with resolution, reading with peripheral vision will be slower than reading with an intact central field. Therefore, as information is being collected, observations related to visual tasks performed within 16 inches from the eyes must be given primary consideration in determining the reading medium, although students with low vision will generally have a closer working distance at near point.

Ophthalmological or low vision findings should be examined by multidisciplinary team members. However, clinical information obtained during an examination by an eye care professional must be used as only one source of information that will contribute to the overall decision. Such information is obtained in a setting that does not, in most cases, parallel the home or school environment in which a student will be reading.

Generally, the clinical environment is ideal (e.g., no glare, good lighting), the visual task is relatively short in duration (e.g., read a few lines of letters, read a few rows of text), and extraneous factors are not present (e.g., noise from other students). Conversely, the student may be intimidated by the clinical or medical setting and results may not be typical of the true level of performance. Also, acuity measurements are often limited to distance vision, which provides little information about how a student will function on most school-related tasks. Therefore, educators must collect information that relates more to the "real" learning environment and use that in conjunction with the clinical findings before making an informed decision on the appropriate reading medium.

During the initial diagnostic teaching phase, information can be collected not only on the current level of functioning but on progress in developing visual efficiency as well. After a vision stimulation/training program has been implemented for several months or more, it is important to examine the student's rate of progress relative to his/her visual potential. This information may be used to predict, as carefully as possible, the level of visual skill that the student is expected to have acquired at the time a formal reading program will begin; such a prediction is a legitimate source of information to be considered by the multidisciplinary team in making the initial decision.

Tactual efficiency

Information related to tactual efficiency should also be collected during the initial diagnostic teaching phase. Some questions the multidisciplinary team may wish to consider include:

- Does the student primarily use his/her tactual sense to explore the environment?
- Does the student use vision to locate and initially identify objects, and then use touch to confirm the initial observation? What is the degree of accuracy for initial identification through use of vision?
- What is the degree of accuracy for subsequent identification through the tactual sense?
- Does the student use his/her vision to locate objects, but then use tactual information to identify the objects?
- Does the student use only tactual information to locate and identify objects in the environment?
- Does the student tactually identify objects of different sizes with accuracy? Large objects (e.g., chair, bed, coffee table)? Medium-sized objects (e.g., teddy bear, toys, shirt, ball)? Small objects (e.g., paper clip, coins, marbles, raisins, cereal)?
- Does the student respond to effective teaching in use of fine motor skills (e.g., cutting, holding spoon, picking up small objects)?
- Does the student tactually discriminate likenesses and differences in objects and geometric shapes?
- Does the student show interest in books embossed in braille when being read to by a parent or teacher?
- Does the student identify his/her name in braille much more readily than in print?

Unlike the area of visual efficiency, there are no widely recognized formal instruments or observation scales that educators can use to assist in collecting information on tactual efficiency. While the *Roughness Discrimination Test* may provide a measure of tactual sensitivity (Harley, Truan, & Sanford, 1987), it does not indicate how a student performs on essential skills involving discrimination and recognition of braille letters and words. A diagnostic teaching approach lends itself to the use of instructional materials for teaching as well as continual assessment, and a number of materials could be used, such as the APH Tactual Discrimination Worksheets, APH Touch and Tell Series, worksheets from the Mangold Developmental Program (Mangold, 1977), and criterion-referenced inventories from Patterns Primary Braille Reading Program (APH, 1982).

As with examining visual efficiency, it is important to consider the student's rate of learning in developing tactual skills necessary for formal reading.

Prognosis of visual impairment

Multidisciplinary team members must consider whether the child's visual condition is stable and not likely to deteriorate in the future (e.g., albinism, optic atrophy) or whether the child's visual condition may be unstable (e.g., uncontrolled glaucoma, detached retinas) or progressive (e.g., retinitis pigmentosa, macular degeneration) and loss of vision in the future is likely. The difficulty for team members at this point is one of "likelihood" of future vision loss. Therefore, it is appropriate and necessary to extend the multidisciplinary team to include eye care professionals that have examined the child and/or to consider clinical low vision/ophthalmological information from the student's file. If current information is not available, a referral should be made immediately to an appropriate eye care professional.

As mentioned previously, no one single member of the multidisciplinary team, including an eye care professional, should make educational decisions for a student. If an eye care professional makes a recommendation regarding educational programming, it must be remembered that the ultimate decision is made by a team of persons familiar with the student. Therefore, it is essential to consider clinical findings and recommendations as one source of information, but not as the sole source. This information is used by the multidisciplinary team, along with information collected from other sources during the diagnostic teaching phase, to make an informed decision about the appropriate reading medium for a student with a visual impairment.

Presence of additional handicaps

In making educational decisions in any area of skill development, the multidisciplinary team must consider the influence of additional handicaps on learning. Of primary consideration is the level of cognitive ability. A cognitive delay or disability makes learning progress more slowly in all areas of development. In the area of reading, the decision that must be considered by the multidisciplinary team is whether a student with a moderate to pro found cognitive disability will benefit from any type of reading program, regardless of whether the medium would be braille or print.

For students with a mild to moderate cognitive disability, decisions will center on the functionality of reading (e.g., use of reading for daily living skills, enjoyment, and job-related skills) and the most appropriate type of reading program to accomplish those functions. For students with any level of cognitive disability, consideration should be given to the value of a reading medium in print or in braille relative to the value of listening/aural reading as a mode of communication.

The presence of motor impairments must also be considered. Motor impairments may affect control of the eyes, although such impairments may be amenable to specific training. Motor impairments may also affect the efficient movements of the hands, which may make braille reading more difficult or, in some cases, functionally impossible. Regardless of the way in which a motor impairment manifests itself, such implications for reading must be one factor that is considered in relationship to the implications of other factors identified in this section.

Synthesizing information and making team decisions

Once information regarding visual efficiency, tactual efficiency, prognosis, and influences of additional handicaps has been collected, it is time to begin the process of synthesizing the information and determining how it will affect the decision on the initial reading medium. It is important to examine carefully the objective findings, rather than to rely on hunches, guesses, and presumptions.

Each member of the multidisciplinary team who has worked with the child during the diagnostic teaching phase, including the parents and regular classroom teachers, should discuss observations and assessment data and contribute to the group discussion of the implications. The team's discussion should focus on the characteristics of the student displayed during the readiness phase, as well as information such as prognosis and presence of other disabilities, to determine whether the student will enter a formal reading program in print or in braille. Characteristics of a student who might be a likely candidate for a print reading program may include:

- uses vision efficiently to complete tasks at near distances;
- shows interest in pictures and demonstrates the ability to identify pictures and/or elements within pictures;
- identifies name in print and/or understands that print has meaning;
- uses print to accomplish other prerequisite reading skills;
- has a stable eye condition;
- has an intact central visual field;
- shows steady progress in learning to use his/her vision as necessary to assure efficient print reading;
- is free of additional handicaps that would interfere with progress in a developmental reading program in print.

Characteristics of a student who might be a likely candidate for a braille reading program may include:

- shows preference for exploring the environment tactually;
- efficiently uses the tactual sense to identify small objects;
- identifies his/her name in braille and/or understands that braille has meaning;
- uses braille to acquire other prerequisite reading skills;
- has an unstable eye condition or poor prognosis for retaining current level of vision in the near future;
- has a reduced or nonfunctional central field to the extent that print reading is expected to be inefficient;
- shows steady progress in developing tactual skills necessary for efficient braille reading;
- is free of additional handicaps that would interfere with progress in a developmental reading program in braille.

For the small number of students who have not displayed characteristics that would support either a print reading program or a braille reading program, the multidisciplinary team may wish to consider a number of options: placing equal emphasis on each medium and reevaluating at some point in the near future (no more than one year as required by Public Law 94-142) to determine a primary reading medium; placing instructional emphasis only on print reading; placing instructional emphasis only on braille reading; placing primary instructional emphasis on print reading and developing braille reading skills as a supplementary medium; or placing primary instructional emphasis on braille reading and developing print reading as a supplementary medium. The efficacy of placing equal emphasis on both media, unless additional time will be available in the school day to teach both effectively, is questionable.

If emphasis must be placed on one medium and the student is truly as efficient in both visual and tactual learning, the multidisciplinary team may wish to give primary consideration to a print reading program, with braille reading instruction reserved as a future option depending on the changing needs of the student. Whatever initial decision is agreed upon, teams should remember that this is not necessarily a final decision and reevaluation must be ongoing.

Continued evaluation

As children grow, their needs and abilities change. The initial decision to teach reading through print or braille is critical; equally as important is a continuing evaluation of progress in the light of the initial decision and changing needs of the student. Education is a fluid process. Teachers must constantly consider new and different options for students as they become appropriate.

In a sense, we are filling a student's "toolbox" with "tools" appropriate to accomplish a variety of tasks. The need for different tools is determined by the tasks that the student must accomplish now and in the future. In some cases it may be appropriate to teach braille to supplement reading and writing tasks for a print reader, while in other cases it may be appropriate to teach print reading/writing for functional activities for braille readers. Additional means for sending and receiving information (e.g., recorded materials, computers, telecommunications) should be considered for all students regardless of their primary reading medium. Again, the emphasis should be placed on developing options for students for both immediate and future use.

There are a number of areas that should be monitored to determine the need for additional or supplemental reading/writing instruction. These include information on visual functioning, academic achievement, comprehension and rate of reading, handwriting, vocational direction, use of technology, functional reading skills for students with multiple disabilities, and use of extremely limited vision.

Additional information on visual functioning

What additional information is available from functional vision evaluations and from ophthalmological/clinical low vision evaluations that has implications for reviewing the student's primary reading medium?

The initial decision concerning a primary reading medium is partly based on the sensory functioning of a student at a young age. Throughout the educational program, a student with low vision should receive instruction designed to increase visual functioning. It is important that the multidisciplinary team continue to evaluate the student's functional vision performance to determine if changes should be made in the reading medium. If there is an increase in visual functioning, as would be expected, changes in the reading medium may include an increase in the print options available to the student (e.g., large print, regular print, regular print with the use of a low vision device).

It is also important to continually examine changing educational demands placed on a student with a visual impairment. In the early years of school, reading materials are already in large type and reading tasks are of relatively short duration. As a student progresses through school, textbooks are printed in smaller type size and the duration of reading tasks increases significantly. The multidisciplinary team should anticipate difficulties with smaller type size and increased fatigue that would indicate that the initial decision should be reconsidered by changing the primary reading medium or, more likely, by adding supplemental tools to assist in the completion of cumbersome assignments.

Team members should continually review new and updated ophthalmological and clinical low vision information and determine the implications for possible changes in, or additions to, the student's reading medium. Braille reading is an important option for students whose vision is deteriorating, and new or different low vision devices may become more appropriate for students as they mature or as their visual functioning changes. Careful attention must always be given to the student's visual prognosis.

Academic achievement

Is the student able to accomplish academic tasks with the current medium with a sufficient level of success? While academic achievement is important, teachers must also examine the amount of time that a student is spending to successfully accomplish academic tasks. A student who must spend a majority of waking hours on schoolwork needs to have options for streamlining work. Regardless of the initial decision, it is likely that a student who is visually impaired will accomplish academic tasks at a slower pace than students who are not visually impaired. It is important to remember that reading braille or reading print are not the only options for communication. There are other means for expressing and receiving information that may make the academic process more efficient for students, such as typing, word processing, readers, recorded textbooks, enlarged print via CCTV or low vision devices, and voice synthesis devices for computers. The key is to explore the range of options that are available, identify the strengths and weaknesses of each, and provide instruction in those that will be of greatest value for the student given immediate and future needs.

Reading braille and reading print for students who are visually impaired are both relatively slow and the teaching of one after the other has been learned (e.g., teaching print after braille has been learned) is time-consuming. A student who is primarily a print reader might benefit from supplemental braille instruction and a braille reader might benefit from supplemental print instruction. However, it is unlikely that a student who is having trouble in academic areas would benefit from instruction designed to teach complete proficiency in an alternate reading medium. The alternate medium should be used as a tool to supplement the primary reading medium when such a supplement can streamline a task.

Comprehension and rate of reading

Does the student read with adequate comprehension in the reading medium initially selected? A comprehension level of at least 75% accuracy is necessary on instructional material (Harley et al., 1987). If a student does not reach this level of comprehension during reading instruction, the teacher must examine closely any factors that might contribute to the problem. In addition to possible explanations that would be considered for any student, teachers of students with visual impairments must examine two factors more closely. First, specific reading skills that influence comprehension may not have been adequately developed even though the reading medium is appropriate. Second, the reading medium selected for the student may be inappropriate and therefore adversely affect comprehension. The first factor will require thorough diagnostic assessment to determine the cause of the reading problem and subsequent implementation of an appropriate remediation program.

A complete discussion of remediation of reading problems for students with visual impairments is presented by Harley et al. (1987). The second factor requires reevaluation of the initial decision on the student's reading medium through additional diagnostic teaching.

Comprehension is related to rate of reading. A reading rate of 10 words per minute is necessary for adequate comprehension (Harley et al., 1987). If the student is not reading at this rate, the multidisciplinary team should consider strategies for increasing reading rate or other options for a primary reading medium.

In some instances, difficulties will occur because of a combination of inadequate comprehension/rate of reading and inappropriate primary reading medium. Professional evaluation and diagnosis will help to determine if one or both represent the significant reason for a lack of comprehension.

Handwriting

Is the student able to read his/her own handwriting? It is important that a person have the ability to communicate with himself (S. Mangold, personal communication, September, 1988). Grocery lists, telephone and address lists, and checkbook registers are examples of things that adults write and must later read. If a student cannot read what he/she has written, a first step is to provide remedial handwriting instruction. If the student is still unable to read his/her own handwriting after sufficient instruction, other options should be systematically explored. Such options may include supplemental instruction in braille writing, typing, computer word processing programs, and use of a tape recorder for note writing. Again, the key element is exploring options and developing appropriate ones given the student's needs.

Vocational direction

Given the student's vocational interests and aptitude, what are the specific demands for expressive and receptive written communication? Does the student have the repertoire of reading and writing skills necessary to achieve projected vocational goals? Consideration of these factors must be ongoing, given the changing nature of developing vocational interests. The multidisciplinary team, including the parents and student, is faced with the dilemma of projecting a likely vocational goal. Considerations for reading and writing options can be safely explored during job exploration and transition activities as part of the secondary school experience. These can be developed prior to leaving the educational system.

For a number of students, the demands of a vocation or profession will be preceded by attendance at a post-secondary vocational school or college program. These students will need to acquire a repertoire of reading and writing skills that will allow them to progress successfully through their course of instruction as well as to have the skills necessary to ultimately accomplish the job tasks when they graduate. Among options to explore are computer word processing skills, use of reader services, use of recorded textbooks, note-taking skills with the slate and stylus, and use of cassette braille devices.

Availability of technology

What, if any, available technology will increase the student's options for efficiently completing reading and writing tasks? The current and future range of computer and related technology has the potential for increasing a student's level of independence by providing more immediate and efficient access to information. The multidisciplinary team must keep abreast of technological advances and have sufficient knowledge of their potential impact in order to evaluate the effectiveness for each student with a visual impairment.

As computer courses become more and more widespread throughout the educational system, it is likely that students will have exposure to them when appropriate access devices are available. However, if such is not the case, it is the responsibility of the teacher of students with visual impairments to provide this exposure, given the relative value of the technology to the student's immediate and future needs. While the options are expensive, some to consider include voice-accessible word processors; large-print word processors; cassette braille devices; portable computer systems; Optacon systems; telecommunications; and optical recognition scanners with conversion to speech, braille, or print, as well as new devices as they become available.

Functional reading skills for students with multiple disabilities

If a student has an additional disability that prevents entering a traditional developmental reading program, would he/she benefit from instruction in reading for functional purposes? Some students with additional handicaps may benefit from learning to read signs, labels, and other words in order to complete functional tasks related to daily living. For example, a student may learn to read "Men" and "Women" in order to locate the correct restroom in a public building or to read common food names to facilitate preparation of simple meals.

Other functional words may be learned to facilitate integration into a work setting. If a multidisciplinary team determines that teaching functional reading will be beneficial to the student, procedures outlined earlier should be used to determine whether reading print or reading braille is most appropriate.

Educators should guard against teaching reading just because it is possible to do so; unless it will serve a functional purpose in the life of a student with multiple disabilities, instructional time may best be used for teaching other essential life skills.

Use of extremely limited vision

Could a student who uses braille as a primary reading and writing medium but who retains any level of visual functioning benefit from a rudimentary level of print reading skill? Even limited skill in reading print, regardless of how tedious, has the potential to increase one's independence by accomplishing functional activities of daily living, such as reading the amount due on bill statements, reading the amount of a paycheck, sorting junk mail from valuable mail, reading short messages, and identifying signs in the environment.

Multidisciplinary teams must evaluate results of functional vision assessments and data collected as part of the ongoing diagnostic teaching procedure to determine the potential for developing a functional level of print reading skill. A further consideration is whether or not this would have sufficient long-term value to justify the instructional time relative to all other priority areas.

Summary

In order for a multidisciplinary team to make informed decisions on the appropriate reading medium for each student with a visual impairment, systematic procedures must be implemented over a period of time to collect needed information. The authors of this article proposed the early implementation of diagnostic teaching practices as a means of collecting the wide range of objective and qualitative data necessary to guide the decision making process.

A continuing process

It was further proposed that decisions be made in two somewhat distinct phases: 1) an initial phase in which the first decision is made on the primary reading medium, and 2) a second phase in which continued evaluation of the initial decision is considered as an ongoing process.

Phase one

During the initial phase, a period of diagnostic teaching begins at the readiness stage and continues into the early part of formal reading instruction in order to consider the following factors:

- the student's demonstrated preference for, and efficiency with, use of the *visual sense* as a primary source of gathering information;
- the student's demonstrated preference for, and efficiency with, use of the *tactual sense* as a primary source-gathering information;
- the prognosis and stability of the visual condition; and
- the possible influences of additional disabilities on learning to read.

Phase two

The second phase confirms or adjusts the initial team decision and examines a number of factors over the period of years which spans the student's educational career. Multidisciplinary team members consider the range of options necessary to meet the student's current and future needs in college, vocational school, or employment and living situation. These considerations include:

- the availability of additional information on visual functioning from an educator of students with visual impairments and from eye care professionals;
- the student's ability to maintain academic progress in the initially selected reading medium;
- the efficiency of reading in the selected medium, i.e., the level of comprehension relative to the rate of reading;
- the student's effectiveness in reading his/her own handwriting;
- the student's vocational interests and goals and the related reading and writing requirements for receptive and expressive communication;
- the use of available technology to increase and/or expand options for communication;
- the usefulness of teaching functional reading skills to a student with multiple disabilities; and
- the usefulness of teaching a rudimentary level of print reading skill to a student with extremely limited vision.

If properly implemented, this two-phase approach assures that instruction in the appropriate reading medium or combination of media is implemented for each student with a visual impairment. The value of initial diagnostic teaching and subsequent continued evaluation provides the multidisciplinary team with a comprehensive process of making an informed decision.

Conclusion

In conclusion, we wish to reiterate the essential elements and guiding principles we believe provide the foundation for making decisions on establishing the reading medium for students with visual impairments:

- Decisions are made on the basis of identified, individual needs of students, not on arbitrary criteria such as the legal definition of blindness.
- Decisions on establishing the reading medium reflect the input from each member of the multidisciplinary team.
- Information on which to base decisions is collected over a period of time through systematic, diagnostic teaching.
- Decisions take into account individual sensory abilities and capabilities of each student, as well as immediate and future needs.
- Decisions to provide additional instruction in other reading media are remade through continuous evaluation as a student's needs change or expand, thereby filling a student's "toolbox" with the appropriate "tools."

Many significant and positive changes have been made in educating students with visual impairments since the days of "sight-saving" classes. The eventual success of students in achieving independent living and employment status to the greatest extent of their abilities must undoubtedly be attributed, at least in part, to the decisions that are made on their behalf during their school years.

Therefore, professionals and parents must jointly endeavor to make a decision as critical as establishing the appropriate reading medium in a climate of reason and professionalism guided by consistent procedures that examine the student's unique abilities as well as immediate and future needs.

References

American Printing House for the Blind (1982). *Patterns, the primary braille reading program: Readiness level.* Louisville, KY: Author.

Barraga, N.C. & Morris, J.E. (1980). *Program to develop efficiency in visual functioning.* Louisville, KY: American Printing House for the Blind.

Harley, R.K., Truan, M.B., & Sanford, L.D. (1987). Communication skills for visually impaired learners. Springfield, IL: Charles C Thomas.

Irwin, R.B. (1920). Sight-saving classes in the public schools. *Harvard Bulletins in Education,* Number 7.

Mangold, S. (1977). *The Mangold developmental program of tactile perception and braille letter recognition.* Castro Valley, CA: Exceptional Teaching Aids.

Roessing, L.J. (1982). Functional vision: Criterion-referenced checklists. In S.S. Mangold (ed.), *A teachers' guide to the special educational needs of blind and visually handicapped children.* New York: American Foundation for the Blind.

Smith, A.J. & Cote, K.S. (1982). *Look at me: A resource manual for the development of residual vision in multiply impaired children.* Philadelphia: Pennsylvania College of Optometry Press.

State of Florida (1983). *Project IVEY: Increasing visual efficiency,* (Volume V–E). Tallahassee, FL: Author.

HOW TO MAKE A BRAILLE WAVE

Bonnie Simons

Braille was a mystery at the elementary school I was assigned to in 1987 as a teacher of students with visual impairments, as were the students who were blind. My students were not as enthusiastic about braille as I, and avoided using it in class. One day I saw a braille book drop out of the arms of one of my students as he crossed campus, and watched in amazement as at least 20 students cautiously and carefully walked around it. When a beginning braille reader enrolled in our school that year, I saw her begin to develop some subtle, negative attitudes toward braille and decided I needed to become part of my students' classroom activities to act as a resource to inform and encourage developing social skills and positive attitudes toward braille.

I taught small groups of students in reading, social studies and science, and found the students were bright, sensitive, and curious. The second-grade children watched in fascination as I worked with my younger student using a variety of braille and tactile materials. They were spellbound by the braillewriter and begged me to teach them how to write their names. One student in second grade, Abby, took a special interest in braille and decided to learn as much about it and the student who was blind as she could. Abby learned a few braille letters every day—some from me, some from the blind student. She learned the basics of using a braillewriter and was also very interested in creating tactile designs using braille dots. The "braille wave" was one of our favorites, originally tapped out by her 4-year-old sister when she came to visit the classroom. It can be made by brailling dots 3, 2, 1, 4, 5, 6 one by one across the page, creating a curving, tactile line.

We designed an independent study class in braille, with the encouragement of her classroom teacher. The blind student blossomed over the next months with the attention she received from her classmates as they came to know her and her special materials better. She was frequently called on to give impromptu demonstrations of her special tools, and gained confidence and status.

The following school year, the blind student, Abby, and another friend asked me to start a braille class. This weekly class of three students quickly grew into two classes of 12 students, thanks to Abby's word-of-mouth publicity. The teachers and staff were extremely patient as our class struggled to get organized. Teachers invited me to their classes to speak about braille. I developed cartoon storyboards that helped tell the story of Louis Braille, explaining the various systems blind people have used before and since the development of braille. Students were fascinated by the knotted string and wooden

Adapted with permission from Bonnie Simons, "How to Make a Braille Wave," paper presented at a meeting of the Association of Education and Rehabilitation of the Blind and Visually Impaired, Dallas, Texas, 1992.

letter alphabets, as well as the talking electronic braille keyboard my sixth-grade student used to take notes in class. They stopped me in hallways to ask me when they could take braille classes.

Classes soon turned into everyday events, with students coming in after school and during their lunch recess to learn braille. Approximately 125 students have attended braille classes over the past three years. The blind students and two of my first braille students were "student teachers" in the Braille Club, but students learned the basics from anyone who knew them. It was not uncommon to see a first grader teaching a fourth grader how to put paper in the braillewriter and braille the alphabet.

Now that the school seemed more comfortable with braille, and the blind students were more relaxed and communicative, we directed our efforts in Braille Club toward helping strenghten the sense of belonging that was developing. Cooperative learning techniques were used to develop team projects students would work on at Braille Club. Bina (1986) feels that cooperative learning techniques help students with special needs improve social skills, and allows them to develop friendships. Students learn strategies for thinking critically and working together toward common goals, to communicate their ideas effectively, and to fairly evaluate the contributions of others. After learning the basics of braille, students were asked to work in teams to develop projects that would be interesting, informative, or helpful to other people.

Flexibility was the key to helping teams develop projects. For example, when students were studying Eastern cultures in social studies, discussions of these cultures in Braille Club led to the idea of designing a project about the abacus. Teams have done research on guide dogs for the blind and made presentations to interested classes, and have designed braille alphabet cards for teachers to give students when reading about or discussing blindness. They wrote print-braille storybooks—wonderfully imaginative stories in print and braille, made by using ink stamp sets—for the teachers of primary-age children to keep in their reading centers, and have copied tactile concept books designed for preschool blind children by a volunteer group in California, donating them to our local preschool for blind children. We have developed presentations and gone to other schools and towns to talk about braille.

The students in Braille Club enjoyed competitions, so children were frequently put in teams to compete against each other in language games for slate and stylus contests. The principal has given certificates of achievement in braille at honors assemblies so that outstanding success can be acknowledged. Students who completed ten projects during the school year received a Braille Club t-shirt decorated with their name in fabric paint and a braillewriter made of silver fabric.

The third year of Braille Club saw more literary projects being completed by students. A team of younger students developed three books, in the style of the *Where's Waldo* books, where the reader has to locate paw prints made of fabric paint hidden on a page of tactile items. Students also worked in teams to make the campus more accessible to visitors who were blind; one team put braille labels on campus doors, while another created a large tactile map of the campus.

I'm not able to relate all the activities and outcomes of our club here. We have undertaken a wide variety of subjects and projects in Braille Club, from social etiquette to how to write a talking computer program. What I hope to relate is the uniquely positive effect Braille Club had on the integration of blind students. One day a student left a sign on my door that read "Braille is cool!" I realized then how the school's attitude toward braille had altered over the months. Students and teachers asked me questions about braille and blindness with ease, and people were talking more to the blind students, giving friendly greetings in the halls, stopping to talk.

Because we were in a relaxed, cooperative learning situation, we observed the growth of positive social interactions between blind and sighted students. When misunderstandings occurred, students felt comfortable asking for clarification of someone else's actions or words. All students learned how to work in teams to complete projects, learning respect for others' ideas and the art of compromise. We all began to understand one another better, and students developed satisfying friendships.

In Braille Club, we have increased sighted students' contact with blind students and the things they use. We have increased awareness, acceptance, and status of blindness on campus, as well as sighted students' level of comfort with blind students. Sighted students have developed empathy because of their close contact with students who are blind, but also have learned to see past the uniqueness of being blind, to view these students as unique in other ways. Blind students have gained sighted peer advocates, but, more important, are beginning to be their own advocates, taking pride in their special school materials and tools.

TEACHING SPECIFIC CONCEPTS TO VISUALLY HANDICAPPED STUDENTS

AMANDA HALL

Students without detailed vision often lack basic concepts and fail to unify integral components in their environment. These concepts must be taught to visually handicapped students so that they can increase their knowledge base and participate equally with sighted peers whenever possible.

It is important to develop systematic methods for teaching concepts in order to determine which concepts to consider for instruction; how to assess these crucial concepts with individual students; what verbal and manipulative procedures best clarify specific concepts for a particular student; and how to reinforce and generalize conceptual understanding once a concept is learned in a specific instructional setting.

The purpose of this chapter is to describe one approach to the systematic teaching of specific concepts. This approach considers logical ways of thinking about concepts that provide direction for the instructional process. Flexibility is the key to the application of the instructional methods described here, since the design of actual lessons will vary with the needs of particular students, the time available for lesson preparation and instruction, and the specific situations in which a concept must be taught.

Selecting specific concepts for instruction

In order to begin the teaching of conceptual skills, it is necessary to identify crucial concepts that a visually handicapped student must understand for full participation in activities and daily life in and out of school. A list of these concepts was developed as a class project in a concept development course for teachers and orientation and mobility instructors of the visually handicapped at San Francisco State University. This list is not exhaustive of all the critical concepts that a visually handicapped student should know, but represents an initial step in the identification of crucial concepts. Additions to this list are encouraged.

List of crucial concepts*

1. **Body Awareness** (concepts pertaining to the body)

top, bottom	middle	relationship of body parts
back, front	wholeness of body	lower part of body
left, right	names of major body parts	upper part of body
	waist-high	

Kinesthetic Awareness
turning
direction of motion
moving, still
gravity in relation to body

Proprioceptive Awareness
bending parts
head up
closed fingers
feet together
posture

Sensations
feelings
smell
taste
touch
hearing
sight

Facial Expressions
smile
frown

Gestures
nod yes
shake no
shrug
point to object
shake hands

2. **Environmental Awareness** (crucial objects in the environment and specific relation-ships among elements in the environment)

divided highway	traffic light	truck, car, bus, wagon
median strip	street signs	tricycle, bicycle
crosswalk	fire hydrant	train
intersection	lamp post	airplane
street	mail box	
sidewalk	trash can	store
driveway	curb	house
block	gutter	porch
pedestrian	corner	tree, grass
yard, back yard	crib, bed	toilet
stairs	table, chair	hallway
doorbell	doorway	desk
	stove	closet
landmark	sink	dresser
shoreline boundaries	refrigerator	
traffic patterns	bathtub	
weather—rain, snow		

3. **Awareness of Object Characteristics** (general properties of objects)

Size
dry, wet
big, little, small, large, medium
fat, thin, narrow, wide
long, short, medium length
deep, shallow

Color
clear, opaque
dark, light
specific colors
hue, tint

Shape
square, rectangle
round, oval
triangle
diamond
straight, curved, crooked
shapes of specific objects
configuration of words

Texture
smooth, rough, flat, hard, soft, sticky,
coarse, fine, bumpy, fuzzy, etc.

Sound
high, low pitch
loud, soft intensity
long, short duration
rhythm

Comparative Characteristics
larger, smaller
fatter, warmer, deeper, etc.
same, different

4. Time Awareness (concepts pertaining to time)

begin, end	today, yesterday, tomorrow
before, after	morning, noon, night, afternoon, evening
first, next, last	sunrise, sunset
during	day, week, month, year
always, never	second, minute, hour
old, new, young	future, past, present, now
time-distance relationships	clock concepts

5. Spatial Awareness (concepts related to position in space)

parallel	degrees of circle or turn	next, to, beside
perpendicular	half turn, whole turn	around
round	about face	in, out
arc	grid pattern	first, last
plane	up, down	toward, away from
middle, center, between	inside, outside	behind
diagonal	on, off	in order
opposite		closed, open

straight, crooked, curved	separated, together	*Directions*
to, from	far, rear, distant, close	north, south
high, low	wide, narrow	east, west
top, bottom	clockwise, counterclock-	northeast
front, back	wise	northwest
left, right	maintaining direction	southeast
forward, backward	maintaining distance	southwest

veering	under, over	across, across from
reference point	underneath, beneath	past, beyond
incline, decline	overhead	through
orientation, disorientation	above, below	here, there
sound localization	upside down, right side up	

6. Actions (concepts pertaining to movement)

writing, typing	swing	veer
buttoning, zipping, snap-ping	duck, bend	turn
	kick	imitate
eating, drinking	slide	
	roll	
skip, run		
jump, hop	stop, start	forward, reverse
climb, crawl	lock, unlock	backward
stand, sit	circle	sideways
step	follow	slow, fast
throw, catch	on, off	
push, pull		

7. Quantity (concepts associated with numbers and number combinations)

specific whole numbers	pair	*Measurement*
half, third, quarter	zero	inch, foot, yard, mile
fractions	increase, decrease	square inch, etc.
least, less (than)	with, without	cubic inches, etc.
most, more (than)	place, value	pound, ounce, ton
enough, only	all, some, none	cup, pint, quart, gallon
several, few, many	infinity	teaspoon, tablespoon
equal		miles per hour
		metric measurements for distance, volume, weight
	Operations	
	addition	
	subtraction	
	multiplication	
	division	

8. Symbol Awareness (crucial symbolic concepts)

compass directions	numbers, zero	*Pronouns*
map reading	signs—shape and design	I, me, mine
letters—print, cursive, braille	pictures	you, yours
	colors (red = stop; green = go)	he, she, his, hers
punctuation signs		we, they, theirs, ours
		it, its

9. Emotional and Social Awareness (concepts associated with psychosocial adjustment)

distinguish *I* from *You*

discriminate parent from stranger

self-concept

human sexuality concepts

manners

grooming

asking assistance, accepting help

initiating questioning

acceptance and rejection of others and by
   others

values

body language

nonverbal communication

voice pitch and intensity

sad, happy, angry

scared, fear, afraid

worried, excited

10. Reasoning (thought processes in which concepts are used)

traffic patterns

right of way

detour

pedestrian traffic

one-way street

lanes of traffic

route

route reversal

patterns in the environment

decision-making

real and make-believe

realistic expectations for self

making judgments—right, wrong, good,
   bad, fair, unfair

orientation, disorientation

estimation

time-distance relationships

functioning of objects and parts of objects

objects with similar parts

all, some, none

any, every

only, either, or

sorting

sequencing (patterns, numbers, sounds)

categorizing, classification

comparing, same, different

conservation (volume, mass, weight, quantity)

use of visual memory

common visual terminology

Assessing conceptual understanding

After determining the concepts to be examined with a particular student by examining the list of concepts, determining curricular needs, and observing the student, it is necessary to assess a student's understanding of these concepts systematically. Both verbal and performance responses should be elicited from the student in the assessment of concrete concepts whenever possible. This serves to clarify the relationship between a student's language ability

*This list was prepared by class members enrolled in Special Education 757 at San Francisco State University, Spring 1978: Rosemary Appel, Pat Davis, Carolyn Brien-Eddins, Jennifer Fitzgerald, Joanne Fong, Scott Johnson, Debbie Kooyer, Joanne Lowe, Sandy Rosen, Debi Ruth, Charles Ryon, Jim Schaer, Margo Simmons, Peggy Williams, Joan Winter. Instructor: Amanda Hall.

Table 3.1 Concepts of Concrete Objects

	Familiar Object Exemplifying Concept	*Unfamiliar Object Exemplifying Concept*
1. Identification:		
Indicate an object named by teacher	_____	_____
Name an object indicated by teacher	_____	_____
2. Describe function of named/indicated object		
3. Describe relationship of named/indicated object to other objects	_____	_____

and performance skills. Students with little or no language ability must be assessed through the use of their available skills, though this makes the assessment process more difficult.

The assessment of concepts requires an examination of the breadth and depth of a student's conceptual understanding. The levels at which concepts are assessed varies with the functioning of the student and the type of concept under consideration. With any concept, the teacher must use his or her judgment to determine which conceptual levels a student can be expected to master, taking into account such factors as past experience and instruction, language ability, visual functioning, and general developmental level. Examples of concept assessment shown in Tables 3.1–3.6 demonstrate different levels at which some basic concepts can be assessed. Since concepts are so varied, these examples cannot cover all types of concepts that must be taught. They can, however, be used as models for developing assessment protocols for other types of concepts.

Students must be able to identify concrete objects represented by concepts before they can be expected to describe functions or relationships (see Table 3.1). Thus the identification of familiar objects represented by a concept is the first level of assessment for concepts of concrete objects. This is followed by the identification of unfamiliar objects represented by a concept. Important for gaining insight into the understanding of very young or low-functioning students, the latter procedure clarifies, for example, whether a student understands the word "table" to signify only one table in a corner of the classroom or whether it signifies all objects with legs and horizontally positioned, flat tops.

A description of the function of objects represented by a concept should be the next step in the assessment of concepts of concrete objects. A table, for example, is used as a place to put things.

Table 3.2 Concepts of Body Parts that can be Touched

	Self	*Other Person*
1. Identification		
Indicate part named by teacher	_____	_____
Name part indicated by teacher	_____	_____
2. Describe function of named/indicated part	_____	_____
3. Describe relationship of named/indicated part to other body parts	_____	_____

It is then necessary to assess the environmental contexts in which the objects represented by a concept are found. This level of assessment is important because it clarifies the conceptual relationships that a student understands. For example, tables are commonly found in homes, schools, restaurants; they are often located in kitchens or dining rooms; chairs are often associated with tables.

Methods for assessing other types of concepts have been summarized in Tables 3.2–3.6.

Table 3.3 Concepts of Object Characteristics

	Clear-Cut Examples	Finer Discrimination
1. Identification		
Indicate characteristic of an object or indicate object with a specific characteristic named by teacher		
Name an object characteristic indicated by teacher		

Table 3.4 Concepts of Actions

	Self	Other Person or Object
1. Identification		
Imitate movement performed by teacher		
Perform movement named by teacher		
Name an indicated movement		
2. Describe function of an action, if appropriate		

Table 3.5 Concepts of Positions

	Own Body Parts Only	Other Person or Object and Own Body Parts	Other Persons or Objects Only
1. Identification			
Move to position named by teacher			
Name a position indicated by teacher			

Table 3.6 Abstract Concepts

1. Describe function	
2. Name class category, if appropriate	
3. Describe similarity or analogy to other known concepts	

Clarifying specific concepts for the teaching process

Many concepts appear obvious, but this cannot be taken for granted. Take, for example, the concept "front." Imagine yourself facing a table with a chair in between your body and the table. The chair is pushed under the table. You are facing the "back" of the chair, but you are facing the "front" of the table. This is so because the chair has a front and a back which are inherent in the definition of chair. Your position in relation to the chair does not determine its front and back, which never change. On the other hand, the front or back of the table is determined by the position of an observer in relation to the table. The front or back of the table changes as the observer changes position. These distinctions could be quite confusing to a student and must be clarified in the instructional process.

To be certain that a concept is presented in a precise manner to a student, a conceptual analysis is performed. This involves two steps. First, a definition of the concept *as it will be used in the teaching process* is developed. This definition may be different from a dictionary definition since its purpose is to simplify or break down a concept for instruction. The definition helps formulate the conceptual goal of the lesson. For some students, "front" would be defined as part of an object directly facing the front of a person's body, when that object does not have a front or a back. This precision in the definition makes it easier to teach, and as a consequence, makes it easier for a student to learn.

The second step in the conceptual analysis process is to identify all the concepts that must be understood in order to achieve the conceptual goal of the lesson. The conceptual goal is determined by the definition of the concept adopted for instruction. Here is an example for the concept "front."

Conceptual Goal: "Front"

The student will be able to indicate (verbally or by pointing or touching) the front of objects that have no designated front or back, either when the student changes position by moving around the objects while facing them, or when the objects are turned while they are in front of the student (Figure 3.1).

Strategies should be devised that teach concepts from the bottom of the conceptual analysis, working upward in the hierarchy. It is not necessary to teach those concepts in the hierarchy that the student already understands. Thus it is important to determine the student's entry level for each conceptual analysis. A student may have more than one en-

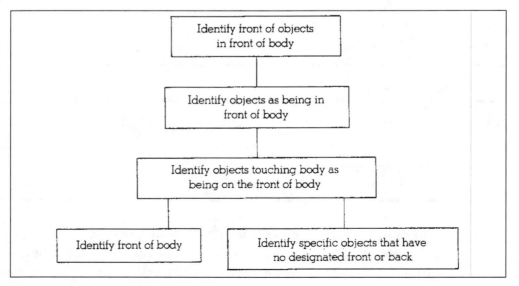

Figure 3.1. Conceptual Goal: "Front"

try level in an analysis, depending on the complexity of the analysis. Concepts should be broken down at least one step below a student's entry level.

Reinforcing and generalizing conceptual understanding

Concepts must be carefully taught to students using both manipulative materials and verbal explanations whenever possible. In addition, it is important to devise methods that help the student transfer his or her understanding of a concept from the specific teaching situation to other situations in the course of a normal day. Cooperation is needed at this point from parents and other professionals. They can be informed of a specific concept that has just been learned by a student and can, in turn, emphasize that concept with the student as relevant situations arise. This procedure reinforces specific concepts and also makes them more meaningful to the student since he or she becomes increasingly aware that certain concepts represent different aspects of daily life.

Examples of teaching specific concepts

Two examples of conceptual analysis follow. One example deals with the deceptively simple concept "first," the other deals with the concept "neighborhood." There are other ways to teach these concepts, but the methods used here worked well for the particular students for whom they were devised.

"First"*

The subject in this case was a six-year-old student whose visual impairment, due to retrolental fibroplasia, left her with minimal light perception. Upon initial observation, the child appeared to lack three important concepts—first, middle, and last. The need to locate things or persons in one's environment necessitates an understanding of order and

---

*Prepared by Toni Provost.

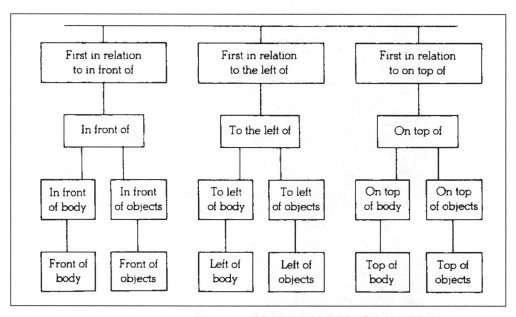

Figure 3.2 Conceptual Goal: "First."

positioning. Because of the student's age, attention span, and the complexity of each of the three concepts, it was decided to begin with one concept—"first."

Conceptual Analysis

Definition of "first": The position or order of an object or person, such that it is preceding all others in space.

Conceptual Goal

Given the directional arrangement of a set (front to back, left to right, top to bottom), the student will demonstrate an understanding of the spatial concept "first" by tactually or verbally identifying the first object or person in the set. (See Figure 3.2.)

In order to determine the entry level of this six-year-old student, the game "Simon Says" was played. The student knew the left and the top of her body, but did not know the front of her body. She did not know left, top, or front of objects. To understand the concept "first," it was necessary to clarify the concepts "left," "top," and "front" for this particular student.

"Neighborhood" *

In this case a 16-year-old blind student was to be taught the concept of "city block." This later grew into the concept of "neighborhood," which is essentially only one step further:

---

*Prepared by Kathryn Weldenfeld-Smith.

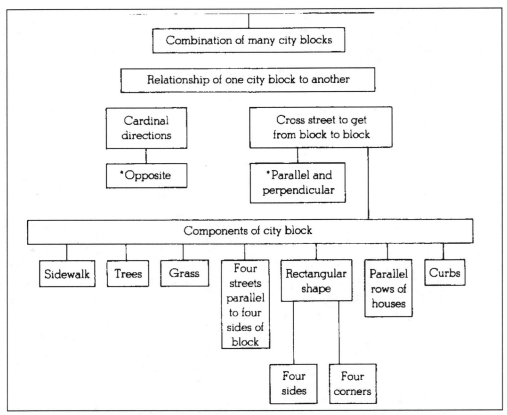

*"Parallel," "perpendicular," and "opposite" are mentioned only once in the analysis to reduce duplication of concepts, although they are prerequisite to the understanding of several other concepts in the analysis.

Figure 3.3 Conceptual Goal: "Neighborhood."

it is an area of many city blocks. From observations of this student, it appeared that she was not familiar with the concept, as she came from a rural environment. This concept is extremely useful in connection with orientation and mobility, and is a challenge which this student was capable of understanding.

Conceptual Analysis

Two definitions are needed for this analysis, since "neighborhood" is closely related to "city block."

Definition of "city block": A rectangular unit immediately bounded by four streets or the length of one side of such a rectangle. Definition of "neighborhood": A district or section of a number of city blocks with people of similar condition and type of habitation living near one another.

Two definitions of "city block" based upon rectangular units were used in this analysis and taught to the student. Some city blocks are not rectangular in shape, but are irregular. This type of city block was not covered in the analysis. Ideally, it should be taught after a student has mastered the more simple (and common) definitions associated with rectangular city blocks.

The original definition of "neighborhood" did not include commercial districts, but the definition was expanded to include commercial districts during the course of the lesson because this particular student was able to make this transition easily.

Conceptual Goal

The student will demonstrate understanding of "neighborhood" in relation to the "city block" concept. (See Figure 3.3.)

From a discussion with the student, it was determined that she was not familiar with the components of a city block, so the lessons began with that point in the analysis.

READING COMES NATURALLY: A MOTHER AND HER BLIND CHILD'S EXPERIENCES

DIANE D. MILLER

I use the word reading in exactly the same sense as when a sighted child picks up a favorite book and thumbs through retelling the story in his or her own words. The child is obviously aware of the meaning and the wholeness of that book. Although the child is not actually reading the words, there is an awareness of the fact that the story comes from these printed words on the page. This activity of retelling a story, dismissed by most as memorization, is actually a very important first step in learning to read. When a child discovers a broom for the first time and then proceeds to wreck the kitchen while "sweeping," mastery begins. But if we do not support and encourage these early approximations, the final skill will never be accomplished. In the same way, a child flips through a book and retells the story, perhaps filling in familiar words for others not yet in his or her vocabulary but retaining the original meaning of the story. The enjoyment and success of these early experiences with books will carry the child through the steps from approximations to final success in deciphering the print—what most people consider "real" reading.

Blindness, and Bridging Concepts

Jamaica was born at home within a close circle of family and friends. Shortly after her birth someone gently said, "You may find out that she is blind." It was true. She was born anophthalmic, or without eyes. Feelings flowed deeply, sadness true, but also good feelings. We were given the unique opportunity to witness the depths of love and understanding unlocked in others by her specialness. It was a time of change, a time of growth, a time of acceptance. And then it was time to get on with making Jamaica's life as full and complete as possible.

Jamaica's brother, Lucky, was only a year-and-a-half old at the time, but already we had spent many hours reading and sharing books. Those were some of our most special times together, times I didn't want to miss with Jamaica. Lucky, like most very young children, spent most of his time looking at and talking about the pictures. What could possibly replace this lure into books for Jamaica? I began to realize that tactual pictures could easily be based on visual representation but also that these would have very little meaning to Jamaica based on her own special kinds of experiences. What could a little piece of fur with four thin strips sticking out of the bottom and pasted on a page have to do with that warm, wiggling, panting mass of fur that she would know as a dog?

Putting my background in graphic design to work, I set out to make Jamaica's first book. She had a little circle puzzle that she liked, so I chose a circle theme. First of all the book had to be durable, able to withstand lots of handling. I used cardboard with fabric cover and filled it with many different textures and sizes of circles, repeating patterns. Most of all I wanted it to feel good; my only mistake was to use sandpaper as one of the textures. I'll never use it again. It sets your teeth on edge . . . not something that encourages tactual exploration. The book was a success. Jamaica and I would "read," tactually following the patterns and saying the same verses each time. On one page we would say "Ring Around the Roses" on another "Round and Round the Mulberry Bush." Then surprise! "What is that square doing in our Circle Book?" Jamaica seemed to enjoy these activities, but I saw a definite increase in her enthusiasm when with big Elmer's Glue dots I added the braille words *Jamaica's Circle Book* to the cover. (Lucky was equally fascinated with picking the new dots off and eating them!) So at eight months, Jamaica and I had begun the process that would eventually lead her into the exciting world of books.

As a mother of two young children, I had very little time to spend making books. So I was constantly searching for appropriate commercially produced books. Golden Books publishes a Touch and Feel Series. These books offer activities such as patting the fuzzy bunny or snapping Santa Claus' rubber band suspenders. We purchased several of these but Jamaica soon lost interest in the activities because the stories were not exciting. I also found that several publishers offer Scratch and Sniff books. These contain stories about children favorites like Bambi and Winnie the Pooh, but with the addition of fragrance labels to the pages. They provided some involvement for Jamaica, as she searched the pages to find the stickers. She even began to recognize some of the books by their general fragrance. We enjoyed the stories and Jamaica often requested these books by name.

Sees Special Need

However, I felt a need for books made especially for a child living in a tactual world. I found *What's That?* by Jensen and Haller. The characters in this book, Little Rough, Little Shaggy, Little Spot, Little Stripe and Little Smooth, all really feel like their names sound. They live in triangles and squares and travel along paths made tactual through a method of printing using thick ink. The book is graphically pleasing, visually as well as tactually. The story is fascinating and includes a fun surprise ending. It is excellent in every respect. Philomel Books in New York publishes this and other books designed especially for blind children. All share similar qualities. We were excited to find these books but wanted more. My search continued.

Due to the scarcity of specially designed books, we spent most of our time reading regular inkprint books. I was always trying different ways to make this reading exciting and meaningful to Jamaica. Whenever we all sat down to read together (including little sister Dixie now), Jamaica's part was to turn the pages. This helped to keep her alert and involved in the process, otherwise she had a tendency to fall asleep. I encouraged Lucky and Dixie to describe to Jamaica what was happening in the pictures, also hoping that this would expand their understanding of her blindness. While reading I would leave words off of the ends of sentences for them to fill in the blanks. I hoped this would help them all to develop the important reading skill of prediction. This was just another way to keep Jamaica actively involved. It was working. She was listening. She could answer questions about what we read. She had favorite books, and would ask for them to be read over and over again.

The bookshelf was one of Jamaica's first landmarks in the house. She would sit on the floor and pull down all of the books. She would hold one in her lap and just flip through feeling the pages. She liked the slick ones best. Books have their own particular smell, a special feel about them, qualities that I seemed to destroy if I did too much pasting and gluing. So I settled for adapting covers only, that left the pages smooth and booklike but still gave Jamaica some independence in choosing which book she wanted at the bookshelf. On the cover of *Pinocchio,* the puppet is holding a match to light the fire inside the whale. I glued a match on that book. There were beans on the cover of *Jack and the Beanstalk.* One day I found Lucky squeezing glue all over the cover of one book. "I'm fixing it so Mai-Mai will know which one it is, Mama." She did indeed learn to recognize that book by its special glue configurations.

Since Jamaica didn't like lumpy books, ones that didn't feel like real books, an alternative was to make "book bags." The book was placed in a paper sack along with as many of the objects mentioned in the story as possible. Why have a picture if you can have the real thing? In Jamaica's favorite story, *Mickey 'n Donald,* the doorbell rang so we had a bell on hand. Robbers stole money from a bank. So we had handcuffs from ropes and money bags with coins tied up in handkerchiefs. Larger items such as a stepladder and a laundry basket were gathered together just before reading. Then with all of our props ready, the family would act out the story as I read. We would tape record the whole performance. The book bag with its contents was returned to the shelf, ready for the next reading.

A Search for Brailled Books

But in spite of all my efforts, Jamaica was still missing some very important pre-reading experiences. First a child grasps the wholeness of the book and its meaning. But gradually the pieces begin to emerge, sentences, words, letters. Dixie would be listening to a story and interrupt to say, "There's my letter," as she pointed to a *D* in the text. I could see that Jamaica needed books with braille so she could find her letter too.

When I went to look, I had difficulty finding appropriate brailled books for Jamaica. Although there were a few braille "readiness" materials such as the ones prepared by the American Printing House for the Blind, very few actual books were available.

I did locate some sources of braille books. The American Brotherhood for the Blind offers, without charge, a lending library of Twin Vision books. These are selected books with print and braille text side by side. In other words, the book is unbound, brailled pages are inserted beside the printed text and then the book is re-bound. Now, with these books Jamaica could follow along as I read, or could she? I was reading the print on one side and there was a whole page of braille beside it. But I didn't even know where to put her hand. How could she possibly follow along? With much time and effort I could maybe pick out a J or was it a J? I wasn't ever sure about where one letter ended and another began. I can remember once trying to decipher a very short sentence using my A.P.H. braille alphabet card. Try as I might, I just couldn't figure what it said. I later learned about contractions and whole word signs, special braille configurations representing frequently used words and letter combinations. You won't find them on an alphabet card. I imagine that many other parents are also unaware of these special characteristics of the code. Other print-braille books are offered by the Library of Congress and Howe Press. But the same problems exist here and are often compounded by the fact that the braille is embossed on clear overlays. This makes the pictures in the book more visible, but the braille is even harder to see than ever. Jamaica and I still preferred our regular ink-print books.

Later on I would have Jamaica's teacher take home some of the books and hand copy the text into each book so we could really begin to use them. Another teacher, upon hearing this said, "I did that too." Why so much duplication of effort? Perhaps, with just a little bit more planning and thought good ready-to-use material could be produced . If quality braille books appropriate for preschool children were accessible, then parents and teachers could spend their time reading with their children.

When Jamaica was three years old, I returned to school seeking my master's degree in Visual Disabilities. As part of my course work I learned to write braille and read it, not tactually but by sight. This was when I learned why I previously had so much trouble figuring out the code. Knowing how to read braille didn't really make it much easier to use available materials. But now I at least knew that the braille word that matched the word I was reading might not even be on the same page.

Jamaica was now in a homebound vision program so we were given a braille writer to use at home. This was very exciting to me. I knew how important paper and pencil experiences were for sighted children in the process of learning to read.

Lucky had invented an ingenious way of making pictures for Jamaica. With the point of a pencil, he would punch holes in a sheet of paper laying on the carpet. The reverse side had nice "braille" dots. Whenever Lucky and Dixie drew or painted, Jamaica did too. Sometimes we used a screen board or raised line drawing kit, so she could feel her marks. But more often than not, Jamaica preferred plain paper and pencil. This is probably because these materials were much more accessible. Also, I was not as likely to try to direct or teach her as she worked. She was allowed more freedom. She would tell me about what she was making. Then, hand-over-hand, we would always sign her name on her work.

She continued to love these activities. But now with the braillewriter, she could also begin to make marks in the medium she would eventually use. Jamaica would "clunk" away on the brailler and dictate letters or stories which I could write down and then read back to her. This activity was similar to a sighted child's scribbling. Gradually lines take on familiar shapes and forms and are refined into letters and words. Jamaica could become familiar with the braillewriter. She pushed the levers and then felt the paper, getting immediate feedback from her actions. "Look Jamaica. You made an A!"

"Home-Made" Books

Now with knowledge of the braille code and access to a braillewriter I could begin to braille materials myself, titles to books and tapes, favorite passages in books. On special occasions I would always try to make a new book for Jamaica. These books would have braille text with the corresponding hand-printed word directly above the braille, the perfect format. As Jamaica's hands moved across the page, I followed reading each word as she touched. We were together at last.

I brailled make-believe stories about Jamaica and her best friend. I wrote about familiar things that she talked about often, our two cats and the dog next door. The picture of the dog, instead of a complicated confusing outline, was simply two bumps for eyes and two floppy pieces of fur for ears. Now our experiences like *Making Banana Bread* became stories and Jamaica had her own braille copy. " 'Jamaica put white flour in her mouth.' 'She looks like a clown.' 'Dixie poured eggs but missed.' 'Lucky, please put the bananas in.' 'Yuk!' " These were very special stories and the children loved to read them over and over again.

Here also we began a "journal" for Jamaica. In a special notebook we would record her experiences, brailling the most important parts of each story in her exact words. Her journal also included letters, newspaper articles, and pictures. One of Jamaica's most prized possessions was her photo album. Like all children she wanted to know all about when she was a tiny baby. In addition, our collection of personal tapes, recordings of places we had visited and people we had met, served as an "auditory experience album." These tapes became Jamaica's favorite bedtime stories. Although she was unable to actually read the braille titles, she would find a tape with no label, "Mama, this one needs braille." Yes, for everything I brailled, there were 20 other things waiting to be brailled.

In efforts to increase the number of books available to Jamaica, I contacted the state center providing instructional materials for the visually impaired. I asked if they would be willing to braille some of Jamaica's favorite books. They found a volunteer who was more than willing. She returned the completed books with a note saying she would be glad to do more whenever we wanted. Suddenly I had 10 or 12 new braille books piled on my desk, pages and pages of braille and no inkprint. Yes, I could read braille but very slowly and painfully. I struggled with each word, sounding like a first grader just beginning to read. So before we could really use our new books I had to hand copy the text into each one. Of course I used the previously described format where the print word was directly above the braille word. It was a slow process. Six months later I had finished only a couple. Then another volunteer offered to do this transcribing for me. Finally Jamaica's library began to grow.

We had already explored the materials available which were developed to promote braille reading readiness. *The Tactual Road to Reading* has books with yarn and stick designs for practicing tracking skills. But Jamaica had to be coaxed to use them. One difficult afternoon I put them away and pulled out one of our new braille books instead. I told Jamaica that I would read while she tracked lines. If her hands stopped, I stopped reading. The next day she came home from school and said, "Mama, don't you think we should practice tracking those words in that book again?" She had never asked to practice on readiness materials. The motivation is intrinsic in the words that tell a story, a whole book.

We learned so much as each new batch of books was made. The first books were brailled horizontally onto whole sheets of braille paper and then bound. The format was wrong. The books were just too big to handle comfortably. The next books we made were smaller. These were much better for Jamaica's little hands and lap. We learned to hand copy in indelible ink so wet fingers wouldn't smear all the words. I found that I was really missing the pictures and the other children showed little excitement over reading in a pictureless book. One of the original books that we had copied was coming unbound, so I cut it up and pasted the pictures into our new braille book. It worked very nicely. Books thrown away by libraries became an incredible resource for producing braille materials with illustrations. Our braillist had another good idea. She xeroxed the pictures from original books and had her own children color and paste them into the new braille books before sending them to us. They were beautiful. Now Jamaica and I had braille inkprint in a format which allowed us to read together and the other children had pictures too. The books were coming together at last.

A Literate Environment

What of all the time and effort that had gone into developing a pre-reading literary environment for Jamaica? How important is this to reading skills? And could my experiences with Jamaica benefit more than one blind child?

Reading and writing are natural extensions of the literacy learning which begins with the acquisition of language. Holdaway (1979) suggests that for a better understanding of the developmental processes involved we should look closely at the ways in which children learn to read (as opposed to the ways in which we teach them). Some children have been observed to learn completely on their own, without any formal instruction.

The common element in the lives of these early readers is described as a "literate environment." Kenneth Goodman (1976) explains this is a place "where kids are constantly exposed to print, made aware of its functions, how it works, its subtle differences and similarities" (p. 2). According to Goodman, children learn to read in much the same way as they learn to talk and to listen: "That is, they become aware first of wholes and their relationship to specific messages. And then with teachers' help they begin to develop a sense of the structure and of the relationship of part to whole" (p. 4).

If we take reading and break it up into letters and words separate from the context of the story, we offer the child the most complex element first. And we expect children to be able to make sense of these abstractions. Conversely, if we offer them a whole book and then proceed to the parts, we are going from the simple to the complex, a logical approach.

If a blind child's experiences have led to adequate and meaningful language development, this will form a sound basis for learning to read and write. However, the literate environment so important in encouraging development of these new skills will not occur naturally for the blind child. Sighted children enter school with five years of experiences with print and books behind them. By the time school starts many children are ready to learn to read, if they haven't done so already. On the other hand, the blind child might come with very few similar braille reading experiences. Is it fair to send

Note to Parent: This is the braille sign for mother—dot 5 m—not all the letters are there. These abbreviations help us save space as we write braille.

Figure 1. An example of an annotated passage from an adapted book to help parents understand the vagaries of braille code.

these children to school with a five-year deficit and expect them to learn something twice as hard?

There are many readily available and untapped resources that lend themselves to our print above the the braille format, the format which allows the parent to read with the child. For example, children's Easy-to-Read books can be adapted by inserting braille copy produced on sticky contact paper directly beneath existing text. These books contain only one or two lines of large print text per page. Thus, the one or two lines of braille will be easier to track than a page full of print lines, but still give the child practice in moving left to right, turning pages, recognizing the top and bottom of the page . . . conventions of print which are prerequisites to reading. More importantly, this offers the blind child a chance to tactually discover the patterns of words and sentences in the context of a whole story as the parent reads aloud. With so many good children's books being published, there are probably many which could be inexpensively and easily adapted.

In addition to adapting books, perhaps a method can be devised to make it easier for sighted parents to easily recognize letter configurations in braille. Here there is the possibility of brailling books on specifically prepared pages of printed squares where each braille configuration falls into its own square. This gives a relationship of the raised dots to the whole braille cell and delineates each character. If parents could begin to recognize certain letters they could point these out to their child as they read. In addition notes and helpful hints to parents about braille code could be printed in the margins or between lines.

Conclusion

Jamaica is now five years old. She is in a regular kindergarten class with itinerant vision services. She is learning braille letters and tactual print letters both. It's not easy. I know it'll probably take longer for her to learn to read than it will for many of her sighted peers. But I'm not worried. She walks around the house and finds the bookshelf, still one of her favorite spots. She pulls down a few books (many of them slick inkprint only). She opens one and says "What is this?" I answer, "Wolfie. Do you know what Wolfie is?" "Oh yes, he's a spider." And I know she knows what a spider is because I've let one crawl on her leg. She might even talk about Wolfie or make up a story of her own as she flips through the book. She's got the basics . . . the meaning of the story, that the story comes from the book and that braille forms the words in the book. She loves books. She's on her way.

References

Goodman, K. (1976). *Reading: A conversation with Kenneth Goodman coauthor of Reading Unlimited.* Glenview, IL: Scott, Foresman & Company.

Holdaway, D. (1979). *The foundations of literacy.* Sydney, Australia: Ashton Scholastic.

Jensen & Haller (1978). *What's That?* New York: Philomel Books.

USING AN INTEGRATED LITERACY CURRICULUM WITH BEGINNING BRAILLE READERS

ANNA M. SWENSON

Blind children learning to read and write face a far more challenging task than their sighted peers. Developing the experiential background necessary for comprehension and mastering the intricacies of the braille code often require much one-on-one instruction. Although the teaching of braille will always necessitate individual attention, recent trends in teaching literacy skills to young sighted children appear to have significant implications for beginning braille readers.

It is now recognized that most sighted children begin school already possessing many literary behaviors, such as left-to-right sequencing, the ability to recognize some letters and produce letterlike forms, and an understanding of the purpose of reading (Wiseman, 1984). Some researchers dismiss the traditional concept of reading readiness, using the term "emergent literacy" to describe reading and writing behaviors seen in young children (Teale, 1985). This new perspective is having a significant impact on kindergarten curricula around the country. In many classrooms, "integrated curriculums" are being tried, stressing the close interconnections of oral language, reading, and writing skills. Kindergarteners no longer "get ready" to read and write—they *are* reading and writing every day, in a wide variety of situations.

> The connection between what is spoken, written, and read becomes even more apparent to children when they are active participants in a print-rich environment where oral language, writing, and reading are important daily activities (Sprunk et al., 1986).

Innovations in teaching language

These children use "big books," collaborative stories, journal writing, story conferencing, and many other activities as a regular part of their instruction. This multifaceted approach produces five-year-olds who are excited about reading and confident in their abilities as writers—results not usually attainable through the sole use of basal readiness materials.

Blind kindergarteners, whether mainstreamed or self-contained, can benefit from much of the integrated-curriculum approach, even if the "Patterns" readiness books continue to be used as a part of the instructional program. However, several special considerations are important in expanding the blind child's early literacy experiences. Blind children certainly do not come to school with the same repertoire of literary behaviors as sighted children. Their lack of exposure to the wealth of written language that surrounds every sighted child, and the relative scarcity of preschool braille materials, may mean that they do not even have the basic concept that spoken language can be written down.

Environmental differences for blind readers

Much can be done to develop this concept during the preschool years by creating a "literature environment" in the home— reading aloud, making simple braille books based on the child's experiences, familiarizing the young blind child with the braillewriter and its purpose, and encouraging approximations of reading and writing behaviors (Miller, 1985).

Equally important for every young child is an understanding of "the functional aspect of literacy" (Teale, 1985). Young blind children often miss out on the purposes of reading and writing because they do not observe other family members reading the newspaper, making shopping lists, jotting down telephone numbers, or consulting a recipe card. Even though print is an abstract concept for blind children, they can be made aware of its many uses of having parents describe in simple terms what they are reading or writing. Later on, when blind children begin to read braille and write on the braillewriter, their basic understanding of why people read and write will give them many reasons to practice and enjoy their new skills.

Once blind children begin kindergarten, much can be done to encourage their participation in an integrated-literacy program. Teachers of visually impaired children tend to spend a great deal of time on the mechanics of reading and writing braille, including manipulative activities to develop finger strength and coordination, tracking drills, and braille character discrimination exercises. While these are important, they do not give a real purpose for reading and writing, nor do they necessarily spark enthusiasm for literary pursuits. They also tend to isolate blind children from the academic activities of their sighted classmates, which are often very social at this level.

Appropriate adaptations

The vision teacher's first task is to select the most meaningful aspects of the "print rich" kindergarten environment to transcribe into braille. These may include the daily message, one or more "big books," collaborative stories, samples of other children's writing, and print books representing the best in children's literature at this level. Preparation of these materials is time-consuming, and often each braille selection must be explored on a one-to-one basis before being used in a classroom group activity. However, the use of such varied written materials adds an important dimension to the blind child's early reading experience, and lays the foundation for future progress and enjoyment.

Daily continuity

In the integrated-language-arts approach used with sighted children, writing is closely tied to oral language and reading. Children discuss their plans for writing at the beginning of a lesson, and later read what they have written in a group "conference," with comments from listeners encouraged. Fluent, uninhibited writing is fostered by making writing a daily activity, allowing children to select their own topics, and emphasizing the importance of the message rather than the mechanics.

Many children keep picture journals where they write a word or sentence about each illustration. All children are encouraged to use "invented spelling," a nonconventional but logical system of sounding out words (Teale, 1985).

Sound/symbol relationships are acquired in real writing situations through sharing, observation, and practice—often making formal instruction in beginning consonant sounds unnecessary. Some of the children's writing is revised and recopied using conventional "book spelling," then bound into attractive books of all shapes and sizes to be enjoyed by the entire class. The direct link between reading and writing is clearly established through the bookmaking process, and the children gain confidence in their abilities as writers and readers.

Essential read/write relationship

Making the reading-writing connection can be equally valuable and exciting for young blind children. Before students are able to use the braillewriter independently, braille language-experience stories dictated to the vision teacher develop the concept that spoken words can be written down. As soon as the children have mastered some basic mechanical skills—finger isolation, knowledge of the dot number associated with each of the six keys, and the ability to write a few words and letters—they can begin composing their own stories with guidance from the vision teacher.

Beginning writing

In the beginning, it is important for the vision teacher to model sounding-out behaviors, teaching the children to listen for consonant sounds in each word and providing the dot numbers for unfamiliar letters when necessary. This should not be a lengthy or a painful process—with the invented-spelling technique, how much of a word is written depends entirely on the child's level. Also, the braille code with its short-form words and special characters for common consonant digraphs actually facilitates the inventive spelling approach, and many young blind children are able to write as fluently as their sighted classmates.

Early writing attempts may consist only of the child's name and the beginning letter of a key word. Later on, whole sentences may be written, made up of one or more consonant letters from each word (e.g., I md a bg—meaning, I made a bridge). Like the early writing of sighted children, these braille stories should be recognized as approximations of mature writing. By providing acceptance, encouragement, and daily opportunities for practice, adults motivate children toward greater independence and skill in literary activities.

Group support

The importance of the message in writing is reinforced by providing children with frequent opportunities to share their writing with others. Blind children can participate easily in small group-writing conferences where each author reads his or her writing to the other children. Basic tracking and phonics skills are practiced during the reading, and critical thinking is developed through a discussion of what was heard. Opportunities to produce other types of meaningful written material—shopping lists for mobility lessons, thank-you letters, labels for cassette tapes—reinforce the many purposes of writing.

Like their sighted classmates, blind children gain further confidence and skills by participating in the bookmaking process. Subjects may be taken from the children's own journal or story writing, with the final copy brailled by the teacher, using conventional spelling and punctuation. Even very young children enjoy numbering the pages and assembling the different parts of their books in order, including the front and back covers, title page, text, and "About the Author" page. At this level, tactual illustrations are often a joint effort by the student and the teacher, providing additional reinforcement of oral language, fine motor skills, spatial awareness, and creative thinking. Books are made to be shared; the children's own braille books should become a temporary part of the classroom or school library, and should be read aloud often before being taken home.

Integrating braille into daily activities

Beginning braille readers who participate in an integrated-language-arts curriculum will continue to require more structure and individual guidance in acquiring literacy skills than their sighted classmates. Becoming a proficient braille reader necessitates practice in tracking, character discrimination, and application of complex rules. However, mastery of these skills should never be regarded as an end in itself. Those blind children whose daily work includes at least some aspects of an integrated curriculum benefit from the global picture of literacy it provides. Oral language, reading, and writing are seen as interrelated, purposeful activities.

References

Miller, D. (1985). Reading comes naturally: A mother and her blind child's experiences. *Journal of Visual Impairment & Blindness, 79,* 1–4.

Strunk, R. (1986). *Integrated language arts guide for kindergarten.* Fairfax, VA: Department of Instructional Service, Fairfax County Public Schools.

Teale, W. (1985). The beginnings of literacy. *Dimensions, 13,* 5–8.

Wiseman, D. (1984). Helping children take early steps toward reading and writing. *The Reading Teacher, 37,* 340–344.

A PROCESS APPROACH TO TEACHING BRAILLE WRITING AT THE PRIMARY LEVEL

ANNA M. SWENSON

Braille literacy is being reaffirmed by many in the field as an educational priority for children with severely limited vision (Schroeder, 1989; Stephens, 1989). The ability to read and write braille maximizes students' chances of educational and vocational success and lays the foundation that they need to benefit from many new technological advances (Stephens, 1989). Those who advocate braille literacy, however, should be aware that traditional approaches to teaching literary skills in regular education are being abandoned as a result of extensive research into the way sighted children achieve literacy. Key components of the new approach to teaching language arts include immersing students in print, giving students greater responsibility for learning, and integrating literary skills with all areas of the curriculum (County School Board of Fairfax County, 1987).

Classes following this approach are sometimes referred to as "reading-writing classrooms" (Butler & Turbill, 1987). Many of the ideas and strategies that characterize instruction in these classrooms may be applied to teaching braille writing at the primary level.

Writing: A process approach

Teaching writing is approached differently in a reading-writing classroom than it is in traditional writing instruction. Rote skill-development exercises from reading, spelling, grammar, and handwriting workbooks are replaced by the students' extensive daily writing on topics they select. This change reflects the belief that children learn to write only by actually writing, not by filling in blanks or copying exercises (Hansen, 1987).

Teachers are less concerned with the final product than with the students' involvement in the *process* of writing—a process that includes the phases of drafting, revising, proofreading, and publishing that are familiar to adult writers. Writing can be thought of as a craft, "a long, painstaking, patient process . . . to learn how to shape material to a level where it is satisfying to the person doing the crafting" (Graves, 1983, p. 6). When writing drafts, students learn to use invented spelling, a nonconventional but logical system of sounding out words (Teale, 1985), that enables them to compose freely using any words in their expressive vocabulary. One or more revisions of selected pieces are undertaken as the writers receive constructive feedback from their audience of peers and teachers. The message, not the mechanics, is the focus for discussion and revision until the work is prepared for publication by its student-author.

Process approach to braille writing

Young children who read braille can also benefit from this approach when the writing process is modified. Because the text should be immediately accessible to both the teacher and the child throughout the drafting and revision stages (Ely, 1989), a teacher who knows braille must assume the major role in teaching writing to a primary-grade child who is blind. When the child has a good understanding of the writing process and is able to transfer writing skills to a talking computer, regular education teachers may become more involved in writing instruction.

The writing samples included in this article are taken from the work of primary grade students who are enrolled in a combination self-contained-resource room for children with severe visual impairments. For part of each day, the children are mainstreamed into regular classes, in which a literature-based, process approach to teaching language arts is used. The vision teacher works closely with the regular education teachers to design a language arts program for each child that includes both mainstream experiences and individual instruction in the resource room. The work samples are exact transcriptions of the invented spelling written by the children on their first drafts. Parentheses indicate a child's use of Grade 2 braille contractions.

The writing program continues to evolve as it is adapted to meet specific students' needs and is expanded to include strategies used in the regular education classrooms. However, a number of key components form the basis for instruction:

1. Because reading and writing influence each other in positive ways (Anderson, Hiebert, Scott, & Wilkinson, 1984), the children are exposed to a wide variety of excellent children's literature, both fiction and nonfiction. They are read to frequently and have access to an expanding classroom library of easy braille books that are suitable for independent reading in the primary grades.

The goal is to develop a feel for the rhythm and pattern of language that the children will transfer to their writing. Most traditional basal reading series do not provide the rich linguistic experiences necessary for developing writers because of their controlled vocabulary and emphasis on rote skills. In the reading-writing classroom, these series have been replaced by a whole language, literature-based language arts program that fully integrates braille reading and writing experiences.

2. Just as students who are sighted are immersed in print in a reading-writing classroom, students who are blind are surrounded by braille to the greatest extent possible. The children are given many functional opportunities to practice their braille reading and writing skills every day—through messages, assignment lists, mainstream schedules, job lists, and letters to read and homework lists, reading logs, journals, thank-you letters, birthday cards, and cassette-tape labels to write. Teachers often leave braille messages for students, and the children quickly imitate this form of communication:

De(ar) Miss Sw(en)son, I ne(ed) (some)
(more) (braille) pap(er) (and) (some) big
(one)s (and) (some) skene <skinny>
(one)s . . . .

De(ar) miss weil, I am (so) soreey (th)et I (for) got to wride (you) a bir(th)(day) c(ar)d ye(st)(er)(day) . . . .

3. Reading and writing strategies are modeled before the children are expected to attempt them on their own. The teacher talks through her thinking process as she demonstrates such skills as selecting a topic, using invented spelling, crossing out and inserting words on a draft, note taking, sequencing ideas, and expanding sentences. The children participate actively, contributing suggestions as the teacher struggles to make choices and examining the braille draft as it takes shape. It is important that the children view the teacher as a fellow writer who requires feedback from the audience to clarify her message (Graves, 1983).

4. Materials for writing are readily available to the children. They include braille paper in various sizes (such as half sheets for short messages and long skinny sheets for lists), braillewriters, a stapler, envelopes, three-ring notebooks for journal entries, and pocket writing folders for each child's current writing project.

5. The writer's message *always* takes precedence over mechanical considerations during the drafting phase of the process. The braille code, with its special characters for consonant digraphs and common words, is well suited to the invented spelling process. In the following journal entry, invented spelling enabled the kindergarten student to relate an entire experience and then read it back to his teacher using phonetic and contextual clues:

my mommy took me to (the) dr
(and) (the)n I w(en)t to (the) dnst
I (had) a kvey (in) my t(th)
my dr gv me a (sh)t
My dr (was) ns dr
hz nm (was) dr frk
I (was) a bzey (ch)d

[My mommy took me to the doctor and then I went to the dentist. I had a cavity in my tooth. My doctor gave me a shot. My doctor was a nice doctor. His name was Dr. Frank. I was a busy child.]

6. Conferences of individual children with the vision teacher are the most common means of revising and proofreading braille drafts. However, opportunities are also provided for the children to share their writing with both sighted and blind peers.

7. Grade 2 braille is used from the beginning of reading and writing instruction. Children are motivated to learn to read and spell words that are of interest to them, regardless of the difficulty of the contractions they may contain.

Writing in kindergarten

Kindergarteners who are blind need to develop the physical skills necessary to operate the braillewriter, the cognitive skills required for independent creative writing, and an awareness of the many purposes of reading and writing braille. If they have been introduced to braille books and the braillewriter as preschoolers, they may already have the concept that spoken language can be written in the form of braille and read back with the fingers. This concept is expanded as they observe their classmates and teachers using braille in a variety of functional ways.

Developing the muscular strength and coordination required to use a braillewriter may take several years. Initially, short daily practice sessions are supplemented with many opportunities to improve fine motor skills through finger plays, art projects, and free play with assembly toys (such as Legos and Tinker Toys). Correct posture should be encouraged, with back support and a footstool provided, if necessary. Children who are unable to press the braillewriter keys without rocking their whole bodies back and forth may benefit from standing and writing at a counter of appropriate height to give them increased leverage. Mechanical skills that they need before they begin to write creatively on the braillewriter include the ability to insert and remove the paper, write a line of full cells using even pressure and correct finger position, isolate the fingers and press each key separately with the correct fingers, and press a combination of keys when the dot numbers for a particular letter or contraction are given.

The cognitive aspects of the writing process should be introduced at the same time as are the drills for the braillewriter, so the children understand that the mastery of mechanical skills is not an end in itself, but a necessary foundation for independent writing. Journal writing is an ideal activity to introduce young children to the pleasure of written expression. The following sequence of learning skills and concepts has been successful in developing independent writing abilities by the end of the kindergarten year.

Dictated writing/"talking writing"
During this first stage, the student dictates one or more sentences about a personal experience to the teacher, who writes the entry in braille. The teacher uses conventional spelling and Grade 2 braille, but models the process of invented spelling by verbally accenting the dominant consonant sounds in words and stating the name of the letter to be written for each sound. Gradually, the student is able to recognize the sounds made by the different consonant letters and to tell the teacher which letters to write. When the entry is complete, the student and teacher may make a simple tactile picture together, and the student reads the sentence with help from the teacher. The teacher points out easy-to-recognize consonant letters, braille contractions, and punctuation marks, and the student searches for other examples.

In the second part of the lesson, the child is encouraged to write freely on the braillewriter. Invariably, children will speak their message as they write, imitating the behavior modeled by their teacher. The result is often a line of seemingly random dots that are equivalent to the scribbles and marks made by sighted children of the same age. It is important to recognize that this "talking writing" represents a valid literary behavior, just as sighted children's first efforts with crayons and paper are crucial steps in the development of literacy (Teale, 1985). Young children who are blind should be permitted to use the braillewriter as much as they like during free time, as long as they treat it with care.

As the children read their teacher's writing and their own "talking writing," they become aware of differences between the two. The teacher explains that "talking writing" is an acceptable form of writing, but it can be read only by the writer. The writing done by the teacher is referred to as "book writing" and can be read by anyone who knows braille. At this point, the children are eager to be shown how to make some of the letters they see in the teacher's "book writing," and these letters begin to appear in their own "talking writing." The teacher conducts frequent informal assessments to determine how many letters the children are able to recognize and write. The children help to choose the next letters to be learned, often by the association of these letters with favorite words or names.

Guided writing

During this stage, the children begin to write words and phrases using invented spelling and conventional braille characters, but still benefit from the teacher's assistance with the formation of characters on the braillewriter. Children who read braille become increasingly aware that characters with special shapes—contractions—may hide the sounds they hear in words or have sounds of their own. For example, the letter "r" does not appear in the word "her" where the "er" contraction is used, and the contraction "sh" makes a new sound altogether. As the children encounter common contractions in their reading, they begin to use them naturally in their writing.

Independent writing

Sighted children can begin to compose independently when they know about six consonants (Graves, 1983). Children who are learning braille often achieve independence in writing on the braillewriter at about the same time as do their sighted peers. The following sequence of journal entries shows one child's movement toward independence during his kindergarten year:

November: I (know) h(ow) to (do) buttons. [Sentence dictated to the teacher followed by a line of "talking writing" and a glued on button]

March: I tk n (the) mkfn

["I talked on the microphone." Sentence written by the child using consonant letters; some help was given with spacing and the contraction "the"]

June:

D(er)edadiho(you)(have)avr(th)rsdalav_
_____

("Dear Dad, I hope you have a very nice Father's Day. Love,—." [Sentence written independently by the child during free time; some contractions and vowels were used, but no spaces between words.])

The invented spelling technique allows young children complete freedom in choosing topics to write about and gives them early confidence in their abilities as independent writers.

The developing writer

As the children move into first grade, they become familiar with the basic steps in the writing process and begin to use the words *draft, revise, proofread,* and *publish* to describe where they are in their work on a particular piece. Children who are blind often write drafts as fluently as do their sighted classmates, using invented spelling to express their ideas. However, during the revision stage, when the students confer with their teachers or classmates and work to improve the clarity of their writing, young children who are blind require additional assistance from a teacher who knows braille. The goal is to maintain the children's lead in revising text while making the concrete part of the process (substituting words, moving text) as easy as possible. For primary-grade children who are blind, this goal can be achieved at several levels of difficulty:

1. The teacher writes in braille while the student revises the piece orally. The student and teacher then read the completed revision (the second draft) together and summarize the reasons for the changes.

2. The teacher and student revise the piece together and make changes directly on the draft. Sentences can be eliminated or rewritten by sticking a long piece of masking tape over the words and writing on top of it if a new version is needed. The sequence of events can also be changed by cutting the draft into separate sentences, placing the sentences in order, and stapling them to a new paper. A similar technique may be used to create space for additional information. Students enjoy helping the teacher manipulate the parts of the text to produce a satisfactory revision.

3. If the piece requires major revisions, the student and teacher may work together, with the student doing the writing. Several drafts may be necessary.

4. Depending on the difficulty and length of the piece and the maturity of the writer, the piece may be revised independently by the student after conferring with the teacher.

Like revision, proofreading can be accomplished most effectively during an individual conference between the student and the teacher. Often the student is asked to mark capitalization, punctuation, and spelling errors on the draft with a crayon before meeting with the teacher. The teacher then helps the student to make corrections using the braillewriter or tactile editing marks. Suggested editing symbols include the following:

- Capital letter: A small piece of Formaline Charting and Graphic Art Tape.
- Period: A small self-adhesive dot label.
- New paragraph: A star.
- Corrected spelling: Brailled on a rectangular file-folder label and stuck over the misspelled word.
- Space needed: A long, thin piece of Formaline tape.

Once the written piece has been revised and proofread, a final copy is prepared for publication. Whether the children copy from a teacher-made draft (as in Level 1) or a draft containing editing marks, they are expected to use correct capitalization, punctuation, spelling, and Grade 2 braille. The children have invested a great deal of effort in their writing by the time it reaches this stage and are so familiar with the text that they can focus carefully on small details. The completed copy is often published as a book, with a title page, dedication, biographical sketch of the author, and tactile pictures, and becomes part of the classroom library for the remainder of the year.

Young children in reading-writing classrooms write daily, but publish only about a fifth of their drafts—one every 10 days to two weeks (Graves, 1983). The learning involved in the revision and proofreading stages is supplemented by minilessons related to their writing style or mechanical skills. During each lesson, the teacher focuses on a specific skill or aspect of writing, often using the student's work to illustrate the problem and possible solutions. The first-grade author of the following draft was asked to think critically about his work by finding the three sentences that said the same thing, choosing the best one, and justifying his decision.

> (the) guiea pig is my fbrt
> I (like) (the) guiea pig (so) (much)
> (the) guiea pig my fvrt anml
> I w(sh)t I (had) a guiea pig
> I (would) tk kv (of) a gu(in)ea pig

Other examples of minilessons that are taught to visually impaired writers at the primary level include grouping like ideas; choosing interesting words; composing a main-idea sentence, followed by support statements; providing more specific information; using quotation marks in dialogue; differentiating between the questions and telling sentences; maintaining the agreement of the subject and the verb in a sentence; and using the contracted form of the word *to*.

The process approach to writing does not ignore the importance of teaching children to spell or use Grade 2 braille correctly. Children understand that conventional "book spelling," not invented spelling, must be used in published pieces. Keeping a running list of words a child misspells during daily writing provides the teacher with a source of weekly spelling lists that are composed of words the student actually uses.

In making up a spelling list, the vision teacher can group words to maximize the practice of specific contractions or to introduce new ones. Children enjoy helping to choose the words for their lists and demonstrate significant improvement in spelling on their written drafts. Correct spelling can also be encouraged by teaching students to use small three-ring notebook "word banks" to record the spelling of words they use frequently or need for a specific topic. The word bank contains one page for each letter and three tabs—"F," "M," and "T"—to help the children locate words quickly.

Diversity in writing

The wide variety of children's literature that developing writers hear and read in a reading-writing classroom leads naturally to diversity in their writing. A favorite literary form is the imitation of rhythms and patterns found in traditional chants like "The More We Get Together," a selection from an early first-grade reading lesson:

> The more we get together, together, together,
> The more we get together, the happier we'll be.
> *Braille variation using the student's favorite food:*
> (The) (more) we eat (the) pizza, (the) pizza, (the) pizza,
> (The) (more) we eat (the) pizza, (the) fatt(er) we'll be!

Primary-grade students can also be introduced to nonfiction, or "information writing," and the techniques of interviewing, developing categories, taking notes, and constructing sentences from notes. A resource-room class project entitled *Frogs: A Search for Information* contained two major parts: "How We Found and Organized Our Information" and "What We Learned about Frogs." The first part was composed in a group as the children recalled the procedures used in researching and writing about frogs:

> When Miss Swenson was reading, we helped her make notes about important information. She used one paper for each kind of information: one paper for body, one for home, one for babies, one for enemies, one for noises, and one for food. We each chose one kind of information to write about. We made the notes into sentences. Then we revised and proofread our writing.

In the second part, each child wrote one chapter. The entire project was published in braille and used for reading instruction before each child took a copy home.

Assessment

The vision teacher should be responsible for the continuous assessment of a young student's progress in braille reading and writing (Rex, 1989). A file of all written drafts for the school year should be maintained, along with records of the minilessons taught, spelling tests administered, revision conferences held, and books published. It is helpful to summarize the information from these records periodically by listing the writing skills a child has mastered (citing specific writing pieces as evidence) and those that are being worked on. This list can be shared with the child and used in parent-teacher conferences along with writing samples. Regular education teachers can also provide useful informal assessment tools that are specifically designed to measure progress in the writing process.

Three times a year—in September, January, and June—a more structured evaluation is suggested. Students can be asked to summarize in writing the content of a short paragraph they have read silently; to write a letter from dictation, paying special attention to the mechanics; to write selected Grade 2 braille contractions that are checked off on a summary sheet; and to write selected Dolch words (220 high-frequency words that make a basic sight vocabulary) that are also checked off on a list. A comparison of data from the three structured assessments provides further information that can be used to plan a child's writing program.

Results

Children who learn to write braille using a process approach develop positive attitudes toward writing. Their attitudes are apparent in the quantity and quality of writing they produce, both at school and at home. They consider the writing not as a type of work assigned a few times each week, but as a useful tool to be employed for many functions throughout the day. The children feel in control of their learning because they are allowed to make important decisions—what topics to write about, which words to learn to spell, what revisions to make, and which pieces to publish. Because they are not constrained by the need to produce a perfect paper during the drafting stage, they are more willing to take risks in choosing topics, vocabulary, and ideas to express. They accept revision as a natural part of the writing process and begin to think critically about their writing as they interact with their text in a variety of ways. Writing samples and periodic structured assessments confirm that the conventions of written expression—spelling, capitalization, and punctuation—*are* mastered when the process approach to writing is used.

Children who write frequently and publish their work learn to make connections between reading and writing. A first grader, writing about a book he read, explained:

> (It) made me (th)ik (of) (some) (of) my books (that) I wrote to (because) I (know) I am a au(th)or to (and) I (know) I wrote lot (of) books (with) pictures (in)side (the)m (and) (ou)tside (the)m.

Authorship sparks children's interest in the adult authors of the books they read and hear read to them. The children develop preferences for the work of particular authors and enjoy discussing the books they read in the same way that they discuss their own writing (Hansen, 1987).

Conclusion

The process approach is a highly effective way of teaching writing to children who are blind. Although it demands additional time from a teacher who knows braille, this method provides young children with a means of creating and thinking about writing that is both pleasurable and challenging. The writing process used in the primary grades establishes a foundation for the development of future literacy skills, including the use of a talking word processor. Its immediate success, however, is reflected in the enthusiasm and confidence with which young children approach the complex task of braille writing.

References

Anderson, R.C., Hiebert, E.H., Scott, J A., & Wilkinson, I.A.G. (1984). *Becoming a nation of readers: The report of the Commission on Reading.* Washington, DC: National Institute of Education.

Butler, A. & Turbill, J. (1987). *Towards a reading-writing classroom.* Portsmouth, NH: Heinemann Educational Books.

County School Board of Fairfax County, Virginia (1987). *Elementary program of studies language arts.* Fairfax County, VA: Author.

Ely, R. (1989). Writing, computers, and visual impairment. *Journal of Visual Impairment & Blindness, 83,* 248–252.

Graves, D.H. (1983). *Writing: Teachers & children at work.* Portsmouth, NH: Heinemann Educational Books.

Hansen, J. (1987). *When writers read.* Portsmouth, NH: Heinemann Educational Books .

Rex, E. J. (1989). Issues related to literacy of legally blind learners. *Journal of Visual Impairment & Blindness, 83,* 306–313.

Schroeder, F. (1989). Literacy: The key to opportunity. *Journal of Visual Impairment & Blindness, 83,* 290–293.

Stephens, O. (1989). Braille—Implications for living. *Journal of Visual Impairment & Blindness, 83,* 288–289.

Teale, W. (1985). The beginnings of literacy. *Dimensions, 13,* 5–8.

TEACHING BRAILLE READING TO STUDENTS WITH LOW VISION

M. CAY HOLBROOK AND ALAN J. KOENIG

It is critical that the present and future reading needs of students with visual impairments are identified and addressed throughout their school years. Koenig and Holbrook (1989) referred to this as "filling a student's 'toolbox' with 'tools' appropriate to accomplish a variety of tasks" (p. 300).

The process of determining the appropriate reading medium for students with visual impairments may be divided into two phases (Koenig & Holbrook, 1989, 1991). In Phase I, an initial decision is made about the primary reading medium for a student who has not received formal reading instruction. When a student's vision is limited, the decision may be difficult and the multidisciplinary team may go through many steps in the process to make the initial decision. Eventually, the team may decide that the student will use either print or braille as his or her only reading medium or that the student will learn to read in both media with equal emphasis. Ongoing evaluations must be made to determine if a student who is being instructed in one medium will receive supplemental instruction in an alternative medium. In Phase II, the team reviews the appropriateness of the initial decision and the need to supplement the initial reading medium with a second medium on the basis of diagnostic information collected in this phase. The reading medium may be changed because the initial decision was incorrect or new information indicates that a change is warranted, or it may be decided that the student should continue to receive instruction in the initial medium with supplemental instruction in a second medium.

This article focuses on teaching braille reading to students with low vision who have the following characteristics:

- Students in Phase I who will learn braille and print reading at the same time with equal intensity.
- Students in Phase II who have a background of formal instruction in print reading but for whom the multidisciplinary team has decided that continued emphasis on print is inappropriate. These students will learn braille reading as a secondary medium that may eventually become the primary reading medium.
- Students in Phase II who will use print as the primary medium and simultaneously learn braille reading as a supplementary tool because braille is needed for particular tasks or print reading may not be effective as the exclusive medium in the long term.

Reprinted from M. C. Holbrook & A. J. Koenig, "Teaching Braille Reading to Students with Low Vision," *Journal of Visual Impairment & Blindness, 86*(1) (January 1992), pp. 44–48. Copyright © 1992, American Foundation for the Blind.

Students in Phase I with some degree of vision may be able to accomplish some distance tasks visually, but cannot complete tasks visually at near point. Braille reading instruction for these students will be similar to that for students who are totally blind and will not be addressed in this article, since these students are considered functionally blind, not students with low vision.

This article explores some aspects of teaching braille reading to students with low vision. First, it discusses the motivation of students to learn braille reading and parents' acceptance of braille and involvement in the process. It then covers instructional approaches and factors to be considered in choosing a program and the phasing in of braille reading throughout the curriculum.

Motivation

Some students with low vision present a dilemma for educators and parents. Although they must be encouraged to develop and use vision as much as possible, they must also be taught to rely on their other senses, including the tactual sense for reading. Several factors may influence both parents' and children's acceptance of braille reading instruction.

Acceptance of visual impairment

It is essential for the parents and child to understand the clinical *and* functional aspects of the child's visual impairment, so appropriate educational decisions can be made and supported. Parents' understanding and acceptance may be increased by the following:

- Teachers' explanations of the educational implications of their child's eye condition.
- Parents' inclusion in the assessment of their child's functional vision to help them understand how their child uses visual information.
- Parents' participation in controlled, appropriate exercises with simulators representing their child's visual impairment and the provision of accurate information during these experiences.
- Parents' and student's ongoing contact with successful adults with a similar type of visual impairment.

Understanding braille

Most people do not know or understand braille as a code for reading and writing and may consider braille a symbol of total blindness. Therefore, parents of a child with low vision may be reluctant to accept braille as a learning medium, since their child has useful vision. These suggestions may help parents to understand and accept braille:

- The most effective route to understanding and acceptance is for parents to learn to read and write in braille through such instructional programs as *Just Enough to Know Better* (Curran, 1988) and *New Programmed Instruction in Braille* (Ashcroft, Henderson, Sanford, & Koenig, 1991). Teachers can provide feedback, reinforcement, and direct instruction.
- Educators can inform parents of the variety of ways that braille can be used by efficient braille users, including note taking, using braille notes in public speaking, and reading braille menus.

- Parents can be encouraged to talk with other parents or to attend parental meetings on the subject.

Parent involvement

The involvement of parents and other family members not only decreases the child's isolation in learning something that most people do not know, but provides an opportunity for increased communication between parents and their child. In addition to learning the braille code, parents can do the following:

- Help the child with his or her homework in braille.
- Show their pride in their child's work by displaying braille homework papers on the refrigerator or placing selected papers in a scrapbook.
- Become involved with their child in public library reading programs. Teachers of students with visual impairments and librarians can facilitate this involvement by establishing a link between the public library and the National Library Service for the Blind and Physically Handicapped.
- Along with educators, advocate for the provision of braille materials in public and private places (such as church bulletins and menus) where the child may need them.

Motivational reading material

Learning braille reading may become tedious if students rely on vision for other activities. It is not enough to use standard, commercially produced reading instructional materials. Students must also be given the opportunity to read material in braille that they want to read for enjoyment or for gaining information on topics they are learning in school or that pertain to their special interests and hobbies. For example, important school materials, such as schedules and menus, can be transcribed and posted beside the print versions, and items, such as records and tapes, can be labeled in braille at home. In addition, children and parents can be encouraged to read twin-version books and educational materials together, and the child can communicate with a pen pal who also reads and writes in braille.

Sleep shades

Some students with low vision will try to use their vision to read braille, rather than learn to decode braille tactually. Decoding braille visually is slow and laborious, since there is little or no contrast between the braille dots and the surrounding paper. If a student consistently reads braille visually over a long period (past the introductory stage) and is reluctant or even refuses to attempt to read braille tactually, the student is demonstrating a high level of visual ability, which may indicate that braille should not be the primary reading medium.

Students who have used their vision for exploration may feel more comfortable using their vision for confirmation during the beginning stages of braille reading instruction. Some educators discourage this use of vision by blindfolding the student during instruction. However, the use of sleep shades should be avoided. Instead, tactual exploration of braille can be encouraged by providing situations, such as these, in which visual examination is not possible:

- The teacher could teach young children to use a "Super Spy Box" (J. Snider, personal communication, January 1991)—a box cut so the student can slip his or her hands into it to find a "clue"—while the teacher watches for the proper techniques and supplies clues through a hole on the opposite side of the box.

- The teacher should place a screen or ledge so it blocks the student's hands from his or her eyes, but is arranged so the teacher can see hand-finger positioning.
- The teacher should encourage proper body positioning (sitting with the back straight and arms parallel to the floor at right angles from the body), so the student cannot view the braille dots.

Instructional approaches

The choice of an instructional approach in teaching braille reading to a student with low vision depends largely on two factors. First, the educator must consider the point at which skill in one reading medium is being developed relative to skill in the other medium. A student in Phase I who is beginning to read in both print and braille will learn readiness skills, word-identification strategies, comprehension skills, and so forth in both media at the same time—an approach we call *parallel instruction*. Parallel instruction implies the equal concentration on reading skills in both print and braille, the only difference being the code used to teach these skills.

Students in Phase II have already acquired basic reading skills in print, so they will be able to apply those skills in braille. We call this approach *nonparallel instruction,* since the student is not acquiring similar skills in both media. The student will continue to develop basic reading skills in print, while instruction in braille will focus on "cracking" a new code. Eventually, the level of braille reading skills will match the level of print reading skills.

Second, the educator must consider the approach with which he or she feels most comfortable and that is consistent with his or her philosophy of teaching reading. Some approaches are more structured and provide specific guidelines for teaching reading, while others are less structured and require the educator to construct a reading program to meet the specific needs of a student. An educator may choose from a variety of approaches, including 1) a basal reading series, 2) language experience, 3) whole language, 4) *Patterns,* and 5) *Read Again.*

Basal reader approach

In the basal reader approach, the educator makes use of a commercial basal reading series (usually the series adopted by the school district) that is designed for teaching reading in print. In most cases, this approach is most appropriate for parallel instruction. It could also be used in nonparallel instruction if it is followed by introductory lessons in essential braille prereading skills and letter-contraction recognition, but a protracted series of introductory lessons may not provide the motivation necessary to sustain interest in reading in braille. (The language experience approach may be used as an alternative or to provide the introductory experiences before using the basal reader approach.)

The primary advantage of the basal reader approach in parallel instruction is that instructional time is used efficiently. Since the child will complete the lessons in print anyway, applying the same skills in braille will extend instructional time only minimally (about 25%) because there are more shared similarities than differences in reading in print and in braille. Another general advantage is that this approach is comprehensive; all essential reading skills are included in carefully sequenced lessons. The teacher of students with visual impairments needs only to supplement it with materials, either teacher made or commercially available, to teach skills that are specific to reading in braille.

Some educators believe that the primary disadvantage of this approach is the lack of control over the introduction of braille contractions, which makes the level of difficulty for vocabulary in braille different from that of print. However, we believe this concern is exaggerated. With adequate readiness, appropriate introductory lessons, and sequential instruction, a student can learn to read efficiently in braille using this approach, as did the generations of students who learned to read in braille before *Patterns* was introduced. Another commonly stated disadvantage of this approach is that stories are often dependent on pictures for meaning. However, for a student with low vision, this disadvantage is greatly minimized or eliminated, since the student can use pictures as part of the process, perhaps learning the crucial visual skill of scanning in conjunction with reading.

In parallel instruction, the teacher of students with visual impairments will introduce new words in both print and braille before reading the story or selection. New contractions in braille should be introduced in meaningful contexts (as they appear in words), since there is little value drilling lists of contractions before they are actually used in reading. The extensive drilling of contractions may cause a student to think that reading in braille is an exercise in calling out isolated bits and pieces of words, rather than in gaining meaning from connected discourse. After appropriate introduction, the student may read the story in print and then in braille or read part of the story in one medium and the rest in the other medium. In reading-strategy lessons following the story, the same options can be applied. Since the student is developing the same reading skills (such as phonics, using context clues, and identifying the main idea) in both print and braille, it makes little difference which reading medium is selected. The essential factor is to maintain a balance, so equal skills are developed in both media.

The basal reader approach offers the educator a great deal of flexibility. If the student is integrated in a reading program, the regular classroom teacher could teach print reading and the teacher of students with visual impairments could teach braille reading using the same materials. Another alternative would be to teach one unit in braille and the next in print. Also, reading in other subjects or for enjoyment could be balanced between print and braille.

If the educator chooses to use a basal reading approach in nonparallel instruction, the sequential presentation of stories in increasing difficulty will be the basis for instruction. It may be desirable to choose a previous grade level from the series (even one the student has already completed) because the student can focus on developing and applying skills in a new code, rather than concentrate on both code skills and reading skills. The teaching of reading-readiness skills in braille before the introduction of stories from a basal reading series will require careful balancing to sustain the child's interest in braille reading while preparing him or her to read in connected discourse in this new medium.

Language-experience approach

The language-experience approach uses the student's actual experiences as the basis for instruction. The student dictates a story about an experience to the teacher, who writes it down while the student observes. The story is then used to develop reading skills (as is done with a basal reading series). Such an approach could be used effectively in either parallel or nonparallel instruction.

There are many advantages to using this approach. First, since the student's actual experiences are used as the basis for reading instruction, the educator is assured that the child has the background needed for comprehending the story. Second, it is a highly motivating approach for a student, since the student dictates the story, knows the content, and can reread the story in a meaningful manner. Because of the high motivational value, teachers may choose to use this approach as a supplement to others. Third, it is a flexible approach that can be used in conjunction with other instructional approaches and in parallel or nonparallel instruction to teach reading-comprehension skills in print, braille, or both.

There are few, if any, disadvantages to this approach. Since the stories are dictated by the student, there can be no control over the presence of difficult words or words with contractions. (In reality, this is a strength of this approach—if the student can *say* a word, he or she can also *read* it.) This lack of control is not a significant concern if adequate, and sequential instruction is provided in the introduction of words. Second, this approach is unstructured. Because there is no prescribed sequence of reading skills, the educator may choose to use this approach in conjunction with a basal reader approach to ensure that all essential reading skills are taught.

The basic instructional procedures are straightforward. First, an experience must take place—one that is either arranged specifically for this purpose (such as a trip to the local firehouse) or that occurs naturally (for example, what happened during recess today). However, educators should keep in mind that students with visual impairments often lack basic experiences, so arranged ones are important. Second, as soon as the experience has occurred, the student dictates a story about it and the teacher writes exactly what the student says using a braillewriter or slate and stylus. Third, the student and teacher read the story together immediately afterward. Fourth, the student and teacher continue to reread the story for a few days. It will be more crucial as this process continues for the teacher to say words only as the student tracks over them, since this is the process by which the student associates certain configurations with the words they represent. Fifth, the teacher can arrange any number of reading strategy lessons using the story as the basis for developing targeted skills. For example, contextual clues can be fostered through the cloze procedure, in which every fifth word is replaced by a blank and the student fills in a word that makes sense as the story is read, or phonics skills can be developed from words present in the story. Hall (1981) is an excellent source of suggestions for reading-strategy lessons to be used with this approach.

Whole-language approach

The whole-language approach is a comprehensive program that integrates reading and writing into the entire curriculum of a classroom, including such activities as choral reading, language experience, journal writing, and uninterrupted sustained silent reading. This approach lends itself to situations in which the classroom teacher works closely with the teacher of students with visual impairments to ensure that the students are fully involved in all aspects of instruction. A residential school classroom in which the teacher knows braille and modifies his or her own materials would be an ideal setting for this approach. In a mainstream classroom, students with low vision are most likely to participate in this approach if the entire curriculum is set up in this type of program. This decision is made by the regular classroom teacher or a school official; the teacher of students with visual impairments will not decide to use this approach, but will respond to the curriculum needs of the mainstream classroom.

There are several advantages to this approach for students who have low vision. First, it uses motivating reading materials and activities. Second, since students participate with their sighted peers in both reading and writing activities, appropriate materials must be provided for all activities. Third, because of the wide variety of activities involving reading and writing, this approach provides opportunities for students with low vision to choose the most effective tool for a particular task.

The disadvantages of this approach are that many materials may need to be adapted or transcribed into braille. The production and adaptation of materials for whole-language classrooms must be ongoing, and options must be available to fulfill the immediate need for spontaneous activities. Finally, the approach is difficult to use in an itinerant teaching model, since constant communication between the classroom teacher and the itinerant teacher is essential for success.

In both parallel and nonparallel instruction, students receive individual instruction in braille reading or the braille code, respectively. In parallel instruction, as much material as possible must be provided in both braille and print and a balance must be maintained between the two media. In nonparallel instruction, the braille code is taught separately from whole-language class, and students continue to use their vision for a majority of tasks until their reading skills in braille are adequate for daily classroom assignments. The whole-language approach to teaching reading is a new system in the United States and requires extensive exploration to determine the most effective way to include students who are learning to read braille.

Patterns

Patterns: The Primary Braille Reading Program is a specially designed basal reading program for young students who are blind. It is intended to introduce basic reading skills through the third-grade level and, by the end of the program, to have introduced all the contractions and short form words in the Grade II braille code. After the third grade, the student is prepared to enter a standard basal reading program or some other approach used by sighted students. This series has recently added the *Patterns Prebraille Program,* which introduces the early concepts and language skills necessary for reading.

One of the primary advantages of *Patterns* is that it is a comprehensive program containing readers, work sheets, a teacher's guide, and criterion tests and is specifically designed to meet the early reading needs of students who are blind. The introduction of new vocabulary and contractions is carefully controlled according to factors known to influence the difficulty of reading in braille. Stories were written to reflect the experiences of young students who are blind and are not dependent on pictures for understanding the content. Finally, beginning teachers may find *Patterns* appealing because it is a structured approach with a complete teacher's guide.

For students with low vision who are learning to read braille, the major disadvantage of using *Patterns*—its incompatibility with other approaches—largely overshadows its advantages. Since *Patterns* was intended to be used as a stand-alone program for young students who are learning to read in braille, it is difficult to combine it with other approaches in a systematic and meaningful manner. Also, its use will prevent integrated reading instruction with sighted peers and will further prevent the use of supplementary and recreational reading materials in braille outside the *Patterns Library Series*.

In parallel instruction, the teacher of students with visual impairments delivers a separate reading program in braille apart from the instructional program in print reading. Therefore, if this approach is used, it will double the amount of instructional time, and multidisciplinary teams must guarantee that this time is set aside for the student.

In nonparallel instruction, the teacher may use *Patterns* only to introduce the unique aspects of reading in braille and eliminate some or all the skills lessons that accompany the series, except for the vocabulary and comprehension skills specific to each story. This strategy assumes that essential reading skills are being taught and acquired in the print reading program. In nonparallel instruction, the amount of instructional time depends on the amount of time devoted to teaching reading skills that are not unique to the braille code.

Read Again

Read Again (Caton, Pester, & Bradley, 1990) is a series of instructional materials that are designed to teach the braille code to individuals with adventitious blindness. It does not purport to teach reading skills per se because it was developed specifically for individuals with established basic reading skills in print who are being introduced to reading in braille. Therefore, it is appropriate only for nonparallel instruction.

An advantage of *Read Again* is that it was designed specifically to teach the braille code to individuals with adventitious blindness who are learning to read in another medium. Therefore, it would meet the similar need for instruction in an alternative reading medium for students with low vision in nonparallel instruction. Also, it is a comprehensive set of materials with practice materials, criterion tests, and a teacher's manual.

A disadvantage of *Read Again* is that since the program was targeted to the vocabulary of teenagers and young adults, it is not appropriate for many younger students. In addition, the contrived reading materials may not sustain the interest of older students.

In nonparallel instruction with older students, the educator will use *Read Again* as a stand-alone program, supplementing the practice exercises with reading materials of importance to the student. These materials may include such items as their class schedule for the upcoming semester and telephone numbers and addresses of friends. It is essential to show the student how braille reading can be useful in completing essential tasks, rather than isolating these skills from day-to-day activities.

Supplementary materials

With all the approaches just discussed and with either parallel or nonparallel instruction, some supplementary materials will be necessary to teach students the unique aspects of reading in braille, including hand movements, tactual discrimination, and braille character recognition. One of the most valuable programs is the *Mangold Program of Tactile Perception and Braille Letter Recognition* (Mangold, 1977)—a carefully sequenced set of materials that teaches efficient and independent hand-movement skills, combined with the quick discrimination and recognition of braille letters.

The Mangold program is a valuable tool for teaching reading in braille to students with low vision *when it is used for its intended purpose*. It is not a reading program per se (and was never intended to be), since it does not teach a student to gain meaning from connected text. It teaches some basic, essential skills that are needed for reading in braille, but does not teach higher-level reading skills, such as vocabulary, word recognition, and comprehension.

Other supplementary materials that may be used as part of a total reading program include the *APH Tactual Discrimination Worksheets, Touch and Tell,* and the *Patterns Prebraille Program*. Also, teacher-made materials that pinpoint specific skills are valuable. Harley, Truan, and Sanford (1987) offer some excellent ideas for teacher-made materials and activities for teaching reading in braille.

Integrating braille into the curriculum

The purpose of reading instruction is not just to teach reading for the sake of reading, but to teach students to use reading to accomplish a variety of daily tasks. The same is true for learning to use braille for reading and writing. If students are to become truly efficient braille users, they must have intensive and extensive experience with braille in all areas of schoolwork.

In parallel instruction, the student must maintain a balance in the use of both print and braille to become effective in both media. Braille reading will not be mastered if braille is used only during reading instruction. Rather, the practice of reading in braille throughout the day and evening is critical to its development. Since the premise of parallel instruction is that both print and braille will be taught at the same time with equal intensity, opportunities must be provided for applied and sustained practice. Print and braille should be integrated into the curriculum with equal frequency, and the student should be encouraged in the early stages to help decide which medium to use for a particular task.

In nonparallel instruction, the focus is on maintaining academic achievement in print reading while developing braille reading skills. It is unreasonable to expect that a child will be able to use braille immediately to achieve academic goals, since in the beginning, braille reading will be slower and less efficient than will print reading. Braille should be phased into the curriculum at various points, while always keeping in mind the time it takes for students to complete the task efficiently in print or in braille. Print reading will continue to be an important tool for students as long as they have sufficient functional vision.

References

Ashcroft, S.C., Henderson, F, Sanford, L., & Koenig, A. (1991). *New programmed instruction in braille.* Nashville, TN: SCALARS Publishing.

Caton, H., Pester, E., & Bradley, E.J. (1990). *Read again.* Louisville, KY: American Printing House for the Blind.

Curran, E.P (1988). *Just enough to know better.* Boston: National Braille Press.

Hall, M.A. (1981). *Teaching reading as a language experience* (3rd ed.). Columbus, OH: Merrill Publishing Co.

Harley, R.K., Truan, M.B., & Sanford, L.D. (1987). *Communication skills for visually impaired learners.* Springfield, IL: Charles C Thomas.

Koenig, A.J. & Holbrook, M.C. (1989). Determining the reading medium for students with visual impairments: A diagnostic teaching approach. *Journal of Visual Impairment & Blindness,* **83,** 296–302.

Koenig, A.J. & Holbrook, M.C. (1991). Determining the reading medium for visually impaired students via diagnostic teaching. *Journal of Visual Impairment & Blindness,* **85,** 61–68.

Mangold, S. (1977). *The Mangold developmental program of tactile perception and braille letter recognition.* Castro Valley, CA: Exceptional Teaching Aids.

Teachers who are providing instruction in braille reading and writing to children who are blind or visually impaired need to have at their fingertips sources of curriculum materials, products, and teaching materials; resources for parents; names of national organizations to which they can turn for help; and more. This resource guide, although not an exhaustive listing, is an attempt to meet that need. It also supplies information about all the products and services and sources of information that are mentioned throughout this book.

In addition to the resources listed here, another resource for teachers of braille reading and writing is the National Literacy Program of the American Foundation for the Blind (AFB). Its goal is to develop programs, products, and strategies to ensure that people who are blind or visually impaired will become literate to the fullest extent possible in the most appropriate media. To this end, the National Literacy Program has developed human resources, training materials, and workshops, among other materials. Through the National Braille Literacy Mentor Project, the initiative has created a national network of expert teachers of braille who can serve as mentors to new teachers. It also publishes a quarterly newsletter, *DOTS for Braille Literacy,* which is available in print, in braille, on computer disk, via e-mail, and online. For more information, see the listing under AFB Southeast under "National Organizations."

The first section, "The Braille Reading Teacher's Bookshelf," includes important books that deal with teaching reading and writing and that are a critical addition to every braille reading teacher's bookshelf. Also included is a listing of courses and materials that will help teachers who have not taught braille recently to refresh their knowledge of the braille code.

"Resources for Teaching Braille" lists sources of materials that are vital to braille instructional programs, such as books, magazines, braille curriculum materials, teaching materials and other products, and braille transcription services. This section also includes resources for teaching braille to students who are bilingual, multilingual, or learning English as a second language and sources of assessment materials that can be used by teachers of braille reading and writing. For additional sources of braille publications, braille transcribers, and listings of the regional Libraries for the Blind around the country, readers can consult the *AFB Directory of Services for Blind and Visually Impaired Persons in the United States and Canada* or contact the National Library Service for the Blind and Physically Handicapped of the Library of Congress. The *Directory* also provides listings of the state instructional materials centers, an additional source of braille books and materials.

The next section lists national organizations that provide information for teachers in the form of publications, conferences, or referrals or that provide professional membership opportunities. This is followed by "Resources for Parents," which lists places to which parents can turn for help, either for learning braille or for support and information.

"Resources for Technology" lists some specific products in several categories of braille access technology, as well as producers and distributors of these products. Because this technology changes so rapidly, and specific products are frequently updated, this can only be an overview of current technology. For additional and up-to-date information, readers are advised to contact the sources for particular products, as well as AFB's National Technology Center at (212) 502-7642.

Finally, at the end of this section, readers will find blank copies of various forms that appear in the chapters for record keeping, assessment, and so forth. These are provided for readers' use and may be copied for educational purposes.

THE BRAILLE READING TEACHER'S BOOKSHELF

The Bookshelf

With a few exceptions, the following books deal with the braille code or braille reading and are recommended for teachers to use as references. Also included are videos and a few books that deal with reading in general.

Anderson, R. D., Hiebert, E. H., Scott, J. A., & Wilkinson, I. A. G. (1985). *Becoming a nation of readers. The report of the Commission on Reading.* Washington, DC: National Academy of Education, National Institute of Education.

Barth, J. (n.d.) *Tactile graphics guidebook.* Louisville, KY: American Printing House for the Blind.

Braille Authority of North America. (1994). *English braille, American edition.* Louisville, KY: American Printing House for the Blind.

Braille Revival League of California. (1991). *Braille: The key to literacy and independence.* Danville, CA: Braille Publishers. (Available from American Council of the Blind.)

Burns, M. F. (1991) *The Burns braille transcription dictionary.* New York: American Foundation for the Blind.

Code of textbook formats and techniques. (1977). Louisville, KY: American Printing House for the Blind.

Edman, P. K. (1992). *Tactile graphics.* New York: American Foundation for the Blind.

Galvin, J., & Scherer, M. (1996). *Evaluating, selecting, and using appropriate assistive technology.* Gaithersburg, MD: Aspen.

Harley, R. K., Truan, M. B., & Sanford, L. D. (1997). *Communication skills for visually impaired learners.* Springfield, IL: Charles C Thomas.

Koenig, A. J., & Farrenkopf, C. (1994). *Providing quality instruction in braille literacy skills: Companion guide to invitations: Changing as teachers and learners K-12.* Houston, TX: Region IV Education Service Center.

Koenig, A. J., & Holbrook, M.C. (1995). *Braille enthusiasts' dictionary.* Nashville, TN: SCALARS Publishing.

Koenig, A. J., & Holbrook, M. C. (1993). *Learning media assessment of students with visual impairment: A resource guide for teachers.* Austin, TX: Texas School for the Blind and Visually Impaired.

Mangold, P. (1993). *Teaching the braille slate and stylus: A manual for mastery (rev. ed.)* Castro Valley, CA: Exceptional Teaching Aids.

Mangold, S. S. (Ed.) (1982). *A Teachers' guide to the special educational needs of blind and visually handicapped children.* New York: American Foundation for the Blind.

Mangold, S. S., & Pesavento, M. E. (1994). *Personal touch* [videotape]. Winnetka, IL: Hadley School for the Blind.

Mangold, S. S., & Pesavento, M. E. (n.d.) *Teaching the braille slate and stylus* [videotape]. Castro Valley, CA: Exceptional Teaching Aids.

Miller, W. H. (1993). *Complete reading disabilities handbook.* West Nyack, NY: Center for Applied Research in Education.

Olson, M. R. (1981). *Guidelines and games for teaching efficient braille reading.* New York: American Foundation for the Blind.

Rex, E. J., Koenig, A. J., Wormsley, D. P., & Baker, R. L. (1994). *Foundations of braille literacy.* New York: AFB Press.

Routman, R. (1994). *Invitations: Changing as teachers and learners K-12.* Portsmouth, NH: Heinemann.

Stratton, J. M., & Wright, S. (1991). *On the way to literacy.* Louisville, KY: American Printing House for the Blind.

Understanding braille literacy [videotape]. (1993). New York: AFB Press.

UNESCO. (1990). *World braille usage.* Washington, DC: National Library Service for the Blind and Physically Handicapped, Library of Congress.

Refresher Courses and Materials for Self-Study of the Braille Code

In addition to the materials listed here, the National Library Service for the Blind and Physically Handicapped and the Hadley School for the Blind (see the "National Organizations" section) offer correspondence courses in braille.

Ashcroft, S., Henderson, F., Sanford, L., & Koenig, A. J. (1994). *New programmed instruction in braille* (2nd ed.). Nashville, TN: SCALARS Publishing.

Kapperman, G., et. al. (1995). *The computerized braille tutor.* Alexandria, VA: Association for Education and Rehabilitation of the Blind and Visually Impaired.

Pesavento, M. E. (1993). *Braille codes and calculations.* Castro Valley, CA: Exceptional Teaching Aids.

Risjord, C. (1995). *Literary braille refresher course for teachers and transcribers.* Rochester, NY: National Braille Association.

RESOURCES FOR TEACHING BRAILLE

Sources of Braille Books for Children and Teenagers
American Action Fund for Blind Children and Adults
18440 Oxnard Street
Tarzana, CA 91356
(818) 343-2022
Has TWIN-VISION books in a lending library, which also includes books up to 12th grade interest and reading levels.

American Printing House for the Blind
1839 Frankfort Avenue
Louisville, KY 40206-0085
(502) 895-2405 or (800) 223-1839
FAX: (502) 899-2274
E-mail: info@aph.org
URL: http://www.aph.org
Has *On the Way to Literacy* books for young children in braille and print with raised-line drawings. Has a wide variety of books in braille, including a large list of high-interest, low- vocabulary books.

Associated Services for the Blind
919 Walnut Street
Philadelphia, PA 19107
(215) 627-0600
FAX: (215) 922-0692
E-mail: asbinfo@libertynet.org
Has cookbooks, computer manuals, and textbooks in braille.

Beach Cities Braille Guild
P.O. Box 712
Huntington Beach, CA 92648
(714) 969-7992
FAX: (714) 960-1815
Has textbooks, recreational reading materials, and children's and adult books in braille.

Bower Hill Braillists Foundation
70 Moffett Street
Pittsburgh, PA 15243
(412) 343-9177
Has fiction, nonfiction, and biography books in braille.

Braille Institute of America
741 North Vermont Avenue
Los Angeles, CA 90029-3594
(213) 663-1111
FAX: (213) 663-0867
E-mail: communications@brailleinstitute.org
Has general-interest fiction and nonfiction books, including books on comput-
ers, cooking, and social studies, mysteries, atlas maps and the *Braille Transcribers'*
Dictionary.

Braille International
The William A. Thomas Braille Bookstore
3290 S.E. Slater Street
Stuart, FL 34997
(561) 286-8366 or (800) 336-3142
FAX: (561) 286-8909
E-mail: braille@gate.net
Has fiction and nonfiction books for children and adults.

Guild for the Blind
180 North Michigan Avenue, #1700
Chicago, IL 60601-7463
(312) 236-8569
FAX: (312) 236-8128
Has books on cooking and hobbies and children's books.

Horizons for the Blind
16-A Meadowdale Shopping Center
Carpentersville, IL 60110
(847) 836-1400 (voice/TDD)
FAX: (847) 836-1443
Has books on crafts and recipes.

Johanna Bureau for the Blind and Physically Handicapped
8 South Michigan Avenue, Suite 300
Chicago, Il 60603
(312) 332-6076
FAX: (312) 332-0780
Has textbooks and general materials.

The Lighthouse
Braille Services Department

111 East 59th Street
New York, NY 10022
(212) 821-9689
Has books on cooking, hobbies, and consumer information in braille.

Louis Braille Center
11050 Fifth Avenue NE, #204
Seattle, WA 98125-6151
(206) 368-8288 (voice and fax)
E-mail: lbcbrl@aol.com
Has books on general literature, poetry, children's books, books about braille, and books by Helen Keller in braille.

Massachusetts Association for the Blind
200 Ivy Street
Brookline, MA 02146
(617) 738-5110 or (800) 682-9200 (in MA)
FAX: (617) 738-1247
(617) 731-6444 (TDD)
E-mail: mablind@tiac.net
URL: http://www.tiac/users/mablind
Has fiction, cookbooks, and children's books in braille.

Metrolina Association for the Blind
704 Louise Avenue
Charlotte, NC 28204-2128
(704) 372-3870 or (800) 926-5466, ext. 123
FAX: (704) 372-3872
E-mail: braille@charlotte.com.infi.net
Has textbooks in braille.

Michigan Braille Transcribing Services
4000 Cooper Street
Jackson, MI 49201
(517) 780-6637
Has textbooks for elementary and high school levels, light reading, and short stories in braille.

National Braille Association
Braille Materials Production Center
3 Townline Circle
Rochester, NY 14623
(716) 427-8260
FAX: (716) 427-0263
Is a depository of braille textbooks; general-interest and vocational materials; music and books on music theory; and technical, scientific, and mathematical tables.

National Braille Press
88 St. Stephen Street

Boston, MA 02115
(617) 266-6160 or (800) 548-7323
FAX: (617) 437-0456
E-mail: orders@nbp.org
Sells a variety of print-braille books for young children and also offers the Children's Braille Book Club.

National Library Service for the Blind and Physically Handicapped
Library of Congress
1291 Taylor Street, N.W.
Washington, DC 20542
(202) 707-5100 or (800) 424-8567
FAX: (202) 707-0712
Has a lending library of print/braille books. Distributes other braille books through state and regional libraries for the blind.

Seedlings: Braille Books for Children
P.O. Box 51924
Livonia, MI 48151-5924
(313) 427-8552 (telephone and fax) or (800) 777-8552
E-mail: seedlink@aol.com
URL: http://www.22cent.com/seedlings
Sells a variety of print-braille books for young children.

Sources of Braille Magazines

American Association for the Deaf-Blind
814 Thayer Avenue, Third Floor
Silver Spring, MD 20910
(301) 588-6545 (TDD)
FAX: (301) 588-8706
E-mail: addb@erols.com
Publishes *The Deaf-Blind American,* a quarterly magazine with information on new communication technology, education, and mobility, and human interest stories.

American Council of the Blind
1155 15th Street N.W., Suite 720
Washington, DC 20005
(202) 467-5081 or (800) 424-8666
FAX: (202) 467-5085
E-mail: ncrabb@access.digex.net
URL: http://www.acb.org
Publishes *Braille Forum* a magazine that covers legislation, human-interest stories, and activities of the American Council of the Blind. Additional braille publications, published by special-interest affiliates, include *BRL Memorandum* from the Braille Revival League, *Log of the Bridgetender* from Friends-in-Art, and *The Blind Teacher* from the National Association of Blind Teachers.

American Foundation for the Blind
11 Penn Plaza, Suite 300
New York, NY 10001
(212) 502-7600 or (800) 232-5463
TDD: (212) 502-7662
FAX: (212) 502-7777
E-mail: afbinfo@afb.org
URL: http://www.afb.org
Publishes *Journal of Visual Impairment & Blindness,* a research journal on visual impairment and blindness and a news service.

American Printing House for the Blind
1839 Frankfort Avenue
Louisville, KY 40206-0085
(502) 895-2405 or (800) 223-1839
FAX: (502) 899-2274
E-mail: info@aph.org
URL: http://www.aph.org
Distributes *Current Events, Current Science, Know Your World EXTRA! My Weekly Reader,* and *Reader's Digest.*

Blindskills
P.O. Box 5181
Salem, OR 97304
(503) 581-4224 or (800) 860-1224
FAX: (503) 581-0178
E-mail: blindskl@teleport.com
URL: http://www.teleport.com/~blindskl
Publishes *Dialogue,* a quarterly general-interest magazine for people who are visually impaired.

Braille Institute of America
741 North Vermont Avenue
Los Angeles, CA 90029-3594
(213) 663-1111
FAX: (213) 663-0867
E-mail: communications@braille institute.org
Publishes *Braille Mirror,* a monthly news magazine and *Expectations,* an annual anthology of stories and poems for grade 3 through 6.

Christian Record Services
4444 South 52nd Street
P.O. Box 6097
Lincoln, NE 68506
(402) 488-0981 or (402) 488-1902 (TDD)
FAX: (402) 488-7582
Is a lending library for children and adults and publishes *Children's Friend, Christian Record, The Student,* and *Young and Alive.*

Clovernook Center/Opportunities for the Blind
7000 Hamilton Avenue
Cincinnati, OH 45231-5297
(513) 522-3860
FAX: (513) 728-3946
E-mail: clovernook@aol.com
Publishes *Tactic,* a quarterly magazine on computer technology for persons with visual impairment.

Guide Dogs for the Blind
P.O. Box 151200
San Rafael, CA 94915-1200
(415) 499-4000
FAX: (415) 499-4035
Publishes *Guide Dog News,* a quarterly newsletter that presents information about the school and the use of dog guides.

Guild for the Blind
180 North Michigan Avenue, #1700
Chicago, IL 60601-7463
(312) 236-8569
FAX: (312) 236-8128
Publishes *Reflections,* a quarterly magazine with articles taken from various spiritual sources.

Helen Keller National Center for Deaf-Blind Youths and Adults
111 Middle Neck Road
Sands Point, NY 11050
(516) 944-8900
(516) 944-8637 (TDD)
FAX: (516) 944-7302
Publishes *Nat-Cent News,* a magazine that discusses the activities of the center.

Maryland Technology Assistance Program (MD TAP)
One Market Center, Box 10
300 West Lexington Street
Baltimore, MD 21201
(800) 832-4827
FAX: (410) 554-9237
E-mail: mdtap@clark.net
URL: http://www.clark.net/pub/mdtap
Publishes *Tapping Technology,* a quarterly that has information on products, services, and resources to assist individuals with disabilities.

Matilda Ziegler Magazine for the Blind
80 Eighth Avenue, Room 1304
New York, NY 10011
(212) 242-0263

FAX: (212) 633-1601
E-mail: zieglermag@ibm.net
URL: http://www.zieglermag.org
A monthly magazine with general-interest articles selected from a broad range of periodicals.

National Braille Association
3 Townline Circle
Rochester, NY 14623
(716) 427-8260
FAX: (716) 427-0263
Publishes *NBA Bulletin.*

National Braille Press
88 St. Stephen Street
Boston, MA 02115
(617) 266-6160 or (800) 548-7323
FAX: (617) 437-0456
E-mail: orders@nbp.org
Publishes *Syndicated Columnists Weekly* and *Our Special,* a bi-monthly women's magazine.

National Council on Disability
1331 F Street N.W., Suite 1050
Washington, DC 20004-1107
(202) 272-2004
FAX: (202) 272-2022
TDD: (202) 272-2074
Publishes *NCD Bulletin,* a monthly magazine with news and issues dealing with independence and empowerment if persons with disabilities.

National Federation of the Blind
1800 Johnson Street
Baltimore, MD 21230
(410) 659-9314
FAX: (410) 685-5653
URL: http://www.nfb.org
Publishes *Braille Monitor,* a monthly magazine that reports on current legislative issues and social concerns affecting people who are blind.

National Federation of the Blind
Writers Division
2704 Beach Drive
Merrick, NY 11566
(516) 868-8718
FAX: (516) 868-9076
Publishes *Slate and Style,* a quarterly magazine with poetry, short stories, articles, and resources of interest to writers who are blind.

National Library Service for the Blind and Physically Handicapped
Library of Congress
1291 Taylor Street, N.W.
Washington, DC 20542
(202) 707-5100 or (800) 424-8567
FAX: (202) 707-0712
Distributes magazines for children, such as *Boys' Life, Jack & Jill, National Geographic World, Children's Digest, Ranger Rick,* and *Seventeen.* Also has magazines for adults.

Braille Curriculum Materials

The following braille curriculum materials all deal with teaching the braille code or teaching reading using braille. All are designed for teaching children or young adults. They are listed by source.

American Printing House for the Blind
1839 Frankfort Avenue
Louisville, KY 40206-0085
(502) 895-2405 or (800) 223-1839
FAX: (502) 899-2274
E-mail: info@aph.org
URL: http://www.aph.org
Touch and Tell
Preparatory Reading Program for Visually Handicapped Children (PREP)
Patterns Prebraille Program
Patterns: The Primary Braille Reading Program
Patterns Library Series
Patterns: The Primary Braille Spelling and English Program
Read Again: A Braille Program for Adventitiously Blinded Print Readers
Braillewriting Dot by Dot

Exceptional Teaching Aids
20102 Woodbine Avenue
Castro Valley, CA 94546
(510) 582-4859 or (800) 549-6999
FAX: (510) 582-5911
The Mangold Developmental Program of Tactile Perception and Braille Letter Recognition
Literary Braille Sentences

Grant Wood Area Education Agency
4401 Sixth Street, S.W.
Cedar Rapids, IA 52404
(319) 399-6700, ext. 493
FAX: (319) 399-6457
URL: http://www.aea10.k12.ia.us
Braille Too

Royal National Institute for the Blind
224 Great Portland Street
London, England W1N6AA
011-71-388-1266
FAX: 011-71-387-2034
Several curricula for British braille are available from RNIB. Write to RNIB for a catalog describing its listings.

Sources of Products and Teaching Materials

The organizations and companies listed in this section carry a wide variety of products, including materials for producing braille, teaching aids, tactile materials, and the like. Listed here are the sources for most of the products mentioned in the text. Products can usually be ordered through catalogs available from the individual companies.

American Printing House for the Blind
1839 Frankfort Avenue
Louisville, KY 40206-0085
(502) 895-2405 or (800) 223-1839
FAX: (502) 899-2274
E-mail: info@aph.org
URL: http://www.aph.org

American Thermoform Corporation
2311 Travers Avenue
City of Commerce, CA 90040
(213) 723-9021
FAX: (213) 728-8877

Ann Morris Enterprises
890 Fams Court
East Meadow, NY 11554
(516) 292-9232 or (800) 454-3175
FAX: (516) 292-2522
E-mail: annmor@netcom.com
URL: http://tribeca.ios.com/~annm2

Canadian National Institute for the Blind
National Office
1929 Bayview Avenue
Toronto, ON M4G 3E8
(416) 480-7580
FAX: (416) 480-7677
E-mail: natgovernment@east.cnib.ca
URL: http://www.cnib.ca

Carolyn's Catalog
1415 57th Avenue

West Bradenton, FL 34207
(800) 648-2266
FAX: (941) 739-5503
E-mail: magnify@bhip.infi.net

Exceptional Teaching Aids
20102 Woodbine Avenue
Castro Valley, CA 94546
(510) 582-4859 or (800) 549-6999
FAX: (510) 582-5911

Flaghouse
601 Flaghouse Drive
Hasbrouck Heights, NJ 07604-3116
(800) 221-5185
E-mail: info@flaghouse.com
URL: http://www.flaghouse.com

Hadley School for the Blind
700 Elm Street
Winnetka, IL 60093-0299, USA
(847) 446-8111 or (800) 323-4238
FAX: (847) 446-9916

Howe Press of Perkins School for the Blind
175 North Beacon Street
Watertown, MA 02172
(617) 924-3490
FAX: (617) 926-2027

Lehigh Valley Braille Guild
614 North 13th Street
Allentown, PA 18102
(610) 264-2141
FAX: (610) 433-4856

The Lighthouse
36-20 Northern Boulevard
Long Island City NY 11101
(718) 786-5620 or (800) 829-0500
FAX: (718) 786-0437

Los Olvidados
P.O. Box 475
Plaistow, NH 03865
(603) 382-1748 or (800) TACTILE (822-5845)
FAX: (603) 382-1748
E-mail: kevin@tack-tiles.com
URL: http://www.tack-tiles.com

LS&S Group
P.O. Box 673
Northbrook, IL 60065
(847) 498-9777 or (800) 468-4789
FAX: (847) 498-1482
E-mail: lssgrp@aol.com
URL: http://www.lssgroup.com

Mary Lou Archer Communications Center
2200 University Avenue West, #240
St. Paul, MN 44114-1840

Maxi-Aids
42 Executive Boulevard
P.O. Box 3209
Farmingdale, NY 11735
(516) 752-0521 or (800) 522-6294
FAX: (516) 752-0689
E-mail: sales@maxiaids.com
URL: http://www.maxiaids.com

Multiple Services Media Technology
11 West Barham Avenue
Santa Rosa, CA 95407

National Federation of the Blind
1800 Johnson Street
Baltimore, MD 21230
(410) 659-9314
FAX: (410) 685-5653
URL: http://www.nfb.org

Region IV Education Service Center
7145 West Tidwell
Houston, TX 77092
(713) 744-8144
FAX: (713) 744-8148
E-mail: dspence@tenet.edu

Repro-Tronics
75 Carver Avenue
Westwood, NJ 07675
(201) 722-1880 or (800) 948-8453
FAX: (201) 722-1881

SCALARS Publishing
P.O. Box 158123
Nashville, TN 37215
(615) 371-0205

Sense-Sations/New Visions
Associated Services for the Blind
919 Walnut Street
Philadelphia, PA 19107
(215) 629-2990
FAX: (215) 922-0692

Texas Education Agency
1701 North Congress Avenue
Austin, TX 78701
(512) 463-9414
URL: http://www.tea.state.tx.us/special.ed/spec~main.ahtm

Texas School for the Blind and Visually Impaired
1100 West 45th Street
Austin, TX 78756-3494
(512) 454-8631
FAX: (512) 454-3395

Commercial Producers/Transcribers of Braille Materials

Associated Services for the Blind
919 Walnut Street
Philadelphia, PA 19107
(215) 627-0600
FAX: (215) 922-0692
E-mail: asbinfo@libertynet.org

Braille, Inc.
184 Seapit Road
P.O. Box 457
East Falmouth, MA 02536-0457
(508) 540-0800
FAX: (508) 548-6116
E-mail: braillinc@c2pecod.net

Braille Institute of America
741 North Vermont Avenue
Los Angeles, CA 90029-3594
(213) 663-1111
FAX: (213) 663-0867
E-mail: communications@brailleinstitute.org

Contra Costa Braille Transcribers
514 Freya Way
Pleasant Hill, CA 94523
(510) 682-4734

Library for the Blind
Canadian National Institute for the Blind
1919 Bayview Avenue
Toronto, ON M4G 3E8, Canada
(416) 480-7520
FAX: (416) 480-7700

National Braille Association
3 Townline Circle
Rochester, NY 14623
(716) 427-8260
FAX: (716) 427-0263

National Braille Press
88 St. Stephen Street
Boston, MA 02115
(617) 266-6160 or (800) 548-7323
FAX: (617) 437-0456
E-mail: orders@nbp.org

QuikScrybe
14144 Burbank Boulevard, #4
Van Nuys, CA 91410
(818) 989-2137
FAX: (818) 989-5602
E-mail: sgstaley@netcom.com

Region IV ESC Computer Braille Center
7145 West Tidwell
Houston, TX 77092-2096
(713) 744-8145

South Dakota Industries for the Blind
Interpoint Braille Printing Service
800 West Avenue North
Sioux Falls, SD 57104-5796
(605) 367-5266 or (800) 658-5441
FAX: (605) 367-5263

Sun Sounds
3124 East Roosevelt Street
Phoenix, AZ 85008
(602) 231-0500
FAX: (602) 220-9335

TFB Publications
238 75th Street
North Bergen, NJ 07047
(201) 662-0956

Visual Aid Volunteers
617 State Street
Garland, TX 75040
(972) 272-1615
FAX: (972) 494-5002

Volunteer Braille Services
3730 Toledo Avenue, North
Robbinsdale, MN 55433
(612) 521-0372
FAX: (612) 588-4912

Resources for Teaching Bilingual, Multilingual and English as a Second Language (ESL) Braille Students

American Econo-Clad Services
P.O. Box 1777
Topeka, KS 66601
(800) 255-3502
Provides multicultural, Spanish, ESL, and bilingual instructional materials.

Arab World and Islamic Resources and School Services
1865 Euclid Avenue, Suite 4
Berkeley, CA 94709
(510) 704-0517
Has instructional materials and books for students and teachers learning about the Arab World.

Barron's Educational Series
250 Wireless Boulevard
Hauppauge, NY 11788
Publishes English, Spanish, and ESL materials for professionals and students.

Bilingual Communications
P.O. Box 649
Odessa, TX 79760
(915) 368-4733
Carries Spanish and English instructional music.

Bilingual Educational Services
2514 South Grand Avenue
Los Angeles, CA 90007
(213) 749-6213 or (800) 448-6032
Carries Spanish literature books for children and adults., as well as textbooks and audiovisual materials in Spanish.

Blind Childrens Center
4120 Marathon Street
P.O. Box 29159

Los Angeles, CA 90029
(213) 664-2153 or in California (800) 222-3566
FAX: (213) 665-3828
Publishes pamphlets on working with young Spanish-speaking children who are blind or visually impaired.

R. R. Bowker
121 Chanlon Road
New Providence, NJ 07974
Publishes catalogs of books in print in most countries.

CHIME—Clearinghouse for Immigrant Education
100 Boylston Street, Suite 737
Boston, MA 02116
(800) 441-7192
Provides articles related to the education of foreign-born students.

Delta Systems
1400 Miller Parkway
McHenry, IL 60050-7030
(800) 323-8270
Carries ESL and foreign language materials.

Dominie Press
5945 Pacific Center Boulevard, Suite 505
San Diego, CA 92121
(619) 546-8899 or (800) 232-4570
Publishes ESL materials for students, resources for teachers, and Spanish books for children.

Ediciones Universal
P.O. Box 450353
Miami, Florida 33245-0353
(305) 642-3234
Has Spanish books for children and Spanish literature books.

Editorial Braille del Comite Internacional Pro Ciegos
Mariano Azuela #218
Co. Santa Maria la Ribera
06400 Mexico, D.F.
Publishes a guide to the braille system in Mexico entitled *Manualde Ensenanza de Escritura y Lectura Braille.*

Estrellita
P.O. Box 20803
Oxnard, CA 93034-0803
(805) 985-9743
Carries Spanish software for the Macintosh.

Fernández USA Publishing Company
1210 East 223rd Street, Suite 309
Carson, CA 90745
(310) 233-4920 or (800) 814-8080
Publishes instructional materials, textbooks, and literature books in Spanish.

Firefly Books
250 Sparks Avenue
Willowdale, Ontario M2H 2S4 Canada
(800) 387-5085
Has stories for children in Spanish.

Fondo de Cultura Económica, USA
2293 Verus Street
San Diego, CA 92154
(800) 5FCE USA
Has Spanish books for children and young adults.

Haitiana Publications
224-08 Linden Boulevard
Cambria Heights, NY 11411
(718) 978-6323
Carries Haitian and Caribbean books, and books about Africa.

Hampton-Brown Company
P.O. Box 223220
Carmel, CA 93923
(800) 333-3510
Has multicultural, Spanish, and bilingual instructional materials.

International Learning Systems
1000 112th Circle North, Suite 100
St. Petersburg, FL 33716
(800) 321-8322 Ext. 15
Has Spanish and English instructional music.

International Software Enterprise
Educational Bilingual Software
P.O. Box 3671
El Paso, TX 79923
(915) 680-2807
Carries educational software in Spanish.

Jostens Learning
7878 North 16th Street
Phoenix, Arizona 85020-4402
(800) 422-4339
Has bilingual software.

Laureate Learning Systems
110 East Spring Street
Winooski, VT 05404-1898
(800) 562-6801
Has talking software.

The Learning Company
6493 Kaiser Drive
Fremont, CA 94555
(800) 852-2255
Carries English and Spanish software.

Lectorum Publications
137 West 14th Street
New York, NY 10011
(212) 929-2833
Carries children's books in Spanish.

Modern Curriculum
4350 Equity Drive
P.O. Box 2649
Columbus, OH 43216
(800) 321-3106
Carries bilingual/ESL instructional materials.

Multilingual Matters
Taylor & Francis
1900 Frost Road, Suite 101
Bristol, PA 19007
(800) 821-8312
Has books for professionals about language learning and bilingualism.

Niños
P.O. Box
Livonia, MI 48151-3398
(800) 634-3304
Has Spanish and English materials.

Northland Publishing
P.O. Box 1389
Flagstaff, AZ 86002-1389
(800) 346-3257
Provides books about Native American stories.

Pan Asian Publications
29564 Union City Boulevard
Union City, CA 94587
(510)-475-1185 or (800) 853-ASIA
Carries books and educational materials available in Asian languages.

Rei America
6355 N.W. 36 Street
Miami, FL 33166
(800) 726-5337
Carries Spanish textbooks and literature books grades K-12, ESL materials for students, and resources for teachers.

Rigby
P.O. Box 797
Crystal Lake, IL 60039-0797
(800) 822-8661
Has Reading Recovery in Spanish.

St. Petersburgh Publishing House
3610 Oceanside Road
Oceanside, NY 11572
(516) 825-2525
Supplies Russian books, dictionaries, and learning materials.

Santillana
942 S. Gerhart Avenue
Los Angeles, CA 90022
(800) 526-1676
Carries books in Spanish.

Scott Foresman
1900 East Lake Avenue
Glenview, IL 60025
(800) 554-4411
Publishes ESL curricula for grades 1–8.

Spanpress
5722 S. Flamingo Road
Suite 277
Cooper City, FL 33330
(800) 585-8384
Has instructional materials, textbooks, and literature books in Spanish.

Syracuse Language Systems
719 E. Genesse Street
Syracuse, NY 13210
(315) 478-6729 or (800) 688-1937
Has talking software in a variety of languages.

Teacher's Discovery
2741 Paldan Drive
Auburn Hills, MI 48326
(800) TEACHER
Carries multicultural, Spanish, and bilingual educational materials.

Sources of Assessment Materials

These assessment tools are listed alphabetically by the name of the product.

Analytic Reading Inventory
Merrill Publishing Company
1300 Alum Creek Drive
Columbus, OH 43216

Assessment of Braille Literacy Skills
Region IV Education Service Center
7145 West Tidwell
Houston, TX 77092-2096

Basic Reading Inventory
Kendall/Hunt Publishing Company
2460 Kerper Boulevard
Dubuque, IA 52001

Basic Reading Rate Scale
American Printing House for the Blind
P.O. Box 6085
Louisville, KY 40206-0085

Blind Learning Aptitude Test (BLAT)
University of Illinois Press
P.O. Box 5081, Station A
Urbana, IL 61820

Braille Assessment Inventory (BAI)
Hawthorne Educational Services
800 Gray Oak drive
Colombia, MO 65201

Braille Unit Recognition Battery
American Printing House for the Blind
P.O. Box 6085
Louisville, KY 40206-0085

Brigance Diagnostic Comprehensive Inventory of Basic Skills— APH Tactile Supplement
American Printing House for the Blind
P.O. Box 6085
Louisville, KY 40206-0085

Burns/Roe Informal Reading Inventory
Houghton Mifflin
1 Beacon Street
Boston, MA 02107

Diagnostic Reading Scale—APH Braille Transcription
American Printing House for the Blind

P.O. Box 6085
Louisville, KY 40206-0085

Dolch Word List—APH Braille Transcription
American Printing House for the Blind
P.O. Box 6085
Louisville, KY 40206-0085

Ekwall/Shanker Reading Inventory
Allyn and Bacon Publishing Company
470 Atlantic Avenue
Boston, MA 02210

Functional Vision and Media Assessment
Consultants for the Visually Impaired
P.O. Box 8594
Hermitage, TN 37076

Minnesota Braille Skills Inventory
Minnesota Educational Services
Capitol View Center
70 West Country Road B2
Little Canada, MN 55117-1402
(612) 483-4442 or (800) 848-4912 Ext. 2401
FAX: (612) 483-0234

**Revised Brigance Diagnostic Inventory of Early Development—
APH Tactile Supplement**
American Printing House for the Blind
P.O. Box 6085
Louisville, KY 40206-0085

Stanford Achievement Test—APH Braille Transcription
American Printing House for the Blind
P.O. Box 6085
Louisville, KY 40206-0085

Wechsler Intelligence Scale for Children, Third Edition
(WISC-III)
The Psychological Corporation
555 Academic Court
San Antonio, TX 78204

Language Proficiency Tests in English and Other Languages

All of these tests have been developed for sighted students and may only be available in print. Individual subtests may depend on the use of illustrations to generate student's answers; therefore, professionals using these tests with students who are blind will have to adapt them and even exclude individual subtests.

Basic Inventory of Natural Language (BINL)

CHECpoint Systems
1520 N. Waterman Avenue
San Bernardino, CA 92404
(800) 635-1235

Measures oral proficiency in English and other languages including Chinese, Japanese, Portuguese, Spanish, and Vietnamese. Instructions for using the test with students who are blind are available from the publisher.

Language Assessment Scales—Oral (LAS-O)

CTB/McGraw-Hill
20 Ryan Ranch Road
Monterey, CA 93940
(800) 538-9547

Measures speaking and listening in either English or Spanish in grades 1-12.

Language Assessment Scales-Reading and Writing (LAS R/W)

CTB/McGraw-Hill
20 Ryan Ranch Road
Monterey, CA 93940
(800) 538-9547

A test of English reading and writing proficiency designed for non-native English speaking students in grades 2-12. There is also a Spanish version to measure literacy levels of Spanish speaking students.

Pre-LAS

CTB/McGraw-Hill
20 Ryan Ranch Road
Monterey, CA 93940
(800) 538-9547

Measures oral language proficiency of preschool, kindergarten, and first grade children.

Preschool Language Scale—3, Spanish Edition

Psychological Corporation
P.O. Box 83954
San Antonio, TX 78283-3954
(800) 228-0752

Is designed for use with young children ranging from birth to 6 years old.

Student Oral Language Observation Matrix (SOLOM)

Los Angeles Unified School District
Office of Instruction
450 North Grand Avenue
Los Angeles, CA 90012
(213) 625-6000

Is an informal rating tool for teacher judgment of oral language proficiency as observed in school.

Woodcock Language Proficiency Battery—Revised
Riverside Publishing Company
8420 Bryn Mawr Avenue
Chicago, IL 60631
(800) 767-8378
Provides an overall measure of English language proficiency.

Woodcock Language Proficiency Battery—Spanish Form
Riverside Publishing Company
8420 Bryn Mawr Avenue
Chicago, IL 60631
(800) 767-8378
Measures oral language, reading, and written language in Spanish.

Woodcock-Muñoz Language Survey
Riverside Publishing Company
8420 Bryn Mawr Avenue
Chicago, IL 60631
(800) 767-8378
Measures oral and written language. This is a screening instrument that available in English and Spanish. It is a screening instrument that measures oral and written language.

Print Tests Available in Non-English Languages

Boehm Test of Basic Concepts-Revised
Psychological Corporation
P.O. Box 83954
San Antonio, TX 78283-3954
(800) 228-0752
Measures the knowledge of 50 basic concepts in young children. There is a Spanish version of the test.

Brigance Assessment of Basic Skills—Spanish Edition
Curriculum Associates
5 Esquire Road
North Billerica, MA 01862-2589
Is a criterion-referenced test for students ranging in grades from Pre-K to 8th grade, available in English and Spanish.

Lista de Destrezas en Desarrollo (La Lista)
CTB/McGraw-Hill
20 Ryan Ranch Road
Monterey, CA 93940
(800) 538-9547
Is a comprehensive checklist that evaluates the skills of Spanish-speaking children from prekindergarten to the end of kindergarten.

Scales of Independent Behavior (SIB)

(Escalas de Conducta Independiente)
Riverside Publishing Company
8420 Bryn Mawr Avenue
Chicago, IL 60631
(800) 767-8378
Is a Spanish version of the Scales of Independent Behavior and includes a test book in Spanish and an interviewer's manual and response booklets in English. Useful when interviewing Spanish speaking family members.

Spanish Assessment of Basic Education, Second Edition (SABE/2)

CTB/McGraw-Hill
20 Ryan Ranch Road
Monterey, CA 93940
(800) 538-9547
Is an achievement test in Spanish for Spanish-speaking students in grades 1-8.

Vineland Adaptive Behavior Scales

American Guidance Service
Circle Pines, MN 55014-1796
Comes in a Spanish version, which is useful when interviewing Spanish-speaking family members.

Woodcock Spanish Psycho-Educational Battery

(Batería Woodcock Psico-Educative en Español)
Riverside Publishing Company
8420 Bryn Mawr Avenue
Chicago, IL 60631
(800) 767-8378
Is a test of cognitive ability and achievement for use with Spanish speaking students ages 4 to 19.

NATIONAL ORGANIZATIONS

American Association of the Deaf-Blind

814 Thayer Avenue, Suite 302
Silver Spring, MD 20910
(301) 588-6545 (TTY/TDD)
FAX: (301) 588-8705
Promotes better opportunities and services for people who are deaf-blind and strives to ensure that a comprehensive, coordinated system of services is accessible to all deaf-blind people, enabling them to achieve their maximum potential through increased independence, productivity, and integration into the community.

American Council of the Blind

1155 15th Street, N.W., Suite 720
Washington, DC 20005

(202) 467-5081 or (800) 424-8666
FAX: (202) 467-5085
E-mail: ncrabb@access.digex.net
URL: http://www.acb.org
Promotes effective participation of blind people in all aspects of society. Provides information and referral, legal assistance, scholarships, advocacy, consultation, and program development assistance. Affiliated groups include the Council of Families with Visual Impairment, the Deaf-Blind Committee, and the Council of Citizens with Low Vision International. Publishes *The Braille Forum.*

American Foundation for the Blind
11 Penn Plaza, Suite 300
New York, NY 10001
Phone: (212) 502-7600 or (800) 232-5463
TDD: (212) 502-7662
FAX: (212) 502-7777
E-mail: afbinfo@afb.net
URL: http://www.afb.net
Provides services to and acts as an information clearinghouse for people who are blind or visually impaired and their families, professionals, organizations, schools, and corporations. Conducts research and mounts program initiatives to improve services to visually impaired persons, including the National Literacy Program; advocates for services and legislation; maintains the M. C. Migel Library and Information Center, the Helen Keller Archives, and a toll-free information line; provides information and referral services; operates the National Technology Center and the Careers and Technology Information Bank; produces videos and publishes books, pamphlets, the *Directory of Services for Blind and Visually Impaired Persons in the United States and Canada,* and the *Journal of Visual Impairment & Blindness.* Maintains the following offices throughout the country in addition to the headquarters office:

AFB Midwest
401 N. Michigan Avenue, Suite 308
Chicago, IL 60611
(312) 245-9961
FAX: (312) 245-9965
E-mail: chicago@afb.net

AFB Southeast
National Literacy Program
100 Peachtree Street, Suite 620
Atlanta, GA 30303
(404) 525-2303
FAX: (404) 659-6957
E-mail: atlanta@afb.net
literacy@afb.net

AFB Southwest
260 Treadway Plaza
Exchange Park
Dallas, TX 75235
(214) 352-7222
FAX: (214) 352-3214
E-mail: afbdallas@afb.net

AFB West
111 Pine Street, Suite 725
San Francisco, CA 94111
(415) 392-4845
FAX: (415) 392-0383
E-mail: sanfran@afb.net

Governmental Relations Group
820 First Street, N.E., Suite 400
Washington, D.C. 20002
(202) 408-0200
FAX: (202) 289-7880
E-mail: afbgov@afb.net

American Printing House for the Blind
1839 Frankfort Avenue
Louisville, KY 40206-0085
(502) 895-2405 or (800) 223-1839
FAX: (502) 899-2274
E-mail: info@aph.org
URL: http://www.aph.org
Produces materials in braille and large print and on audiocassette; manufactures computer-access equipment, software, and special education devices for persons who are visually impaired; maintains an educational research and development program and reference-catalog service providing information about volunteer-produced textbooks in accessible media.

Association for Education and Rehabilitation of the Blind and Visually Impaired
4600 Duke Street, Suite 430
Alexandria, VA 22304
(703) 823-9690
FAX: (703) 823-9695
E-mail: aernet@laser.net
Promotes all phases of education and work for people of all ages who are blind and visually impaired, strives to expand their opportunities to take a contributory place in society, and disseminates information. Publishes *RE:view* and *AER Report*.

Braille Authority of North America
c/o Phyllis Campana, Chairperson

American Printing House for the Blind
1839 Frankfort Avenue
Louisville, KY 40206-0085
(502) 899-2274 or (800) 223-1839
URL: http://www.brailleauthority.org
Serves as a U.S.-Canadian standard-setting organization whose member agencies strive to promulgate codes regarding usage of braille and to promote and facilitate its use, teaching, and production. Publishes an *Annual Directory*.

Braille Revival League
c/o Kim Charlson, President
57 Grandview Avenue
Watertown, MA 02172
(617) 926-9198
E-mail: klcharlson@delphi.com
Fosters the use, production, and instruction of braille. Encourages people who are blind to read and write in braille and advocates mandatory braille instruction in educational facilities for individuals who are blind. Publishes the newsletter *BRL Memorandum*.

California Transcribers and Educators of the Visually Handicapped
741 North Vermont Avenue
Los Angeles, CA 90029
(213) 666-2211
Serves as a national organization of braille transcribers and educators. Provides support to teachers, holds a yearly conference, and publishes a quarterly journal.

Closing the Gap
P.O. Box 68
Henderson, MN 56044
(612) 248-3294
FAX: (612) 248-3810
Holds conferences and workshops on technology for disabled people. Publishes a bi-monthly newsletter, *Closing the Gap*.

Council for Exceptional Children
Division of the Visually Impaired
1920 Association Drive
Reston, VA 22091-1589
(703) 620-3660 or (800) 328-0272
FAX: (703) 264-9494
Acts as a professional organization for individuals serving children with disabilities and children who are gifted. Is the largest such international organization, with 17 specialized divisions. Primary activities include advocating for appropriate government policies; setting professional standards; providing continuing professional development; and helping professionals obtain conditions and resources necessary for effective professional practice. Publishes numerous related materials, journals, and newsletters.

Council of Schools for the Blind
c/o St. Joseph's School for the Blind
253 Baldwin Avenue
Jersey City, NJ 07306
(201) 653-0578
FAX: (201) 653-4087
Serves as an organization of chief executive officers of residential schools for the blind and visually impaired in the United States and Canada.

C-SUN Technology and Persons with Disabilities Conference Center on Disabilities
18111 Nordhoff Street
Northridge, CA 91330-8340
(818) 677-2578
FAX: (818) 677-4929
Sponsors a national conference on disabilities and technologies.

DB-LINK
The National Information Clearinghouse on Children Who Are Deaf-Blind
c/o Teaching Research Division
Western Oregon State College
345 North Monmouth Avenue
Monmoputh, OR 97361
(800) 438-9376
TTY/TDD: (800) 854-7013
FAX: (503) 838-8150
Identifies, coordinates, and disseminates information on topics related to children and youths from birth through age 21 who are deaf-blind.

DO-IT (Disabilities, Opportunities, Internetworking and Technology)
University of Washington
4545 15th Avenue, N.E., Room 206
Seattle, WA 98105-4527
(206) 685-DOIT (685-3648) (Voice/TTY)
FAX: (206) 685-4045
E-mail: doit@u.washington.edu
URL: http://weber.u.washington.edu/~doit/
Supports high school students with disabilities to prepare for academic study and careers in science, engineeering, and mathematics, through the loan of computers and adaptive technology, mentoring, and summer study programs. Provides information, publications, videos, and resources on related issues and financial aid for students with disabilities. Publishes *DO-IT News*.

Foundation Fighting Blindness
Executive Plaza, Suite 800
11350 McCormick Road
Hunt Valley, MD 21031-1014
(410) 785-1414 or (800) 683-5555

TTY/TDD: (410) 785-9687
FAX: (410) 771-9470
Provides public education, information and referral, workshops and research through its main office and 60 affiliates. Raises funds for research into the cause, prevention, and treatment of retinitis pigmentosa. Publishes *Fighting Blindness News.*

Hadley School for the Blind
700 Elm Street
Winnetka, IL 60093-0299
(847) 446-8111 or (800) 323-4238
FAX: (847) 446-9916
Provides tuition-free home studies in academic subjects as well as vocational and technical areas, personal enrichment, parent-child issues, compensatory rehabilitation education, and Bible study.

Helen Keller National Center for Deaf-Blind Youths and Adults
111 Middle Neck Road
Sands Point, NY 11050
(516) 944-8900
TDD: (516) 944-8637
FAX: (516)944-7302
Provides diagnostic evaluations, comprehensive vocational and personal adjustment training, and job preparation and placement for people from every state and territory who are deaf-blind through its national center and 10 regional offices. Provides technical assistance and training to those who work with deaf-blind people. Publishes *Nat-Cent News.*

International Association for Education of Deaf-Blind People
c/o Sense
311 Gray's Inn Road
London WC1X 8PT
England
(011) 44 171-278-1005
FAX: (011) 44 171-837-3267
Serves educators and other interested individuals, including family members, of children and youths who are deaf-blind. Conducts international conferences on educational issues and related topics on deaf-blindness. Publishes *Deaf-Blind Education* and *Talking Sense* newsletter.

International Council for Education of People with Visual Impairments
c/o Lawrence Campbell
Overbrook School for the Blind
6333 Malvern Avenue
Philadelphia, PA 19151
(215) 878-3252
FAX: (215) 877-2709

Promotes opportunities for children and adults with visual impairments throughout the world.

International Reading Association
800 Barksdale Road
P.O. Box 8139
Newark, DE 19714-8139
(302) 731-1600
FAX: (302) 731-1057
Serves as the professional membership organization for reading teachers. Publishes several journals and is a source of information and publications on the teaching of reading.

National Association for Bilingual Education
1220 L Street, N.W., Suite 605
Washington, DC 20005-1829
(202) 898-1829
Serves as the professional organization of bilingual educators and a source of information on bilingual education.

National Braille Association
3 Townline Circle
Rochester, NY 14623
(716) 427-8260
FAX: (716) 427-0263
Assists all involved in the development of skills and techniques required for the production of reading materials for individuals who are print handicapped.

National Coalition on Deaf-Blindness
175 North Beacon Street
Watertown, MA 02172
(617) 972-7347
TTY/TDD: (617) 924-5525
FAX: (617) 923-8076
Advocates on behalf of children and adults who are deaf-blind through contact with legislators and policymaking agencies. Members are national organizations that have an interest in services to deaf-blind people, as well as professionals, parents, and consumers interested in influencing such services.

National Federation of the Blind
1800 Johnson Street
Baltimore, MD 21230
(410) 659-9314
FAX: (410) 685-5653
URL: http://www.nfb.org
Strives to improve social and economic conditions of blind persons, evaluates and assists in establishing programs, and provides public education and scholarships. Affiliated groups include the National Organization of Parents of Blind

Children and the Committee on the Concerns of the Deaf-Blind. Publishes *The Braille Monitor* and *Future Reflections.*

National Library Service for the Blind and Physically Handicapped
Library of Congress
1291 Taylor Street, N.W.
Washington, DC 20542
(202) 707-5100 or (800) 424-8567
FAX: (202) 707-0712
Conducts a national program to distribute free reading materials of a general nature to individuals who are blind or who have physical disabilities. Provides reference information on all aspects of blindness and other physical disabilities that affect reading. Conducts national correspondence courses to train sighted persons as braille transcribers and blind persons as braille proofreaders.

RESNA Technical Assistance Project
1700 N. Moore Street, Suite 1540
Arlington, VA 22209-1903
(703) 524-6686
TTY: (703) 524-6639
FAX: (703) 524-6630
Serves as an information center to address research, and the development, dissemination, integration, and utilization of knowledge in rehabilitation and assistive technology.

Teachers of English to Speakers of Other Languages (TESOL)
600 Cameron Street, Suite 300
Alexandria, VA 22314
(703) 836-0774
Serves as the professional organization of teachers of English as a second language (ESL) and a source of information on ESL education.

RESOURCES FOR PARENTS

American Council of the Blind
1155 15th Street, N.W., Suite 720
Washington, DC 20005
(202) 467-5081 or (800) 424-8666
FAX: (202) 467-5085
E-mail: ncrabb@access.digex.net
URL: http://www.acb.org
See under "National Organizations."

American Foundation for the Blind
11 Penn Plaza, Suite 300
New York, NY 10001
Phone: (212) 502-7600 or (800) 232-5463
TDD: (212) 502-7662

FAX: (212) 502-7777
E-mail: afbinfo@afb.org
URL: http://www.afb.org
See under "National Organizations."

Blind Childrens Center
4120 Marathon Street
Los Angeles, CA 90029
(213) 664-2153 or in California (800) 222-3567
FAX: (213) 665-3828
Provides services to young children who are visually impaired.

Exceptional Parent
Psy-Ed Corporation
209 Harvard Street, Suite 303
Brookline, MA 02146-5005
(613) 951-1581
FAX: (613) 951-1584
Publishes a magazine devoted to issues of interest to families of exceptional children, including resources and support information.

Hadley School for the Blind
700 Elm Street
Winnetka, IL 60093-0299
(847) 446-8111 or (800) 323-4238
FAX: (847) 446-9916
See under "National Organizations."

National Association for Parents of the Visually Impaired
P.O. Box 317
Watertown, MA 02272-0317
(800) 562-6265
FAX: (617) 972-7444
Provides support to parents and families and youths who have visual impairments. Operates a national clearinghouse for information, education, and referral. Publishes a newsletter, *Awareness.*

National Federation of the Blind
1800 Johnson Street
Baltimore, MD 21230
(410) 659-9314
FAX: (410) 685-5653
URL: http://www.nfb.org
See under "National Organizations."

National Information Center for Children and Youth with Disabilities
P.O. Box 1492
Washington, DC 20013-1492
(202) 884-8200

Voice/TTY/TDD: (800) 695-0285
FAX: (202) 884-8441
Serves as a national information clearinghouse on subjects relating to children
and youths with disabilities. Provides information and referral to national, state,
and local resources. Disseminates numerous free publications.

National Organization for Rare Disorders
100 Route 37, P.O. Box 8923
New Fairfield, CT 06812-8923
(203) 746-6518 or (800) 999-6673
TTY/TDD: (203) 746-6927
FAX: (203) 746-6491
E-mail: orphan@nord-rdb.com
URL: http://www.NORD-RDB.com/~orphan
Serves as an information clearinghouse on thousands of rare disorders. Brings to-
gether families with similar disorders for mutual support. Promotes research, ac-
cumulates and disseminates information about special drugs and devices, and
maintains a database on rare diseases.

National Parent to Parent Support and Information System
P.O. Box 907
Blue Ridge, GA 30513
(706) 632-8822 or (800) 651-1151 (TDD available)
Fax: (706) 632-8830
E-mail: judd103w@wonder.em.cdc.gov
URL: http://www.nppsis.org
Links families of children with a rare disorder or special health care need for
mutual support. Maintains a database of parents from all states and many coun-
tries. Provides health care information, resources, and referrals for families and
professionals.

RESOURCES FOR TECHNOLOGY

Products

Products are listed alphabetically by type of product. Product sources are refer-
enced in each listing. The listing of manufacturers and distributors of technology includes sources of additional products mentioned in the text.

Braille Notetakers and Computer Products

Braille Lite Has a 20-character refreshable braille display. *Blazie Engineering*

BrailleMate 2 Includes an appointment book, calculator, and clock and has 2 megabytes of RAM. *TeleSensory Corporation*

Braille 'n Speak Includes a calculator, calendar, and stopwatch. The Braille 'n Speak 640 contains additional memory and the ability to run auxiliary programs such as a spellchecker and scientific calculator. *Blazie Engineering*

David PC 386 DOS-compatible notebook computer with a braille keyboard, 40-cell braille display, and built-in synthetic speech. *TeleSensory Corporation*

Notex 25 and 40 Portable braille notetakers. *Adaptec*

Personal Touch Braille notetaker with a 20-cell braille display. *Blazie Engineering*

SuperBraille Pentium laptop computer with a 40-character braille display and/or synthetic speech. Options include a CD-ROM, multimedia sound, 32 megabytes of memory, and a model that includes just a braille display and keyboard that can serve as a braille access terminal to another PC. *Advanced Access Devices*

Braille Printers

Braille Blazer Small braille printer with synthetic speech output; handles 8.5-by-11-inch paper. *Blazie Engineering*

Braille Bookmaker Fifty-pound interpoint braille printer. *Enabling Technologies Company*

Braillo Interpoint Braille embosser designed for large volume use. Different models include the **Braillo Comet, Braillo 200,** and **Braillo 400.** *American Thermoform Corporation*

Index Basic 50 and **Everest** *E.V.A.S.*

Juliet 40-CPS interpoint braille embosser. *Enabling Technologies*

Marathon Brailler High-speed, 200-CPS, braille embosser. *Enabling Technologies*

Mountbatten Brailler Braille printer and an electronic braille typewriter that accepts characters from a standard QWERTY keyboard. Includes optional forward and reverse translators. *HumanWare*

Ohtsuki Printer Produces braille and print on the same page. *American Thermoform Corporation*

Resus Braille Printer Braille embosser that prints at 140 CPS. *American Thermoform Corporation*

Romeo Braille Printer (RB-20, RB-25 and RB-40) Single-sided braille embossers that print at 20, 25, and 40 CPS respectively. *Enabling Technologies*

TED 600 High-speed interpoint braille embosser (350 CPS). *Enabling Technologies*

Thiel Beta X/3 Braille Printer Medium-speed embosser (130 CPS). **Thiel BAX-10 interpoint Braille Printer** High-speed interpoint embosser (400 CPS). **Porta-**

Thiel Small, lightweight printer that can print on single sheets or continuous paper at 20 CPS. *Sighted Electronics*

Thomas Brailler Single-sided printer that prints at 40 CPS. *Enabling Technologies*

VersaPoint Braille Embosser Prints 40 CPS, single-sided. **VersaPoint Duo** Sixty CPS interpoint braille embosser. *TeleSensory Corporation*

Braille Translators: Hardware

Braille-n-Print Attaches to a Perkins Braillewriter and includes a back-translator that translates Braille into ASCII code and transmits to ink printer. *HumanWare*

MPRINT Attaches to a Perkins Braillewriter and back translates for printing on an ink-print printer. *TeleSensory Corporation*

Ransley Braille Interface *Humanware*

Braille Translators: Software

Bex *Raised Dot Computing*

Braille Talk PC IBM-compatible system. *GW Micro*

Duxbury Braille Translator IBM-compatible DOS, Windows 3.x, and Macintosh systems available. *Duxbury Systems*

MegaDots Braille translator that includes word processing capabilities. Imports many file types and uses "Braille styles" to format. *Raised Dot Computing*

Pokadot *National Braille Association*

OCR Systems and Scanners

First Reader Reconditioned, discounted OCR system. *Arkenstone*

Omni 1000 Stand-alone or PC-based OCR system that functions in the Windows 95 environment. *Kurzweil Educational Systems*

Omni Page Pro OCR software. *Caere*

Open Book OCR system that comes bundled with a specially designed PC. **Open Book Unbound** PC-based OCR system. *Arkenstone*

OsCaR PC-based OCR system. *TeleSensory Corporation*

Rainbow Reading Machine Stand-alone system. *Technologies for the Visually Impaired*

Reading AdvantEdge PC-based OCR system. **Reading Edge** Stand-alone OCR system. *Xerox Imaging Systems*

ReadMan Stand-alone and PC-based system. *Schamex Research*

Portable Computers/Personal Organizers

Aria DOS-compatible, palmtop computer. *Technologies for the Visually Impaired*

Keynote Companion Palmtop personal organizer that includes word processor, diary/calendar, calculator, and address list manager. *HumanWare*

Myna Palmtop personal organizer with built-in DECtalk speech synthesizer and two PCMCIA Type II slots. Can run DOS applications with the edition of RAM cards. *T.F.i. Engineering*

Type 'n Speak Same as the Braille 'n Speak 640 with a computer-style keyboard instead of a braille keyboard. *Blazie Engineering*

TransType Personal organizer with built-in Artic speech synthesizer. *Artic Technologies*

Refreshable Braille Displays

Alva Braille Terminal 40- and 80-cell braille displays. **Alva Braille Terminal** (portable) Available as 20- or 40-cell models, with batteries. *HumanWare*

Braillex 2D 80-cell braille display. *Adaptec*

DM80 and DM80/FM 80-cell desktop braille displays. *TeleSensory Corporation*

INKA 40-cell braille keyboard/braille display that plugs into the keyboard port. *TeleSensory Corporation*

KTS Braillotherm 40- or 80-cell desktop braille displays. *American Thermoform Corporation*

KeyBraille 25 and 45-cell desktop and/or portable Braille displays. **Mini Braille** A 20-cell braille portable display that can interface with the Braille 'n Speak as well as with PCs. *HumanWare*

PowerBraille 40-, 65-, and 80-character battery-powered braille displays. *TeleSensory Corporation*

Speech Synthesizers

Accent Internal and external units available; also Messenger-IC card for PCMCIA slot on laptops and notebook computers. *AICOM*

Apollo Speech Synthesizers Internal and external units. Several languages available. *E.V.A.S.*

Artic P-27 PCMCIA card. **Artic SynPhonix** Internal cards for desktop and laptop computers. **Artic TransBook** External, portable model including 20-key keypad, battery; allows user to upload, download, store and read files on RAM cards.

Artic TransPort External, portable model including battery; has ability to upload a screen review program to the computer. *Artic Technologies*

Audapter Speech System External unit with battery. *Personal Data Systems*

DECtalk Express Small, battery-powered synthesizer. **DECtalk PC** Internal card. *Digital Equipment Corporation*

Double Talk PC Internal speech synthesizer card. *R.C. Systems*

KeyNote Gold Internal and external units for desktop and laptop computers, also **VoiceCard** a PCMCIA card. *HumanWare*

Litetalk External unit. *MicroTalk Software*

SmartTalk Small external, battery-powered synthesizer. *Automated Functions*

Sounding Board Internal card. **Speak-Out** Small, battery-powered unit. *GW Micro*

Speaqualizer External Unit. *American Printing House for the Blind*

Synthetic Speech Programs—Apple Macintosh-based

outSPOKEN *Alva Access Group*

Synthetic Speech Programs—DOS-based

Artic Vision, Artic Business Vision *Artic Technologies*

ASAP (Automatic Screen Access Program) *MicroTalk Software*

IBM Screen Reader *IBM Special Needs Systems*

JAWS (Job Access with Speech) *Henter-Joyce*

MasterTouch Comes with optional touch tablet. *HumanWare*

PC Master Designed for use with Braille 'n Speak. *Blazie Engineering*

ScreenPower *TeleSensory Corporation*

SLIMWARE *Syntha-Voice Computers*

Tinytalk Shareware, works with SoundBlaster speech card. *OMS Development Systems*

Vocal-Eyes *GW Micro.*

Synthetic Speech Programs—Microsoft Windows-based

ASAW Windows 3.x and 95. *MicroTalk Software*

Artic WinVision Windows 3.x and 95. *Artic Technologies*

JAWS for Windows Windows 3.x and 95. *Henter-Joyce*

outSPOKEN for Windows *Alva Access*

ScreenPower for Windows Windows 3.x and 95. *TeleSensory Corporation*

SLIMWARE Window Bridge Windows 3.x and 95. *Syntha-Voice Computers*

Window-Eyes Windows 3.x and 95. *GW Micro*

Synthetic Speech Programs—OS/2-based

IBM Screen Reader/2 *IBM Special Needs Systems*

Web Browser

pwWebSpeak Windows-based web browser designed for blind and visually impaired users. Does not require the use of a synthetic speech program. *The Productivity Works*

Sources of Products

Adaptec Systems
6909 Rufus Drive
Austin, TX 78752-3123
(512) 451-1717
E-mail: tecraig@bga.com

Advanced Access Devices
2066-C Walsh Avenue
Santa Clara, CA 95050
(408) 970-9760
FAX: (408) 727-9351
E-mail: aadbrl@aol.com

AICOM Corporation
2381 Zanker Road, Suite 160
San Jose, CA 95131
(408) 577-0370
Fax: (408) 577-0373

Alva Access
5801 Christie Avenue, Suite 475
Emeryville, CA 94608
(510) 923-6280
FAX: (510) 923-6270
E-mail: info@aagi.com
URL: http://www.aagi.com

American Printing House for the Blind
1839 Frankfort Avenue
Louisville, KY 40206-0085
(502) 895-2405 or (800) 223-1839
FAX: (502) 899-2274
E-mail: info@aph.org
URL: http://www.aph.org

American Thermoform Corporation
2311 Travers Avenue
City of Commerce, CA 90040
(213) 723-9021
FAX: (213) 728-8877

Arkenstone
555 Oakmead Parkway
Sunnyvale, CA 94086-4023
(408) 245-5900 or (800) 444-4443
FAX: (408) 745-6739
URL: http://www.arkenstone.org

Artic Technologies
55 Park Street, Suite 2
Troy, MI 48083-2753
(810) 588-7370 or (810) 588-1425
FAX: (810) 588-2650
BBS: (810) 588-1424

Arts Computer Products
145 Tremont Street, Suite 407
Boston, MA 02111
(617) 482-8248 or (800) 343-0095
FAX: (617) 547-5597

Automated Functions
7700 Leesburg Pike, Suite 420
Falls Church, VA 22043
(703) 883-9797
FAX: (703) 883-9798

Blazie Engineering
101 East Jarretsville Road
Forest Hill, MD 21050
(410) 893-9333
FAX: (410) 836-5040
URL: http://www.blazie.com

Caere
100 Cooper Court
Los Gatos, CA 95030
(800) 535-7226

Digital Equipment Corporation
P.O. Box 9501
Merrimac, NH 03054
(800) 344-4825
FAX: (800) 234-2298

Dunamis
3423 Fowler Boulevard
Lawrenceville, GA 30044
(770) 279-1144

Duxbury Systems
P.O. Box 1504
435 King Street
Littleton, MA 01460
(508) 486-9766
FAX: (508) 586-9712

Enabling Technologies Company
1601 N.E. Braille Place
Jensen Beach, FL 34957
(561) 225-2687 or (800) 777-3687
FAX: (561) 225-3299 or (800) 950-3687

E.V.A.S.
16 David Avenue
P.O. Box 371
Westerley, RI 02891
(401) 596-3155 or (800) 872-3827
FAX: (401) 596-3979
URL: http://www.evas.com

GW Micro
725 Airport North Office Park
Fort Wayne, IN 46825
(219) 489-3671
FAX: (219) 489-2608
E-mail: vv@gwmicro.com
URL: http://www.gwmicro.com

Henter-Joyce
2100 62nd Avenue, North
St. Petersburg, FL 33702
(813) 528-8900 or (800) 336-5658
FAX: (813) 528-8901
E-mail: info@hj.com
URL: http://www.hj.com

Hewlett Packard Company
3495 Deer Creek Road
Palo Alto, CA 94304
(800) 538-8787

HumanWare
6245 King Road
Loomis, CA 95650
(916) 652-7253 or (800) 722-3393
FAX: (916) 652-7296
E-mail: infor@humanware.com
URL: http://www.humanware.com

IBM Special Needs System
11400 Burnett Road
Building 904/6 Internal Zip 9448
Austin, TX 78758
(512) 838-4598 or (800) 426-4832

Infogrip
1411 East Main Street
Ventura, CA 93001
(805) 652-0880 or (800) 397-0921
FAX: (805) 652-0880
E-mail: infogrip@infogrip.com
URL: http://www.infogrip.com/infogrip

IntelliTools
55 Leverom Court
Novato, CA 94949
(415) 382-5959
FAX: (415) 382-5950
E-mail: info@intellitools.com
URL: http://www.intellitools.com

Kurzweil Educational Systems
411 Waverly Oaks Road
Waltham, MA 02154
(617) 893-8200 or (800) 894-5374
FAX: (617) 893-4157
E-mail: info@kurzweiledu.com
URL: http://www.kurzweiledu.com

MicroTalk Software
721 Olive Street
Texarkana, TX 75501
(903) 792-2570
FAX:(903) 792-5140
BBS: (903) 832-3722
E-mail: larry@screenaccess.com
URL: http://www.screenaccess.com

National Braille Association
Braille Materials Production Center
3 Townline Circle
Rochester, NY 14623
(716) 427-8260
FAX: (716) 427-0263

OMS Development Systems
1921 Highland Avenue

Wilmette, IL 60091
(708) 251-5787

Personal Data Systems
P.O. Box 1008
Campbell, CA 95009-1008
(408) 866-1126
FAX: (408) 866-1128

Productivity Works
7 Belmont Circle
Trenton, NJ 08618
(609) 984-8044
FAX: (609) 984-8048
E-mail: info@prodworks.com
http://www.prodworks.com

Raised Dot Computing
408 South Baldwin Street
Madison, WI 53703
(608) 257-9595 or (608) 241-2498
FAX: (608) 257-4143
URL: http://www.well.com/www/dnavy

R.C. Systems
1609 England Avenue
Everett, WA 98203
(206) 355-3800

Schamex Research
19201 Parthenia Street, Suite H
Northridge, CA 91324
(818) 772-6644
FAX: (818) 993-2946

Sighted Electronics
464 Tappan Road
Northvale, NJ 07647
(201) 767-3977
FAX: (201) 767-0612
E-mail: sighted@village.ios.com

Syntha-Voice Computers
800 Queenstone Road, Suite 304
Stony Creek, ON L8G 1A7
(905) 662-0565 or (800)263-4540
BBS: (905) 662-0569
FAX: (905) 662-0568

Technologies for the Visually Impaired
9 Nolan Court
Hauppauge, NY 11788
(516) 724-4479
E-mail: tvii@concentric.net
URL: http://villagenet/~tvinc

T.F.i. Engineering
529 Main Street
Boston, MA 02129
(617) 242-7007

TeleSensory Corporation
P.O. Box 7455
455 North Bernardo
Mountain View, CA 94039-7455
(415) 960-0920 or (800) 286-8484
Fax: (415) 969-9064
http://www.telesensory.com

Unicorn Engineering
5221 Central Avenue, Suite 205
Richmond, CA 94804
(510) 528-0670 or (800) 899-6687

Xerox Imaging Systems
Adaptive Technology Products
9 Centennial Drive
Peabody, MA 01960
(800) 248-6550
FAX: (508) 977-2148
E-mail: doiron@xis.xerox.com
URL: http://www.xerox.com

Publications on Technology

Access Review
Sensory Access Foundation
385 Sherman Avenue, Suite #2
Palo Alto, CA 94306

Bitstream
Shrinkwrap Computer Products
11706 Saddle Crescent Circle
Oakton, VA 22124
(800) 377-0774

Bumpy Gazette
Repro-Tronics
75 Carver Avenue

Westwood, NJ 07675
(201) 722-1880 or (800) 948-8453
FAX: (201) 722-1881

Closing the Gap
P.O. Box 68
Henderson, MN 56044
(612) 248-3294
FAX: (612) 248-3810

JVIB News Service
AFB Press
11 Penn Plaza, Suite 300
New York, NY 10001
Phone: (212) 502-7649 or (888) 522-0220
FAX: (212) 502-7774
E-mail: afbinfo@afb.org
URL: http://www.afb.org

Tactic
Clovernook Center/Opportunities for the Blind
7000 Hamilton Avenue
Cincinnati, OH 45231
(513) 522-3860

Voice of Vision
GW Micro
725 Airport North Office Park
Fort Wayne, IN 46825
(219) 489-3671
FAX: (219) 489-2608
E-mail: vv@gwmicro.com
URL: http://www.gwmicro.com

COMPREHENSION RECORD SHEET

Student's name _____ Book _____

Date	Story & page numbers	Characterization	Classification	Comparison	Conclusion	Context clues	Creative thinking	Detail	Emotional reaction	Empathy	Forecasting	Generalization	Inference	Literary point of view	Main idea	Paragraph meaning	Personal evaluation	Personal experience	Personal reaction	Pitch, stress, juncture	Previous knowledge	Recall	Relationship	Sentence meaning	Sequence	Summarizing	Word meaning	Recall from previous day	Total/%
Total/%																													

D. P. Wormsley and F. M. D'Andrea, Eds., *Instructional Strategies for Braille Literacy*, New York: AFB Press, 1997. This page may be copied for educational use.

DAILY RECORD SHEET

Student's name _____

Book _____

Date	Page #	Miscue	Actual Word	Time (wpm)	Comments	Date	Page #	Miscue	Actual Word	Time (wpm)	Comments

D. P. Wormsley and F. M. D'Andrea, Eds., *Instructional Strategies for Braille Literacy*, New York: AFB Press, 1997. This page may be copied for educational use.

MECHANICS OF USING A BRAILLEWRITER
Assessment and Sequence of Skills

Recording Procedures: I = Skill introduced
A = Skill achieved with assistance
M = Skill achieved with mastery

Skills	I	A	M
01. Identifies and uses the following parts of the brailler:			
embossing bar			
spacing keys			
backspacing key			
paper release levers			
paper feed knob			
embossing head lever			
line spacing key			
support bar			
feed roller			
left paper stop			
warning bell			
handle			
cover			
margin stop			
02. Operates braillewriter:			
Positions brailler correctly on work surface.			
Moves embossing head to correct positions.			
Rotates paper feed knob away from self.			
Pulls paper release levers all the way toward self.			
Holds paper against paper support with one hand and closes paper release with the other.			
Rolls paper into brailler until stopped by left paper stop.			
Depresses the line spacing key to lock paper position.			
Removes paper from the brailler.			
Leaves brailler in rest position when not in use (moves embossing head to the right as far as possible, leaves paper release lever open, and covers machine).			

D. P. Wormsley and F. M. D'Andrea, Eds., *Instructional Strategies for Braille Literacy*, New York: AFB Press, 1997. This page may be copied for educational use.

READING-INTEREST INVENTORY

Student _____ Date _____

Please fill out this survey to let me know what you think about reading and books.

1. In my free time I like to _____ .

2. The kinds of books I like to read best are _____ .

3. The activity I like to do best at school is _____ .

4. I usually read about _____ times a week.

5. When I go to the library, I _____ .

6. When I read material that is too difficult for me, I _____ .

7. When my teacher reads to the class, I _____ .

8. My reading class is _____ .

9. My teacher helps me the most when _____ .

10. I worry about school when _____ .

11. My least favorite kinds of books are _____ .

12. Here's how I feel about the following kinds of books:

a. mysteries	love	1	2	3	4	5	6	7	8	9	10	hate
b. poetry	love	1	2	3	4	5	6	7	8	9	10	hate
c. plays	love	1	2	3	4	5	6	7	8	9	10	hate
d. biographies	love	1	2	3	4	5	6	7	8	9	10	hate
e. sports stories	love	1	2	3	4	5	6	7	8	9	10	hate
f. comedies	love	1	2	3	4	5	6	7	8	9	10	hate
g. romances	love	1	2	3	4	5	6	7	8	9	10	hate
h. essays	love	1	2	3	4	5	6	7	8	9	10	hate
i. science	love	1	2	3	4	5	6	7	8	9	10	hate
j. animal stories	love	1	2	3	4	5	6	7	8	9	10	hate
k. nature stories	love	1	2	3	4	5	6	7	8	9	10	hate
l. other_____	love	1	2	3	4	5	6	7	8	9	10	hate

D. P. Wormsley and F. M. D'Andrea, Eds., *Instructional Strategies for Braille Literacy,* New York: AFB Press, 1997. This page may be copied for educational use.

BRAILLE ASSESSMENT CHECKLIST
FOR PERSONS WITH MULTIPLE DISABILITIES

Directions

In the *general visual information* category, information from the learning media assessment is noted. Information from the eye report should be listed, including the eye condition (if known), and whether it is stable, unstable, or deteriorating. Distance and near acuities should be noted, as well as visual field information (note any central or peripheral field losses, as well as blind spots). Also in this area the teacher should report results of the functional vision assessment, including use of current vision for reading print or seeing small objects. Environmental modifications such as lighting preferences, use of color and contrast, etc. are important and can be listed on the form. Use of low vision devices (if any) such as hand-held magnifiers, monocular telescopes, CCTVs, or others the student may have had prescribed should be listed, including how well they are used. The teacher should also add information about the individual's use of tactile channels, especially if he or she has already been a braille reader. Current literacy skills should be noted, as should efficiency in current media, such as reading rate, accuracy, fatigue, distance from page (if using print), and ability to read own handwriting. The teacher can then list academic and vocational requirements of literacy (how will the student use reading and writing?), as well as recreational and personal requirements (functional literacy). It should be noted that the teacher may not have all the information already at his or her fingertips and will need to do the standard assessment procedures first. Other areas may not seem to be immediately applicable for a student but by having them on the form, the teacher can be reminded to consider their importance.

The second area to consider is *physical considerations* for reading and writing braille. The individual's medical records will be helpful to you, if you have access to them, as well as reports from an occupational and physical therapist (OT and PT). Is there a medical diagnosis of the physical condition? Note the student's body posture: is she able to sit up straight, or is she positioned in a different way? Consider the student's endurance and stamina. Does the student have use of two hands, or is hand movement restricted? Can the student maintain a relaxed, curved hand and finger position? Can the student maintain a consistent light touch on the braille dots? Assess the learner's arm/hand movements: does she have a full range of motion up/down and right/left? Can she cross midline? How is the learner's muscle strength? Is coordination affected? Is the student's tactile sensitivity affected? Other useful information could include whether the learner is taking any medications that may effect general health, alertness, or fatigue.

The third area of consideration is *cognitive abilities*. There may be some evidence in the student's records that the cognitive disability is congenital or acquired (for example, from a brain injury). Some factors that may affect the individual's braille reading ability are memory, perception and attention, organization, abstract thinking skills, and generalization. If the learner has a current psychological report, you may be able to find some of this information there. Some of these areas may be more difficult for you as a teacher to assess, but a staff psychologist or psychometrist may be able to assist you. Also observe the learner's behaviors, and note signs of confusion, short attention span, etc. These will not necessarily preclude teaching braille to this individual, but may help you plan your lessons and suggest strategies that will help your student learn. For example, this individual may need shorter lessons, more frequent breaks, extra practice on certain skills, and suggestions for organizing materials.

Language is the fourth area to consider. In this space, the teacher can record information from a Speech/Language Pathologist (SLP) report, or results of any testing the teacher may have done. If the learner speaks English as a Second Language, this information can also be recorded here, as well as the learner's primary language, and literacy level in both the primary language and English.

The last area that should be considered is the category of *auditory skills*. Does the learner have a hearing impairment? There are several combinations to consider. Does your student have a congenital visual impairment (VI) and an acquired hearing impairment (HI) (perhaps from the effects of aging, or a syndrome)? Does your student have a congenital hearing impairment (such as a person with Usher's syndrome)? Perhaps your student has both a congenital hearing and visual impairment, or perhaps your student has acquired both a hearing and visual impairment (for example, from an accident, reaction to medication, or effects of aging). Each of these scenarios will have an effect on learning to read and write braille, and should be noted in your assessment. An audiologist's report will be helpful to you, if available.

D. P. Wormsley and F. M. D'Andrea, Eds., *Instructional Strategies for Braille Literacy,* New York: AFB Press, 1997. This page may be copied for educational use.

BRAILLE ASSESSMENT CHECKLIST
FOR PERSONS WITH MULTIPLE DISABILITIES

Name _____ Date of Birth _____

Address _____ School/Facility _____

City _____ State _____ Zip _____ Completed by _____ Date _____

Key: I = Impairment/difficulty
OK = No impairment
NA = Not applicable

I. General Category	I	OK	NA	Comments (including assessment dates)
Eye condition: _____				Eye report information:
_____				
Stable	☐	☐	☐	
Unstable	☐	☐	☐	
Deteriorating	☐	☐	☐	
Acuity	☐	☐	☐	
Central loss	☐	☐	☐	
Use of current vision: Reading print/ Seeing small objects	☐	☐	☐	Functional vision assessment:
				Environmental modifications:
Use of low vision devices: Type & competency:	☐	☐	☐	Low vision evaluation:

D. P. Wormsley and F. M. D'Andrea, Eds., *Instructional Strategies for Braille Literacy,* New York: AFB Press, 1997. This page may be copied for educational use.

Use of tactile channel: ☐ ☐ ☐   Sensory channel assessment:

Affective status: ☐ ☐ ☐   Interview:

Current literacy skills: Learning media assessment:
   Conventional   ☐ ☐ ☐
   Functional   ☐ ☐ ☐
   Literacy readiness

Efficiency in current media:
   Distance from page   ☐ ☐ ☐
   Reading rate   ☐ ☐ ☐
   Accuracy   ☐ ☐ ☐
   Fatigue   ☐ ☐ ☐
   Able to read own handwriting   ☐ ☐ ☐

Literacy requirements across
   environments: ☐ ☐ ☐   Ecological assessment for braille literacy:

Other information: ☐ ☐ ☐

II. Physical Category	I	OK	NA	Comments
Physical condition:	☐	☐	☐	Medical report:

D. P. Wormsley and F. M. D'Andrea, Eds., *Instructional Strategies for Braille Literacy,* New York: AFB Press, 1997. This page may be copied for educational use.

Endurance/stamina: ☐ ☐ ☐

Body posture/position: ☐ ☐ ☐ PT report:

Use of two hands: ☐ ☐ ☐ OT report:

Finger/hand position: ☐ ☐ ☐

Light touch on braille: ☐ ☐ ☐

Arm/hand movement:
   Range of motion ☐ ☐ ☐
   Muscle strength ☐ ☐ ☐
   Coordination ☐ ☐ ☐

Tactile perception: ☐ ☐ ☐

Other information: ☐ ☐ ☐

III. Cognitive Category	I	OK	NA	*Comments*
Intellectual status: Type of impairment: _____ _____ ☐ Congenital ☐ Acquired	☐	☐	☐	Psychological report:
Memory	☐	☐	☐	
Perception/attention	☐	☐	☐	
Organization	☐	☐	☐	
Abstract thinking	☐	☐	☐	
Generalization	☐	☐	☐	
Other information:	☐	☐	☐	

IV. Language Category	I	OK	NA	*Comments*
Language & communication:	☐	☐	☐	SLP report:
Other information:	☐	☐	☐	

V. Auditory Category	I	OK	NA	*Comments*
Hearing impairment:				Audiological & medical report:
Congenital VI & acquired HI	☐	☐	☐	
Congenital HI & acquired VI	☐	☐	☐	
Congenital VI & HI	☐	☐	☐	
Acquired VI & HI	☐	☐	☐	
Other information:	☐	☐	☐	

D. P. Wormsley and F. M. D'Andrea, Eds., *Instructional Strategies for Braille Literacy,* New York: AFB Press, 1997. This page may be copied for educational use.

STUDENT PROFILE
Students with Limited English Proficiency Who Are Blind or Visually Impaired

1. General Information

Student's name _____

Age _____ School _____ Grade _____

Name and title of person completing form _____

Date completing form _____

Date student entered program _____

Date student first entered U.S. school system_____

Did student attend school in another country before entering school in the United States?

    ☐ Yes ☐No If Yes, how long? _____

Language(s) spoken at home _____

Language(s) understood by the student (answer even if the student is not verbal) _____

_____

Language(s) spoken by the student _____

Type of instruction the student has received in the United States related to his or her native language and English-language development:

Type of Service	Length of Service	
☐ Native language instruction	from _____	to _____
☐ English as a second language	from _____	to _____
☐ Content-area ESL	from _____	to _____
☐ Speech/language therapy	from _____	to _____
☐ Other _____	from _____	to _____

Type of instruction currently provided to the student related to his or her native language and English language development:

Type of Service	How Frequently?
☐ Native language instruction	_____
☐ English as a second language	_____
☐ Content-area ESL	_____
☐ Speech/language therapy	_____
☐ Other _____	_____

D. P. Wormsley and F. M. D'Andrea, Eds., *Instructional Strategies for Braille Literacy,* New York: AFB Press, 1997. This page may be copied for educational use.

2. Language Skills: Listening, Speaking, Reading, and Writing

The student receives information through   ☐ Voice   ☐ Signs

What strategies do school personnel use to ensure understanding?

_____

_____

_____

_____

The student communicates expressively through

☐ Voice   ☐ Signs   ☐ Communication board   ☐ Other

If the student uses voice, what is known about the phonology and grammar structure of the student's primary language that may influence the clarity and quality of the student's oral communication?

_____

_____

_____

_____

_____

The student writes information in
☐ Regular print   ☐ Large print   ☐ Braille   ☐ Both print and braille

Did the student learn to write in the primary language?
☐ Yes   ☐ No

If the student writes in print (regular or large), what specific information is known about the student's primary language that may influence the quality and clarity of the student's writing? (directionality, type of alphabet, and so forth.)

_____

_____

_____

_____

_____

The student gains access to written information through
☐ Regular print   ☐ Large print   ☐ Braille   ☐ Both print and braille

If the student uses braille, did he or she learn it in the primary language?

☐ Yes   ☐ No

If yes, what are some differences between the braille code in the student's primary language and the braille code taught at school?

_____

_____

_____

_____

_____

(To answer questions about the braille code of the student's primary language, teachers may want to consult *World Braille Usage,* 1990, published by the Library of Congress.)

What else is known about the educational history of the student that will facilitate understanding of student's current functioning? (Some important factors may be past educational experiences, history of the ethnic group in the community, medical problems, school attendance, family's educational and social levels, and siblings' contributions to the student's education.)

_____

_____

_____

_____

_____

_____

_____

_____

_____

_____

3. Language Proficiency Levels: Listening, Speaking, Reading, and Writing

Proficiency Levels in Language Other than English			
Date	Instrument	Area	Results

D. P. Wormsley and F. M. D'Andrea, Eds., *Instructional Strategies for Braille Literacy,* New York: AFB Press, 1997. This page may be copied for educational use.

Proficiency Levels in English

Date	Instrument	Area	Results

4. Instructional Goals for the Primary Language and English

Goals for Language Other than English

Date	Area	Goals

Goals for English

Date	Area	Goals

OBSERVATION RECORD

Student _____ Date _____

Location _____ Observer _____

Time	Observations	Notes

SELF-ASSESSMENT OF READING

Name _____ Date _____

The following piece of work demonstrates my strengths in reading. These strengths are _____

_____

_____

_____

_____

I will work to improve my reading by _____

_____

_____

_____

_____

SELF-ASSESSMENT OF WRITING

Name _____ Date _____

The following piece of work demonstrates my strengths in writing. These strengths are _____

_____

_____

_____

I will work to improve my writing by _____

_____

_____

_____

_____

RECORD OF INDEPENDENT READING

Student _____

Date	Title of Book	Notes

QUESTIONNAIRE FOR TEACHERS

Directions: The following questions are an essential part of the assessment of _____. You have had _____ in your classes and have observed him [or her] in many settings at school. To help meet his/her educational needs, the IEP team would like to have some input from each of his/her teachers. As teachers, you know that each part of the student's day at school is important when assessing the educational needs of students. Please take the time to jot down some thoughts on each of the following questions. _____ will benefit from the time you took to help ensure that his/her educational needs are addressed to maximize his/her strengths. Please regard this written questionnaire as a confidential part of the assessment report. Feel free to write additional thoughts and comments on the back of these pages. After you complete this form, please return it in the enclosed self-addressed envelope. Thank you for your time and interest.

Teacher's name _____ Subject _____

Student's name _____ Date _____

1. What are this student's learning strengths?

2. What learning strategies work best for this student?

3. What kinds of materials are most effective with this student?

4. What types of learning situations are most beneficial for this student?

5. What type of reading material does this student prefer?

6. Are there any specific observations that you can make regarding the student's current literacy needs?

7. What kind of literacy tasks does this student need to complete during the daily school routine?

D. P. Wormsley and F. M. D'Andrea, Eds., *Instructional Strategies for Braille Literacy*, New York: AFB Press, 1997. This page may be copied for educational use.

PARENT INTERVIEW

Directions: The following questions are an essential part of the assessment of your child, _____.
To help meet his/her educational needs, the IEP team would like to have some input from you as a parent.
Each part of the student's day is important when assessing the educational needs of students. Your
observations are extremely valuable to the overall planning for your child. Please take the time to jot down
some thoughts on each of the following questions. If you prefer to give your comments in person, contact
your child's vision teacher or counselor, who will record your comments for you. _____ will
benefit from the time you take to help ensure that his/her educational needs are addressed to maximize
his/her strengths. Feel free to write additional thoughts and comments on the back of these pages. After you
complete this form, please return it in the enclosed self-addressed envelope. We value your comments.
Thank you for your time.

Parent's Name _____ Interviewer _____

Student's Name _____ Date _____

1. How well do you think your child is doing in school?

2. Please describe your concerns about your child's work in school.

3. Does your child engage in leisure activities?
   If so, what kind?

   Does he or she do these activities independently or with other children?

4. Does your child participate in household responsibilties and chores?

5. What social activities interest your child?

6. Does your child require help with homework?
   If so, what is the best way to help your child?

7. What type of leisure reading materials does your child prefer?

8. Are there any specific observations you can make regarding your child's current literacy needs?

9. Do you have any comments or suggestions about additional support that is needed to help your child
   succeed in school or in daily living?

D. P. Wormsley and F. M. D'Andrea, Eds., *Instructional Strategies for Braille Literacy*, New York: AFB Press, 1997. This page may be copied for educational use.

STUDENT INTERVIEW

Directions: Your answers to the following questions will play an essential part in planning your instruction and schedule at school and determining educational goals that you think are the most important. Please take the time to jot down some thoughts on each question. After you complete this form, please return it to your vision teacher.

Name _____ Date _____

1. How well do you think you are doing in school?

2. Please describe your concerns about your schedule and the subjects you are taking.

3. Do you like to read during your free time?
   What kind of material do you like to read?

4. Do you enjoy doing schoolwork that involves reading and writing?

5. Are you able to finish your work in a reasonable amount of time?
   If your answer is no, what do you think is the problem?

6. What kind of help do you think you need?

7. Do you think your braille skills are adequately developed?

8. Do you require help with your homework?
   If so, what is the best way to get this help?

9. What are your plans when you graduate from high school?

D. P. Wormsley and F. M. D'Andrea, Eds., *Instructional Strategies for Braille Literacy,* New York: AFB Press, 1997. This page may be copied for educational use.

MISCUE ANALYSIS CHART

No.	Error	Text	Graphic/Tactile Similarity Yes	Context Acceptable	Context Unacceptable	Self-Correction
1.						
2.						
3.						
4.						
5.						
6.						
7.						
8.						
9.						
10.						
11.						
12.						
13.						
14.						
15.						
		Column Total				
		Number of Errors Analyzed				
		Percentage				

D. P. Wormsley and F. M. D'Andrea, Eds., *Instructional Strategies for Braille Literacy,* New York: AFB Press, 1997. This page may be copied for educational use.

A HANDY GUIDE TO CALCULATING TOTALS AND PERCENTAGES

Graphic/tactile similarity

a. Column total (number of checks in the Yes column)   _____

b. Number of errors analyzed (total boxes without *Xs*)   _____

c. Percentage of miscues with graphic similarity (a ÷ b)   _____ %

Acceptability in context

a. Column total (number of checks in the Acceptable column)   _____

b. Number of errors analyzed (total number of errors analyzed)   _____

c. Percentage of miscues acceptable in context (a ÷ b)   _____ %

Correction strategy

a. Column total (number of unacceptable miscues self-corrected)   _____

b. Number of errors analyzed (total unacceptable miscues)   _____

c. Percentage of unacceptable miscues self-corrected (a ÷ b)   _____ %

D. P. Wormsley and F. M. D'Andrea, Eds., *Instructional Strategies for Braille Literacy,* New York: AFB Press, 1997. This page may be copied for educational use.

PROFILE

PREDICTION
STRATEGY
_____

CORRECTION
STRATEGY
_____

Graphic/Tactile Similarity	*Errors Acceptable in Context*	*Unacceptable Errors, Self-Corrected*
100 % _____	100 % _____	100 % _____
90 % _____	90 % _____	90 % _____
80 % _____	80 % _____	80 % _____
70 % _____	70 % _____	70 % _____
60 % _____	60 % _____	60 % _____
50 % _____	50 % _____	50 % _____
40 % _____	40 % _____	40 % _____
30 % _____	30 % _____	30 % _____
20 % _____	20 % _____	20 % _____
10 % _____	10 % _____	10 % _____
0 % _____	0 % _____	0 % _____

D. P. Wormsley and F. M. D'Andrea, Eds., *Instructional Strategies for Braille Literacy,* New York: AFB Press, 1997. This page may be copied for educational use.

ASSISTIVE TECHNOLOGY ASSESSMENT
FOR VISUALLY IMPAIRED STUDENTS
Background Referral Information

Identifying Information: Please type or print

Student's name _____ Date of birth _____ Age ___

School system _____ School _____

Classroom teacher _____ Grade level _____

Vision teacher _____ Telephone No. _____

Educational Information

Primary Disability

☐ Orthopedically impaired   ☐ Hearing impaired

☐ Mildly intellectually disabled   ☐ Deaf

☐ Moderately intellectually disabled   ☐ Vision impaired

☐ Severely intellectually disabled   ☐ Blind

☐ Profoundly intellectually disabled   ☐ Other health impaired

☐ Speech-language impaired   ☐ Severely emotionally disturbed

☐ Learning disabled   ☐ Has a behavior disorder

☐ Autistic

Secondary Disability

☐ Orthopedically impaired   ☐ Hearing impaired

☐ Mildly intellectually disabled   ☐ Deaf

☐ Moderately intellectually disabled   ☐ Vision impaired

☐ Severely intellectually disabled   ☐ Blind

☐ Profoundly intellectually disabled   ☐ Other health impaired

☐ Speech-language impaired   ☐ Severely emotionally disturbed

☐ Learning disabled   ☐ Has a behavior disorder

☐ Autistic

Time in Regular Education Class (hours per week)

☐ 0–5   ☐ 6–10   ☐ 11–15

☐ 16–20   ☐ 21–25   ☐ 26–30

Medical Diagnosis

☐ Cerebral palsy   ☐ Closed head injury

☐ Down's syndrome   ☐ Neurological disease (specify)_____

☐ Other syndrome (specify) _____

☐ Unknown

Vision: Please complete with input from vision teacher if appropriate

Date of most recent eye exam _____

Visual status: Right/OD - _____   Left/OS - _____

Field loss (please describe in detail) _____

D. P. Wormsley and F. M. D'Andrea, Eds., *Instructional Strategies for Braille Literacy,* New York: AFB Press, 1997. This page may be copied for educational use.

Optimal placement of stimuli _____

Age/date of onset _____

Cause of visual impairment (etiology) _____

Is visual condition stable? _____

Describe any deficiencies in color vision _____

Date of most recent low vision exam _____

Was a low vision aid prescribed? Specify _____

Vision concerns

_____ Acuity   _____ Tracking   _____ Visual field

_____ Nystagmus   _____ Scanning   _____ Strabismus

Date of most recent learning media assessment _____

Results _____

_____

Accessing Print

How does the student access printed information?

☐ Acetate overlays for "dittos": Specify color(s) _____

☐ Materials produced with felt-tip pen on bold-line paper

☐ Materials enlarged on photocopying machine: Specify (i.e., 130%, 3 times) _____

☐ Large-print books   Optimal point size _____

☐ Large-print materials   Preferred point size/viewing distance _____

☐ Others (size/distance) _____

☐ Optical aids

    ☐ Eyeglasses   ☐ Contact lens

    ☐ Handheld/stand magnifier—power _____

    ☐ Telescope—power _____

    ☐ Large-print

    ☐ Closed-circuit television (CCTV)

☐ Braille books and materials. Briefly describe student's braille skills: _____

_____

☐ Books on tape and other recorded materials

☐ Tactile graphics: maps, graphs, charts, geometry figures

☐ Large print/talking calculator

☐ Talking dictionary

How does student gain access to information presented on a chalkboard or overhead projector?

☐ Gets copy from teacher   ☐ Gets copy from other students

☐ Uses handheld or spectacle-mounted telescope   ☐ Sits close enough to read from the chalkboard

☐ Computerized materials when provided with adaptations

    ☐ Computer networks   ☐ Books on disk

    ☐ CD-ROM   ☐ Optical scanner

    ☐ Online information provided via telephone lines

Does the student experience reading fatigue? (Describe conditions under which fatigue occurs.) _____

_____

D. P. Wormsley and F. M. D'Andrea, Eds., *Instructional Strategies for Braille Literacy*, New York: AFB Press, 1997. This page may be copied for educational use.

Producing Written Communication

How does the student produce written communications?

☐ Bold-line paper   ☐ Raised-line paper

☐ Felt-tip pens   ☐ White boards

☐ Braillewriter   ☐ Slate and stylus

☐ Mountbatten brailler   ☐ Typewriter

☐ Computer

    ☐ Apple (specify) _____ ☐ Macintosh (specify) _____

    ☐ IBM-compatible (specify) _____

    ☐ How is computer accessed?

        ☐ Regular print   ☐ Large print

        ☐ Speech   ☐ Braille display

Note Taking

How does the student take notes in class?

☐ Bold-line paper and felt-tip pen (Can student read his/her handwritten notes?)

☐ Braillewriter   ☐ Slate and stylus

☐ Tape recorder   ☐ Notebook computer

☐ Braille 'n Speak   ☐ Braille Mate

☐ Type 'n Speak   ☐ Keynote Companion

☐ Mountbatten brailler   ☐ Other (specify) _____

Background information provided by

Name _____ Position _____

Computer-Access Evaluation

Computer Functions

Specify the activities for which the student will use the computer.

☐ Vocational (specify) _____

☐ Writing (specify) _____

☐ Reading (specify) _____

☐ Mathematics (specify) _____

☐ Communication (specify) _____

☐ Recreation/leisure activities (specify) _____

☐ Other (specify) _____

Input

Standard Keyboard

☐ Student can use the standard keyboard without adaptations.

☐ Student can use the standard computer keyboard with adaptations.

    ☐ Keyguard   ☐ Finger guard/pointer

    ☐ Keylatch   ☐ Wrist/arm support _____

    ☐ Moisture guard   ☐ Tactile locator dots _____

- ☐ Braille keyboard
- ☐ Other (specify) _____
☐ Student cannot use the standard keyboard (with or without adaptations).

If the student can use the keyboard (with or without adaptations), please provide the following information:

- ☐ Student can identify alphanumeric keys.
- ☐ Student can identify function keys.
- ☐ Student can activate two keys simultaneously.
- ☐ Student can activate/deactivate keys without causing key repeats.

    Method of access
    - ☐ Right hand   Fingers used _____
    - ☐ Left hand   Fingers used _____

Typing speed (specify) _____ words per minute

- ☐ Student can touch type without looking at keys.

Specify appropriate keyboard utilities for this student:

☐ Sticky keys   ☐ Repeat keys   ☐ Slow keys   ☐ Toggle keys   ☐ Mouse keys

Alternative Keyboards

If the student cannot use the standard keyboard effectively with or without the above adaptations, please indicate which type of keyboard(s) the student can use to access the computer independently.

- ☐ Break-apart keyboard
- ☐ Expanded keyboard (specify) _____
- ☐ Miniature keyboard (specify) _____
- ☐ One-handed keyboard
- ☐ On-screen keyboard with a mouse. Indicate type of mouse: _____
- ☐ TouchTablet (e.g., Power Pad)
- ☐ Braille input device (keyboard)

Standard Mouse and Mouse Alternatives

- ☐ Student can use the standard computer mouse.
- ☐ Student cannot use the standard computer mouse.

Output

- ☐ Student can see information on the standard computer monitor without adaptations.
- ☐ Student can see information on the standard computer monitor with adaptations.
    - ☐ Screen-enlarging hardware (specify) _____
    - ☐ Flexible-arm monitor stand
    - ☐ Enlarged font   ☐ Double spacing
    - ☐ Screen-enlarging software (specify): _____
        Magnification _____ Viewing distance _____
        Preferred color combination _____
        Preferred viewing mode (e.g., full screen, line, area) _____

If the student cannot use the standard computer monitor with adaptations, indicate which hardware/software the student can use:

- ☐ Screen-reading/access software (specify) _____

D. P. Wormsley and F. M. D'Andrea, Eds., *Instructional Strategies for Braille Literacy*, New York: AFB Press, 1997. This page may be copied for educational use.

☐ Talking word processing (specify) _____

☐ Speech synthesizer (specify) _____

☐ Student can understand speech produced by speech synthesizer.

☐ Braille display

☐ Student prefers to read print from a standard computer printer, with other adaptations, such as a CCTV or magnifier.

If the student cannot read the print from a standard computer printer, please specify the following:

☐ Student can read the print when enlarged. (Specify preferred font size): _____

☐ Student requires a braille printer.

Computer Operations

Indicate which computer operations the student can do:

☐ Turn central processing unit on and off   ☐ Turn monitor on and off

☐ Insert disk in disk drive   ☐ Eject disk from disk drive

☐ Turn printer on and off   ☐ Retrieve desired program for on-screen menu

Software Applications

Specify the software applications the student requires:

Vocational

☐ Word processing   ☐ Database   ☐ Spreadsheet

☐ Desktop publishing   ☐ Computer-assisted design

☐ Other (specify) _____

Writing

☐ Word processing   ☐ Grammar checker   ☐ Spell checker

☐ Outlining software   ☐ Word prediction

☐ Other (specify) _____

Mathematics

☐ Access to Math—Apple IIe   ☐ Math Scratch Pad—Apple IIc

☐ Math CAD—IBM   ☐ Other (specify) _____

☐ On-screen calculator

Cognitive and language

☐ Cause and effect (specify) _____

☐ Language development (specify) _____

Communication

☐ Write OutLoud—Macintosh   ☐ Speaking Dynamically—Macintosh

☐ EZ Keys—IBM   ☐ Handiword—IBM

☐ Other (specify) _____

Recreation/Leisure

☐ Cause-and-effect games

☐ Other (specify) _____

D. P. Wormsley and F. M. D'Andrea, Eds., *Instructional Strategies for Braille Literacy*, New York: AFB Press, 1997. This page may be copied for educational use.

☐ *Other (specify)* _____

Computer Access Recommendations

Input mode

☐ Standard keyboard

☐ Standard keyboard with adaptations (specify) _____

☐ Alternative keyboard (specify) _____

☐ Switch input (specify) _____

☐ Mouse or mouse alternative (specify) _____

☐ Voice recognition (specify) _____

Output mode

☐ Standard computer monitor—optimal size _____

☐ Standard computer monitor with adaptations (specify) _____

☐ Screen enlarging software/hardware (specify) _____

☐ Talking word processing (specify) _____

☐ Screen-reading/access software (specify) _____

☐ Speech synthesizer/sound card (specify) _____

☐ Braille display (specify) _____

Software needs

Specify any software the student needs: _____

_____

_____

_____

Additional comments/recommendations:

_____

_____

_____

_____

_____

_____

_____

_____

Computer Access Evaluation conducted by

Name _____   Position _____

D. P. Wormsley and F. M. D'Andrea, Eds., *Instructional Strategies for Braille Literacy,* New York: AFB Press, 1997. This page may be copied for educational use.

SKILLS NEEDED TO OPERATE EQUIPMENT

Student's name _____

Instructor's name _____

Training date(s) _____

Name and version of device _____

The following checklist will serve as an indicator of the tasks
that this student has learned:

* I - independently performs the task
* N - uses notes ( )% of the time to complete tasks
* V - needs verbal coaching ( )% of the time to complete task
* U - unable to consistently perform the task assigned
* — student has not been shown that particular feature of the device

	Pretest Date					Posttest Date
Major Components The student can						
—identify and locate all the alpha keys						
—identify and locate all the number keys						
—identify and locate the special function keys such as help						
—identify and connect the power charger						
—describe and perform the charging procedure						
—state name and manufacturer of device						
—find information in the manual						
—get technical support						
Operating the Menus The student can						
—select menu choices						
—exit menus and return to document						
Creating and Writing a File The student knows the procedures for						
—creating a new file						
—opening an existing file						
—describing the cursor and its function						
—moving the cursor to the top or bottom of a file						
—quitting and saving a file						

D. P. Wormsley and F. M. D'Andrea, Eds., *Instructional Strategies for Braille Literacy,* New York: AFB Press, 1997. This page may be copied for educational use.

	Pretest Date						Posttest Date	
Editing Commands								
The student knows the procedures for								
—positioning the cursor for properly inserting letters, words, and sentences								
—deleting the current word								
—deleting the current character								
—deleting the previous character								
—deleting to the end of a sentence								
—deleting to the end of a paragraph								
—deleting from the cursor to the end of a file								
New Pages, Search Procedures, and Place Markers								
The student knows the procedures for								
—starting a new page								
—searching forward for a specific string of text								
—searching backward for a specific string of text								
—searching and replacing text forward								
—searching and replacing text backwards								
Operating the Disk Drive								
The student knows the procedures for								
—touching the disk properly without affecting its storage capability								
—positioning and inserting a disk								
—formatting a disk								
—removing the disk safely from the disk drive								
—setting the write-protect tab on the diskette								
—transferring files between the device and the disk drive								
File Commands								
The student knows the procedures for								
—reading the disk directory								
—reading subdirectories on disks								
—spelling file names or directory names								
—copying from disk to memory								
—erasing files from memory or disk								
—renaming files								

D. P. Wormsley and F. M. D'Andrea, Eds., *Instructional Strategies for Braille Literacy,* New York: AFB Press, 1997. This page may be copied for educational use.

	Pretest Date					Posttest Date	

Printing a File

The student knows the procedure for

—loading the paper into the printer

—connecting the printer cables to the device and the printer

—selecting a specific print driver (if appropriate)

—printing a single page

—printing multiple pages

—printing a single file

—printing groups of files

Calculator Functions

The student knows the procedures for

—entering and exiting the calculator mode

—entering calculations

—operating adding, subtraction, multiplying, and dividing functions

—operating negation, percentages, and parentheses

—operating trigonometric functions (if available)

—operating the square and square-root functions (if available)

—operating the logarithmic functions (if available)

—operating the power and root functions (if available)

Advanced Editing Features

The student knows the procedures for

—moving a block of text

—copying a block of text

—deleting a block of text

—merging documents

—centering text

—underlining text

—making a line right justified

—moving to the start of the next line

—moving to the next tab setting

—inserting the time and date into a file

—inserting the calculated result

D. P. Wormsley and F. M. D'Andrea, Eds., *Instructional Strategies for Braille Literacy*, New York: AFB Press, 1997. This page may be copied for educational use.

	Pretest Date					Posttest Date
—editing directly from disk						
—exiting a file without saving text						
Other Features The student knows the procedures for						
—using spell checking, if available						
—adding, deleting, and changing a word in the dictionary						
—saving and retrieving a dictionary file to disk						
—deleting the current dictionary						
—running another application program						
—setting the time and date						
—formatting disks						
—renaming disks						
—copying disks						
Using the Help Key The student knows the procedures for						
—entering and exiting the help mode						
Miscellaneous The student knows the procedures for						
—reinitializing, resetting, warm-booting the device						
—installing new application programs						
—updating software						

D. P. Wormsley and F. M. D'Andrea, Eds., *Instructional Strategies for Braille Literacy,* New York: AFB Press, 1997. This page may be copied for educational use.